'Éxva Teméeku:
Where We Began

Dear Readers,

Pechanga established the Great Oak Press in order to provide an avenue by which Native voices and topics of significance and of importance to Native Americans could find their way into the contemporary discourse and become both a growing and permanent part of recorded knowledge.

As a publisher of scholarly and academic books, Pechanga's Great Oak Press is dedicated to working with the leading experts and also the up and coming experts in a wide range of fields, ranging from the arts to the sciences and from history to languages. Our focus, though broad in topics, is finely centered on publishing works of great importance that preserve and expand knowledge as well as encourage creative thought and intellectual exploration.

However, Great Oak Press is not focused solely on producing scholarly titles that only the academic and higher education community find accessible. Rather, Great Oak Press is committed to producing books of exceptional quality that literally begin with First Readers for children and will include works for the entire range that comprises the K-12 reading levels. After all, the health of society is directly related to its efforts at raising and educating its youth.

In this work, one of the first Great Oak Press publications, Myra Masiel-Zamora (Pechanga), presents her findings on the 'Éxva Teméeku archaeological materials, which had been excavated in 1952, and until recently, had been stored in a museum. This book provides not only a detailed archaeological analysis of the ancient 'Éxva Teméeku village, of equal importance is that it also provides a Native Voice on what village life was like for Luiseño people prior to the Spanish through United States colonization of this land.

We thank you for your support.

Mark Macarro

Tribal Chairman of the Pechanga Band of Luiseño Indians

'Éxva Teméeku: Where We Began

Myra Ruth Masiel-Zamora

Great Oak Press, Pechanga, California

A CIP catalog record for this book is available from the Library of Congress.

ISBN: 978-1-942279-04-4

Publisher: Great Oak Press, Pechanga, California

Printed in the United States of America

DEDICATION

This book is dedicated to Raymond Basquez-Caparapish Sr.

ABSTRACT

Precontact Archeological studies have primarily explored lithic, ceramic, faunal, shell and adornment artifacts. The 'éxva Teméeku collection includes material remains from each of these study areas. Excavated in 1952, the collection was considered a museum archaeological collection and remained in storage since that time. A brief site report was published immediately after the excavation that analyzed only a portion of the collection, leaving many questions unanswered about the overall picture of this village site. The unanswered questions include insight about the lithic technology, diet, hunting strategies, trade and adornment that can be garnered from the existing material remains. This book provides a detailed archaeological analysis of the entire prehistoric portion of the 'éxva Teméeku collection and has led to new conclusions about what village life was like for the Luiseño people before contact. The brief analysis in the 1950s was insufficient and a complete cataloguing of the collection did not occur until 2010. Unfortunately, many artifacts mentioned in the site report are no longer part of the collection and there is no information as to where these artifacts might be housed. The loss of artifacts motivated the author to request the collection in order to verify what remains of the collection and complete a detailed analysis of its content. The result of this analysis is outlined here and provides a greater picture of what village life was like before contact. This information in turn provides Temecula residents a greater cultural awareness of the people of this area and advances the discipline of anthropology by developing a more detailed understanding of the Luiseño people living in Temecula during precontact times. Of equal significance, the analysis has provided the author an opportunity to preserve her Luiseño ancestors' village through knowledge and affirmation of their thriving presence.

Keywords: Precontact Archaeology, 'éxva Teméeku, and Luiseño Indians

TABLE OF CONTENTS

APPENDIX

LIST OF TABLES

ACKNOWLEDGMENTS

I would like to thank everyone who has helped me along the way. This project would not have been possible without the staff at the Pechanga Cultural Resource Center, especially all the interns who assisted with the analysis and cataloguing of the 'éxva Teméeku collection at the San Bernardino County Museum, and the San Bernardino County Museum staff for their corporation to allow the collection to be on loan to Pechanga for further study. A special thanks to Jim McPherson for all your hard work, dedication, and guidance on the collection and all the hours you spent helping me with the analysis: Thanks, Jim, for pushing me to take on such a task. I offer a special thanks to my family for their support in this journey, especially my husband and mother. Thank you Dr. Peréz and Dr. Mayes for all your guidance, support, and dedication to this important project: It would have never been possible without you two. Thank you Dr. Schellenberg for serving as a member of my thesis committee. Lastly, I would like to thank Amy Gusick for your editorial review.

1

INTRODUCTION

View of the Santa Margarita River at 'Éxva Teméeku.

This book investigates the Luiseño Indian village site, 'éxva Teméeku, with an analysis of the precontact archaeological materials that were excavated in 1952 by B.E. McCown and his crew under the direction of the Archaeological Survey Association of Southern California. Since the time of the excavation, the collection was originally stored at the San Bernardino Historical Society's Museum in Redlands, California and was later moved to the San Bernardino County Museum. Gerald Smith, the president of the San Bernardino Historical Society in 1952, deemed the entire collection available to all students of Anthropology for research purposes.

On July 16, 1951 the excavation at 'éxva Teméeku began. The area was surveyed and divided into ten-foot squares, the squares were numbered northerly, and its southeast corner designated each square. Each excavator was assigned a five-foot square that was excavated at six-inch levels. All excavators screened soil with quarter inch screens (McCown 1955). After the excavation was complete McCown published a report on the findings in 1955 titled "Temeku: A Page from the History of the Luiseño Indians" through the Archaeological survey association of Southern California. After careful review of this document and a detailed inventory of the 'éxva Teméeku collection, I determined that many of the artifact counts did not match up. Much of the provenience has been lost, most likely due to the lack of a collection catalogue or numbering system for the collection. I will discuss this issue in more detail in the Museum Ethics section in Chapter 8.

The Luiseño Creation Story ultimately justifies the importance of the 'éxva Teméeku site and its collections. According to the Creation Story of the Luiseño Indians, 'éxva Teméeku, is where the first beings were born. This includes people, trees, animals, rocks, and rivers (DuBois 1908). This narrative yields insight into the construction of the past and allows for archaeological interpretations of the 'éxva Teméeku village. Utilizing ethnographic and archaeological materials together reveals the power archaeology holds in the way the "past is interpreted, discussed, and presented" (Watkins 2003).

The version of the Luiseño creation story that is included here was derived from Constance Dubois (1904, 1908). It contains ethnographic accounts of the Luiseño creation story recorded from informants of the Rincon Band of Luiseño Indians. Since the ethnographic account of the story originated from a different Luiseño band, the version below was loosely based on Dubois' ethnographic account with a few characters and events in the story modified to fit the Pechanga Band's public version of the story. This version of our creation story had to be agreed upon by all cultural representatives at Pechanga and has never been in print for the public until now.

In the Luiseño Creation Story, the world is believed to have begun in Temecula. It is believed that in the beginning all was empty space. Kíwvish 'atáxvish was the only being. This period was called 'óomay Yáamay and it signified emptiness. Then things came into shape, working in darkness. There was a gray glimmering, like the whiteness of frost and the dimness of twilight. Then Kíwvish 'atáxvish made a man, Túukumit, (the sky); and a woman, Tamáayawut, (the Earth). Tamáayawut (the Earth) became the mother of all things. She gave birth to the Káamalam. Her first born children were: Ṣíivat (crystal), Pávyut (sacred pointed knife), 'úshla (wild rose), Píkwla (blackberry), Néenixyal (sedge), Páachayal (bulrush), Tóopal (mortar), and Támyash (sacred bowl) (Dubois 1904).

Then came forth all other things: people, animals, trees, rocks, and rivers, but they were not as we see them today. All things then were people. Then Temét (the Sun) was born and gave tremendous light, which struck the people in agony and caused them to roll on the ground. Tamáayawut (the Earth) witnessed this, so she caught the Sun and hid him (Dubois 1906).

At first the Káamalam rolled, like newborn babies. They began to crawl. For food they ate tóovish (white clay). Then Tamáayawut (Earth-Mother) made the sea so that her children could bathe in it. The breeze from the sea filled their lungs with air (Dubois 1904).

The Káamalam moved to a place called Nachíivo Pomíisavo, but it was too small so they moved to a place called 'exva Teméeku, the place now known as Temeku. Here they settled while everything was still in darkness (DuBois 1908).

Tamáayawut (Earth-Mother) took Temét out of his hiding place and immediately there was light. Everyone could see each other. While the Sun was standing among them, they decided that he must go east and west to give light all over the world. Everyone raised their arms to the sky, and cried out, "xá' xá' xá'," and Temét went up into the sky (DuBois 1904).

While the Káamalam were living at Temecula, there was a man, Wuyóot, who was very wise and was their teacher. He watched over them.

There was a beautiful woman whom Wuyóot had especially admired. Her name was Waxáawut (frog). She had a beautiful face and long hair that fell to her feet. Wuyóot watched her one day when she jumped into the water and he saw that her back was hollow and flat like that of a frog; his admiration quickly turned to disgust (DuBois 1904).

Waxáawut saw Wuyóot; she read his thoughts and was filled with anger. When she told káarawut (earthworm), móota (gopher) and yóovish (meadow mouse) of his feelings towards her, they conspired together and decided to kill Wuyóot with witchcraft.

As soon as they witched him, Wuyóot fell sick. Many tried to help, but all remedies were useless. The Káamalam tried to cure him, so they took him to the seven Hot Springs of the valley (DuBois 1904).

Wuyóot's condition worsened and he called for his best friend Chixéemal (kingbird). He told Chixéemal (kingbird) that he had been poisoned. At this point in life, there had been no death. Wuyóot told Chixéemal (kingbird) how his death should be handled. He told Chixéemal (kingbird) that after he died, he would come back. Wuyóot died at Paayáchi (Elsinore).

Chixéemal arranged the cremation for Wuyóot on Pu'éska Mountain. The Káamalam built a pyre for the cremation. Kúyvaxash (glowworm), an old woman, brought a little fire hidden under her arm to light the pyre. Kangaroo rat (pa'ásh) made a carrying net to lift Wuyóot's body.

The Káamalam did not want their brother 'anó' (Coyote) around during the cremation. They told 'anó' to go to the north to get fire; while he was gone, the Káamalam lit the pyre. The men carried the body in the net and laid it on the pyre. 'anó' turned around, saw smoke, and he ran back (DuBois 1906).

When 'anó' got to the cremation site, the Káamalam took sticks to drive him away. They stood in a circle close together around the fire. 'anó' jumped directly over húunal (badger) and snatched Wuyóot's heart from the fire. It was the only part of the body that had not burned; he ran off and devoured it. The Káamalam tried to chase him.

The people took Wuyóot's ashes, put them in a basket, and buried it in the ground. While burying it, they sang songs and danced. This was the first time there had been singing and dancing for the dead. Tóovit (rabbit) sang first and 'álwut (crow) was the first to dance. Qaxáal (quail) was the first to cut his hair as a sign of mourning (DuBois 1906).

Chixéemal told the Káamalam of Wuyóot's plan for the order of life in the world.

This is how the animals, plants and the entire world came to be. The people that were left as people were called 'atáaxum. Chixéemal rose to the highest mountain (Piiwípwi), and began to tell the people that Wuyóot was coming back and to look towards the east for him. When the people looked, to their surprise they saw him. He came up in the shape of Móyla (the Moon) (DuBois 1908). To this day he lights the night as a promise he will always be with his 'atáaxum—the people—the Payómkawichum.

The 'éxva Teméeku village is important in the creation story, as it is believed to be one of the first villages of the Luiseño people as they were traveling their way through the world. These artifacts are the first-born children and the animals involved in the centering of the world. They have an integral role in the development of the Luiseño culture. Two of the first-born artifacts are a crystal and a mortar, which are in the 'éxva Teméeku collection. The story affirms the concept of death and establishes funeral ritualism (Bean and Shipek 1978). This narrative gives importance to the relationship that Luiseño people have with the sky above them and the earth that surrounds them. This story explains the environmental, social, and spiritual relations of the Luiseño people. The 'éxva Teméeku site is not only archaeologically significant in the density and diversity of artifacts collected from the site, it is the center of the Luiseños' origin and, thus, of their world.

The analysis of the precontact archaeological materials from the 'éxva Teméeku collection provides insight into what life was like for the Luiseño people living at 'éxva Teméeku before contact. More specifically, the faunal analysis provides insight to diet while also highlighting the specific utilization of animals and hunting strategies. The analysis of the lithic artifacts provides information about the materials utilized. Obsidian hydration dating was conducted on obsidian artifacts to determine an age for the collection. Additionally, x-ray fluorescence was used to identify trace elements in the obsidian to determine the source of material. The shell analysis reveals the patterns needed for dating cultural deposits, trade routes, relations among cultures, and it also provides insight into the reconstruction of social and political organization. Lastly, the human remains provide insight into Luiseño burial practices.

Providing a descriptive analysis is the goal of this book. It is important that all prehistoric elements of the collection are accounted for and analyzed in this study in order to provide new knowledge for the discipline of anthropology and for future researchers. The prehistoric material analysis of the 'éxva Teméeku collection will aid in any future direct references to 'éxva Teméeku in Southern California archaeological site reports while also providing an argument for the significance of the site and need for protection of the 'éxva Teméeku site in the event of future development.

2

ARCHAEOLOGY

The area that was excavated in 1952 by B.E. McCown under the direction of the Archaeological Survey Association of Southern California.

A detailed summary of 'éxva Teméeku's site reports and recordings are discussed in order to provide background information about this site. Information on the sites within a two-mile radius will also be discussed to provide a regional context.

The 'éxva Teméeku site was originally placed on The National Register in the early 1940s by Dorothy Luhrs. Luhrs noted artifact fragments on the site's surface and remarked that 'éxva Teméeku was an old village near the Pechanga Reservation (Luhrs 1940). In 1947, the Smithsonian Institution requested an excavation of 'éxva Teméeku under the direction of the Archaeological Survey Association of Southern California (McCown 1955). In 1952, 'éxva Teméeku was revisited by Pilling and recorded as a Historical site. In 1965, 'éxva Teméeku was revisited and recorded by J. K. Chartkoff and L. Kona as a Historical Luiseño Village site, which included ramadas, fire rings and Spanish structure features. They reported that more information could be gathered from the 'éxva Teméeku site (Chartkoff and Kona 1965). In 1981, 'éxva Teméeku was revisited and recorded by Stein as a "Prehistoric site" with a lithic scatter, midden soil, bedrock milling, slicks, granite boulders, and artifacts that included scrapers, flakes of granite and quartz, and pottery sherds (Stein 1981). The following year L.L. Bowles revisited 'éxva Teméeku and concluded that there was evidence of habitation, an extensive area of dark soil, fire-affected rocks, flakes, and bedrock features (Bowles 1982). Bowles recorded the site as both prehistoric and historic, with evidence of pot hunting. Bowles also noted that if the area on which 'éxva Teméeku is located were ever developed, it would result in a massive loss of information (Bowles 1982). All of the records above are part of the Eastern Information Center's site records database at the University of California, Riverside. Cheryl Bowden-Smithy last recorded 'éxva Teméeku in 2002 in the State of California, Resource Agency Department of Parks and Recreation annual report. Bowden recorded 22 additional milling features on site, and further expanded the border of the 'éxva Teméeku site (Bowden 2002). This further expanded the borders of the 'éxva Teméeku Village site. Based on the 'éxva Teméeku site records it is evident that the Luiseño people inhabited this site for many years (Carrico 2008).

A total of 108 recorded sites (Appendix A) are located within a two-mile radius of the 'éxva Teméeku site. There are 32 sites that contained bedrock millings and/or slicks; 46 sites had evidence of grinding tools such as manos, metates, mortars, and pestles; five sites had projectile points or projectile point fragments; seven sites contained stone tools such as hammerstones, cores or core tools; 12 sites had pottery sherds; 22 sites showed evidence of tool production with a lithic scatter, or isolated flakes; six had fire-affected rocks; two had shell fragments; 12 sites contained evidence of midden; three sites had pictographs; and two sites had petroglyphs, rock images made by carving or pecking. Only eight sites were recorded as precontact habitation sites, and 10 sites as temporary campsites. After careful review of the site records, it can be construed that any lithic scatter or isolated artifacts not in association with bedrock milling have been labeled as a temporary campsite, and habitation sites are only noted in site records if there is more than one bedrock milling. This industry standard, however, deserves to be reevaluated on a regional level. I argue here that the high number of sites near and around 'éxva Teméeku provide evidence that the majority of these labeled temporary campsites are actually connected to the 'éxva Teméeku site (Appendix B).

If we looked at these sites not as isolates from one another, but rather in connection to each other, we begin to see a bigger picture. It is evident, in my opinion, that many of the smaller sites with only debitage that are in close proximity to bedrock mortars (i.e. cooking areas), need to be considered in relation to larger sites, or rather, the rest of the site. For instance, differentiation of work and living areas, does not infer separate sites: making or refining tools, would not necessarily take place in an area where food is prepared, cooked or served. The five sites that contained isolated projectile points could possibly be hunting areas or pathways that people took in returning to the main living area. When looking at the vast geographical area of the original Luiseño territory, one begins to understand that this was not a simple hunter and gatherer society of passive collectors, but rather, a society which controlled its vegetation with burning management, knew when to replenish the soil, moved seasonally to maximize foraging returns, and consumed a wide variety of food to ensure adequate nutrition. This type of subsistence and settlement patterning documented during historic times has been practiced for thousands of years (Carrico 2008).

It is important to note that much of the work recording and placing sites on the National Historic Register is driven by development, is project specific, and is subject to time constraints. The archaeological work itself is not driven by larger research questions but is strictly limited to the project area. I believe this has given rise to the identification of bedrock mortars or slicks as temporary campsites and is the reason why a larger number of individual sites surround the 'éxva Teméeku site. Contract archaeologists are ending site boundaries when no surface artifacts are visible after 25 meters (Glassow 1985). This limited interpretation of what a Luiseño village looked like based on site records or site reports is a direct result of the Contract Archaeology practiced in California since the 1970s. Glassow stated that "contract funded archaeology site evaluations are extremely limited since the contract of these excavations has usually been small-scale testing programs for purposed of significance assessment" (Glassow 1985:61). The process of Cultural Resource Management reports evaluating significance has become a debate between the Academic field of Archaeology and Contract Archaeologists. Glassow highlights that, in order to understand the larger settlement pattern system, one must note all the activities that were practiced on these small sites (Glassow 1985). This lack of research has unfortunately resulted in destruction of an unknown number of Luiseño sites along with research data. Glassow explains that many smaller sites are not investigated further and are being destroyed by land development with no data (Glassow 1985). In the future, the 'éxva Teméeku data that has been generated, could be used in a comparison study with other sites that are in close proximity to 'éxva Teméeku.

3

PROJECT OVERVIEW

The 'éxva Teméeku collection was sorted and identified at the San Bernardino County Museum in 2010 by employees from Pechanga Cultural Resources Center (PCRC), including the author. The collection was unprocessed and stored in 2,050 bags with limited provenience information. The PCRC staff sorted all material, noting any provenience information provided. In cases where no provenience was recorded on the bag, or the writing had become too faint for legibility, material was marked as unknown provenience. Each bag was sorted, counted, weighed, and entered into the San Bernardino County Museum database system. The selected items that were individually measured and weighed included ground stone, milling stone, lithic tools, modified bone, decorated pottery, and adornment artifacts. Once a complete catalogue was generated, the PCRC submitted a loan request for further analysis to be completed at the Pechanga Cultural Resource Center. San Bernardino County Museum agreed to release the collection on loan to Pechanga until 2013 with the possibility of an extension.

In February 2011, the collection was housed at Pechanga Cultural Resource Center and was further sorted by artifact type, material, and site location. The individuals involved included the author along with several colleagues from both history and archaeological backgrounds and are referred to as the PCRC staff throughout this thesis. All unit and level references in this chapter can be located on the excavation map (Appendix B).

The 'éxva Teméeku collection proved to have evidence of years of habitation with over 8,000 catalogued data entries of lithics, faunal, shells, and ceramics. 'Éxva Teméeku has been described as a village site in Luiseño oral histories, and the archaeological assemblage reflects an intensity of occupation with a density and diversity of material indicative of extensive and/or intensive site use. Site deposits at 'éxva Teméeku have been described as a well-developed dark greasy midden around bedrock outcrops that support 10 to 21 milling features (Oxendine 1983). The midden deposits, density and diversity of cultural material, and the Luiseño oral history support the assumption that 'éxva Teméeku is a village site that experienced extensive habitation for several hundred years.

4

LITHIC ANALYSIS

Tool Production

Stone tools are a large part of the earliest record of human material culture, and as such, the manufacture and modification of lithic material are an integral part of modern archaeology (Odell 2003). The initial acquisition of raw materials from a quarry or mine provides insight into the pathways of my Luiseño ancestors. Location of raw material source can help define trade routes and infer trade relations. In the 'éxva Teméeku assemblage, there is a wide range of variability with many different local stone types represented. The identification and analysis of stone tools and debitage involves specialized knowledge and interpretive techniques that can inform on the technology development and manufacturing process of the people who inhabited the 'éxva Teméeku site. This analysis gives insight into production intensity, types of technologies, and stages in the reduction sequence represented at the site, along with the types of material used in stone tool production (Sutton and Arkush 2006).

Odell's (2003) lithic manual was used for outlining the fundamentals of the lithic analysis. The lithic analysis began with debitage analysis to identify stages of tool production. Lithic debitage types were then organized into technological types based on both Andrefsky (2001) and Odell's (2003) lithic debitage classification system. The debitage classification includes: biface early percussion, biface edge modified, biface early pressure, biface early percussion, biface margin removal, biface outré passé, burin spall, complete cortical, complete cortical outré passé, flake fragment cortical, flake fragment no cortex, no cortex, no cortex alternate, no cortex blub removal, no cortex edge modified, no cortex margin removal, no cortex outré passé, no cortex undulation removal, partially cortical, partially cortical alternate, partially cortical edge, partially cortical margin removal, shatter, shatter cortical, and shatter no cortex. Additional identification includes platform types: platform absent, natural platform, multifaceted platform, and single faceted platform. Other identification includes material, count and weight in grams. In this analysis, there are many data entries that contain a variety of debitage types of the same material with the same catalogue number. These were not given new individual numbers due to time constraints; however, each debitage type was kept separate within the bag. For example, in the database there may be five basalt debitage-type entries all with the same catalogue number.

The analysis of the flakes will contribute to the overall research findings of this project as it was structured to generate data that will ultimately function as a descriptive account of the activities that occurred on site. The flakes constituted 2,151 data entries (Appendix C-I). Debitage analysis results are limited due to the large number of flakes that had no recorded provenience. Items that were catalogued separately include bifaces, projectile points, flake tools, cores, and hammerstones. Due to the large volume of flakes in the collection, analyzing every flake proved to be an arduous procedure, so a representative sample was taken from flakes that had a provenience. All flakes that did not have a provenience were not analyzed but were entered into a database for possible future study.

Lithic Materials

The local materials in the collection are from the general area of Southern California and are common material types. The materials identified include quartz, cryptocrystalline quartz, metavolcanic, basalt, metasedimentary, Santiago Peak Metavolcanic and metaquartzite. Most of these materials are abundant in various locations around Southern California, with the exception of the metavolcanic material, which is only found on Santiago Peak located in Orange County, California. All of the local materials were compared with other local lithic collections stored at the Pechanga Cultural Resource Center. Due to the wide range of availably of these materials and the close proximity of 'éxva Teméeku, it is possible that some materials were traded with other Luiseño villages.

Imported Material

Six obsidian artifacts from the 'éxva Teméeku collection were sent to the Northwest Research Obsidian Studies Laboratory for further study. At the lab, the imported material was researched using a large database of sourced obsidian from California and dated using obsidian hydration measurements.

Obsidian Dating

The six obsidian artifacts from 'éxva Teméeku were analyzed using energy dispersive X-ray fluorescence (XRF) trace element analysis. The XRF analysis identified the geological sources of the obsidian. Five of the specimens were also dated using obsidian hydration.

XRF analysis is a nondestructive trace element test that uses a Spectrace 5000 energy dispersive XRF spectrometer. The diagnostic trace element values used to characterize the samples were compared directly to known obsidian sources reported in the Northwest Research Obsidian Studies Laboratory geological source samples database. The samples were correlated to a parent obsidian source, or geochemical source group. If the trace elements fell within two standard deviations of the known upper and lower limits of chemical variability, then it was attributed to that source. Currently the Northwest Research Obsidian Studies Laboratory has over 100,000 analyzed and sourced samples for comparison (Skinner and Thatcher 2011).

The method for obsidian hydration analysis includes cutting an appropriate section of each artifact and selecting it for a hydration slide. Two parallel cuts are made at the edge of the obsidian artifact using a lapidary saw equipped with a .004 inch thick diamond blade. This results in a cross section removal of about 1 millimeter. This sample is then mounted on a petrographic microscope slide with Lakeside thermoplastic cement and ground into a thickness of 30-50 microns. The prepared slide is measured using an Olympus BHT petrographic microscope with a video micrometer unit and a digital imaging video camera. Next, a clear hydration layer is identified. Averages of four rim measurements are typically needed for examination. Hydration thicknesses are reported to the nearest 0.1μm. The standard deviation is recorded for each measured surface hydration thickness for the rim values (Skinner and Thatcher 2011).

XRF spectroscopy was performed using energy dispersive or wavelength-dispersive modes. This only affects the surface of the artifact and is non-destructive. In this process, the sample is irradiated by a beam of x-rays that excite electrons into higher energy levels (Odell 2003). These then drop back into their normal levels, leading the second rays to become fluorescent. These fluorescent waves are measured by the intensities of the x-rays different wave-lengths.

The results of the XRF analysis correlate with three geochemical groups of known obsidian sources. The locations indicate that three samples come from Obsidian Butte and two come from Coso Volcanic field. Both locations are approximately 300 miles away from the 'éxva Teméeku site. One of the bifaces was not included in Table 1 because it was burned. This type of modification prevents accurate XRF analysis. It was conjectured by the Northwest lab researchers that this biface is possibly from an obsidian source in Mexico, but their database is currently not sufficient to make a definitive source location. Four of the six specimens analyzed using XRF were also prepared for obsidian hydration analysis. These specimens yielded four measurable rims.

The obsidian dating results provide a time frame for the 'éxva Teméeku site's oldest occupation component dating to at least 6,000 years before the present (YBP). In California, one must factor in bioturbation and animal activity which can cause a reworking of the soil and sediments and lead to disruption of the chronological sequence in the site deposits. The results in Table 1 appear to reflect this situation, with some of the older dates occurring in higher levels. For instance, levels 3 and 4 have obsidian hydration dates of 2,800 and 2,600 respectively, while level 5 has a date of 1,800. Due to the apparent mixing of the datable material within the deposit at 'éxva Teméeku, a fine-grained chronological analysis will not be published.

Table 1. Obsidian Results

Cat #	Unit	Level	Artifact Type	Obsidian Source	Rim Measurement	Date Range
184-3442	100F5	4	Biface	Obsidian Butte	2.6 ± 0.1	2,600 ± 100 yrs
184-3452	110I5	3	Flake	Obsidian Butte	2.8 ± 0.1	2,800 ± 100 yrs
184-3492	95E5	7	Flake	Coso (West Sugarloaf)	6.0 ± 0.1	6,000 ± 100 yrs
184-3415	95E5	5	Flake	Obsidian Butte	1.8 ± 0.1	1,800 ± 100 yrs

Cores

A core is defined as any rock mass that shows flake scar patterning with a removal of flakes taken from all sides (Andrefsky 2005). The classification of cores includes material type, multidirectional or unidirectional flake removal, original form of cobble, flake or tabular, the number of negative flake scars, secondary tool functions such as hammerstone or scraper, and the number of edges modified. Core length, width, and thickness is measured in millimeters and the core was weighed in grams using a digital scale. The secondary tool function category is necessary because no additional categories were created for scrapers or core tools. If a core is identified as exhausted in the comments section, it means no additional flaking can occur on that rock mass.

McCown (1955) found a total of 73 scrapers made from dacite, quartz, rhyolite, agate and granite. Twenty-five of these were from level 1, 19 from level 2, 16 from level 3, six from level 4, one from level 6, two from both level 7 and level 9. In my analysis, I did not have a category for scrapers but noted cores with a secondary tool function as a scraper because of their similar core/flake scar patterning.

A total of 102 cores were identified from levels 1 through 6 (Appendix M). The breakdown included: 38 quartz, 26 cryptocrystalline quartz, seven metaquartzite, six metavolcanic, four obsidian, two Santiago Peak Metavolcanic, one quartz crystal, one metasedimentary and one wonderstone. The cores identified were flaked off from large masses of materials not found near the 'éxva Teméeku site. Only 23 have a secondary tool function, such as a hammerstone, and nine were used as scrapers. The majority of the cores have three or more flake scars showing edge modification, and 20 cores are classified as exhausted. It is evident by the large amount of cores identified that the initial stage of tool manufacture was taking place on site.

Hammerstones

Hammerstones were used in both tool manufacturing and food processing for crushing a variety of stone and plant materials. A total of 22 hammerstones were accounted for in McCown's (1955) report. The breakdown of material included: three dacite in level 1, four porphy and one quartz in level 2, three quartz in level 3, four granite, one rhyolite and one quartz in level 5, one granite and one quartz in level 7, one granitic in level 8 and one rhyolite in level 9. Currently, 20 hammerstones are accounted for in the collection (Appendix N). Out of these, 15 have no recorded provenience and five are recorded in levels 2, 6, and 8. The variety of materials includes basalt, granitic, cryptocrystalline quartz, metaquatzite, metasedimentary, quartz and rhyolite. The majority, were manufactured from cobbles with all edges modified. One hammerstone is recorded with a secondary tool function as a scraper with one sharp edge.

Flakes

McCown (1955) noted that flakes of both agate and rhyolite were found in levels 1 through 8. Obsidian from an unknown source was found in levels 6 and 7. A large amount of flakes were identified in levels 1 through 3 and a significantly lower number were identified in levels 4 through 10. Previous research considered the inconsistency in flake recovery rates throughout the deposit puzzling and struggled with identifying tool manufacture processes on the 'éxva Teméeku site (McCown 1955). The current analysis presented focuses on these inconsistencies and possible conclusion for the variation will be discussed in the last chapter.

The flakes were analyzed by material type (Appendix C-H). Only flakes with a recorded provenience are classified by type and platform. Due to the large list of classification types (Appendix C-H) they are grouped as bifaces, percussion flakes and shatter flakes for interpretation purposes. The flake type results are recorded in percentages in Table 2. A breakdown of the total number of flakes that are present in the collection is included, but the results presented in this thesis are only for the flakes with a recorded provenience. The lack of recorded proveniences for the flakes resulted in very limited data for the flake types.

Based on the identification of the flake types, it is evident that the occupants of 'éxva Teméeku were quarrying their raw materials off site and transporting them home. This conclusion is made based on the lack of cortex in every material on site. With the lack of pressure flaking on site it can be inferred that all finishing touches were completed outside the excavated area. This is a limited conclusion based on the large amount of flakes with no provenience and the lithic material that was smaller than the quarter inch screens used at the time of the excavation. The current findings indicate that there is no evidence of projectile points being manufactured at the excavated area of 'éxva Teméeku. These conclusions have been derived from the limited spectrum of the flake analysis.

Table 2. Flake Type Analysis

Material Type	Total #	Analyzed	Biface	Percussion	Shatter
Basalt	2,161	85%	7.60%	50.90%	41.40%
Cryptocryalline Quartz	2,469	60%	16.10%	57.80%	25.40%
Metasedimentary	447	0.01%	0%	60%	40%
Metavolcanic	555	48%	0.30%	52.90%	40%
Metaquartzite	2,408	23%	6.90%	66.30%	25.80%
Obsidian	634	21%	20%	18.50%	61.50%
Quartz	6,867	5%	4%	56%	40%
Ryholite	2	100%	0%	50%	50%
Santiago Peak Metavolcanic	71	75%	15%	45.20%	39.60%
Wonderstone	26	100%	19.20%	69.20%	11.50%

Flake Tools

A flake tool is identified as any flake that exhibits modified edges by intentional modification. These modifications are small or large flake scars at the edges, and vary from highly to slightly modified. The number of altered edges ranges from one to three. The type of modification is recorded as bifacial or unifacial. All measurements are recorded in millimeters and weighed in grams using a digital scale. Flake tools were not identified in McCown's (1955) report, so no comparisons can be made. The majority of the flake tools were identified at the Pechanga Cultural Resource Center from bags of debitage.

A total of 88 flake tools were identified (Appendix L). Thirty-seven have no recorded provenience, and the remaining 51 were recovered in levels 1 through 7. The majority of the flakes are made from basalt or metaquartzite. Other materials utilized included: 16 cryptocrystalline quartz, 11 metavolanic, six quartz, five Santiago Peak Metavolanic, five metasedimentary, one granitic, and one wonderstone. All flake tools have one to three edges modified, and the preferred type of modification is unifacial. These tools were used for cutting or scraping.

Bifaces

A biface is produced by flaking opposite sides of a stone for thinning production of a stone tool (Andrefsky 2005). Once a stone tool was defined as a biface based on the above criteria, it was further classified based on material, condition, portion, and flaking method. The biface measurements of length, width, and thickness are recorded in millimeters and the biface weight is recorded in grams using a triple balance beam scale. The portion category for the biface notes the presence of the middle or end section of the biface fragment. The flaking method is identified as either percussion or pressure, or in some cases, both. Percussion flaking is the method of striking with a precursor to detach flakes from the objective pieces. Pressure flaking removes flakes with pressure from the detached piece (Andrefsky 2005).

A total of 206 bifaces were identified (Appendix J). The largest quantities were in levels 1 through 4. In the deeper levels biface quantities were low, with five in level 5, two in level 6, and one in level 7. The dominant material is quartz, with 99 bifaces identified. The other predominant material is cryptocrystalline quartz with 77 bifaces identified. The remaining materials that were sporadically found include 15 basalt bifaces, eight metaquartzite bifaces, four obsidian bifaces, two metavolcanic, two metasedimentary, and one wonderstone biface. The biface fragments identified total 160. Only 19 are noted as nearly complete with sixty percent of the biface fragment present. A total of 17 are identified as whole. Out of the 160 biface fragments, 73 are recorded with the end section present and 40 with the medial section present. The dominant flaking method is a combination of pressure and percussion. Only 21 bifaces have evidence of pressure flakes, and three show evidence of percussion flaking. The scarcity of pressure flakes found in the flake types suggests that tools were refined in another location.

McCown (1955) did not define any bifaces in his report. It is possible that the excavation team classified bifaces as projectile points; however this only accounts for a small percentage since the majority of bifaces identified were sorted out from larger bags of flakes at the San Bernardino County Museum and the Pechanga Cultural Resources Center.

Projectile Points

Projectile points are defined as bifacially flaked stones that show evidence of hafting (grooved) elements at the proximal end that allowed for attachment to another object with sinew or twine (Andrefsky 2005). Projectile points' overall shape is triangular and occurs in broad and narrow forms. The classification of each projectile point includes material, condition, flaking method, flaking pattern, and shape. The length, width, and thickness of the projectile points are measured in millimeters and each point was weighed in grams using a triple beam scale. The descriptive categories for the flaking method includes, pressure flaking and both percussion and pressure flaking. The flaking patterns are recorded as collateral, random, or transverse parallel (Andrefsky 2005). The points are further classified by shape based on Odell's (2003) description of projectile points. Some modifications were made so descriptions reflect the exact characteristics of each projectile point's shape, edges, and base modification (Appendix K). Shapesare described as triangular or Elko-eared with the sides being round, notched, or serrated and the base as concave (in), convex (out), or straight.

McCown (1955) accounted for 754 complete and partial projectile points in the seven upper levels. McCown classified 391 projectile points and of those, 300 were recorded as triangular straight to deep indented base, the

Left: In 1952, B.E. McCown reported that over 700 projectile points were uncovered in the excavation. Sadly, only 93 projectile points were identified in the current 'Éxva Teméeku collection. Right: A trio of cryptocrystalline quartz projectile points.

typical types from the local area. Some of the projectile points had serrated edges. Blades were described as having a straight to rounded base, and atypical types were noted as having side notches with a square base (McCown 1955). McCown (1955) suggested some of the projectile points from the deeper levels are from an entirely different culture than the Luiseño. While the points recovered from the lower levels at the site are considered older based on deposit chronology, point style, and form, I argue that the Luiseño people are responsible for their manufacture based on the longevity of 'éxva Teméeku site occupation described in the Luiseño Creation Story. These points may represent an earlier projectile point form in the technology development of the Luiseño inhabitants at the 'éxva Teméeku site.

A total of 93 projectile points were identified in the collection (Appendix K). This value is vastly different from McCown's previous recordings. Out of the 93 projectile points identified, 25 are whole, 38 are nearly complete with sixty percent of the projectile point present, and 30 fragments have less than sixty percent present. The majority of the projectile points were recovered from levels 1 through 5. Over a third of the projectile points have no provenience recorded and only three came from the lower levels. Quartz and cryptocrystalline quartz are the two dominant materials for projectile point manufacture. Other materials that are in the collection included: 11 basalt, five metavolcanic, three obsidian, two metaquartzite, and one metasedimentary. Over half of the projectile points show evidence of pressure flaking, and 38 show evidence of both pressure and percussion flaking. The majority of the flaking patterns are random. Out of the whole and nearly complete projectile points, the following types were identified: 18 triangular with a concave base, seven triangular with a concave base, five triangular serrated with a concave base, five triangular side notch concave base, four triangular straight base, three triangular serrated with a convex base, two Elko-eared side notch with a concave base, one Elko eared side notch with a straight base, one triangular serrated straight base, and one triangular serrated convex base. Two of the points are recorded as possible learning projectile points in the comment section. Although this observation is based on my exposure to lithic technology of the Luiseño people, this type of observation has been debated in the literature on the knowledge of understanding lithic industries. It is believed that this type of learning took place where the raw material was located, not at the place of home-based workings. The majority of the projectile points identified are the correct size for attaching to arrows used to hunt small game. The older Elko eared style was used for larger game hunting and would be attached to a spear or atlatl.

McCown's (1955) report identified over 700 whole and fragmented projectile points. This count does not

Granite mano and metate.

match what was found in the collection. If counts from the projectile points and bifaces are added together, the numbers still fail to match up with the total reported bifaces collected by McCown (1955). A total of 455 projectile points or projectile point fragments are currently missing from the 'éxva Teméeku collection. This issue of accountability for collections will be discussed further in Chapter 8, Ethics, under the subheading Archaeologists.

Groundstones

The ground stone analysis will contribute to the understanding of precontact Luiseño lifestyle. The analysis will focus on technology as a reflection of life history and draw attention to the importance of individuals as "social agents who are making culturally constituted choices concerning design, use, and disuse" (Adams 2002:3). The ground stone and milling stone analysis includes identification of design, manufacture, use, wear, material, and object size. Each groundstone and millingstone artifact was measured in millimeters and weighed in grams with a digital scale. It is appropriately noted in the comment section for each catalogued entry if an artifact had a secondary use or was burned. The ground stone assemblage includes manos, pestles, heating stones, pipes, beads and pottery anvils. All will be discussed in this section except the pottery anvils, which are included in the ceramic section. The milling stones include metate and mortar fragments.

The classification system used for the ground stone and milling stone analysis is based on Adams (2002) percussion tool guidelines. Some of the descriptive terms were modified to accommodate the specific shape and possible function of the ground stone identified in the collection.

Groundstone function

Groundstone and milling stones were part of the daily routine for the Luiseño people living during precontact times. Manos, pestles, metates and mortars were all utilized for food processing. The variety of food types pulverized and crushed included nuts, seashells, seeds, plants, bones, and meats. Heating stones were used for cooking, heating food, and heating dwellings. The steatite stones were warmed on the open fire then placed in a basket or bed for cooking and heating. Beads were also constructed of stone and typically measured from three to five millimeters (Iovin 1963). There are two stone beads in the collection made from soapstone (Appendix T). One of them has no provenience and the other is from level 3 or 4. These were used for adornment purposes.

Manos

McCown (1955) reported 58 manos, with a breakdown of material as follows: 46 granite, five quartz, two rhyolite and five basalt. Twenty-four of the manos were unifacially shaped, 30 bifacially shaped and five were wedge-shaped. Each of the biface manos was shaped on the edges. McCown provided a chart for each mano material and depth of recovery. The deepest was found in level 8, while the majority in levels 2 and 4. It is important to take into account that McCown does not define between whole and fragmented manos.

The identified manos in the collection do not match McCown's original findings. In the collection there are 82 mano and mano fragments made from six local materials: basalt, gabbro, granite, quartzite, schist and vesicular basalt (Appendix O). Out of the 82 manos, 18 were recorded in levels 1 through 5 and 64 were recorded with an unknown provenience. Fifty of those are identified as bifacally shaped, 29 as unifacially shaped and two with multiple ground surfaces. The manufacturing form includes: 48 modified from cobbles, 29 were of natural cobble form, and three original forms were indeterminate. The manos' shapes include: 33 ovoid, one rectangular, one triangular, one round, three irregular, and 41 are of unknown shapes due to their fragmentary state. All manos were identified with a milling surface use pattern and milling as their primary function. A total of 44 manos are considered fragments with fifty percent or less of the mano present, ten are nearly complete with less than thirty percent missing, and twenty-six are considered whole. A secondary tool function was identified for 30 manos (Adams 2002). The secondary tool function includes fifteen hammerstones, eight anvils, four pecking, and four pestles. Out of the 82 manos, seven are burned and one has a drilled biconical hole.

Metates

A total of nine metate fragments were identified. These were made from granitic, slate, and vesicular basalt. Five are recorded with no provenience but could be surface findings as suggested above. Two are from level 2 and two are from levels 5 and 6. Two of the granitic metate fragments are recorded with anvil as a secondary use. Anvils were used for cracking or pounding smaller or singular nuts. Only one metate fragment is recorded as burned with an unknown provenience. When cataloging at the San Bernardino County Museum, the Curator expressed that one of the whole metates in the collection was from 'éxva Teméeku, but based on McCown's (1955) report, no whole metates were uncovered in the excavation. This whole metate is possibly not from 'éxva Teméeku, but it was cataloged with the collection under the direction of the San Bernardino County Museum curator.

The majority of the metates in the collection were made of the local granite from Temecula and the mortars from vesicular basalt which is likely from the Santa Rosa Plateau about 20 miles northwest of the 'éxva Teméeku site.

Pestles

McCown (1955) did not provide the number of pestles or their exact location in his report. He reported that pestles were found in levels 2, 3, 5, and 6. The current research identified a total of 20 pestles, with five found in levels 2 through 4 and 15 with an unknown provenience (Appendix P). Nine pestles are recorded as whole, four are nearly complete with less than thirty percent missing, and seven are considered fragments with fifty percent or more missing. The shapes of the pestles includes one rectangular, two cylindrical, eight conical and three of indeterminate shapes based on their fragmentation. Pestle fragments are recorded with medial or ends present. This includes nine fragments with neither end, 11 with both ends, and one medial section. Only eight whole pestles are accounted for in the current collection. A total of 30 pestles were used for food or material processing and seven are ceremonial. The ceremonial pestles will be discussed further in the ceremonial section. Six pestles have a secondary tool function. Two pestles are natural in shape, two have evidence of multiple areas of original surface changes, and nine have changes to the medial section surface. One of the pestles is recorded as burned.

Mortars

McCown (1955) noted portions of portable stone mortars found in the excavation.

He questioned why mortar and metate fragments were not found in the deeper levels since manos were located in level 8. Half of the granite metates were found on the surface. Basalt metate fragments were located in section 105F level 2. McCown noted a portion of a bowl was found at 13 centimeters. He suggested the artifact was part of a bowl used during a Tolache Ceremony. An additional half basalt mortar was located in 110G level 3 (McCown 1955). McCown's finding on stone mortars does not match up with the current collection.

Based on the current findings, it is believed that many of the metate fragments McCown (1955) identified are mortar fragments. A total of 39 mortar fragments were identified (Appendix S). This includes 22 vesicular basalt, 14 granitic and three basalt. Four of these are burned rim fragments located in levels 4 through 6. Overall, 13 were found in levels 5 through 6, which is deeper than McCown previously reported. Seven are from level 4, two from level 3, and an additional seven from level 4. A total of ten mortar fragments are recorded with no provenience. McCown's (1955) report stated that many fragments were found on the surface, so the unknown provenience mortar fragments from the current research may be the surface findings. The two half mortar fragments that McCown referenced are large for Luiseño ceremonial bowls.

Heating stones

McCown (1955) described a portion of heating stones in section 55-I5 at level 3 (Appendix B). This included a fragment with a portion of the hole. Another fragment was located in section 150-F5 in level 2 (Appendix B). They were noted as being two different heating stones. A total of six heating stone fragments were identified with no recorded provenience (Appendix Q). It is possible that number 2011.28.7174 or 7175 is the heating stone fragment from section 55-I5 in level 3 and 2011.28.7176 or 7177 is the fragment from 150-F5 level 2. Five of the heating stone fragments are made from steatite and one from soapstone. The portions are recorded as two medial section fragments and two end section fragments. All heating stone fragments show evidence of ground edges.

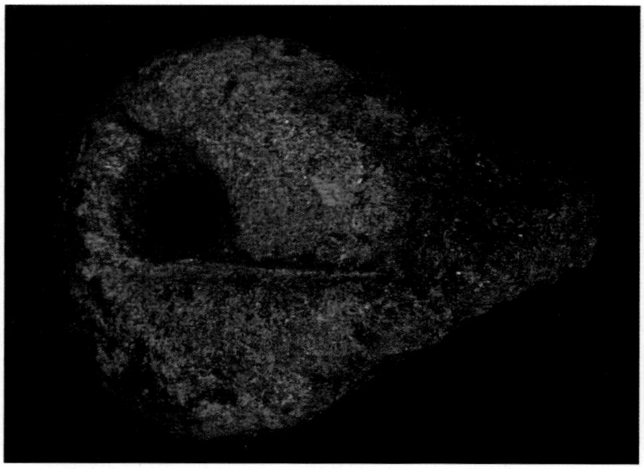

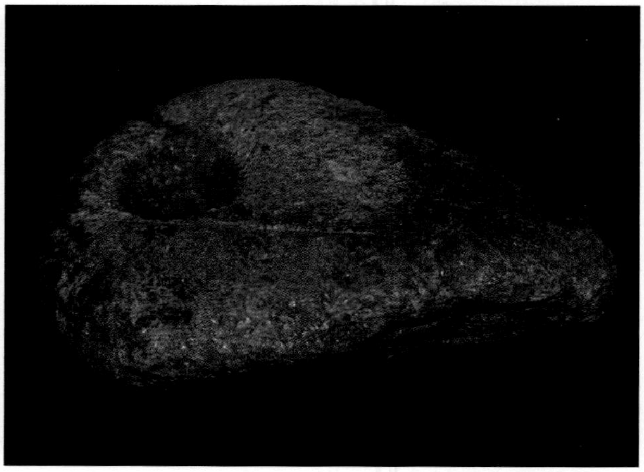

A total of five steatite heating stones were uncovered from 'Éxva Teméeku.

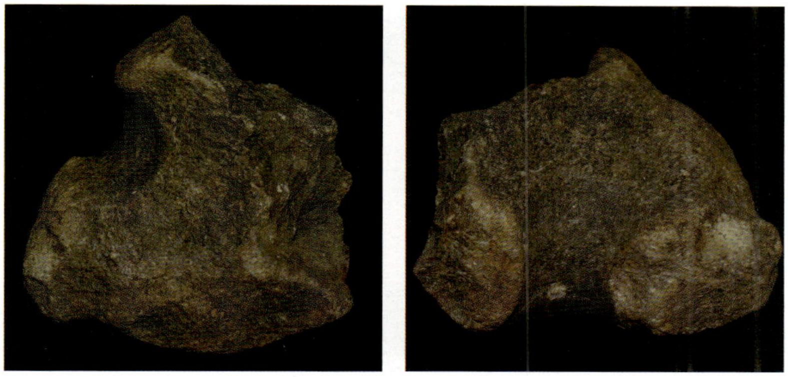

A steatite heating stone fragment.

Ceremonial Artifacts

Ceremonial items in this section include: small pestles, pipes, and a flat-bottomed spherical stone. A total of seven pestles were identified as ceremonial based on their significantly smaller size in relation to food processing pestles (Appendix P). Their length is less than 70 millimeters and their width less than 38 millimeters with a thickness of less than 27 millimeters. The smallest weighs 21.8 grams and the heaviest 107.2 grams. Six of these were in levels 2 through 4 and one has no provenience. Based on my own cultural and ethnographic information, these smaller pestles were used in a "tamyush", a small stone bowl that was exclusively used by medicine men for pounding roots or mixing paint during ceremonies (Sparkman 1908). For example, a small mortar would be used during the boys' puberty ceremony to mix the root jimson weed for the boys to drink (Sparkman 1908). Sparkman (1908) describes these pestles and mortars as neatly shaped and polished with the bowls being exactly round.

Four of the steatite pipes (Appendix R) are believed to be sucking tubes based on their wide cylinder diameter and greater length. A sucking tube was used only by medicine men for healing purposes. These types of sacred items require proper spiritual care for the Luiseño people and should not be mixed in with non-sacred or mundane items.

The flat-bottomed spherical granitic stone in the collection was likely used in the boys' puberty ceremony. During the ceremony, these stones would be heated, and the boys would jump across them in a demonstration of courage (Kroeber 1976). The flat spherical stone is considered a sacred item because of its integral role in the puberty ceremonies, which were part of a religious passage ceremony for the Luiseño people.

Pipes

McCown (1955) recorded two steatite pipes in section 100-E5 level 6 and 100 E level 5. His descriptions included the steam and bowl portions of the pipe. This does not match the findings in the 'éxva Teméeku collection because the majority of steatite pipes were whole with only one fragment. A total of five steatite stone pipes were identified (Appendix R). The closest steatite raw material source is approximately 15 miles north of the 'éxva Teméeku site. Four of these are recorded as ceremonial. The one pipe that is not ceremonial appears to be a smoking pipe; it is burned and has cross-hatching etched on the sides. It is possible that the whole pipes are not from 'éxva Teméeku but are possibly from another collection that the San Bernardino County Museum had recorded from the Temecula area. Two of these pipes have Temecula written directly on them, which leads me to believe that they are from another collection because none of the other artifacts from the 'éxva Teméeku collection have such markings. Since there is no original catalogue for the 'éxva Teméeku collection, it is difficult to determine if the pipes are actually from the 'éxva Teméeku site. This issue will be addressed further in the ethics chapter.

5

FAUNAL AND SHELL ANALYSIS

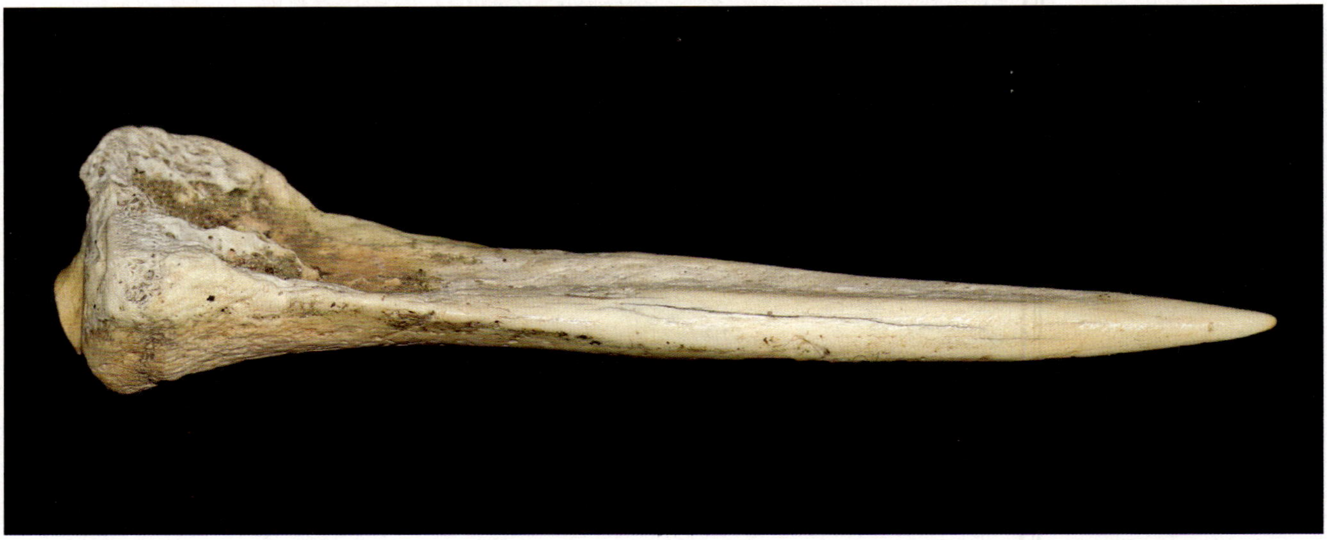

A total of 65 animal bone awls were included in the 'Éxva Teméeku archaeological collection. Side view of a deer bone awl.

Due to the high volume of faunal bone in the collection, it was initially sorted by unit and level for organizational purposes (Appendix B). During the sorting process, it became clear that human remains were mixed in with the faunal material. The human remains were removed from the faunal material and bagged separately: They will be discussed in detail in the human remains section.

The amount of bone analyzed for this project was over 1,500 whole and fragmented pieces, which resulted in the examination of 1,521 numbers of individual specimens (NISP) (Appendix U). The faunal bone that had no provenience, had multiple levels not in sequence, was recorded with a unit not located on the excavation map, or had illegible writing on the bag is all considered unprovenienced. A total of 154 pieces of bone fall into this category. The majority of the faunal material do have a provenience, including 1,192 NISP from levels 1 through 10. Sorted faunal material was placed in categories of identified bone and unidentified bone. The faunal material was counted and weighed using a triple beam scale and grouped into categories based on animal weight classes. The weight classes include: extra small (10lb and under) animals represented by rat, wood rat, kangaroo rat, ground squirrel, grey squirrel, mouse, jack rabbit, cotton tail rabbit, brush rabbit, gopher, chipmunk, western pond turtle, fish and bird; small (10-30lbs) animals represented by skunk, raccoon and badger; medium (30-200lbs) animals represented by mule deer, bobcat, sheep, mountain lion, coyote; and large (200+lbs) animals represented by horse and cow. The bulk of the material was unidentifiable by species, so it was placed into an unidentifiable mammal categories based on the weight classes. The teeth are completely separated since the identification process is easier to define. The identified bone is classified according to genus and species and placed into the weight categories described above. The faunal material is classified according to France's (2009) guideline on bone morphology to determine if the bone is human or animal. The teeth are identified according to Elbroch's (2006) skull guidelines of North American animal species. The identification process was aided by previous knowledge of the species present around the site and reports on the identified species with the collection.

For the purpose of this analysis, some bags are mixed with more than one size mammal since many items were so fragmentary. This was the only option for achieving results in the time allotted for this project. The combination categories are meant to represent both size mammals and are not a new category itself. Many of the fragments that fall into combination categories are between 10-20 millimeters in length and were identified by the thickness of the cortical bone. Another category was created for the unknown size mammal, which ultimately became the largest category. If bone is burned, it is noted in the comment section and is catalogued separately from the unburned. Modifications such as cut marks are noted. The cut marks are all light cuts presumably made by a chopper during the butchering process. Rixson (1989) articulates this exact cutting process by explaining that light cuts are made using a chopper when cutting through animal flesh as opposed to fine knife cuts. Mammalian bone that was modified by polishing, etching or grinding is catalogued separately (Appendix V). This also includes any bone used for tools such as awls (Appendix W).

The non-mammalian materials were identified by the use of a comparative collection. This included turtle shell, fish, and bird. No distinction is made between the specific species of fish and bird. All the turtle shell was identified as the western pond turtle, which is significant to the Luiseño culture for ceremonial use.

Human Diet

Analysis of the type of animals present indicates the primary source of meat was obtained from smaller game animals along with the occasional large animal such as the mule deer and fresh and salt water shellfish varieties. The presence of badgers, squirrels, rabbits and rats are an indication of the variety of small game species. These smaller game animals are considered an additional protein resource for the Luiseño diet. Based on the optimal foraging model, people try to maximize the amount of energy in the most cost-efficient manner (Smith 1983). In this respect, it can be interpreted that the smaller mammal was the primary source of protein as it was more abundant around the site. The larger game may have not been readily available near the site, making these animals a supplemental subsistence pursuit for the occupants of the 'éxva Teméeku site. Other faunal remains identified suggest that the Luiseño people utilized all aspects of their surrounding environment, which included streams and riverine environments in the area. The tools suggest that hunting was done year round, with seasonal harvesting of black and scrub oak acorns, cherries, blackberries, elderberries, wild grapes, prickly pear cactus, sumac berries, yucca, chia, mustard greens and miner's lettuce, to name a few from Bean and Shipek's (1978) Luiseño ethnographic record.

The 'éxva Teméeku faunal results match with Bean and Shipek's (1978) findings that the "principal game animals were deer, rabbit, jackrabbit, wood rat, mice, and ground squirrels" (552). Additional food sources included acorns, Manzanita, sunflower, saga, chia, lemonade berry, wild rose, holly leaf cherry, and pine nuts. Miners lettuce and white sage where also eaten and dried. The berries that were consumed included: elderberries, wild strawberries and thimbleberries. Bulbs and roots from yucca were also roasted in the spring and summer months (Bean and Shipek 1978).

Based on the shell fragments that were found on site, the shellfish consumed at 'éxva Teméeku included: fresh water bean Pismo, hard shell clams, black abalone, pectin, mussel, and volcano limpet. These included both salt and fresh water species. All shellfish varieties were eaten and used for purposes of adornment (White 1963).

Faunal

The bulk of the faunal material recovered was mammalian, and the majority identified is Cottontail rabbit and small unidentified mammal (Appendix U). There are 175 bags of medium size mammals that cannot be identified by species due to their fragmented state.

The identified animals are summarized in the faunal appendix (Appendix U). They are presented in order from highest to lowest NISP. The taxon and the NISP for each animal are included in Table 3. In order to achieve correct and definite identification of all species, careful attention to morphology of the bone fragments and whole bones was crucial for accuracy. The distinction between adult and sub-adult is not identified in the faunal analysis.

The unidentified mammals are placed into categories based on their weight, and include: 14 extra small

Table 3. Faunal Analysis

Faunal	Frag #	Mandi-ble	Maxil-lary	Teeth	Skull	Long Bones	Rib	Scap-ula	Meta-carpal	Metatar-sal	Pha-lange	Vertebra
Bobcat	9	x				x			x		x	
Chipmunk	1	x										
Cotton Tail Rabbit	101	x	x	x	x	x	x	x	x	x		
Coyote	3			x		x				x		
Grey Squirrel	53	x										
Jack Rabbit	7	x		x								
Kangarro Rat	2	x										
Mountain Lion	3											x
Mouse	1				x							
Mule Deer	42	x		x		x	x			x		x
Rat	41	x	x	x		x		x		x	x	
Sheep	9					x		x	x	x	x	x
Skunk	5	x				x						
Wood Rat	7	x		x								

(10lb and under), 59 small (10-30lbs), 120 medium (30-200lbs), and 87 large (200+lbs). The combination weight categories include two extra small/small (30lbs and under), eight extra small/large (200lbs and under), 102 small/medium (10-200lbs), 11 small/large (10-200lbs+), and 63 medium/large (30-200lbs+). A total of 42 bags are mixed with mammals of all sizes, and 611 bags contain bones of mammals of unknown size due to their fragmented state. A total of 523 NISP are burned (Appendix X). The burned coloring in the collection varies based on the temperature to which the faunal was exposed. Gilchrist and Mytum, (1986) provide examples of the color changes that occur in animal bone at specific temperatures in an archaeological experimental study. Their results show dark brown (300°C), black (350°), dark blue grey (420°), bluish grey (420°), light blue grey (420°C), and white (700°C). Therefore, the firing temperatures ranged from 300°C to 700°C at the 'éxva Teméeku site. Gilchrist and Mytum (1986) also provide a detailed analysis on the typical shrinkages of bone during the firing process. This data comparison was insightful when identifying degrees of burning and typical shrinkages on the bone from the 'éxva Teméeku collection.

During the initial inventory at the San Bernardino County Museum, many bags of mixed bone were labeled as possible human cremation due to the grey blue coloring. During the identification process, the PCRC staff identified these remains as human or faunal.

In McCown's (1955) report, he recorded that the bone found within the village excavation was extremely fragmentary and that all bone had been broken through subsistence processing. According to McCown's report, 49 bone specimens were sent to the Department of Mammal, U.S. National Museum, Smithsonian Institution, Washington, D.C. for identification (McCown 1955). In this analysis bear, badger, wildcat, coyote, pocket gopher, jackrabbit, cottontail, deer, cow, sheep and fish were identified. It is not known which specimens were sent out, but is assumed that the faunal specimens (n=12) with written species identification on the bone were part of this analysis. In my analysis, bear was not identified, but it may be missing from the collection.

Table 4. Minimum Number of Individuals (MNI)

Species	MNI
Mammals	
Canus latrans (Coyote)	1
Diapodamys (Kangaroo Rat)	2
Lepus (Jack Rabbit)	2
Lynx rufus (Bob cat)	2
Mephitidae (Skunk)	1
Mus musculus (Mouse)	1
Neotoma (Wood Rat)	3
Odocoileus hemionus (Mule Deer)	2.5
Otospermophilus beecheyi (Ground Squirrel)	2
Ovis aries (Sheep)	1
Procyon lotor (Raccoon)	1
Puma concolor (Mountain Lion)	1
Rattus (Rat)	2
Sciurus carolinensis (California Grey Squirrel)	1
Sylvilagus (Cotton Tail Rabbit)	9
Sylvilagus bachmani (Brush Rabbit)	1
Tamias (Chipmunk)	1
Taxidea taxus (Badger)	1
Reptiles	
Actinemys marmorata (Western Pond Turtle)	1
Birds	
Unidentified (Bird)	1
Fish	
Unidentified (Fish)	1

Minimum Number of Individuals

The minimum number of individuals (MNI) in Table 4 is derived from skeletal elements present (i.e. two same-sided mandibles, femurs, and humerus).

It is evident from the faunal identification that large game, while present, does not, despite its size and potential for preservation in the archaeological record, make up the majority of the available bone. Therefore, it can be loosely inferred that large game was not a daily dietary staple. This is a limited conclusion based on the small number of large game faunal remains identified. The analysis indicates that there was a heavy reliance on smaller game animals such a rabbits and wood rats. Although it is important to remember that the high number of unidentifiable faunal remains limits these results, they do give insight into the early Luiseño diet at the 'éxva Teméeku site.

Hunting Strategies

Hunting was considered an individual and group activity. A shoulder-height bow was used with a stone tip arrow for larger game. Deer decoys were also used to attract deer during hunting. A hunter would attach a stuffed deer head to his own head, cover his body with a deer pelt, and attract a deer in order to get closer for a guaranteed kill. "Smaller game was caught with a curved throwing stick, rabbit nets, slings, traps, or the spring pole or pit type of deadfall (Bean and Shipek 1978:552). Throwing sticks were flat, curved sticks similar in style to a boomerang. Many other smaller animals were trapped in this fashion. Fish were caught with a net or spearing harpoon (Sparkman 1908).

Modified Bone

The modified bone was identified by unnatural shapes, modification on the bone and manufacturing marks such as scratches, grooves, or polishing, on the surface (Sutton and Arkush 2006). Modified faunal remains at 'éxva Teméeku would have served many purposes, from textile tools such as awls to tools used in lithic production and food procurement. As with lithic technology, bone tools are manufactured in a reductive manner, which means they are shaped by the removal of raw material (Bean and Shipek 1978). A total of 104 pieces of faunal bone have been identified as modified with polishing or grinding (Appendix W). Out of those, 40 are burned, one is drilled, and one is grooved. One matches the description of shape for a ceremonial "scratching stick", which was used in the girls' puberty ceremony (DuBois 1904). Out of the 104 identified pieces of modified bone, only 64 have proveniences. The majority (n=62) are from levels 1 through 5 (Appendix V).

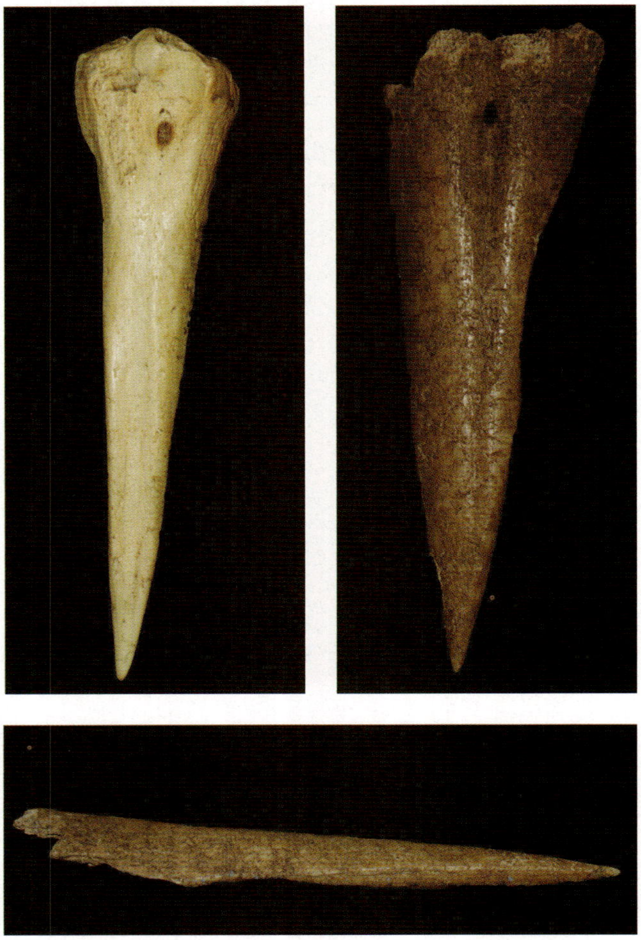

Deer bone awls used for basket weaving. There was one awl in the collection with a conical drill hole (right). Awl fragment (bottom).

Awls

Awls were made from bone, and occasionally of wood. They were used as household utensils, as punches, and as needles (Iovin 1963). Awls were also used for weaving baskets. Baskets are weaved by coiling and wrapping sumac (Rhus ovata) or juncas (Juncas acutus) on a deergrass (Muhlenbergia rigens) foundation. The awl is then used to puncture a hole in the coil for the next stitch to pass through. Basket weaving is a highly skilled and tedious process. Patterns on the baskets represent cultural symbolism and religious significance. Basketry is an important utilitarian part of the Luiseño culture and is highly prized today.

There were 65 bone awl fragments identified. The mammal bone used to create the awls includes one bobcat and 12 deer antlers, with 52 awls made from unidentified mammals. Only one awl has a drilled hole near the top and six are highly polished. The majority (n=58) have no provenience, and seven were found in levels 1 through 8. In McCown's (1955) report, he noted that worked bone, including awls, was recovered from levels 1 through 9. He explained that awls made from antler tips were located in levels 2, 4 and 6. Although McCown provided provenience in his report, this detail was not recorded on the individual awl artifact bags. Due to the lack of an artifact catalogue from the 1950s excavation, no artifacts were numbered, so the proveniences could not be matched in the current study.

Shell fragments

The shell fragments were sorted and identified by taxon using a Southern California comparative shell collection housed at the San Diego Archaeological Center. Each shell fragment was identified based on attributes common for that specific shell such as color, size, and texture. Specimens identified were then verified using Dance's (1992) Smithsonian handbook on shells. Shells that were not located in Dance's handbook were identified by Keep's (1881) descriptions and drawings of common seashells found in California.

Black abalone (*Haliotis cracherodii*) and fresh water clam (*Anodonta sp.*) were the dominant shell types found in levels 1 through 9. Overall the variety of shell fragments identified includes: fresh water clam (*Anodonta sp.*), bean clam (*Donax gouldii*), hard shell clam (*Chione succincta*), black abalone, (*Haliotis cracherodii*), red abalone (*Haliotis rufescens*), green abalone (*Haliotis fulfens*), pecten (*Pectinidae*), mussel (*Mytilus sp.*), California mactra (*Mactra Californica*), pismo clam (*Tivela stultorum*), California mussel (*Mytilus Californianus*), volcano limpet (*Fissurella volcano*), sand dollar (*Clypeasteroida*), crab (*Brachyura*), and unknown shell (Appendix Z). The unknown shell was too small to make a definitive identification. All shell was counted and weighed with a triple beam balance scale.

McCown's (1955) shell identification was limited due to the fragmentary conditions of the shell. He identified clam in the 5 upper levels, pecten in the upper 7, abalone only in level 4, mussel in level 3, and one hard shell cockle in level 4. Miscellaneous fresh water shell, possibly clam, was found in level 8. All shell sources were left unknown. Although the shell is in a fragmented state, comparing the specimens to a typed reference collection made identification possible. Sourcing was not part of the shell analysis.

Shell Beads

For centuries, people have used the beautiful properties of shells to create an array of beads and ornaments (Vellanoweth 2001). Beads, in particular, have been one of the forms of ornamentations for humans for more than 35,000 years. They are present in many cultures in a various forms and often serve beyond personal adornment, acting as a economic reflection in many social systems (Gibson 1992). Shell beads are not just simple decoration but were particularly important in the trade economy in the precontact Luiseño culture. Additionally, beads can be used as time markers, allowing archaeologists to develop time-space frameworks for exchange systems.

The shell bead analysis followed the classification based on bead shape, material, perforation, dimension, incising, and grinding that was developed by Bennyhoff and Heizer (1958) and refined by Bennyhoff and Hughes (1987), King (1990), and Gibson (1992). The typology developed by King will be used to place the shell beads in chronological order. King organizes the forms of beads and ornaments into specific time periods termed Early Period, Middle period and Late Period for Southern California (Gibson 1992). King describes the Early Period shell manufacture as represented by rectangular, two-holed pendants and cylinder disc beads. Circular disc/saucer beads and one-hole pendants characterize the Middle Period. The Late Period is defined by callus, clam disc, barrel-cap and cylinder beads (King 1990). The *Olivella biplicata* is the most common shell species from which shell beads were produced in the Santa Barbara Channel region and is the most abundant shell bead found at 'éxva Teméeku (King 1990).

There were 59 shell beads identified in the collection (Appendix Y). Shell beads were also compared with identified beads from southern Luiseño collections stored at the San Diego Archaeological Center. A total of 14 different Olivella shell bead types were identified out of the 59 beads (Appendix Y). Each bead diameter and thickness was measured in millimeters and each bead was weighed in grams on a triple beam balance scale. If a bead is burned, it is recorded in the comments section.

The Olivella shell beads in the collection exhibit a variety of types (see Table 5). This includes the Olivella spire removed perpendicular (Type A1). The defining characteristic of this bead is the removal of the apex. This type is distinguished by three different sizes: one small spire-lopped (Type A1a) ranging from 3 to 6.5 millimeters in length was identified from the Late Period; one medium spire-lopped (Type A1b) ranging from 6.51 to 9.5 millimeters was identified from an unknown period; and14 large spire looped (Type A1c) ranging from 9.5 to 14 millimeters were identified from all time periods. Three type E1 Olivella thin-lipped beads manufactured from the callus and wall portions were identified. One of these is burned, and all are from the Late Period. One type

E2a, a full-lipped oval bead with central perforation drilled conically, was identified from the Late Period. Two type E2b, a deep-lipped bead made from the higher portion of the Olivella shell, are from the Late Period. Type G saucer circular beads made from the wall are drilled conically and retouched on the exterior edges (Bennyhoff and Hughes 1987).

Table 5. Olivella Shell Bead Types

Type	Period	Date (YBP)
Small spire-lopped (A1a)	Late	800-400 ybp
Medium spire-lopped (A1b)	Unknown	N/A
Large spire-lopped (A1c)	All	N/A
Thin lipped (E1)	Late	800-400 ybp
Full lipped (E2a)	Late	800-400 ybp
Deep lipped (E2b)	Late	800-400 ybp
Saucer circular (G)	Late	800-400 ybp
Tiny saucer (G1)	Late	800-400 ybp

Source: Bennyhoff, James A., and Richard E. Hughes 1987 Shell Bead and Ornament Exchange Networks Between California and the Western Great Basin. New York: American Museum of Natural History.

A total of nine Type G1 beads, tiny saucers, were identified from the Late Period. Two are burned, and one is etched with lines on the outside ground surface. The crosshatched parallel lines along the edge make the bead stand out in the Late Period (King 1990). One type H1a, a semi ground disk circular bead with ground edges, is from the Late/ Historic Period in Central California. Seven semi-ground disk type H1b with partially ground edges were identified. Three are etched, two are burned, six are drilled biconically and one is conical. Four type H2, a small, rough, irregular disk with chipped edges were identified in the collection. One is burned. All are from the Late Period. Three are from Central California based on their size, and the other is from Southern California. Ten type J, a medium round disk with ground edges, were identified from the Late Period. Three of these are burned. The K type is the callus bead, made from the upper callus portion of the Olivella shell, so it is thicker compared to classes G and H and J. Three type K1, a cupped small circular bead with central perforation, were identified from the Late Period. Only one type K3, a cylinder bead, was identified from the Late Period.

The N type is a bead manufactured from the wall portion of the shell and varies in shaped from rectangular to ovoid (Gibson 1992). Rather than drilling, the bead maker sawed a hole with an abrasive stone (Vellanoweth 2001). In Bennyhoff and Hughes' (1987) analysis, there are two different beads in the N class although a new variety has been suggested as N3 (Vellanoweth 1995). This third type has a length of 2-3 millimeters and a width of 3-4 millimeters. The most defining characteristic of this bead is its groove. The manufacture of this type has been found in the largest quantities on San Nicolas Island (Vellanoweth, 1995). N3 beads are considered rare in other locations, and may indicate a status marker or group affiliation (Vellanoweth 2001). In the 'éxva Teméeku collection, a bead blank was identified that met the exact measurements of an N3 bead, including a sawed out hole. This leads to questions about bead manufacturing at 'éxva Teméeku, as well as trading and relations between the inhabitants of San Nicolas Island and the Luiseño people living at 'éxva Teméeku. It is believed that Juana

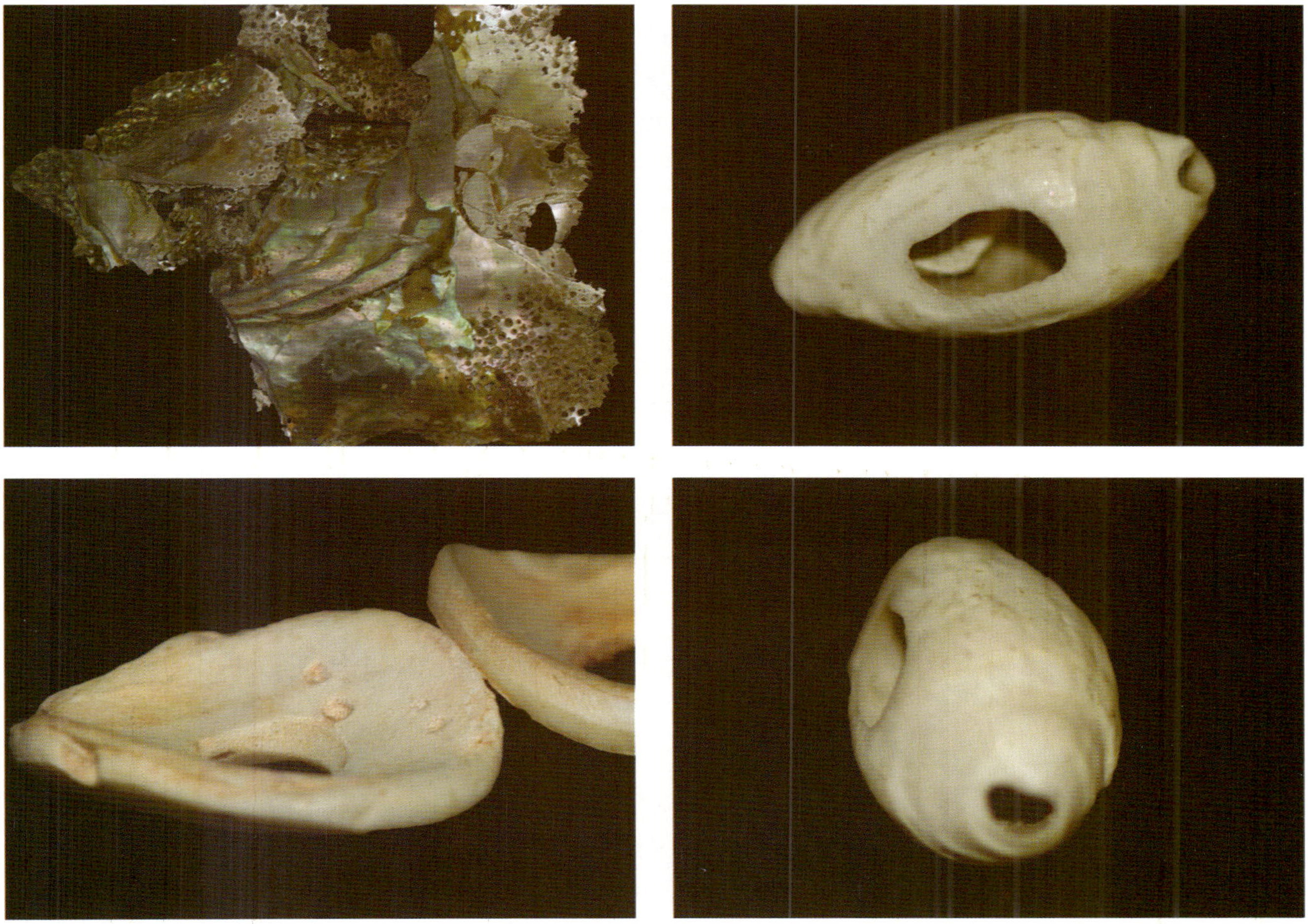

Above Left: Green abalone (Haliotis fulfens) fragments. Below Left: Two Late Period Tiny Saucer Olivella Disk beads (Type G1) Above and Below Right: An Olivella (N Type) bead blank from 'Éxva Teméeku. With very few exceptions, this type of bead blank is only found on San Nicolas Island.

Maria, the last Native woman from San Nicolas Island, was speaking a Takic language when she was recorded after leaving the island (Munro 2002). The current research on the transcription from linguist Eric Elliot will reveal the linguistic family that Juana Maria belonged to. This could indicate a connection between the inhabitants of 'éxva Teméeku and San Nicolas Island.

According to McCown's (1955) report, there were several varieties of shells found on site, including 15 flat, circular Olivella shells recovered from levels 1 through 4 and three larger flat circular Olivella beads recovered from levels 1 and 2. An additional 11 beads were noted as Olivella shell beads but not described in detail. Two *Donax gouldii* shell beads were found in levels 1 and 4, but were never located in the collection. McCown does not provide the total number of Olivella shell beads found at 'éxva Teméeku, so current shell bead counts could not be compared.

Beads as trade goods

Shell beads have been considered an important commodity and were traded as a luxury item (Vellanoweth 2001). The majority of the shell beads in the 'éxva Teméeku collection were likely traded from the Channel Islands, with the exception of a few originating from Central California. None of the Olivella shell beads identified originated from Southern California. Ethnographic examples of Olivella bead exchange are included to familiarize the reader of their cultural significance. An example from Strong (1929) documents shell beads in the economic exchange system of the Cahuilla of Palm Springs where the chief of the clan keeps several strings of shell beads as money. These strands were seven meters long and were valued at 50 cents each in 1912. Another example from Strong (1929) includes a strand of this type given to the leaders of each invited clan during an image burning ceremony. In addition, a string of beads one meter long would be given to clan leaders when a death occurred in his clan. The type of Olivella bead involved in these types of exchanges were disc beads (Strong 1929). King (1990) provides examples of smaller strings of beads exchanged for large food stores that were kept to feed the household for the entire year. This allowed for smaller scale trading between households. In King's example, smaller strings of the Olivella callus beads were used to obtain baskets of acorns, dried meat, basketry material, spices, tools, and pigments (Gibson 1992).

Beads as status markers

Shell beads were a marker of status, rank, and group affiliation and functioned as elaborate ornamentation (King 1990). Shell beads were often strung together, worn singularly, or applied to other items such as stone bowls. In Southern California, shell beads played a variety of roles in the economic, social, political, and spiritual arenas of people's daily lives. The shell beads from 'éxva Teméeku were likely a status symbol due to the limited quantities.

Pendants

The pendants in the collection are made from shell, stone, bone, or clay. These were sorted by material type and noted if burned or etched. Pendant condition is recorded as fragmented, nearly complete, or whole. There are a total of 47 pendant fragments in the collection. The variety of materials includes slate, soapstone, bone, green abalone, clay, and pecten shell (Appendix T). Out of these, 37 show evidence of burning, one is etched and one has ground, scalloped edges. The clay pendant fragments were from levels 1 and 3. The slate pendant fragments were spread out in levels 2, 3 and 6. The abalone pendant fragments were found in levels 3 and 4. A total of 12 pendants have no provenience. McCown (1955) does not provide a description or provenience of any pendants.

6

CERAMIC ANALYSIS

There were over 12,000 pottery sherds uncovered during the 'Éxva Teméeku excavation. The dominant ware type manufactured there was Tizon Brown Ware.

Typical Luiseño pottery vessels include shallow dishes, bowls, narrow-topped jars, dippers, and miniatures (Bean and Shipek 1978). The smaller size pots were used for carrying small amounts of drinking water when out gathering. Pottery was constructed using the coiling method, but in some cases smaller bowls were shaped by hand (Iovin 1963). Pottery shape was further refined using the paddle and anvil technique and fired in shallow open-pit fires (Bean and Shipek 1978). Pottery decoration was simple geometric patterns made with a stick or fingernail. It is considered rare to have incised designs on Luiseño pottery (Iovin 1963). There is evidence of pottery repair in the collection, with a number of pottery patches drilled with one or two holes. Additionally, five granite pottery anvils were identified that contain traces of clay on the surface that are visible under a microscope.

The ceramics were identified by material, sorted by provenience, counted, and weighed with a triple beam balance scale. Several attributes were recorded from each sherd: ceramic ware type, vessel part and surface finish (painted or etched). When the rim contained a measurable curve, an approximate diameter was recorded using a diameter chart that also indicated the percentage of vessel remaining. The maximum length of the rim was measured and the thickness of the rim was recorded in millimeters. The initial sort of the sherds was performed at the San Bernardino County Museum, but additional sherds were found to be mixed in with the debitage and faunal material during cataloging at the Pechanga Cultural Resource Center. Sherds were also sorted by ware type at the Pechanga Cultural Resource Center, which proved to be very time consuming. The ware types include Tizon Brown and Lower Colorado Buff. Description of the ceramics in the 'éxva Teméeku collection will be included, but further analysis is outside the scope of this thesis.

There is a total of 12,083 Tizon Brown Ware and 660 Lower Colorado Buff Ware body sherds, 765 Tizon Brown Ware and 30 Lower Colorado Buff Ware rim sherds. A total of 77 pieces of pottery, both Tizon and Buff, are marked as etched, contain a pottery patch, have ground edges, or have a drill hole (Appendix AA).

According to McCown's (1955) report, pottery sherds were recorded in all 10 levels, although the frequency declined in level 5 and was lowest in levels 6 through 10. There was also a large portion of pottery anvils; a tool used in pottery manufacture, recovered from section 105 E level 2. Out of the 660 Lower Colorado Buff Ware pottery sherds, a portion are painted with reddish brown paint made of ochre, which is often used for paint on pottery (Appendix BB). Pottery decoration includes crosshatching, impressions of wavy lines, and one basket imprint. McCown (1955) stated that pottery figurine fragments of arms, legs and heads were recovered. Only two possible figurine fragments were identified in the current collection. These fragments are two small, round, fired clay fragments less than 3 centimeters in length. The possible figurine fragments were from level 2, indicating a possible chronology dating to the Spanish period. McCown provided a picture of a figurine fragment in the site report, but after careful analysis, it was identified as a candlestick holder from the Spanish Period.

660 Lower Colorado Buff Ware pottery sherds were identified in the 'Éxva Teméeku collection.

Misinterpretation

A misinterpretation about the pottery at 'éxva Teméeku was cited by Cameron (1999) in her study of potsherds in Southern California. Cameron (1999) stated that no buff ware ceramics were found at 'éxva Teméeku, which is incorrect according to McCown's site report and the current findings. Misinterpretation will hopefully be avoided in the future with a complete catalogue of the pottery. With a complete catalogue, information that was lacking in McCown's (1955) site report will be significant to the interpretations made in reference to the Luiseño people who occupied the 'éxva Teméeku site.

7

HUMAN REMAINS AND ASSOCIATED GRAVE ITEMS

The previous studies, including an inventory of the 'éxva Teméeku collection, did not identify human remains (McCown 1955). Identification and cataloging for the human remains from the collection was completed during the current investigation, which involved researchers with experience in human osteology. The treatment of the human remains in the 'éxva Teméeku collection will need to comply with the Native American Graves Protection and Repatriation Act (NAGPRA). NAGPRA, passed in 1990, prohibits trade, transport, or sale of Native American human remains and directs federal agencies and museums to take inventory of any Native American or Native Hawaiian remains and, if identifiable, the agency or museum is to return them to the tribal descendants (43 CFR 10.10). NAGPRA has been a heated debate between Indians and the non-Indian scientific and museum communities. These issues are deeply rooted in complex historical and cultural concerns for collections (Getches et al. 1998). This is part of the rift between Native Americans and many Anthropologists about the fundamentals of discovery for reconstructing the past (White 2005; Mayes 2010). The analysis made here combines the perspectives that I, as a Native Luiseño and trained archaeologist, understand, and I agree that the tensions not only exist but continue to define many relationships between the various groups.

Identification of human remains

Human remains were identified while sorting through the unidentified faunal bone under the direction of Dr. Arion Mayes, a forensic anthropologist in the Department of Anthropology at San Diego State University. The identification of the human bone was based on morphological variation and radiographic analysis. The inclusion of human bone in the collection was first publically noted in the newspaper article about the 'éxva Teméeku site entitled, "San Diegans Find Lost Indian City" the San Diego Union, October 7, 1951. The article clearly stated, "At the cremation scenes only small particles of human bone are present". Small amounts of burned human bone are an indication of a cremation. McCown expressed in this article that personal items were also burned during Luiseño cremations. This affirmed that at the time of excavation, the individuals involved were knowledgeable about the human remains and associated grave items unearthed.

According to McCown's (1955) report, several ash deposits containing small amounts of burned human bone were located in two locations. In sections 65H5 and 65I, a bed of ash lay at a depth of 16 inches and extended to seven and half feet wide. The greatest depth of cremation was three inches, which was above the floor of Ramada 1(Appendix B). The other cremation was located in sections 100D and 105D at 18 inches. This cremation fire contained the remains of an entire body. The area covered by the fire was seven feet wide. Charred remains of at least one turtle shell rattle were found with the cremation. Additional areas of the site not excavated have evidence of charcoal and small fragments of human bone that have been burned (McCown 1955).

The human remains were identified by morphology, assessments of approximate age, sex, and pathology for each individual. Upon the completion of this catalogue of the human remains, the 'éxva Teméeku collection fell under the requirements of the NAGPRA guidelines. An agreement was reach in 2015 between the San Bernardino County Museum and the Pechanga Cultural Resource Center for the permanent transfer of ownership of the entire 'éxva Teméeku collection.

Description of Individual

Over 100 human bone fragments were identified (Appendix CC). All human remains were transported for one day to the Physical Anthropology Lab at San Diego State University for identification and x-ray verification. Under the direction of Dr. Arion Mayes, each fragment was identified based on morphological traits. Four references including, Bass's *Human Osteology* (2009), White's *Human Bone Manual* (2005), *Standards for data collection from Human Skeletal Remains* edited by Buikstra and Ubelaker (1994), and *The Analysis of Burned Human Remains* (2008) edited by Schmidt and Symes were used for comparison. The Buikstra and Ubelaker (1994) form for recording burned bone was used for color description and surface texture. The color is important to note because it describes how hot the fire was at the time of cremation. The surface texture is equally important because all cremated bones exhibit cracking, checking, and longitudinal cracking (Schultz et al. 2008).

The first identified human remain was an adult mandible fragment located in section 105F, level 1 (Appendix B). The mandible fragment analyzed is a right body mandible fragment from the anterior mental foramen to the base with the gonial angle. The overall morphology, including the root sockets, indicates that the bone is definitely human. The bone is in good condition considering its age. It is black and tan in coloring. The length measured at 54.04 millimeters. There is evidence of old post-mortem breaks, both mesially and distally, as well as superiorly along the alveolar margin. The breaks along the alveolar margin give the illusion of a shortened body height, but this is a taphonomic change. More recent post-mortem breakage is evident, but it is differentiated from the old breaks by the lighter colored exposed bone, whereas the old breaks maintain the same color as the rest of the bone, indicating equal exposure to the soil for extended periods of time. The lingual surface of the mandible's distal end and the mylohyoid line is a characteristic of human morphology. Indications of human morphology are illustrated by the following finding; on the buccal surface, the oblique line is identifiable with the appropriate depression posteriorly and inferiorly and with the mental foramina below the pre-molar region. Present are the well-defined root sockets for three permanent teeth, missing postmortem, and one partial socket. The root socket morphology represents: the second premolar, the first molar with two roots split, the second molar with two roots compressed. The third molar root socket is also present but incomplete, and shows the depression for the third molar as compressed and appears to be a single socket. Overall, the root socket morphology is indicative of human. Individual assessment as well as comparative anatomy demonstrates that the mandible is human.

Radiographic analysis was done for documentation and identification purposes on the mandible fragment. The x-rays analysis supports morphological observations regarding the body and root sockets. Radiographic analysis showed the internal bone structure, with the trabecular bone irregular in pattern and cortical thickness within normal range of human morphology. The x-rays also showed that the bone maintained its density and integrity over time. Comparative analysis with another human mandible, using radiographs was also carried-out. Additionally, the radiographic analysis shows no signs of pathological change, and supports the observation that the alveolar bone was healthy.

Two adult frontal cranium fragments with an unknown provenience were identified based on the sutures. Three femoral head fragments were identified based on the visibility of the fovea capita. Long bone fragments were identified in the same bag recorded at 95D level 5. These burned long bone fragments were identified, ranging from black (cooler portion of the fire) to white (hottest portion of the fire) (Devlin and Herrmann 2008).

One bag containing over 860 burned human and faunal remains was identified in the 'éxva Teméeku collection. The burned faunal bone and other non-bone pieces were bagged separately. The color of the burned human bone ranges from dark blue to white and indicates sustained exposure to the hottest portions of the fire, as seen in cremations. All human bone fragments included in this bag are adult. The human dentition present includes 17 burned blue-to-white colored tooth fragments. Out of these 17 dentition fragments, 11 have a single root and seven have two roots present. Four dentition fragments have the enamel crown present and were identified as pre molars with two cusps. Six of the 11 fragments have two roots and are molars. All six of these have the complete enamel and complete crowns visible. None of the roots are complete, but do show evidence of the two-root characteristics.

Also present in this bag are metacarpal and phalanges, including: five metacarpal fragments and three complete phalanges. All metacarpal and phalange fragments are burned and are blue to white in color. A total of 33 fragments of cranium were identified using three morphological features: sutures, meningeal grooves, and frontal crest. All morphological cranium features are not complete but are partially visible. Four additional mandible fragments have root sockets and body pieces present. All mandible fragments are burned with a blue to white tint. The 11 vertebrae fragments were identified using the following features: spinous process, vertebral body, and transverse process. Vertebrae fragments were not identified by vertebrae type due to their fragmentation. All vertebrae fragments are burned with a blue to white tint. A total of 57 long-bone fragments from the shaft or diaphysis were identified and 12 fragments from the epiphysis, or joint areas, of the long bones. Specific morphological traits could not be identified for the long bone fragments due to the small size of the bones. All of these fragments were bagged separately for identification purposes. More than 100 bone fragments were bagged together and are considered part of the cremation due to coloring and context, but they are too fragmented for morphological identification. The provenience on this bag was marked with an unknown unit number and levels 3 and 4. Based on McCown's (1955) description of the cremation, it is likely that this bag is from one of the two areas previously identified as the cremation location.

An additional three bags were identified as human cremation but are too fragmented for any morphological identification. The three bags have different proveniences. The first has a provenience of 165I level 2 and contains four fragments of black and white burned bone with longitudinal and transverse checking. The second has a provenience of 175I level 1 and contains over ten fragments of black and white burned bone with surface texture cracking. The third bag has a provenience of 110E5 level 7 and contains two fragments of blue to gray burned bone with longitudinal and transverse checking.

One cranium fragment with a provenience of 100D has sutures present and is black in coloring. An additional vertebra fragment with a provenience of 90D level 4 has only the spinous process present and is blue to gray in color.

Based on the human remains identified and their proveniences according to the excavation map and McCown's (1955) identification of the two cremation areas, it is evident that there are at least three cremation areas in the excavation area of the 'éxva Teméeku site. This additional area 165I and 175I levels 1 and 2 is a new discovery in the current investigation of 'éxva Teméeku (Appendix B). Due to the fragmentation of all human cremations, except for the right mandible fragment (SBCM 184-1005), it is difficult to narrow down the minimum number of individuals identified in the 'éxva Teméeku collection.

Burial Practices

It is evident based on the human remains from 'éxva Teméeku that the burial practice on site was cremation. All of the human remains exhibited a high-temperature firing process. Based on the ethnographic information, the act of cremation began with the dying of our god Wuyóot. The First People burned his body, which affirms the concept of death and the establishment of funerary ritualism (Bean and Shipek 1978).

Associated Grave Items

Once the three areas of cremation were identified based on the 11 specific areas of identified cremation, each of the 11 locations were separated out on a spreadsheet, along with the associated grave items from that same unit and level (Appendix DD). All of the locations are located on the excavation map (Appendix B).

The first area of cremation is based on McCown's (1955) identification of 65H5 and 65Hlevels 1 through 3. The associated items include two black abalone shells, one hard shell clam and one pecten, Tizon pottery sherds, two bags of charcoal, ochre fragments, and over 300 mammals of various sizes.

The second area consists of proveniences 100D and 105D level 3, 100D level 5, 105F level 1, 95D level 5, 90D level 4, and 110E level 5. The associated items include two projectile points, two bone awl fragments, two black abalone shells, one red abalone shell, one fresh water clam shell, Tizon and Buff ware pottery fragments, a flake tool, one slate pendant, a pipe fragment, and over 100 small and medium mammal fragments.

The third cremation area includes two locations: 165I level 2 and 175I level 1. The associated items include

Tizon and Buff ware pottery, turtle shell rattle fragments, two bags of charcoal, one black abalone shell, one fresh water clam shell, and about 200 fragments of mammals that include mountain lion, cotton tail rabbit, and small and medium sized mammals. The turtle shell rattle fragments were found in section 95D in levels 3 and 4 (Appendix B).

During the cremation process, many of the deceased person's personal possessions are burned with them. This symbolizes the transport of one's possessions to the After Place and validates the concept of ownership and personal property for the Luiseño culture. According to White (1963), material possessions, including those of personal manufacture and trade items, were burned during the cremation of that owner. White (1963) listed personal items such as bows, arrows, fishhooks, stone knives, nets, rabbit sticks, clothing, and personal adornments. In some cases, personal adornments were also given to family members. It is believed that if personal items were not burned, spirits would come back demanding their property (White 1963). It is interesting that there is a high volume of burned animal bone that was found with the human cremations. This animal bone was similar in coloring of the cremation, which proved it was fired at a high temperature. It is possible that, in some cases, burned animal remains found with human remains were an offering in the cremation process (Iovin 1963).

8

ETHICS

Many people believe that ethics are the same as the law. While they are connected, the law is different because it is enforceable and sets the bar for good behavior at the lowest threshold (Vitelli 1996). The only law that is directly applicable to the 'éxva Teméeku collection is NAGPRA. Ethics on the other hand, are often obligatory but unenforceable. In the field of Anthropology, the code of ethics differs depending on the organization, but many still reflect similar experiences, circumstances and concerns (http://www.aaanet.org/issues/policy-advocacy/code-of-ethics.cfm location of the current code of ethics of the American Anthropological Association). In respect to the 'éxva Teméeku project's excavators, it is uncertain what code of ethics they followed, but such a code did exist within the American Anthropological Association during that period.

Based on my research, the ethics in salvage or rescue archaeology conducted during the time that 'éxva Teméeku was excavated focused simply on digging up new discoveries. At the time of the excavation, the property of the 'éxva Teméeku site was privately owned and was not subject to any archaeological protection laws: the Antiquities Act of 1906 had passed but was limited to federal and Indian lands. This allowed for limited protection of the site and potentially questionable ethics for the individuals who excavated 'éxva Teméeku. The excitement of digging up a new discovery appears to have been the mind frame of many individuals who participated in the excavation of 'éxva Teméeku. Many newspaper articles from the time sensationalized the find with titles such as "Legendary Indian City Believed Discovered" (source unknown) and "San Diegans Find Lost Indian City". These articles portray the excavation of the 'éxva Teméeku site as a remarkable discovery. While the general public may not have been aware of the 'éxva Teméeku site, the Luiseño Creation Story describes 'éxva Teméeku as the first place the people settled, demonstrating that the site was well known to the Luiseño people. The newspaper articles and researchers who worked on the excavation left an important stakeholder completely out of the equation: the direct descendants. All the newspaper articles from the 1950s about the 'éxva Teméeku site are written as if the original descendants of 'éxva Teméeku were no longer living. In fact, many elderly people from the Pechanga Indian Reservation remember the 'éxva Teméeku excavation, having watched the archeologist team excavate the site every weekend for almost two years. It is evident that the descendants were not considered during the excavation.

Archaeologist ethics

The Register of Professional Archaeologists has an extensive code of conduct. The three sections of the code that are relevant to the ethical issue in the 'éxva Teméeku collection include: being responsible for all manners when conducting research, being respectful towards the concerns of groups under study, and processing all research materials in a timely manner. This code of conduct is necessary, but in the case of 'éxva Teméeku, all the excavators were considered amateur archaeologists and thus did not heed these ethical standards.

The issue of artifact counts not matching up to the collection was most difficult in the projectile point analysis. A large amount (n=455) of projectile points are deemed missing from the 'éxva Teméeku collection based on the recent analysis. The question remains as to where these projectile points are located. Based on a projectile point's small size it can easily be lost or stolen. Projectile points are often a desired artifact among the general public due to their esthetic value and uniqueness. Considering the amount of projectile points that were in the upper levels it can easily be assumed that many projectile points that were on the surface or in these upper levels were taken from the site. Although there were laws on the books that should have protected 'éxva Teméeku (American Antiquities Act), there was less enforcement of them. It is important to note that the code of ethics for the Society of American Archaeology (SAA) prohibits selling antiquities on the black market (http://www.saa.org/Aboutthesoceity/PrincipalesofArchaeologicalEthics/tabid/203/Default.aspx). This rule would not have been made if this were not an issue in archaeology that people have actively worked to change. This is an unfortunate occurrence and leaves limited information for future researchers.

Museum ethics

The catalogue generated in 2010 for the 'éxva Teméeku collection at the San Bernardino County Museum failed to match up with McCown's (1955) report of artifact totals. Many artifacts were missing from the collection, with little evidence as to their locations or how they went missing. For example, out of the 49 specimens of faunal material McCown (1955) set to the Department of Mammal, U. S. National Museum, Smithsonian Institution, Washington, D. C. only a dozen are currently accounted for in the collection. This may be an example of the mismanagement in the collections department at the San Bernardino County Museum or an error from McCown's records. Overall, the cataloguing of collections by museums and other such institutions is a significant mandate as noted under the National Park Service of the Federal Department of Interior. Before 2010, the San Bernardino County Museum failed to generate a catalogue of the 'éxva Teméeku collection, which is a reflection of what Barker (2003:80) termed the "Mañana Mentality" of museums when they hold material for posterity and justify that it is safe. Unfortunately, this trend has occurred countless times in the museum sector: collections are accepted, stored, and then forgotten (Barker 2003). The issue here is the lack of curation of the 'éxva Teméeku collection, which is, ironically, one of the original collections housed at the San Bernardino County Museum.

The parties with the greatest investment in this collection include the San Bernardino County Museum, the Luiseño Indians, specifically the Pechanga Band, and researchers within Anthropology. This is an example of a complex and "multifaceted past that is owned by no one but controlled by many" (Barker 2003). It is important to highlight that the 'éxva Teméeku site report serves as an example of how the descendent community was not involved in the excavation of their own people's culture. This leaves questions about whom the responsible stakeholders are. In my opinion, the responsible stakeholder is the Pechanga Tribe for funding the curation and analysis of the 'éxva Teméeku collection.

In the groundstone section of this thesis, I raised the issue of a metate that was catalogued with the 'éxva Teméeku collection, but based on McCown's (1955) report it is possible that the metate was miscataloged. Additionally, McCown (1955) had pictures of all the larger mortar fragments and the three metates that were found. Sadly, two of the three metates were never located by the Museum, and when questioned about their location, the assistant curator directed me to "annex storage", where a large number of metates, mortars, and manos were left sitting under a tree, open to the elements, on the side the museum curation facility! It was explained to me that all unprovenienced metates, mortars, and manos were put outside in the "annex storage" to weather in the elements. The search for the two missing metates was distressing to my two colleagues and myself. We spent two hours uncovering whole metates and mortars, all made from local Southern California materials. It was astonishing and heartbreaking that due to a storage issue, the Museum had decided that outside under a tree was where their unprovenienced metates would be the safest. Considering the many local educational outreach programs, I asked the logical question: Why not lend them to schools that are learning about the local Native culture, or even better, a Southern California tribe? As a representative of my tribe, I felt it necessary to inquire about the issue and to suggest a more appropriate storage solution. I felt that the response I received was insincere; however, I was a guest at their facility, so I did not pursue the issue further at that time. I intend to explore the issue of appropriate treatment of cultural material by the museum in the future.

In addition, I noted that there was an issue with the steatite pipes described by McCown (1955). This brings about the question as to whether these previously undocumented pipes are from the 'éxva Teméeku site or from the Temecula area in general. My concern is that the word "Temecula" is written on the three steatite pipes. This marking does not match with any of the catalogue markings on the other artifacts in the 'éxva Teméeku collection of over 8,000 items. This could be an example of an error by the Museum in identification and the lack of an inventory or catalogue of the 'éxva Teméeku collection. Without a complete catalogue, the exact contents of the 'éxva Teméeku collection have been unknown for decades. The combination of misidentified artifacts, the lack of an inventory, and minimal analysis has resulted in the collection being non-compliant under NAGPRA.

Many students expect museums to be a great resource for archaeological research, but if their collections are not curated, it becomes difficult to account for all the assemblages included in the collection. In many ways, lack of a complete catalogue can be a limiting factor to any conclusion made about the 'éxva Teméeku site and its inhabitants. That said, I am grateful that the San Bernardino County Museum was able to house the collection for over **60** years for use by researchers.

Tribal responsibility

As a tribal member of the Pechanga Indian Reservation and a consultant for the Pechanga Cultural Resource Center, I clearly recognize our responsibility to the 'éxva Teméeku collection. As a Cultural Resources Department, our job is to protect and preserve what is culturally relevant to the Luiseño people. We consider this responsibility our duty, and we have stood as the responsible stakeholder for countless projects in Cultural Resources and Development projects. One may ask why we did not pursue this project before if it is so important for our history. The answer is simple: working with the museum has been a difficult task, as they have sought to limit the questions that this thesis poses. Additionally, acquiring a large number of lab technicians and completing the analysis of such a large collection in a timely manner were all issues that precluded an earlier request to catalogue the 'éxva Teméeku collection. As a tribe, we needed to wait until our curation department was able to take on such a large task. This project was not something we were going to pursue before we were equipped, as it reflects not only pieces of our culture, history, and sense of self, but also, and perhaps of greatest significance, is the understanding of exactly what the collection is—our point of origin as a people.

9

CONCLUSION

Observed Patterns

When looking at all of the assemblages together, over 1,000 artifacts did not have a provenience so could not be part of the observed cultural patterns. The missing proveniences are from data lost during the excavation and during curation due to illegible information on the individual artifacts bags. Despite this, the unprovenienced material is still included in the overall picture presented in the individual sections above. Based on the artifacts that have a recorded provenience, it is evident that the highest concentration of artifacts was in levels 1 through 3. This included pottery, faunal material, debitage, charcoal, and shell. The cremations in levels 1 through 5 represent ceremonial activities involved in a funeral, including cremation of food and offerings with the deceased. In levels 4 through 6, the amount of artifacts dramatically lessens but the types of artifacts represented remains consistent. In levels 7 through 10, an additional drop in volume is present, but it is interesting to note that pottery was recovered as low as level 10. Based on the obsidian dates from level 7 (6,000 ± 100), there is a relatively clear indication that pottery may have been used by the Luiseño people much earlier than what is projected in the current literature (1,500 years).

Site Significance

Based on the current findings, I posit that 'éxva Teméeku was a site occupied during the creation of the world, was a living habitation site for years, and later became a ceremonial burial site based on the cremation evidence in the five upper levels. It is evident that the site was used by hundreds of people throughout the centuries.

The Luiseño Creation Story places the first beings at 'éxva Teméeku. The scientific evidence supports the great length of time described in the creation story, with an obsidian hydration date of 6,000 ± 100 yrs. The archaeology further supports the richness of life and culture in the area, as well as continuity of burial practices, which not only corresponds to the creation story, but to the ethnographic evidence as well.

In the lower levels of the site deposit, there is a density of cultural material that shows years of habitation activities such as food processing and cooking. Taking into account the landscape surrounding the excavated area of 'éxva Teméeku, many mortar holes, which were used for subsistence processing, are in close proximity to the excavated area. Water sources are also so close to the excavated area that you can still hear the water running today. The abundance of natural resources and the slope and location of 'éxva Teméeku made it an ideal living area. So, when did the shift to a ceremonial area occur? The exact timing of the shift is difficult to determine; however, evidence recovered from the upper four levels of the site indicates that a certain area of the site may have shifted to ceremonial use approximately 1,800-2,600 YBP. Levels 1 through 4 contained evidence of cremation, including human bone, ceremonial pestles, and personal items such as shell beads, pendants, and pipes, which are all fire-affected and were likely cremated along with the deceased. The lower levels, which date earlier in time, do not present evidence of ceremonial activity.

Taking into account that Luiseño ceremonial burial practices are accompanied by an extensive ritual that lasts for a number of days and includes a feast for a large group of people, the evidence from the 'éxva Teméeku site supports use of the site for funerary practices. Additionally, McCown (1955) accounted for over 100 bedrock mortars in close proximity to the excavated area of 'éxva Teméeku. The abundance of these food-processing locations indicates that the site accommodated a large number of people.

Implications

This detailed analysis on the 'éxva Teméeku collection has generated new evidence, and therefore **new** interpretations of the events that were taking place on site. The data that has been produced will provide new research ideas for future studies and give current researchers a concrete reference to cite when discussing the 'éxva Teméeku site. The obsidian hydration dates verifies the long existence of the Luiseño people in the Temecula valley. I hope that future references made to the 'éxva Teméeku collection in the literature will include the new, corrected data that has developed from this thesis research.

In the completion of this analysis, the inventory of human remains and associated grave goods will be compliant under NAGPRA. This is one of the most important new findings in the 'éxva Teméeku collection. An agreement between the San Bernardino County Museum and the Pechanga Band of Luiseño Indians for permanent storage of the 'éxva Teméeku collection was agreed upon in 2015. This is considered a private matter between the Pechanga Tribe and the San Bernardino County Museum and will not be discussed further.

Benefits to the Community

All findings will be shared with the community, and a copy of this book will be given to the San Bernardino County Museum and the Pechanga Cultural Resource Center for their records. This book will aid in the protection of the 'éxva Teméeku area based on the in-depth analysis of the sacred items and important findings that the analysis generated. These findings will help to justify the protection of burial sites and hopefully encourage other tribal people to look further into to the vast amounts of collections currently stored in museum repositories.

APPENDIX A

'ÉXVA TEMÉEKU SURROUNDING SITES

Appendix A: 'Éxva Teméeku Surrounding Sites				
CA-Riv # sites			Primary # sites	
Ca-Riv-50	Ca-Riv-3391	Ca-Riv-7867	33-11072	33-14929
Ca-Riv-115	Ca-Riv-3410	Ca-Riv-7868	33-11222	33-14930
Ca-Riv-116	Ca-Riv-3411	Ca-Riv-7869	33-11443	33-14931
Ca-Riv-270	Ca-Riv-3649	Ca-Riv-7883	33-11811	33-14932
Ca-Riv-364	Ca-Riv-3650	Ca-Riv-7902	33-11812	33-14933
Ca-Riv-365	Ca-Riv-3933	Ca-Riv-7903	33-11813	33-17637
Ca-Riv-1071	Ca-Riv-3980	Ca-Riv-7904	33-12517	33-17649
Ca-Riv-1382	Ca-Riv-4166	Ca-Riv-7905	33-12520	33-17848
Ca-Riv-1384	Ca-Riv-4264	Ca-Riv-7906	33-12731	
Ca-Riv-1460	Ca-Riv-4707	Ca-Riv-7907	33-12732	
Ca-Riv-1520	Ca-Riv-4949	Ca-Riv-7908	33-23742	
Ca-Riv-1522	Ca-Riv-5055	Ca-Riv-7909	33-12742	
Ca-Riv-1728	Ca-Riv-5229	Ca-Riv-8026	33-12790	
Ca-Riv-1729	Ca-Riv-5230	Ca-Riv-8027	33-13096	
Ca-Riv-1742	Ca-Riv-5463	Ca-Riv-6499	33-12112	
Ca-Riv-1753	Ca-Riv-5464	Ca-Riv-6645	33-13135	
Ca-Riv-1860	Ca-Riv-7848	Ca-Riv-6655	33-13511	
Ca-Riv-1861	Ca-Riv-7849	Ca-Riv-6656	33-13541	
Ca-Riv-2134	Ca-Riv-7859	Ca-Riv-6657	33-13686	
Ca-Riv-2189	Ca-Riv-7860	Ca-Riv-6658	33-13712	
Ca-Riv-2536	Ca-Riv-7861	Ca-Riv-6659	33-13726	
Ca-Riv-3063	Ca-Riv-7862	Ca-Riv-6660	33-13838	
Ca-Riv-3330	Ca-Riv-7863	Ca-Riv-2376	33-14892	
Ca-Riv-3376	Ca-Riv-7864		33-14893	
Ca-Riv- 3390	Ca-Riv-7865		33-14894	

APPENDIX B

'ÉXVA TEMÉEKU EXCAVATION MAP

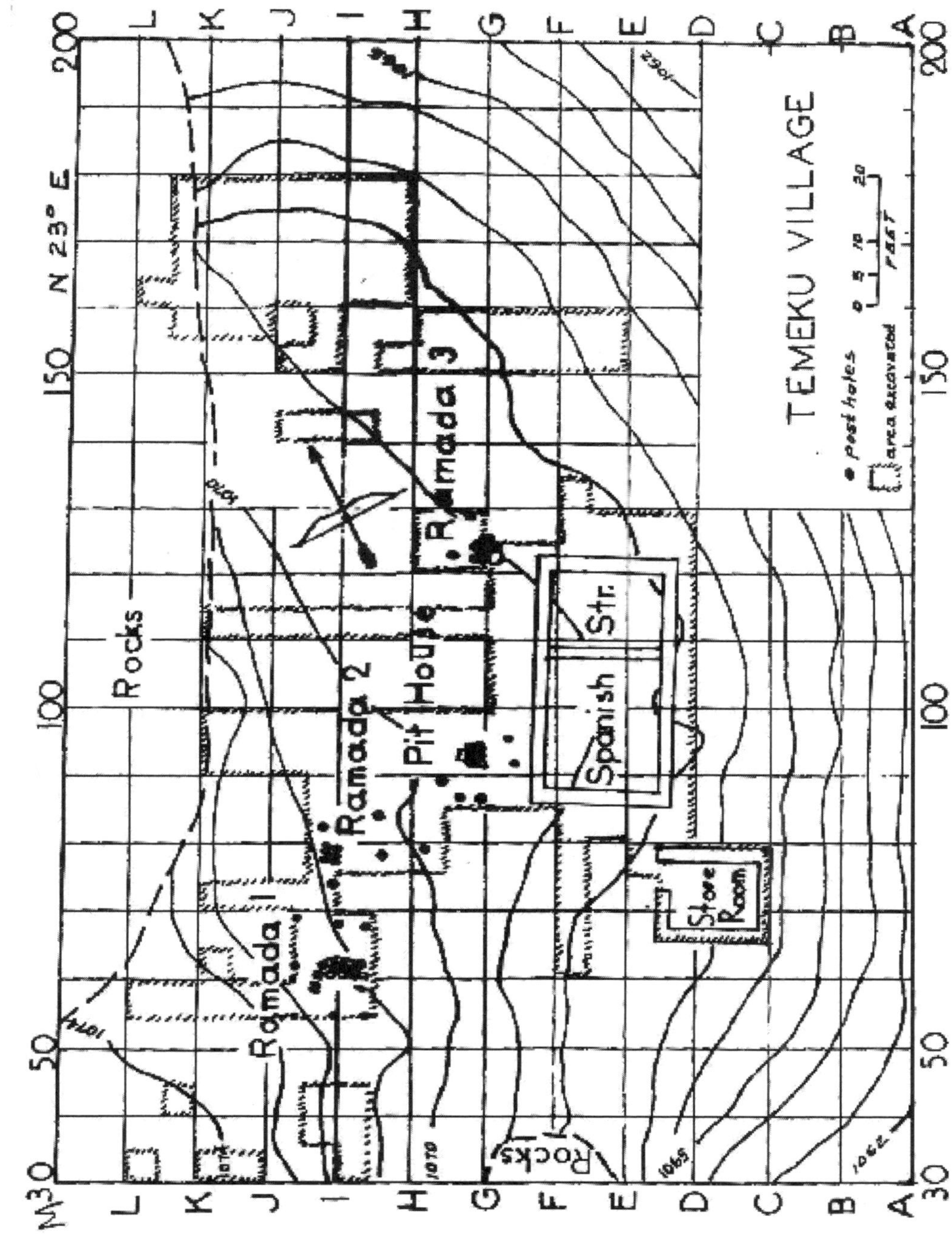
TEMEKU VILLAGE
N 23° E
Rocks
Ramada 1
Ramada 2
Ramada 3
Pit House
Spanish Str.
Store Room
post holes
area excavated
0 5 10 20
FEET

APPENDIX C

BASALT DEBITAGE

Appendix C: Basalt Debitage									
2011.28	**SBCM**	**Cat. #**	**Unit**	**Level**	**Qty**	**MTRL**	**DEB TYPE**	**PLAT**	**WT/g**
7269	184	4906	80D5	1	1	BSLT	BF/EDGE	MFP	
7302	184	4976	85F5	5	1	BSLT	BF/EDGE		
7326	184	1237	95G	3	1	BSLT	BF/EDGE		
7569	184	2492	105D5	5	1	BSLT	BF/EPERC	MFP	
7563	184	1002	105F	1	1	BSLT	BF/EPERC	MFP	
7086	184	4953	110E5	8	2	BSLT	BF/EPERC	MFP	2
6904	184	3185	110F5	4	1	BSLT	BF/EPERC	MFP	1.9
7124	184	1921	110H5	5	1	BSLT	BF/EPERC	MFP	0.9
7188	184	3176	115F	2	1	BSLT	BF/EPERC	MFP	3.2
7231	184	1652	115F5	3	1	BSLT	BF/EPERC	MFP	
7220	184	2540	120E5	1	1	BSLT	BF/EPERC	MFP	
6993	184	945	120G	1	2	BSLT	BF/EPERC	MFP	2
7283	184	1148	140I5	2	1	BSLT	BF/EPERC	MFP	
7187	184	17	160H	2	1	BSLT	BF/EPERC	MFP	
7566	184	2778	170I5	2	1	BSLT	BF/EPERC	MFP	
7119	184	241	170J5	1	3	BSLT	BF/EPERC	MFP	2
7168	184	1572	40I	3	3	BSLT	BF/EPERC	MFP	6.7
7164	184	1182	45I	4	3	BSLT	BF/EPERC	MFP	44
7293	184	2006	55I	2	1	BSLT	BF/EPERC	MFP	
7282	184	1660	55K5	1	20	BSLT	BF/EPERC	MFP	
7208	184	2737	70E5	3	1	BSLT	BF/EPERC	MFP	

2011.28	SBCM	Cat. #	Unit	Level	Qty	MTRL	DEB TYPE	PLAT	WT/g
6902	184	2553	70E5	6	1	BSLT	BF/EPERC	MFP	2.3
7269	184	4906	80D5	1	1	BSLT	BF/EPERC	MFP	
7278	184	128	85E	3	1	BSLT	BF/EPERC	MFP	
7263	184	3572	85F5	3	1	BSLT	BF/EPERC	MFP	1.5
7250	184	1603	85G5	2	2	BSLT	BF/EPERC	MFP	3.5
7033	184	3357	90D	2	1	BSLT	BF/EPERC	MFP	1
7279	184	3217	90E	5	2	BSLT	BF/EPERC	MFP	
7565	184	2016	90E5	4	1	BSLT	BF/EPERC	MFP	
7037	184	4174	90I5	1	1	BSLT	BF/EPERC	MFP	1
7254	184	4162	90I5	2	1	BSLT	BF/EPERC	MFP	1.9
7289	184	2310	95D	2	1	BSLT	BF/EPERC	MFP	
6876	184	1997	95D	5	4	BSLT	BF/EPERC	MFP	3.7
7581	184	2150	95E	4	3	BSLT	BF/EPERC	MFP	
7270	184	3338	95E5	6	1	BSLT	BF/EPYPE	MFP	
7290	184	1210	95H5	3	1	BSLT	BF/EPERC	MFP	
6958	184	1095	110E5	4	3	BSLT	BF/EPERC	PA	2
6998	184	3100	95G	3	1	BSLT	BF/EPERC	PA	0.8
7183	184	2569	160H	1	1	BSLT	BF/EPERC	SFP	
7221	184	5522	160I5	2	1	BSLT	BF/EPERC	SFP	
6887	184	1670	175J5	2	2	BSLT	BF/EPERC	SFP	2.2
7205	184	178	100F	1	4	BSLT	BF/EPERC		
7266	184	434	125E5	3	1	BSLT	BF/EPERC		

2011.28	SBCM	Cat. #	Unit	Level	Qty	MTRL	DEB TYPE	PLAT	WT/g
7209	184	1884	170H5	1	2	BSLT	BF/EPERC		
7228	184	1617	55J	2	1	BSLT	BF/EPERC		
7199	184	27	70J5	2	2	BSLT	BF/EPERC		
7191	184	2437	95D5	3	1	BSLT	BF/EPERC		
7190	184	1975	95E	3	2	BSLT	BF/EPERC		
7186	184	3142	95E5	3	1	BSLT	BF/EPERC		
7297	184	4210	110D	2	1	BSLT	BF/EPREC	MFP	
7257	184	6487	35H5	1	2	BSLT	BF/EPREC	MFP	
7318	184	1476	40K	3	1	BSLT	BF/EPREC	MFP	
7068	184	1407	55K	3	2	BSLT	BF/EPREC	MFP	1.7
5217	184	6185	65I	1	3	BSLT	BF/EPREC	MFP	1.7
7229	184	4669	85G5	4	2	BSLT	BF/EPREC	MFP	19.1
7296	184	2608	90F	3	1	BSLT	BF/EPREC	MFP	
7312	184	2211	95E	6	1	BSLT	BF/EPREC	MFP	
6927	184	891	85F	2	1	BSLT	BF/EPREC	SFP	0.5
6915	184	2536	100D5	1	1	BSLT	BF/EPRES	MFP	0.4
6885	184	1670	175J5	2	3	BSLT	BF/EPRES	MFP	0.7
7279	184	3217	90E	5	1	BSLT	BF/EPRES	MFP	
7043	184	830	105E5	1	1	BSLT	BF/EPRES		0.5
7009	184	6442	160J	1	1	BSLT	BF/EPRES		0.5
6890	184	155	165I5	1	1	BSLT	BF/EPRES		0.6
7218	184	2178	55H5	2	1	BSLT	BF/EPRES		

2011.28	SBCM	Cat. #	Unit	Level	Qty	MTRL	DEB TYPE	PLAT	WT/g
7003	184	2712	55I5	3	1	BSLT	BF/EPRES		2
6954	184	1445	70I	1	1	BSLT	BF/EPRES		1.3
7155	184	1712	80D5	5	2	BSLT	BF/EPRES		2
7280	184	275	85E	3	1	BSLT	BF/EPRES		
7158	184	3229	95E	5	1	BSLT	BF/EPRES		1
7270	184	3338	95E5	6	2	BSLT	BF/EPRES		
7088	184	4953	110E5	8	1	BSLT	BF/LPERC	MFP	2
6934	184	2156	20J5	4	1	BSLT	BF/LPERC	MFP	1.6
7291	184	4715	55J5	4	1	BSLT	BF/LPERC	MFP	
7589	184	1590	55K5	1	1	BSLT	BF/LPERC	MFP	
7243	184	119	95D	1	1	BSLT	BF/LPERC	MFP	
6921	184	924	1E+07	1	1	BSLT	BF/LPERC	PA	0.9
6982	184	2500	165I5	2	1	BSLT	BF/Lperc	PA	2
7316	184	4816	65E5	2	1	BSLT	BF/LPERC	PA	
7269	184	4906	80D5	1	1	BSLT	BF/LPERC		
7016	184	319	85D5	4	1	BSLT	BF/LPERC		1
7227	184	2370	85H5	1	1	BSLT	BF/LPERC		
7200	184	1442	75N	1	3	BSLT	BF/MARG	MFP	
6937	184	2156	20J5	4	1	BSLT	BF/MARG		1.4
6941	184	4036	80E	2	1	BSLT	BF/MARG		1.1
7567	184	4044	80E	2	1	BSLT	BF/MARG		
7302	184	4976	85F5	5	1	BSLT	BF/MARG		

2011.28	SBCM	Cat. #	Unit	Level	Qty	MTRL	DEB TYPE	PLAT	WT/g
5240	184	682	115	1	1	BSLT	CC	NP	13.7
7270	184	3338	95E5	6	1	BSLT	CC	NP	
7140	184	3587	90E	8	1	BSLT	CC	PA	1
7194	184	790	110F5	6	1	BSLT	FF		3.1
7247	184	591	110E5	2	1	BSLT	FF/C		4.5
7242	184	5082	100D	7	1	BSLT	FF/NC		7.2
6923	184	924	100E5	1	2	BSLT	FF/NC		1.1
7167	184	4579	105E5	5	1	BSLT	FF/NC		
7294	184	623	105F	5	1	BSLT	FF/NC		1
7184	184	4991	110E5	7	2	BSLT	FF/NC		
7224	184	4780	110G	5	1	BSLT	FF/NC		
7561	184	4863	110G5	3	1	BSLT	FF/NC		
5713	184	5713	110I	1	1	BSLT	FF/NC		
7588	184	3000	110I5	4	1	BSLT	FF/NC		
7188	184	3176	115F	2	1	BSLT	FF/NC		
6985	184	4059	115F	2	2	BSLT	FF/NC		1.4
7166	184	2958	115F	4	4	BSLT	FF/NC		
7231	184	1652	115F5	3	5	BSLT	FF/NC		
7213	184	1986	120F	5	4	BSLT	FF/NC		
6972	184	3328	120G	2	1	BSLT	FF/NC		1
7271	184	514	125D5	3	1	BSLT	FF/NC		2.3
7219	184	6522	140I5	1	5	BSLT	FF/NC		

2011.28	SBCM	Cat. #	Unit	Level	Qty	MTRL	DEB TYPE	PLAT	WT/g
7187	184	17	160H	2	5	BSLT	FF/NC		14.5
7222	184	2588	170I5	1	3	BSLT	FF/NC		
7081	184	3597	175H5	3	2	BSLT	FF/NC		1
7051	184	2982	175I	1	2	BSLT	FF/NC		1
3346	184	3346	175I	2	4	BSLT	FF/NC		
7192	184	4731	20J5	2	1	BSLT	FF/NC		6.4
7232	184	1514	40K	1	3	BSLT	FF/NC		
7164	184	1182	45I	4	5	BSLT	FF/NC		
7195	184	611	55I	4	3	BSLT	FF/NC		
7292	184	2748	55I5	2	2	BSLT	FF/NC		
7163	184	373	60J5	2	6	BSLT	FF/NC		8.3
7323	184	1698	70C	3	1	BSLT	FF/NC		
7578	184	1668	70D	2	1	BSLT	FF/NC		4.3
7162	184	2702	70E5	4	1	BSLT	FF/NC		2
7129	184	646	70J	1	1	BSLT	FF/NC		1
7246	184	3313	75C	4	1	BSLT	FF/NC		
7285	184	3567	75D	1	2	BSLT	FF/NC		
7200	184	1442	75N	1	3	BSLT	FF/NC		
7286	184	46	90D5	4	1	BSLT	FF/NC		3.7
7189	184	2041	90E5	6	1	BSLT	FF/NC		
7139	184	5922	90E5	8	1	BSLT	FF/NC		4
7265	184	2129	95D5	2	3	BSLT	FF/NC		4

2011.28	SBCM	Cat. #	Unit	Level	Qty	MTRL	DEB TYPE	PLAT	WT/g
2123	184	2123	95D5	4	3	BSLT	FF/NC		
7190	184	1975	95E	3	10	BSLT	FF/NC		
7186	184	3142	95E5	3	2	BSLT	FF/NC		
7267	184	229	100D	5	1	BSLT	NC	MFP	
6907	184	1961	100D5	5	1	BSLT	NC	MFP	1.5
7233	184	1088	105E	4	1	BSLT	NC	MFP	
7041	184	830	105E5	1	1	BSLT	NC	MFP	2
7094	184	1780	110D5	3	1	BSLT	NC	MFP	0.7
7264	184	5227	110G	2	1	BSLT	NC	MFP	
7288	184	1461	110H5	4	1	BSLT	NC	MFP	12.9
7313	184	3019	115F	3	2	BSLT	NC	MFP	25.6
7597	184	266	120-E5	3	2	BSLT	NC	MFP	172
7220	184	2540	120E5	1	1	BSLT	NC	MFP	6.2
7048	184	2011	120F	3	2	BSLT	NC	MFP	2
7154	184	2400	120F5	6	1	BSLT	NC	MFP	2
7266	184	434	125E5	3	1	BSLT	NC	MFP	
7221	184	5522	160I5	2	1	BSLT	NC	MFP	
7008	184	6442	160J	1	1	BSLT	NC	MFP	4
7182	184	569	165H	1	1	BSLT	NC	MFP	
7274	184	2100	170H	1	2	BSLT	NC	MFP	
6858	184	1890	170H5	2	2	BSLT	NC	MFP	1.1
7120	184	241	170J5	1	1	BSLT	NC	MFP	2

2011.28	SBCM	Cat. #	Unit	Level	Qty	MTRL	DEB TYPE	PLAT	WT/g
3346	184	3346	175I	2	1	BSLT	NC	MFP	
7318	184	1476	40K	3	3	BSLT	NC	MFP	19.5
7329	184	1967	60E5	1	1	BSLT	NC	MFP	
6964	184	6390	65I	5	1	BSLT	NC	MFP	1
7156	184	1712	80D5	5	1	BSLT	NC	MFP	8
7567	184	4044	80E	2	1	BSLT	NC	MFP	
7302	184	4976	85F5	5	1	BSLT	NC	MFP	
7302	184	4976	85F5	5	1	BSLT	NC	MFP	
7189	184	2041	90E5	6	1	BSLT	NC	MFP	14
2123	184	2123	95D5	4	2	BSLT	NC	MFP	36.9
7301	184	6046	95E	8	1	BSLT	NC	MFP	9
6866	184	3055	95E5	8	1	BSLT	NC	MFP	3.1
5898	184	2146	95E	4	1	BSLT	NC	NP	2.4
7006	184	186	100D	2	1	BSLT	NC	PA	4
6909	184	1961	100D5	5	1	BSLT	NC	PA	4.8
7310	184	2289	100D5	6	1	BSLT	NC	PA	9.2
5229	184	823	100E5	6,7	2	BSLT	NC	PA	2.1
7056	184	767	100F5	8	1	BSLT	NC	PA	2
7040	184	830	105E5	1	1	BSLT	NC	PA	0.7
6990	184	1013	105E5	3	39	BSLT	NC	PA	6
7563	184	1002	105F	1	1	BSLT	NC	PA	14.6
5894	184	871	105F	3	1	BSLT	NC	PA	2.6

2011.28	SBCM	Cat. #	Unit	Level	Qty	MTRL	DEB TYPE	PLAT	WT/g
7297	184	4210	110D	2	1	BSLT	NC	PA	
7096	184	1780	110D5	3	1	BSLT	NC	PA	1
7184	184	4991	110E5	7	1	BSLT	NC	PA	
6906	184	3185	110F5	4	1	BSLT	NC	PA	2
7194	184	790	110F5	6	1	BSLT	NC	PA	
7185	184	1917	110H	2	2	BSLT	NC	PA	17
7272	184	1798	110H5	5	1	BSLT	NC	PA	
7143	184	4884	115E	6	1	BSLT	NC	PA	
6883	184	3307	120F	4	1	BSLT	NC	PA	2
7266	184	434	125E5	3	3	BSLT	NC	PA	
7219	184	6522	140I5	1	1	BSLT	NC	PA	
7221	184	5522	160I5	2	1	BSLT	NC	PA	
7010	184	6442	160J	1	2	BSLT	NC	PA	2
7216	184	1165	160J5	2	1	BSLT	NC	PA	15
7223	184	2624	165I	2	2	BSLT	NC	PA	16.3
7274	184	2100	170H	1	3	BSLT	NC	PA	9.6
6857	184	1890	170H5	2	1	BSLT	NC	PA	2
7612	184	2599	175H	3	1	BSLT	NC	PA	0.5
6929	184	5534	175J5	1	1	BSLT	NC	PA	2.8
7210	184	2008	20J5	6	2	BSLT	NC	PA	
7067	184	4744	30J5	1	1	BSLT	NC	PA	1
7257	184	6487	35H5	1	1	BSLT	NC	PA	6

2011.28	SBCM	Cat. #	Unit	Level	Qty	MTRL	DEB TYPE	PLAT	WT/g
6970	184	1908	40I	1	1	BSLT	NC	PA	2
7168	184	1572	40I	3	1	BSLT	NC	PA	
7232	184	1514	40K	1	2	BSLT	NC	PA	
6946	184	2046	55I	1	3	BSLT	NC	PA	2.3
7235	184	1388	55J5	3	1	BSLT	NC	PA	5.9
7291	184	4715	55J5	4	4	BSLT	NC	PA	78.1
7591	184	1399	55K	2	1	BSLT	NC	PA	8.7
7282	184	1660	55K5	2	2	BSLT	NC	PA	30.1
7329	184	1967	60E5	1	1	BSLT	NC	PA	4.5
7163	184	373	60J5	2	1	BSLT	NC	PA	
7323	184	1698	70C	3	3	BSLT	NC	PA	
7215	184	1841	70C5	1	6	BSLT	NC	PA	
6956	184	1445	70I	1	1	BSLT	NC	PA	1.2
6898	184	2508	70J5	1	1	BSLT	NC	PA	1.4
7246	184	3313	75C	4	1	BSLT	NC	PA	6.6
6966	184	803	80D5	2	2	BSLT	NC	PA	2
7278	184	128	85E	3	1	BSLT	NC	PA	7
7211	184	4907	85F5	1	1	BSLT	NC	PA	6.1
7302	184	4976	85F5	5	1	BSLT	NC	PA	
7322	184	2081	90D5	3	2	BSLT	NC	PA	21.8
7565	184	2016	90E5	4	2	BSLT	NC	PA	
7262	184	2413	90E5	5	1	BSLT	NC	PA	9.5

2011.28	SBCM	Cat. #	Unit	Level	Qty	MTRL	DEB TYPE	PLAT	WT/g
6952	184	2032	95E	3	1	BSLT	NC	PA	2
7312	184	2211	95E	6	3	BSLT	NC	PA	11.8
6919	184	2221	95E	7	1	BSLT	NC	PA	1.1
7590	184	3268	95E5	7	1	BSLT	NC	PA	2.8
7036	184	1821	95F	9	2	BSLT	NC	PA	4
7326	184	1237	95G	3	2	BSLT	NC	PA	
7267	184	229	100D	5	1	BSLT	NC	SFP	
7100	184	3063	100D5	1	1	BSLT	NC	SFP	2
5870	184	924	100E5	1	1	BSLT	NC	SFP	0.6
7196	184	705	100E5	9	1	BSLT	NC	SFP	8
7205	184	178	100F	1	6	BSLT	NC	SFP	28.3
7258	184	3789	100F5	6	1	BSLT	NC	SFP	10.6
7260	184	1018	100O5	9	3	BSLT	NC	SFP	
7599	184	958	105D5	1	1	BSLT	NC	SFP	3.8
7304	184	972	105D5	2	3	BSLT	NC	SFP	17
7594	184	720	105D5	4	1	BSLT	NC	SFP	9.2
7569	184	2492	105D5	5	3	BSLT	NC	SFP	9.4
7233	184	1088	105E	4	1	BSLT	NC	SFP	10.8
6991	184	1013	105E5	3	39	BSLT	NC	SFP	8
6987	184	863	105F5	4	2	BSLT	NC	SFP	3
7297	184	4210	110D	2	4	BSLT	NC	SFP	10
6957	184	1095	110E5	4	1	BSLT	NC	SFP	2

2011.28	SBCM	Cat. #	Unit	Level	Qty	MTRL	DEB TYPE	PLAT	WT/g
7085	184	4953	110E5	8	1	BSLT	NC	SFP	0.9
7580	184	1222	110F	6	1	BSLT	NC	SFP	1.7
6905	184	3185	110F5	4	1	BSLT	NC	SFP	5.8
7224	184	4780	110G	5	1	BSLT	NC	SFP	14
7561	184	4863	110G5	3	2	BSLT	NC	SFP	2.8
7185	184	1917	110H	2	1	BSLT	NC	SFP	
7123	184	1921	110H5	5	1	BSLT	NC	SFP	1.8
5713	184	5713	110I	1	1	BSLT	NC	SFP	
7588	184	3000	110I5	4	4	BSLT	NC	SFP	
7217	184	535	115D	1	1	BSLT	NC	SFP	3
7574	184	417	115D	2	1	BSLT	NC	SFP	1.6
7595	184	764	115D5	4	2	BSLT	NC	SFP	24
7207	184	2169	115F	1	1	BSLT	NC	SFP	25.2
6983	184	4059	115F	2	3	BSLT	NC	SFP	2
7166	184	2958	115F	4	1	BSLT	NC	SFP	25
7251	184	2332	120D	7	1	BSLT	NC	SFP	1.8
7021	184	5292	120F	1	5	BSLT	NC	SFP	4
6882	184	3307	120F	4	1	BSLT	NC	SFP	1.7
7213	184	1986	120F	5	3	BSLT	NC	SFP	32.8
7152	184	2400	120F5	6	3	BSLT	NC	SFP	10
7281	184	927	120F5	7	5	BSLT	NC	SFP	12.9
6973	184	3328	120G	2	2	BSLT	NC	SFP	1.7

2011.28	SBCM	Cat. #	Unit	Level	Qty	MTRL	DEB TYPE	PLAT	WT/g
7601	184	743	125D5	1	3	BSLT	NC	SFP	21.9
7266	184	434	1.25E+07	3	3	BSLT	NC	SFP	20.6
7273	184	4842	125G5	3	1	BSLT	NC	SFP	1.2
7045	184	1805	140I	3	1	BSLT	NC	SFP	1
7219	184	6522	140I5	1	2	BSLT	NC	SFP	31
7183	184	2569	160H	1	7	BSLT	NC	SFP	
7187	184	17	160H	2	2	BSLT	NC	SFP	
6925	184	2476	160H5	1	2	BSLT	NC	SFP	2.7
5989	184	2527	160H5	2	1	BSLT	NC	SFP	0.5
7216	184	1165	160J5	2	1	BSLT	NC	SFP	
6547	184	1161	160J5	2	1	BSLT	NC	SFP	7.6
7182	184	569	165H	1	1	BSLT	NC	SFP	
7223	184	2624	165I	2	2	BSLT	NC	SFP	
6888	184	155	165I5	1	7	BSLT	NC	SFP	8.8
6981	184	2500	165I5	2	1	BSLT	NC	SFP	2
7335	184	43	165K	1	1	BSLT	NC	SFP	3.6
6860	184	1890	170H5	2	2	BSLT	NC	SFP	15.3
7222	184	2588	170I5	1	1	BSLT	NC	SFP	
7566	184	2778	170I5	2	3	BSLT	NC	SFP	13.6
7587	184	2428	170J	1	1	BSLT	NC	SFP	7.3
7214	184	2887	175H	1	1	BSLT	NC	SFP	8.5
7082	184	3597	175H5	3	2	BSLT	NC	SFP	2

2011.28	SBCM	Cat. #	Unit	Level	Qty	MTRL	DEB TYPE	PLAT	WT/g
3346	184	3346	175I	2	2	BSLT	NC	SFP	
7327	184	3224	175J	2	4	BSLT	NC	SFP	25.6
7295	184	3112	175J	3	1	BSLT	NC	SFP	2
6930	184	5534	175J5	1	2	BSLT	NC	SFP	6
7192	184	4731	20J5	2	1	BSLT	NC	SFP	
6936	184	2156	20J5	4	1	BSLT	NC	SFP	0.8
7210	184	2008	20J5	6	1	BSLT	NC	SFP	9.5
7065	184	4744	30J5	1	3	BSLT	NC	SFP	8
7149	184	1414	30J5	3	2	BSLT	NC	SFP	6
7257	184	6487	35H5	1	2	BSLT	NC	SFP	
6949	184	5678	35I	3	1	BSLT	NC	SFP	0.5
6968	184	1908	40I	1	3	BSLT	NC	SFP	2
7232	184	1514	40K	1	7	BSLT	NC	SFP	52.6
7101	184	3364	40K	4	2	BSLT	NC	SFP	2
7005	184	1582	40K	5	1	BSLT	NC	SFP	1
7164	184	1182	45I	4	6	BSLT	NC	SFP	
6947	184	2046	55I	1	2	BSLT	NC	SFP	8
7292	184	2748	55I5	2	2	BSLT	NC	SFP	
7228	184	1617	55J	2	1	BSLT	NC	SFP	7.1
7235	184	1388	55J5	3	1	BSLT	NC	SFP	
7577	184	4393	55J5	4	1	BSLT	NC	SFP	
7071	184	1384	55K	4	1	BSLT	NC	SFP	1

2011.28	SBCM	Cat. #	Unit	Level	Qty	MTRL	DEB TYPE	PLAT	WT/g
7282	184	1660	55K5	2	3	BSLT	NC	SFP	
7203	184	2029	60H5	4	1	BSLT	NC	SFP	
6871	184	2061	60H5	6	2	BSLT	NC	SFP	2.9
7163	184	373	60J5	2	1	BSLT	NC	SFP	
7316	184	4816	65E5	2	1	BSLT	NC	SFP	3.8
5218	184	6185	65I	1	1	BSLT	NC	SFP	2
7592	184	3853	70C	2	3	BSLT	NC	SFP	14.2
7215	184	1841	70C5	1	2	BSLT	NC	SFP	12.8
7321	184	1789	70C5	3	3	BSLT	NC	SFP	20
7208	184	2737	70E5	3	1	BSLT	NC	SFP	6.3
6903	184	2553	70E5	6	2	BSLT	NC	SFP	1.4
6955	184	1445	70I	1	3	BSLT	NC	SFP	6
7307	184	87	70J	1	1	BSLT	NC	SFP	
7127	184	646	70J	1	3	BSLT	NC	SFP	2
6896	184	2508	70J5	1	1	BSLT	NC	SFP	1.3
7199	184	27	70J5	2	2	BSLT	NC	SFP	10
7285	184	3567	75D	1	1	BSLT	NC	SFP	3
7198	184	3200	75D	5	1	BSLT	NC	SFP	
6895	184	195	75I	3	4	BSLT	NC	SFP	10.3
7200	184	1442	75N	1	3	BSLT	NC	SFP	17.4
6967	184	803	80D5	2	4	BSLT	NC	SFP	2
7241	184	1082	80D5	2	6	BSLT	NC	SFP	

2011.28	SBCM	Cat. #	Unit	Level	Qty	MTRL	DEB TYPE	PLAT	WT/g
6942	184	4036	80E	2	2	BSLT	NC	SFP	10
7567	184	4044	80E	2	1	BSLT	NC	SFP	
6963	184	602	80E	3	1	BSLT	NC	SFP	1
7146	184	4080	80E	4	1	BSLT	NC	SFP	2
7583	184	424	84-85H	6	1	BSLT	NC	SFP	1.4
7015	184	319	85D5	4	4	BSLT	NC	SFP	6
7280	184	275	85E	3	2	BSLT	NC	SFP	3
7268	184	206	85E5	4	1	BSLT	NC	SFP	7.3
6872	184	3126	85F	5	2	BSLT	NC	SFP	2.8
7302	184	4976	85F5	5	2	BSLT	NC	SFP	12.7
7031	184	3357	90D	2	1	BSLT	NC	SFP	1.4
7279	184	3217	90E	5	1	BSLT	NC	SFP	
7585	184	3282	90E	7	1	BSLT	NC	SFP	1
7141	184	3587	90E	8	1	BSLT	NC	SFP	4
7262	184	2413	90E5	5	2	BSLT	NC	SFP	
7038	184	4174	90I5	1	1	BSLT	NC	SFP	2
7243	184	119	95D	1	2	BSLT	NC	SFP	22.5
6875	184	1997	95D	5	6	BSLT	NC	SFP	7.2
7190	184	1975	95E	3	5	BSLT	NC	SFP	52
6951	184	2032	95E	3	5	BSLT	NC	SFP	30
7581	184	2150	95E	4	6	BSLT	NC	SFP	68.9
7159	184	3229	95E	5	8	BSLT	NC	SFP	8

2011.28	SBCM	Cat. #	Unit	Level	Qty	MTRL	DEB TYPE	PLAT	WT/g
7586	184	3288	95E	5	3	BSLT	NC	SFP	2.6
7312	184	2211	95E	6	1	BSLT	NC	SFP	
6863	184	3055	95E5	8	2	BSLT	NC	SFP	1.3
7043	184	1821	95F	9	1	BSLT	NC	SFP	0.8
7326	184	1237	95G	3	4	BSLT	NC	SFP	7.9
7057	184	767	100F5	8	1	BSLT	NC/ALT		1
6997	184	1056	100O5	7	2	BSLT	NC/ALT		2.2
7304	184	972	105D5	2	1	BSLT	NC/ALT		
7233	184	1088	105E	4	1	BSLT	NC/ALT		
7091	184	4953	110E5	8	1	BSLT	NC/ALT		
6868	184	690	120G	1	4	BSLT	NC/ALT		10.4
7131	184	1024	125D	3	1	BSLT	NC/ALT		2
7566	184	2778	170I5	2	1	BSLT	NC/ALT		
7295	184	3112	175J	3	1	BSLT	NC/ALT		
7164	184	1182	45I	4	1	BSLT	NC/ALT		
7292	184	2748	55I5	2	2	BSLT	NC/ALT		
7291	184	4715	55J5	4	1	BSLT	NC/ALT		
7269	184	4906	80D5	1	1	BSLT	NC/ALT		4.7
7138	184	5922	90E5	8	1	BSLT	NC/ALT		2
6919	184	2221	95E	7	1	BSLT	NC/ALT		0.5
7186	184	3142	95E5	3	1	BSLT	NC/ALT		
7270	184	3338	95E5	6	2	BSLT	NC/ALT		

2011.28	SBCM	Cat. #	Unit	Level	Qty	MTRL	DEB TYPE	PLAT	WT/g
6944	184	4036	80E	2	1	BSLT	NC/BULB		1.7
7248	184	4137	110D	3	1	BSLT	NC/EDGE		0.3
6996	184	945	120G	1	1	BSLT	NC/EDGE		1
7044	184	1805	140I	3	1	BSLT	NC/EDGE		2
7001	184	2712	55I5	3	1	BSLT	NC/EDGE		0.8
7282	184	1660	55K5	2	1	BSLT	NC/EDGE		
7314	184	66	90D5	4	2	BSLT	NC/EDGE		27.2
7184	184	4991	110E5	7	1	BSLT	NC/MARG	SFP	
7237	184	2485	55I	4	1	BSLT	NC/MARG		1.3
6961	184	1095	110E5	4	1	BSLT	NC/UNDL		0.5
7130	184	646	70J	1	1	BSLT	NC/UNDL		2
7182	184	569	165H	1	2	BSLT	NN/FF		
6922	184	924	100E5	1	1	BSLT	PC	MFP	3.3
7244	184	2115	110D5	4	1	BSLT	PC	MFP	40.9
7111	184	6540	70C	1	1	BSLT	PC	MFP	4
7319	184	146	85E	4	1	BSLT	PC	MFP	1.8
7290	184	1210	95H5	3	1	BSLT	PC	MFP	2.1
7267	184	229	100D	5	1	BSLT	PC	NP	12.4
7098	184	3063	100D5	1	1	BSLT	PC	NP	0.5
7570	184	1041	100E5	3	2	BSLT	PC	NP	41.2
6913	184	2912	100E5	4	2	BSLT	PC	NP	9
7305	184	3011	100E5	5	6	BSLT	PC	NP	34.5

2011.28	SBCM	Cat. #	Unit	Level	Qty	MTRL	DEB TYPE	PLAT	WT/g
5231	184	823	100E5	6,7	3	BSLT	PC	NP	7.1
7059	184	767	100F5	8	3	BSLT	PC	NP	2
7260	184	1018	100O5	9	1	BSLT	PC	NP	
7599	184	958	105D5	1	2	BSLT	PC	NP	
7304	184	972	105D5	2	2	BSLT	PC	NP	
6989	184	1013	105E5	3	39	BSLT	PC	NP	30
7095	184	1780	110D5	3	1	BSLT	PC	NP	0.9
7598	184	5724	110E5	2	2	BSLT	PC	NP	12
6960	184	1095	110E5	4	1	BSLT	PC	NP	1
7184	184	4991	110E5	7	2	BSLT	PC	NP	
7090	184	4953	110E5	8	1	BSLT	PC	NP	2.4
7264	184	5227	110G	2	2	BSLT	PC	NP	16.5
7185	184	1917	110H	2	1	BSLT	PC	NP	
7142	184	4884	115E	6	1	BSLT	PC	NP	2
7313	184	3019	115F	3	1	BSLT	PC	NP	
7023	184	5292	120F	1	1	BSLT	PC	NP	2
7047	184	2011	120F	3	1	BSLT	PC	NP	44
7180	184	2066	120F	7	1	BSLT	PC	NP	
6869	184	690	120G	1	2	BSLT	PC	NP	17.4
7011	184	6442	160J	1	5	BSLT	PC	NP	16
7216	184	1165	160J5	2	1	BSLT	PC	NP	
7564	184	4999	160J5	3	2	BSLT	PC	NP	

2011.28	SBCM	Cat. #	Unit	Level	Qty	MTRL	DEB TYPE	PLAT	WT/g
6932	184	451	165H	2	4	BSLT	PC	NP	8
6980	184	2500	165I5	2	1	BSLT	PC	NP	2
7209	184	1884	170H5	1	7	BSLT	PC	NP	
6859	184	1890	170H5	2	2	BSLT	PC	NP	4
7122	184	241	170J5	1	3	BSLT	PC	NP	2
7079	184	3597	175H5	3	1	BSLT	PC	NP	2
7619	184	1762	40I	1	4	BSLT	PC	NP	2.3
7218	184	2178	55H5	2	2	BSLT	PC	NP	11
7069	184	1407	55K	3	1	BSLT	PC	NP	1
7073	184	1384	55K	4	5	BSLT	PC	NP	12
7282	184	1660	55K5	2	6	BSLT	PC	NP	
7303	184	2422	60J5	5	5	BSLT	PC	NP	
7323	184	1698	70C	3	2	BSLT	PC	NP	10.5
7308	184	5634	70E	5	2	BSLT	PC	NP	
7307	184	87	70J	1	2	BSLT	PC	NP	
7198	184	3200	75D	5	1	BSLT	PC	NP	13.9
7181	184	5598	75J	1	5	BSLT	PC	NP	
6940	184	4036	80E	2	1	BSLT	PC	NP	1.6
7582	184	2994	85D	3	2	BSLT	PC	NP	8.5
7126	184	104	85E	1	2	BSLT	PC	NP	10
7211	184	4907	85F5	1	1	BSLT	PC	NP	
7315	184	5902	85F5	3	2	BSLT	PC	NP	9

2011.28	SBCM	Cat. #	Unit	Level	Qty	MTRL	DEB TYPE	PLAT	WT/g
7206	184	1770	85G5	3	4	BSLT	PC	NP	
7322	184	2081	90D5	3	1	BSLT	PC	NP	
7279	184	3217	90E	5	5	BSLT	PC	NP	6.6
7565	184	2016	90E5	4	4	BSLT	PC	NP	81.3
7204	184	5407	90I	1	2	BSLT	PC	NP	40.4
5212	184	2228	95E	1	7	BSLT	PC	NP	2.9
7190	184	1975	95E	3	1	BSLT	PC	NP	
7581	184	2150	95E	4	2	BSLT	PC	NP	
7312	184	2211	95E	6	3	BSLT	PC	NP	
6919	184	2221	95E	7	4	BSLT	PC	NP	9.7
6865	184	3055	95E5	8	2	BSLT	PC	NP	13.5
7616	184	3119	Tile 11	2	1	BSLT	PC	NP	0.6
7610	184	2922	100D	5	1	BSLT	PC	PA	5.1
5272	184	961	100E	2	1	BSLT	PC	PA	3.9
6912	184	2912	100E5	4	2	BSLT	PC	PA	1.5
7305	184	3011	100E5	5	1	BSLT	PC	PA	
7304	184	972	105D5	2	2	BSLT	PC	PA	
7264	184	5227	110G	2	1	BSLT	PC	PA	
7224	184	4780	110G	5	1	BSLT	PC	PA	
7229	184	6209	110H5	1	1	BSLT	PC	PA	7.7
5257	184	5322	110J5	3	1	BSLT	PC	PA	1.7
7180	184	2066	120F	7	1	BSLT	PC	PA	

2011.28	SBCM	Cat. #	Unit	Level	Qty	MTRL	DEB TYPE	PLAT	WT/g
7255	184	249	120F5	2	2	BSLT	PC	PA	3.8
7012	184	6442	160J	1	6	BSLT	PC	PA	6
7620	184	6402	160J5	1	1	BSLT	PC	PA	8
7564	184	4999	160J5	3	3	BSLT	PC	PA	3.8
6933	184	451	165H	2	4	BSLT	PC	PA	4
7209	184	1884	170H5	1	4	BSLT	PC	PA	
7049	184	2982	175I	1	1	BSLT	PC	PA	4
6950	184	5678	35I	3	1	BSLT	PC	PA	2
7591	184	1399	55K	2	1	BSLT	PC	PA	
7308	184	5634	70E	5	1	BSLT	PC	PA	
7230	184	2580	70I	1	1	BSLT	PC	PA	
7307	184	87	70J	1	3	BSLT	PC	PA	37.7
7181	184	5598	75J	1	3	BSLT	PC	PA	
7241	184	1082	80D5	2	2	BSLT	PC	PA	
6873	184	3126	85F	5	1	BSLT	PC	PA	3.9
7206	184	1770	85G5	3	3	BSLT	PC	PA	32.1
7227	184	2370	85H5	1	1	BSLT	PC	PA	4.4
7262	184	2413	90E5	5	1	BSLT	PC	PA	
7581	184	2150	95E	4	1	BSLT	PC	PA	
5897	184	2146	95E	4	1	BSLT	PC	PA	0.6
7186	184	3142	95E5	3	1	BSLT	PC	PA	
7270	184	3338	95E5	6	1	BSLT	PC	PA	19.1

2011.28	SBCM	Cat. #	Unit	Level	Qty	MTRL	DEB TYPE	PLAT	WT/g
7275	184	783	100F5	1	2	BSLT	PC	SFP	10.2
7150	184	776	100F5	3	1	BSLT	PC	SFP	30.9
7258	184	3789	100F5	6	1	BSLT	PC	SFP	
7593	184	714	105F5	2	1	BSLT	PC	SFP	1.7
7184	184	4991	110E5	7	2	BSLT	PC	SFP	47.4
7185	184	1917	110H	2	1	BSLT	PC	SFP	
7272	184	1798	110H5	5	1	BSLT	PC	SFP	22.9
7333	184	1424	110I	2	1	BSLT	PC	SFP	31.8
7236	184	5558	110I5	2	2	BSLT	PC	SFP	4.2
7225	184	409	115D5	3	2	BSLT	PC	SFP	7.2
7231	184	1652	115F5	3	1	BSLT	PC	SFP	15
7603	184	1071	125D	2	1	BSLT	PC	SFP	4.8
6891	184	155	165I5	1	1	BSLT	PC	SFP	8.4
7274	184	2100	170H	1	3	BSLT	PC	SFP	
7121	184	241	170J5	1	1	BSLT	PC	SFP	6
7080	184	3597	175H5	3	4	BSLT	PC	SFP	8
7053	184	2982	175I	1	1	BSLT	PC	SFP	28
7293	184	2006	55I	2	1	BSLT	PC	SFP	4
7573	184	4128	80I	2	1	BSLT	PC	SFP	21.1
7268	184	206	85E5	4	1	BSLT	PC	SFP	
6938	184	3273	90E	2	1	BSLT	PC	SFP	1.9
7137	184	5922	90E5	8	3	BSLT	PC	SFP	14

2011.28	SBCM	Cat. #	Unit	Level	Qty	MTRL	DEB TYPE	PLAT	WT/g
7190	184	1975	95E	3	2	BSLT	PC	SFP	
7083	184	3045	95E5	2	1	BSLT	PC	SFP	1.4
7186	184	3142	95E5	3	1	BSLT	PC	SFP	105.4
7014	184	319	85D5	4	2	BSLT	PC		18
6908	184	1961	100D5	5	1	BSLT	PC/ALT		1.7
5228	184	823	100E5	6,7	1	BSLT	PC/ALT		4.1
7234	184	795	105F	1	1	BSLT	PC/ALT		5.6
7605	184	870	105F	3	2	BSLT	PC/ALT		4.7
7288	184	1461	110H5	4	1	BSLT	PC/ALT		
7024	184	5292	120F	1	2	BSLT	PC/ALT		2
7151	184	2400	120F5	6	1	BSLT	PC/ALT		2
7216	184	1165	160J5	2	1	BSLT	PC/ALT		
6862	184	1890	170H5	2	1	BSLT	PC/ALT		0.8
7214	184	2887	175H	1	1	BSLT	PC/ALT		
7592	184	3853	70C	2	1	BSLT	PC/ALT		
7323	184	1698	70C	3	2	BSLT	PC/ALT		
7216	184	1165	160J5	2	1	BSLT	PC/MARG		
7588	184	3000	110I5	4	2	BSLT	PC/NC		11.3
7577	184	4393	55J5	4	2	BSLT	PC/NC		
6994	184	945	120G	1	1	BSLT	PC/outré		12
2123	184	2123	95D5	4	1	BSLT	PC/outré		
7596	184	2701	100D	1	1	BSLT	SHT		0.6

2011.28	SBCM	Cat. #	Unit	Level	Qty	MTRL	DEB TYPE	PLAT	WT/g
6914	184	2536	100D5	1	3	BSLT	SHT		19
7570	184	1041	100E5	3	23	BSLT	SHT		
6911	184	2912	100E5	4	12	BSLT	SHT		15.2
7660	184	907	105F5	3	2	BSLT	SHT		3.3
6986	184	863	105F5	4	4	BSLT	SHT		18
7207	184	2169	115F	1	3	BSLT	SHT		
7153	184	2400	120F5	6	2	BSLT	SHT		4
6867	184	690	120G	1	5	BSLT	SHT		11
7221	184	5522	160I5	2	1	BSLT	SHT		11.8
6931	184	451	165H	2	15	BSLT	SHT		20
6886	184	1670	175J5	2	6	BSLT	SHT		6.9
7148	184	1414	30J5	3	6	BSLT	SHT		10
7004	184	1582	40K	5	1	BSLT	SHT		2
7218	184	2178	55H5	2	4	BSLT	SHT		
7002	184	2712	55I5	3	1	BSLT	SHT		3.8
7070	184	1384	55K	4	1	BSLT	SHT		2
7303	184	2422	60J5	5	3	BSLT	SHT		16.1
5216	184	6185	65I	1	9	BSLT	SHT		12.4
7308	184	5634	70E	5	6	BSLT	SHT		29
7206	184	1770	85G5	3	2	BSLT	SHT		
7565	184	2016	90E5	4	4	BSLT	SHT		
7204	184	5407	90I	1	1	BSLT	SHT		

2011.28	SBCM	Cat. #	Unit	Level	Qty	MTRL	DEB TYPE	PLAT	WT/g
7243	184	119	95D	1	8	BSLT	SHT		
6874	184	1997	95D	5	8	BSLT	SHT		4.1
7212	184	2246	95E	2	5	BSLT	SHT		32.8
5899	184	2146	95E	4	2	BSLT	SHT		3.3
7160	184	3229	95E	5	12	BSLT	SHT		14
7270	184	3338	95E5	6	4	BSLT	SHT		
5271	184	961	100E	2	3	BSLT	SHT		2.2
7180	184	2066	120F	7	8	BSLT	SHT		17.3
7241	184	1082	80D5	2	12	BSLT	SHT		36.6
7267	184	229	100D	5	1	BSLT	SHT/C		
7099	184	3063	100D5	1	1	BSLT	SHT/C		2
7249	184	895	100D5	8	1	BSLT	SHT/C		4.6
7305	184	3011	100E5	5	2	BSLT	SHT/C		
5230	184	823	100E5	6,7	1	BSLT	SHT/C		2.3
7055	184	767	100F5	8	3	BSLT	SHT/C		30
6992	184	1013	105E5	3	39	BSLT	SHT/C		12
7563	184	1002	105F	1	1	BSLT	SHT/C		
7229	184	6209	110H5	1	2	BSLT	SHT/C		
7288	184	1461	110H5	4	3	BSLT	SHT/C		
7022	184	5292	120F	1	3	BSLT	SHT/C		12
7132	184	1024	125D	3	1	BSLT	SHT/C		6
7571	184	4832	125E	1	1	BSLT	SHT/C		2

2011.28	SBCM	Cat. #	Unit	Level	Qty	MTRL	DEB TYPE	PLAT	WT/g
7219	184	6522	140I5	1	5	BSLT	SHT/C		
6924	184	2476	160H5	1	1	BSLT	SHT/C		4
7216	184	1165	160J5	2	3	BSLT	SHT/C		
7274	184	2100	170H	1	2	BSLT	SHT/C		
3346	184	3346	175I	2	1	BSLT	SHT/C		26.3
6969	184	1908	40I	1	1	BSLT	SHT/C		1
7292	184	2748	55I5	2	1	BSLT	SHT/C		10.4
7291	184	4715	55J5	4	2	BSLT	SHT/C		
7589	184	1590	55K5	1	1	BSLT	SHT/C		11.6
7282	184	1660	55K5	2	3	BSLT	SHT/C		
7110	184	6540	70C	1	1	BSLT	SHT/C		2
7181	184	5598	75J	1	7	BSLT	SHT/C		54.2
7125	184	104	85E	1	1	BSLT	SHT/C		26
7211	184	4907	85F5	1	2	BSLT	SHT/C		
6939	184	3273	90E	2	1	BSLT	SHT/C		4
7136	184	5922	90E5	8	1	BSLT	SHT/C		4
7296	184	2608	90F	3	1	BSLT	SHT/C		6.1
2123	184	2123	95D5	4	3	BSLT	SHT/C		
5210	184	2228	95E	3	7	BSLT	SHT/C		9.3
7312	184	2211	95E	6	3	BSLT	SHT/C		
7301	184	6046	95E	8	2	BSLT	SHT/C		
6999	184	3100	95G	3	1	BSLT	SHT/C		2

2011.28	SBCM	Cat. #	Unit	Level	Qty	MTRL	DEB TYPE	PLAT	WT/g
7097	184	3063	100D5	1	4	BSLT	SHT/NC		8
7238	184	2639	100D5	2	3	BSLT	SHT/NC		5.1
6910	184	1961	100D5	5	1	BSLT	SHT/NC		6.9
7310	184	2289	100D5	6	3	BSLT	SHT/NC		
7305	184	3011	100E5	5	3	BSLT	SHT/NC		
7205	184	178	100F	1	9	BSLT	SHT/NC		
7608	184	215	100F	1	1	BSLT	SHT/NC		0.2
7058	184	767	100F5	8	5	BSLT	SHT/NC		10
7260	184	1018	100O5	9	1	BSLT	SHT/NC		18
7599	184	958	105D5	1	1	BSLT	SHT/NC		
7304	184	972	105D5	2	5	BSLT	SHT/NC		
7613	184	494	105D5	3	3	BSLT	SHT/NC		1.2
7233	184	1088	105E	4	3	BSLT	SHT/NC		
7042	184	830	105E5	1	1	BSLT	SHT/NC		0.8
6988	184	1013	105E5	3	21	BSLT	SHT/NC		16
7167	184	4579	105E5	5	2	BSLT	SHT/NC		3
7297	184	4210	110D	2	3	BSLT	SHT/NC		
7598	184	5724	110E5	2	1	BSLT	SHT/NC		
6959	184	1095	110E5	4	8	BSLT	SHT/NC		4
7184	184	4991	110E5	7	6	BSLT	SHT/NC		
7087	184	4953	110E5	8	2	BSLT	SHT/NC		2
7264	184	5227	110G	2	1	BSLT	SHT/NC		

2011.28	SBCM	Cat. #	Unit	Level	Qty	MTRL	DEB TYPE	PLAT	WT/g
5713	184	5713	110I	1	5	BSLT	SHT/NC		32.4
7588	184	3000	110I5	4	3	BSLT	SHT/NC		
6984	184	4059	115F	2	2	BSLT	SHT/NC		1
7313	184	3019	115F	3	5	BSLT	SHT/NC		
7166	184	2958	115F	4	3	BSLT	SHT/NC		
7231	184	1652	115F5	3	4	BSLT	SHT/NC		
7252	184	1983	120D	2	1	BSLT	SHT/NC		0.9
7220	184	2540	120E5	1	1	BSLT	SHT/NC		
7165	184	2545	120E5	2	1	BSLT	SHT/NC		22
7046	184	2011	120F	3	12	BSLT	SHT/NC		32
7213	184	1986	120F	5	5	BSLT	SHT/NC		
7281	184	927	120F5	7	5	BSLT	SHT/NC		
6995	184	945	120G	1	1	BSLT	SHT/NC		4
6342	184	1732	140I	2	2	BSLT	SHT/NC		1.5
7283	184	1148	140I5	2	5	BSLT	SHT/NC		11.1
7183	184	2569	160H	1	3	BSLT	SHT/NC		18
7187	184	17	160H	2	2	BSLT	SHT/NC		
7604	184	2767	160I	2	2	BSLT	SHT/NC		2.1
7007	184	6442	160J	1	5	BSLT	SHT/NC		14
7223	184	2624	165I	2	7	BSLT	SHT/NC		
6892	184	155	165I5	1	8	BSLT	SHT/NC		10
7209	184	1884	170H5	1	18	BSLT	SHT/NC		35.2

2011.28	SBCM	Cat. #	Unit	Level	Qty	MTRL	DEB TYPE	PLAT	WT/g
6861	184	1890	170H5	2	2	BSLT	SHT/NC		1.4
7222	184	2588	170I5	1	1	BSLT	SHT/NC		11.5
7566	184	2778	170I5	2	3	BSLT	SHT/NC		
7587	184	2428	170J	1	2	BSLT	SHT/NC		
7259	184	2520	170J	1	4	BSLT	SHT/NC		4.3
7118	184	241	170J5	1	8	BSLT	SHT/NC		10
7214	184	2887	175H	1	4	BSLT	SHT/NC		
7050	184	2982	175I	1	3	BSLT	SHT/NC		2
3346	184	3346	175I	2	5	BSLT	SHT/NC		
7327	184	3224	175J	2	5	BSLT	SHT/NC		
6928	184	5534	175J5	1	3	BSLT	SHT/NC		4
7392	184	2392	20J5	3	2	BSLT	SHT/NC		7.1
7210	184	2008	20J5	6	2	BSLT	SHT/NC		
7066	184	4744	30J5	1	1	BSLT	SHT/NC		2
7257	184	6487	35H5	1	3	BSLT	SHT/NC		
6948	184	5678	35I	3	2	BSLT	SHT/NC		8
6971	184	1908	40I	1	2	BSLT	SHT/NC		2
7232	184	1514	40K	1	13	BSLT	SHT/NC		
7318	184	1476	40K	3	6	BSLT	SHT/NC		
7102	184	3364	40K	4	2	BSLT	SHT/NC		16
7164	184	1182	45I	4	1	BSLT	SHT/NC		
6945	184	2046	55I	1	5	BSLT	SHT/NC		50

2011.28	SBCM	Cat. #	Unit	Level	Qty	MTRL	DEB TYPE	PLAT	WT/g
7195	184	611	55I	4	1	BSLT	SHT/NC		8.6
7292	184	2748	55I5	2	3	BSLT	SHT/NC		
7228	184	1617	55J	2	2	BSLT	SHT/NC		
7577	184	4393	55J5	4	2	BSLT	SHT/NC		15.2
7291	184	4715	55J5	4	3	BSLT	SHT/NC		
7072	184	1384	55K	4	2	BSLT	SHT/NC		2
7282	184	1660	55K5	3	20	BSLT	SHT/NC		
7203	184	2029	60H5	4	5	BSLT	SHT/NC		29.7
6870	184	2061	60H5	6	6	BSLT	SHT/NC		23.4
7592	184	3853	70C	2	1	BSLT	SHT/NC		
7323	184	1698	70C	3	3	BSLT	SHT/NC		
7215	184	1841	70C5	1	6	BSLT	SHT/NC		
7321	184	1789	70C5	3	1	BSLT	SHT/NC		
7256	184	1828	70C5	5	1	BSLT	SHT/NC		1.2
7208	184	2737	70E5	3	3	BSLT	SHT/NC		
7162	184	2702	70E5	4	4	BSLT	SHT/NC		1
7230	184	2580	70I	1	3	BSLT	SHT/NC		16.2
7307	184	87	70J	1	3	BSLT	SHT/NC		
7128	184	646	70J	1	1	BSLT	SHT/NC		2
6897	184	2508	70J5	1	2	BSLT	SHT/NC		6.6
7246	184	3313	75C	4	1	BSLT	SHT/NC		
7198	184	3200	75D	5	4	BSLT	SHT/NC		

2011.28	SBCM	Cat. #	Unit	Level	Qty	MTRL	DEB TYPE	PLAT	WT/g
6894	184	195	75I	3	1	BSLT	SHT/NC		3.1
7181	184	5598	75J	1	2	BSLT	SHT/NC		
7200	184	1442	75N	1	3	BSLT	SHT/NC		
6965	184	803	80D5	2	3	BSLT	SHT/NC		3
7000	184	1464	80D5	2	1	BSLT	SHT/NC		2
7157	184	1712	80D5	5	7	BSLT	SHT/NC		12
6943	184	4036	80E	2	3	BSLT	SHT/NC		8
7567	184	4044	80E	2	3	BSLT	SHT/NC		9
6962	184	602	80E	3	5	BSLT	SHT/NC		8
7147	184	4080	80E	4	1	BSLT	SHT/NC		6
6979	184	1863	80I	1	1	BSLT	SHT/NC		2.4
7573	184	4128	80I	2	3	BSLT	SHT/NC		
7013	184	319	85D5	4	9	BSLT	SHT/NC		20
7018	184	319	85D5	4	1	BSLT	SHT/NC		0.7
7278	184	128	85E	3	1	BSLT	SHT/NC		
7280	184	275	85E	3	2	BSLT	SHT/NC		
7268	184	206	85E5	4	1	BSLT	SHT/NC		
7253	184	2950	85F	1	1	BSLT	SHT/NC		1.7
6926	184	891	85F	2	4	BSLT	SHT/NC		30.4
7211	184	4907	85F5	1	2	BSLT	SHT/NC		
7032	184	3357	90D	2	2	BSLT	SHT/NC		4
7322	184	2081	90D5	3	1	BSLT	SHT/NC		

2011.28	SBCM	Cat. #	Unit	Level	Qty	MTRL	DEB TYPE	PLAT	WT/g
7309	184	3298	90E	1	1	BSLT	SHT/NC		2.8
7279	184	3217	90E	5	3	BSLT	SHT/NC		
7262	184	2413	90E5	5	3	BSLT	SHT/NC		
7189	184	2041	90E5	6	5	BSLT	SHT/NC		
7611	184	4726	90E5	7	1	BSLT	SHT/NC		1.7
7575	184	4151	90I5	3	2	BSLT	SHT/NC		52
7191	184	2437	95D5	3	2	BSLT	SHT/NC		15.7
7190	184	1975	95E	3	11	BSLT	SHT/NC		
6953	184	2032	95E	3	1	BSLT	SHT/NC		2
5211	184	2228	95E	3	7	BSLT	SHT/NC		3.9
7581	184	2150	95E	4	18	BSLT	SHT/NC		
7312	184	2211	95E	6	3	BSLT	SHT/NC		
6918	184	2221	95E	7	2	BSLT	SHT/NC		13.5
7084	184	3045	95E5	2	4	BSLT	SHT/NC		4
7186	184	3142	95E5	3	3	BSLT	SHT/NC		
6864	184	3055	95E5	8	3	BSLT	SHT/NC		2.6
7035	184	1821	95F	9	1	BSLT	SHT/NC		1
7326	184	1237	95G	3	4	BSLT	SHT/NC		
7276	184	1736	95H	2	1	BSLT	SHT/NC		3.1

Basalt Debitage Notation Key

2011.28: Pechanga Cultural Resource catalogue number

SBCM: San Bernardino Collection catalogue number					
CAT #: Catalog number					
UNIT: Location					
	According to excavation map				
	TEST: Test Hole				
LEVEL: Depth					
	SURF: Surface				
	Levels 1-10 (Increments of 6 inches each level)				
	N/A: Not applicable				
QTY: Quantity					
MTRL: Material					
	BSLT: Basalt				
DEB TYPE: Debitage Type					
	BF: EPERC: Biface early percussion flake				
	BF/EDGE: Biface edge modified flake				
	BF/EPRES: Biface early pressure flake				
	BF/LPERC: Biface late percussion flake				
	BF/MARG: Biface margin removal flake				
	BF/outré: Biface outré passé				
	Burin spall				
	CC: Completely Cortical				
	CC/outré: Completely cortical outré passé				
	FF/C: Flake fragment cortical				

	FF/NC: Flake Fragment no cortex				
	NC: No Cortex				
	NC/ALT: No Cortex alternate flake				
	NC/BULB: No Cortex bulb removal flake				
	NC/EDGE: No cortex edge modified flake				
	NC/MARG: No Cortex margin removal flake				
	NC/outré: No cortex outré passé				
	NC/UNDI: No Cortex undulation removal flake				
	PC: Partially Cortical				
	PC/ALT: Partically cortical alternate flake				
	PC/EDGE: Partially cortical edge modified flake				
	PC/MARG: Partially cortical margin removal flake				
	SHT: Shatter				
	SHT/C: Shatter Cortical				
	SHT/NC: Shatter No Cortex				
PLAT: Platform					
	PA: Platform absent				
	NP: Natural Platform				
	MFP: Multi-faceted platform				
	SFP: Single faceted platform				
WT/g: Weight measured in grams					

APPENDIX D

CRYTOCRYSTALLINE QUARTZ DEBITAGE

Appendix D: Crytocrystalline Quartz Debitage									
2011.28	**SBCM**	**Cat. #**	**Unit**	**Level**	**Qty**	**MTRL**	**DEB TYPE**	**PLAT**	**WT/g**
5424	184	4885	115E	6	1	CCQZ	BF/ALT	MFP	1.3
5748	184	2028	60H5	4	1	CCQZ	BF/ALT	MFP	0.7
5730	184	4405	75C	2	1	CCQZ	BF/ALT		0.7
6284	184	1091	105E	4	4	CCQZ	BF/EDGE	MFP	0.8
5621	184	3001	110I5	4	3	CCQZ	BF/EDGE	MFP	1.2
6041	184	4007	115-E	1	1	CCQZ	BF/EDGE	MFP	0.5
6548	184	1161	160J5	2	1	CCQZ	BF/EDGE	MFP	0.6
5984	184	505	165H	3	1	CCQZ	BF/EDGE	MFP	0.5
6555	184	2103	170H	1	3	CCQZ	BF/EDGE	MFP	1.9
6226	184	1886	170H5	2	2	CCQZ	BF/EDGE	MFP	0.6
5879	184	3598	175H5	3	1	CCQZ	BF/EDGE	MFP	0.5
5597	184	4477	30J5	1	1	CCQZ	BF/EDGE	MFP	0.7
5840	184	1493	40H5	2	1	CCQZ	BF/EDGE	MFP	0.6
5531	184	2176	55H5	2	1	CCQZ	BF/EDGE	MFP	0.6
5409	184	6052	55H5	3	1	CCQZ	BF/EDGE	MFP	0.9
6323	184	4717	55J5	4	1	CCQZ	BF/EDGE	MFP	0.9
6197	184	4438	55J5	5	1	CCQZ	BF/EDGE	MFP	0.6
6252	184	372	60J5	2	2	CCQZ	BF/EDGE	MFP	0.7
5691	184	6105	65I	2	1	CCQZ	BF/EDGE	MFP	0.4
5706	184	1446	70I	1	1	CCQZ	BF/EDGE	MFP	0.7
5840	184	1079	80D5	2	1	CCQZ	BF/EDGE	MFP	0.6

2011.28	SBCM	Cat. #	Unit	Level	Qty	MTRL	DEB TYPE	PLAT	WT/g
6349	184	6283	85F5	6	1	CCQZ	BF/EDGE	MFP	0.4
5422	184	2369	85H5	1	1	CCQZ	BF/EDGE	MFP	0.2
5505	184	3284	90E	7	1	CCQZ	BF/EDGE	MFP	0.2
6301	184	2149	95E	4	2	CCQZ	BF/EDGE	MFP	1.4
5627	184	3233	95E	5	1	CCQZ	BF/EDGE	MFP	0.5
6278	184	5262	95H5	2	1	CCQZ	BF/EDGE	MFP	0.9
5671	184	2819	55I5	4	2	CCQZ	BF/EDGE	PA	0.9
6288	184	6182	65I	1	2	CCQZ	BF/EDGE	PA	0.9
6279	184	5262	95H5	2	1	CCQZ	BF/EDGE	PA	1.1
5572	184	964	100E	2	1	CCQZ	BF/EDGE		0.7
5888	184	5695	175K	1	1	CCQZ	BF/EDGE		0.6
6007	184	574	70-5	2	1	CCQZ	BF/EDGE		0.6
6556	184	3900	70C5	2	1	CCQZ	BF/EDGE		0.8
5649	184	5653	75E5	1	1	CCQZ	BF/EDGE		0.5
5886	184	4799	75E5	2	1	CCQZ	BF/EDGE		0.3
6608	184	512	85F	4	1	CCQZ	BF/EDGE		0.5
6312	184	2320	90E5	3	1	CCQZ	BF/EDGE		1.1
5752	184	2292	100D5	6	2	CCQZ	BF/EPERC	MFP	1.3
5645	184	3013	100E5	2	11	CCQZ	BF/EPERC	MFP	1.2
5756	184	855	100F5	7	1	CCQZ	BF/EPERC	MFP	1.4
6260	184	975	105D5	2	1	CCQZ	BF/EPERC	MFP	0.7
5817	184	862	105F5	4	2	CCQZ	BF/EPERC	MFP	2.5

APPENDIX D

2011.28	SBCM	Cat. #	Unit	Level	Qty	MTRL	DEB TYPE	PLAT	WT/g
6200	184	5340	110D	3	1	CCQZ	BF/EPERC	MFP	0.8
5475	184	1778	110D5	1	9	CCQZ	BF/EPERC	MFP	0.6
5960	184	5556	110I5	2	1	CCQZ	BF/EPERC	MFP	1.1
6333	184	1566	115D5	2	1	CCQZ	BF/EPERC	MFP	1.8
5589	184	4873	115E5	8	1	CCQZ	BF/EPERC	MFP	0.7
5638	184	2957	115F	4	1	CCQZ	BF/EPERC	MFP	1.2
5620	184	1654	115F5	3	1	CCQZ	BF/EPERC	MFP	0.7
5521	184	2848	120E5	1	1	CCQZ	BF/EPERC	MFP	1.2
6266	184	5135	140H5	3	1	CCQZ	BF/EPERC	MFP	1
5972	184	5047	140I	1	1	CCQZ	BF/EPERC	MFP	0.6
6275	184	6525	140I5	1	2	CCQZ	BF/EPERC	MFP	1.89
5664	184	6408	160J5	1	2	CCQZ	BF/EPERC	MFP	1.3
5986	184	505	165H	3	3	CCQZ	BF/EPERC	MFP	1.5
5555	184	2239	170H	2	1	CCQZ	BF/EPERC	MFP	1.2
5721	184	2429	170J	1	2	CCQZ	BF/EPERC	MFP	0.6
5551	184	3253	175H5	1	1	CCQZ	BF/EPERC	MFP	0.7
5993	184	2985	175I	1	1	CCQZ	BF/EPERC	MFP	1.3
6179	184	5547	175I5	2	3	CCQZ	BF/EPERC	MFP	3.3
6018	184	3225	175J	2	2	CCQZ	BF/EPERC	MFP	1.7
5562	184	6356	40H5	1	1	CCQZ	BF/EPERC	MFP	0.8
6025	184	1573	40I	3	4	CCQZ	BF/EPERC	MFP	1.2
5607	184	1176	45I	4	2	CCQZ	BF/EPERC	MFP	1.3

2011.28	SBCM	Cat. #	Unit	Level	Qty	MTRL	DEB TYPE	PLAT	WT/g
5533	184	2176	55H5	2	2	CCQZ	BF/EPERC	MFP	1
6220	184	2483	55I	4	1	CCQZ	BF/EPERC	MFP	1.6
5684	184	2747	55I5	2	3	CCQZ	BF/EPERC	MFP	1.4
5471	184	2709	55I5	3	4	CCQZ	BF/EPERC	MFP	2.9
5883	184	1408	55K	3	1	CCQZ	BF/EPERC	MFP	0.9
6038	184	1951	60H5	1	2	CCQZ	BF/EPERC	MFP	1.4
5915	184	2087	60H5	3	2	CCQZ	BF/EPERC	MFP	2
6195	184	2054	60H5	6	1	CCQZ	BF/EPERC	MFP	0.7
5659	184	4551	65E	1	2	CCQZ	BF/EPERC	MFP	2.5
5689	184	6105	65I	2	2	CCQZ	BF/EPERC	MFP	1.1
5982	184	6320	65I	4	1	CCQZ	BF/EPERC	MFP	0.7
6003	184	574	70-5	2	3	CCQZ	BF/EPERC	MFP	2.7
6583	184	3851	70C	2	1	CCQZ	BF/EPERC	MFP	0.6
6282	184	2866	70E5	2	1	CCQZ	BF/EPRC	MFP	0.6
5825	184	2727	70I	2	2	CCQZ	BF/EPERC	MFP	1.6
5918	184	389	70J5	1	2	CCQZ	BF/EPERC	MFP	0.9
5857	184	4763	75H5	1	3	CCQZ	BF/EPERC	MFP	3
6180	184	1711	80D5	5	1	CCQZ	BF/EPERC	MFP	1.5
5909	184	281	85E5	1	2	CCQZ	BF/EPERC	MFP	2.4
5933	184	886	85F	2	1	CCQZ	BF/EPERC	MFP	1.3
5583	184	3570	85F5	3	1	CCQZ	BF/EPERC	MFP	1.3
6215	184	3356	90D	2	1	CCQZ	BF/EPERC	MFP	0.6

2011.28	SBCM	Cat. #	Unit	Level	Qty	MTRL	DEB TYPE	PLAT	WT/g
6308	184	2320	90E5	3	1	CCQZ	BF/EPERC	MFP	1.2
6209	184	3292	95E	5	1	CCQZ	BF/EPERC	MFP	0.7
5623	184	3233	95E	5	1	CCQZ	BF/EPERC	MFP	1.7
5677	184	2213	95E	6	1	CCQZ	BF/EPERC	MFP	0.6
6238	184	5679	35I	3	2	CCQZ	BF/EPERC	PA	1.6
6222	184	2483	55I	4	1	CCQZ	BF/EPERC	PA	1
9150	184	3902	70C5	2	1	CCQZ	BF/EPERC	PA	0.7
5744	184	4497	95E5	4	2	CCQZ	BF/EPERC	PA	1.1
6151	184	3902	70C5	2	1	CCQZ	BF/EPERC	SFP	1.3
5737	184	3292	95E	5	3	CCQZ	BF/EPERC	SFP	2.7
5600	184	819	100E5	6,7	2	CCQZ	BF/EPERC		1.1
5528	184	3022	115F	3	1	CCQZ	BF/EPERC		0.7
5981	184	6320	65I	4	2	CCQZ	BF/EPERC		1.5
5169	184	1091	105E	4	1	CCQZ	BF/EPREC	MFP	2.3
5479	184	431	125E5	3	1	CCQZ	BF/EPREC	MFP	0.6
5605	184	554	165H5	1	1	CCQZ	BF/EPREC	MFP	0.4
5488	184	4628	20J5	4	1	CCQZ	BF/EPREC	MFP	0.5
5429	184	648	70J	1	1	CCQZ	BF/EPREC	MFP	2.3
5610	184	6222	80E	7	1	CCQZ	BF/EPREC	MFP	0.5
5679	184	318	85D5	4	1	CCQZ	BF/EPREC	MFP	0.7
5421	184	2369	85H5	1	1	CCQZ	BF/EPREC	MFP	0.3
5927	184	152	165I5	1	2	CCQZ	BF/EPREC	PA	1.8

2011.28	SBCM	Cat. #	Unit	Level	Qty	MTRL	DEB TYPE	PLAT	WT/g
5443	184	2494	105D5	5	2	CCQZ	BF/EPREC		0.6
5412	184	689	120G	1	2	CCQZ	BF/EPREC		3
6190	184	2237	170H	2	1	CCQZ	BF/EPREC		0.6
5407	184	6052	55H5	3	1	CCQZ	BF/EPREC		0.1
5219	184	6185	65I	1	2	CCQZ	BF/EPREC		0.9
5665	184	6432	85G	3	1	CCQZ	BF/EPREC		0.4
5438	184	59	85G5	4	1	CCQZ	BF/EPREC		0.1
5502	184	2533	100D5	1	1	CCQZ	BF/EPRES		0.2
5871	184	921	100E5	1	1	CCQZ	BF/EPRES		0.6
6243	184	1040	100E5	3	1	CCQZ	BF/EPRES		0.4
5477	184	1778	110D5	2	9	CCQZ	BF/EPRES		0.2
5640	184	2957	115F	4	1	CCQZ	BF/EPRES		0.4
6569	184	3170	115F	5	1	CCQZ	BF/EPRES		0.5
5971	184	5047	140I	1	1	CCQZ	BF/EPRES		0.4
6571	184	2759	165J	2	1	CCQZ	BF/EPRES		0.7
6553	184	2103	170H	1	2	CCQZ	BF/EPRES		0.6
5557	184	2239	170H	2	1	CCQZ	BF/EPRES		0.4
6231	184	2894	170J	2	1	CCQZ	BF/EPRES		0.6
5994	184	2985	175I	1	1	CCQZ	BF/EPRES		0.5
5652	184	4742	30J5	1	2	CCQZ	BF/EPRES		0.7
5565	184	6356	40H5	1	2	CCQZ	BF/EPRES		0.5
5692	184	6105	65I	2	1	CCQZ	BF/EPRES		0.5

2011.28	SBCM	Cat. #	Unit	Level	Qty	MTRL	DEB TYPE	PLAT	WT/g
5729	184	4405	75C	2	1	CCQZ	BF/EPRES		0.4
5835	184	4692	85G	5	1	CCQZ	BF/EPRES		0.5
6338	184	3066	100D5	1	1	CCQZ	BF/LPERC	MFP	0.9
6316	184	956	105D5	1	3	CCQZ	BF/LPERC	MFP	2.3
6032	184	4606	125G	2	1	CCQZ	BF/LPERC	MFP	2.6
6337	184	3738	125G5	4	1	CCQZ	BF/LPERC	MFP	3.3
6019	184	5521	160I5	2	1	CCQZ	BF/LPERC	MFP	1.4
5881	184	3598	175H5	3	1	CCQZ	BF/LPERC	MFP	0.8
6303	184	6412	30M	1	1	CCQZ	BF/LPERC	MFP	1.2
5923	184	1606	55K	1	1	CCQZ	BF/LPERC	MFP	1.2
5474	184	1778	110D5	1	1	CCQZ	BF/LPERC		0.6
5529	184	3022	115F	3	1	CCQZ	BF/LPREC		0.4
5733	184	880	105F	4	1	CCQZ	BF/LPRES	MFP	1.6
5540	184	942	120G	1	1	CCQZ	BF/LPRES		0.6
5445	184	655	55I	3	1	CCQZ	BF/LPRES		0.3
5869	184	6120	80E5	3	1	CCQZ	BF/LPRES		0.5
6242	184	1040	100E5	3	2	CCQZ	BF/MARG	MFP	2
5849	184	3287	95E	5	13	CCQZ	BF/MARG	MFP	0.7
6574	184	3483	75C5	2	1	CCQZ	BF/PERC	MFP	1.1
6622	184	4158	90I5	2	2	CCQZ	BF/PERC	MFP	1.7
5845	184	2552	70E5	6	1	CCQZ	BURIN SPALL		0.6
5743	184	3111	175J	3	1	CCQZ	CC	NP	0.7

2011.28	SBCM	Cat. #	Unit	Level	Qty	MTRL	DEB TYPE	PLAT	WT/g
6262	184	583	55I	4	1	CCQZ	CC	NP	2.2
6265	184	583	55I	4	1	CCQZ	CC/outré		1.2
5917	184	2087	60H5	3	4	CCQZ	FF/NC		1.8
5442	184	5319	110J5	3	1	CCQZ	FF/C		0.7
5423	184	4885	115E	6	1	CCQZ	FF/C		2.4
6241	184	5679	35I	3	1	CCQZ	FF/C		0.7
5859	184	1905	40I	1	1	CCQZ	FF/C		1.5
5480	184	1390	55J5	3	5	CCQZ	FF/NC		1.9
5699	184	1383	55K	4	2	CCQZ	FF/NC		1.1
6339	184	3066	100D5	1	4	CCQZ	FF/NC		2.3
5872	184	921	100E5	1	2	CCQZ	FF/NC		1
6246	184	1040	100E5	3	3	CCQZ	FF/NC		1.5
5648	184	3013	100E5	4	11	CCQZ	FF/NC		1.7
6145	184	180	100F	1	3	CCQZ	FF/NC		1.5
5612	184	769	100F5	8	4	CCQZ	FF/NC		3.4
5613	184	769	100F5	8	1	CCQZ	FF/NC		1.7
6261	184	975	105D5	2	1	CCQZ	FF/NC		0.7
6598	184	1233	105E	2	1	CCQZ	FF/NC		0.5
6286	184	1091	105E	4	2	CCQZ	FF/NC		1
6011	184	824	105E5	1	4	CCQZ	FF/NC		1.8
6155	184	1010	105E5	3	2	CCQZ	FF/NC		0.7
5967	184	4580	105E5	5	1	CCQZ	FF/NC		0.8

2011.28	SBCM	Cat. #	Unit	Level	Qty	MTRL	DEB TYPE	PLAT	WT/g
5968	184	4580	105E5	5	5	CCQZ	FF/NC		2.7
5436	184	901	105F5	3	1	CCQZ	FF/NC		0.4
6336	184	4212	110D	2	2	CCQZ	FF/NC		1.5
6287	184	4142	110D	3	1	CCQZ	FF/NC		3.9
5476	184	1778	110D5	2	9	CCQZ	FF/NC		0.8
5512	184	5727	110E5	2	2	CCQZ	FF/NC		0.7
5670	184	1096	110E5	4	4	CCQZ	FF/NC		2
6176	184	4993	110E5	7	1	CCQZ	FF/NC		0.5
6562	184	792	110F5	6	1	CCQZ	FF/NC		0.9
6617	184	1867	110H	1	1	CCQZ	FF/NC		1.6
5959	184	5556	110I5	2	1	CCQZ	FF/NC		2.1
6561	184	5830	110J5	1	1	CCQZ	FF/NC		1.3
6315	184	681	115	1	1	CCQZ	FF/NC		1.5
3987	184	3987	115 E	3	2	CCQZ	FF/NC		3.5
6182	184	5143	115E5	7	2	CCQZ	FF/NC		0.9
6167	184	398	115F	1	2	CCQZ	FF/NC		1
5537	184	4058	115F	2	2	CCQZ	FF/NC		1.2
5637	184	2957	115F	4	3	CCQZ	FF/NC		2
5616	184	5328	115F5	6	1	CCQZ	FF/NC		1.5
5566	184	5960	120D	1	2	CCQZ	FF/NC		1.4
6581	184	2449	120D	6	1	CCQZ	FF/NC		2.3
5864	184	5286	120F	1	2	CCQZ	FF/NC		1.5

2011.28	SBCM	Cat. #	Unit	Level	Qty	MTRL	DEB TYPE	PLAT	WT/g
5703	184	5221	120F5	1	4	CCQZ	FF/NC		3.4
5411	184	689	120G	1	4	CCQZ	FF/NC		4.3
5541	184	942	120G	1	5	CCQZ	FF/NC		2.4
5414	184	3329	120G	2	1	CCQZ	FF/NC		2.4
6033	184	4606	125G	2	2	CCQZ	FF/NC		1.2
5836	184	4700	125G5	1	1	CCQZ	FF/NC		1.3
6277	184	6525	140I5	1	1	CCQZ	FF/NC		1.1
5458	184	6372	160I	1	1	CCQZ	FF/NC		0.2
6029	184	2764	160I	2	1	CCQZ	FF/NC		1.6
5954	184	6443	160J	1	3	CCQZ	FF/NC		2.5
5663	184	6408	160J5	1	1	CCQZ	FF/NC		0.5
5434	184	4998	160J5	3	1	CCQZ	FF/NC		0.2
5739	184	6090	160K	1	1	CCQZ	FF/NC		0.7
5941	184	569	165H	1	2	CCQZ	FF/NC		1.5
5403	184	616	165H	2	2	CCQZ	FF/NC		1.2
5988	184	505	165H	3	3	CCQZ	FF/NC		2
5603	184	554	165H5	1	6	CCQZ	FF/NC		5.5
5928	184	152	165I5	1	2	CCQZ	FF/NC		1.9
6045	184	2835	165J	3	2	CCQZ	FF/NC		1.1
5876	184	38	165J5	2	2	CCQZ	FF/NC		2.2
6551	184	2103	170H	1	4	CCQZ	FF/NC		2
6229	184	1886	170H5	2	3	CCQZ	FF/NC		1

2011.28	SBCM	Cat. #	Unit	Level	Qty	MTRL	DEB TYPE	PLAT	WT/g
6001	184	2775	170I5	2	2	CCQZ	FF/NC		0.7
5723	184	2429	170J	1	2	CCQZ	FF/NC		0.8
6280	184	2852	170J	2	2	CCQZ	FF/NC		1.8
5554	184	242	170J5	1	3	CCQZ	FF/NC		2.2
5539	184	2676	175H	2	1	CCQZ	FF/NC		1.8
5552	184	3253	175H5	1	2	CCQZ	FF/NC		1.1
5880	184	3598	175H5	3	1	CCQZ	FF/NC		0.9
5996	184	2985	175I	1	2	CCQZ	FF/NC		0.9
6178	184	5547	175I5	2	1	CCQZ	FF/NC		0.7
6017	184	3225	175J	2	4	CCQZ	FF/NC		3.6
5523	184	1669	175J5	2	4	CCQZ	FF/NC		1.5
5889	184	5695	175K	1	4	CCQZ	FF/NC		1.5
5687	184	4733	20J5	2	1	CCQZ	FF/NC		0.8
5716	184	5704	30I	2	3	CCQZ	FF/NC		2.1
5595	184	4477	30J5	1	3	CCQZ	FF/NC		1.5
6236	184	5679	35I	3	5	CCQZ	FF/NC		2
5842	184	1493	40H5	2	1	CCQZ	FF/NC		0.7
6021	184	1573	40I	3	6	CCQZ	FF/NC		2.6
6621	184	1471	40K	3	1	CCQZ	FF/NC		1.3
5410	184	6052	55H5	3	3	CCQZ	FF/NC		1.3
5509	184	2051	55I	1	4	CCQZ	FF/NC		2.9
5963	184	2004	55I	2	2	CCQZ	FF/NC		0.7

2011.28	SBCM	Cat. #	Unit	Level	Qty	MTRL	DEB TYPE	PLAT	WT/g
5448	184	655	55I	3	1	CCQZ	FF/NC		2.6
6225	184	2483	55I	4	5	CCQZ	FF/NC		2.2
5683	184	2747	55I5	2	6	CCQZ	FF/NC		2.2
5468	184	2709	55I5	3	6	CCQZ	FF/NC		3.7
5673	184	2819	55I5	4	2	CCQZ	FF/NC		1.1
5570	184	2809	55I5	5	2	CCQZ	FF/NC		1.3
6324	184	4717	55J5	4	5	CCQZ	FF/NC		2.3
6198	184	4438	55J5	5	2	CCQZ	FF/NC		1.5
5750	184	2028	60H5	4	1	CCQZ	FF/NC		0.4
5715	184	5975	60I5	3	1	CCQZ	FF/NC		1.9
6251	184	372	60J5	2	5	CCQZ	FF/NC		1.4
5658	184	4551	65E	1	3	CCQZ	FF/NC		2.1
5992	184	92	65H5	5	1	CCQZ	FF/NC		0.8
6294	184	6182	65I	1	10	CCQZ	FF/NC		3.8
5693	184	6105	65I	2	1	CCQZ	FF/NC		1.2
5631	184	6137	65I	3	5	CCQZ	FF/NC		3
5495	184	1245	65I	4	1	CCQZ	FF/NC		0.3
5979	184	6320	65I	4	4	CCQZ	FF/NC		1.5
6009	184	574	70-5	2	1	CCQZ	FF/NC		0.5
6345	184	1843	70C5	1	1	CCQZ	FF/NC		1.6
6618	184	1788	70C5	3	3	CCQZ	FF/NC		3.3
6192	184	2734	70E5	3	2	CCQZ	FF/NC		0.9

2011.28	SBCM	Cat. #	Unit	Level	Qty	MTRL	DEB TYPE	PLAT	WT/g
5519	184	2688	70E5	5	1	CCQZ	FF/NC		0.2
6283	184	2795	70E5	7	1	CCQZ	FF/NC		2.9
5829	184	2727	70I	2	2	CCQZ	FF/NC		1
5642	184	88	70J	1	4	CCQZ	FF/NC		3.1
5430	184	648	70J	1	3	CCQZ	FF/NC		1.3
5920	184	389	70J5	1	7	CCQZ	FF/NC		3.5
5487	184	2507	70J5	1	2	CCQZ	FF/NC		0.7
6172	184	28	70J5	2	2	CCQZ	FF/NC		1.6
5650	184	5653	75E5	1	1	CCQZ	FF/NC		0.7
5452	184	5575	75I	1	4	CCQZ	FF/NC		0.3
5712	184	5600	75J	1	4	CCQZ	FF/NC		5.5
5599	184	3620	80D	6	3	CCQZ	FF/NC		3.4
6217	184	805	80D5	2	2	CCQZ	FF/NC		4.2
5838	184	1079	80D5	2	2	CCQZ	FF/NC		1
6181	184	1711	80D5	5	2	CCQZ	FF/NC		1.5
5636	184	4046	80E	2	2	CCQZ	FF/NC		1.8
6213	184	4078	80E	4	5	CCQZ	FF/NC		2.1
6203	184	5024	80E5	3	3	CCQZ	FF/NC		1.7
5867	184	6120	80E5	3	2	CCQZ	FF/NC		1.3
5680	184	318	85D5	4	2	CCQZ	FF/NC		1
5704	184	106	85E	1	1	CCQZ	FF/NC		0.8
6295	184	274	85E	3	3	CCQZ	FF/NC		1.1

2011.28	SBCM	Cat. #	Unit	Level	Qty	MTRL	DEB TYPE	PLAT	WT/g
5936	184	886	85F	2	3	CCQZ	FF/NC		1.3
5847	184	4919	85F5	1	2	CCQZ	FF/NC		1.3
5727	184	4973	85F5	5	2	CCQZ	FF/NC		0.8
5667	184	6432	85G	3	2	CCQZ	FF/NC		1.1
5755	184	1600	85G5	2	1	CCQZ	FF/NC		2.1
5405	184	1772	85G5	3	1	CCQZ	FF/NC		
6579	184	3527	90D	4	1	CCQZ	FF/NC		1.7
6037	184	3159	90E	3	1	CCQZ	FF/NC		1.2
5736	184	3218	90E	4	2	CCQZ	FF/NC		0.8
6311	184	2320	90E5	3	1	CCQZ	FF/NC		0.6
6616	184	5920	90E5	8	1	CCQZ	FF/NC		0.7
5866	184	4541	90G	2	1	CCQZ	FF/NC		1.4
5575	184	6239	90H5	5	1	CCQZ	FF/NC		0.2
5875	184	2312	95D	2	2	CCQZ	FF/NC		1.2
5719	184	2127	95D5	2	1	CCQZ	FF/NC		1.6
5944	184	341	95D5	5	2	CCQZ	FF/NC		0.6
5428	184	1978	95E	3	4	CCQZ	FF/NC		1.6
6300	184	2149	95E	4	1	CCQZ	FF/NC		0.9
5624	184	3233	95E	5	4	CCQZ	FF/NC		1.9
5851	184	3287	95E	5	1	CCQZ	FF/NC		4.8
6916	184	3384	95E	6	1	CCQZ	FF/NC		1.1
5820	184	3047	95E5	2	3	CCQZ	FF/NC		0.9

2011.28	SBCM	Cat. #	Unit	Level	Qty	MTRL	DEB TYPE	PLAT	WT/g
5746	184	4497	95E5	4	6	CCQZ	FF/NC		2.6
5824	184	3622	95I	1	2	CCQZ	FF/NC		1.2
6047	184	1114	95I	2	1	CCQZ	FF/NC		0.4
5437	184	901	105F5	3	2	CCQZ	FF/PC		4.5
5585	184	6168	115F5	5	2	CCQZ	FF/PC		4.9
6588	184	250	120F5	2	2	CCQZ	FF/PC		4.2
6232	184	2894	170J	2	1	CCQZ	NC	MFP	1.6
5576	184	700	100E5	9	1	CCQZ	NC	MFP	1
6144	184	180	100F	1	1	CCQZ	NC	MFP	1.7
6012	184	824	105E5	1	1	CCQZ	NC	MFP	0.6
5514	184	5727	110E5	2	1	CCQZ	NC	MFP	1.3
6174	184	4993	110E5	7	1	CCQZ	NC	MFP	1.5
5591	184	1527	110I5	4	1	CCQZ	NC	MFP	0.8
6165	184	398	115F	1	1	CCQZ	NC	MFP	1.1
5534	184	4058	115F	2	1	CCQZ	NC	MFP	0.9
6580	184	2449	120D	6	1	CCQZ	NC	MFP	0.7
5459	184	6372	160I	1	1	CCQZ	NC	MFP	0.5
6027	184	2764	160I	2	1	CCQZ	NC	MFP	0.9
5985	184	505	165H	3	2	CCQZ	NC	MFP	1.9
5686	184	4733	20J5	2	1	CCQZ	NC	MFP	0.9
5844	184	1493	40H5	2	1	CCQZ	NC	MFP	5.5
5508	184	2051	55I	1	1	CCQZ	NC	MFP	1

2011.28	SBCM	Cat. #	Unit	Level	Qty	MTRL	DEB TYPE	PLAT	WT/g
6224	184	2483	55I	4	1	CCQZ	NC	MFP	0.7
6327	184	4717	55J5	4	1	CCQZ	NC	MFP	0.9
5990	184	92	65H5	5	2	CCQZ	NC	MFP	1.5
6291	184	6182	65I	1	1	CCQZ	NC	MFP	0.9
6329	184	1697	70C	3	2	CCQZ	NC	MFP	1.7
5830	184	2727	70I	2	2	CCQZ	NC	MFP	2.9
6572	184	4788	75H5	2	3	CCQZ	NC	MFP	3.1
6219	184	805	80D5	2	1	CCQZ	NC	MFP	1.5
5852	184	3287	95E	5	4	CCQZ	NC	MFP	2.7
5578	184	700	100E5	9	2	CCQZ	NC	PA	1.5
6147	184	180	100F	1	1	CCQZ	NC	PA	1
5499	184	4415	105B	2	1	CCQZ	NC	PA	0.2
6576	184	4633	105D	1	1	CCQZ	NC	PA	0.8
6010	184	824	105E5	1	3	CCQZ	NC	PA	1.2
6031	184	4865	110G5	3	1	CCQZ	NC	PA	1.1
6256	184	1540	110I5	1	2	CCQZ	NC	PA	2.2
5617	184	6252	110I5	3	1	CCQZ	NC	PA	1.2
6183	184	5143	115E5	7	1	CCQZ	NC	PA	0.9
5535	184	4058	115F	2	1	CCQZ	NC	PA	1
5588	184	6168	115F5	5	1	CCQZ	NC	PA	0.9
5543	184	942	120G	1	1	CCQZ	NC	PA	0.8
6268	184	5135	140H5	3	1	CCQZ	NC	PA	0.5

2011.28	SBCM	Cat. #	Unit	Level	Qty	MTRL	DEB TYPE	PLAT	WT/g
5973	184	5047	140I	1	1	CCQZ	NC	PA	0.7
5490	184	4573	150G5	1	1	CCQZ	NC	PA	0.5
5940	184	569	165H	1	2	CCQZ	NC	PA	6.8
6207	184	2589	170I5	1	2	CCQZ	NC	PA	3.6
5718	184	5704	30I	2	3	CCQZ	NC	PA	1.6
6237	184	5679	35I	3	2	CCQZ	NC	PA	2.7
5561	184	6356	40H5	1	2	CCQZ	NC	PA	1.5
5843	184	1493	40H5	2	2	CCQZ	NC	PA	1
5860	184	1905	40I	1	1	CCQZ	NC	PA	0.7
5510	184	2051	55I	1	1	CCQZ	NC	PA	0.7
5444	184	655	55I	3	3	CCQZ	NC	PA	3.3
6223	184	2483	55I	4	3	CCQZ	NC	PA	1.2
5482	184	1390	55J5	3	2	CCQZ	NC	PA	0.6
5602	184	4389	55J5	4	4	CCQZ	NC	PA	2.8
5832	184	1589	55K5	1	5	CCQZ	NC	PA	3.2
6254	184	372	60J5	2	1	CCQZ	NC	PA	2.7
5460	184	5	65H5	1	1	CCQZ	NC	PA	1.1
5632	184	6137	65I	3	1	CCQZ	NC	PA	0.6
6348	184	1843	70C5	1	2	CCQZ	NC	PA	2.1
6559	184	3900	70C5	2	1	CCQZ	NC	PA	1
5643	184	88	70J	1	1	CCQZ	NC	PA	0.9
5486	184	2507	70J5	1	1	CCQZ	NC	PA	0.4

2011.28	SBCM	Cat. #	Unit	Level	Qty	MTRL	DEB TYPE	PLAT	WT/g
6171	184	28	70J5	2	2	CCQZ	NC	PA	2.4
6566	184	4424	75C	6	1	CCQZ	NC	PA	0.3
6211	184	4078	80E	4	1	CCQZ	NC	PA	0.7
5858	184	5945	85E	4	1	CCQZ	NC	PA	2
6610	184	2413	90E5	5	1	CCQZ	NC	PA	0.5
5675	184	2042	90E5	6	1	CCQZ	NC	PA	1
5930	184	5408	90I	1	1	CCQZ	NC	PA	0.7
6210	184	3292	95E	5	1	CCQZ	NC	PA	0.7
5854	184	3287	95E	5	1	CCQZ	NC	PA	1.7
5676	184	2213	95E	6	1	CCQZ	NC	PA	1
5823	184	3622	95I	1	2	CCQZ	NC	PA	1.5
5573	184	964	100E	2	2	CCQZ	NC	SFP	1.6
5579	184	700	100E5	9	2	CCQZ	NC	SFP	0.8
6148	184	180	100F	1	1	CCQZ	NC	SFP	1.5
5506	184	3790	100F5	6	1	CCQZ	NC	SFP	0.5
5951	184	5758	105E	3	1	CCQZ	NC	SFP	0.9
6152	184	1010	105E5	3	5	CCQZ	NC	SFP	2.7
5970	184	4580	105E5	5	3	CCQZ	NC	SFP	5.7
5435	184	901	105F5	3	1	CCQZ	NC	SFP	0.5
6335	184	4212	110D	2	1	CCQZ	NC	SFP	1.6
5426	184	587	110E5	2	2	CCQZ	NC	SFP	22.5
5732	184	440	110E5	3	2	CCQZ	NC	SFP	3.2

APPENDIX D

2011.28	SBCM	Cat. #	Unit	Level	Qty	MTRL	DEB TYPE	PLAT	WT/g
6257	184	1540	110I5	1	2	CCQZ	NC	SFP	3.9
5501	184	5560	110I5	2	1	CCQZ	NC	SFP	1.3
6314	184	681	115	1	1	CCQZ	NC	SFP	4.3
6042	184	4007	115-E	1	1	CCQZ	NC	SFP	2.2
6163	184	398	115F	1	6	CCQZ	NC	SFP	4.1
5615	184	5328	115F5	6	1	CCQZ	NC	SFP	0.4
5404	184	2448	120D	6	1	CCQZ	NC	SFP	0.4
6582	184	2449	120D	6	1	CCQZ	NC	SFP	4.1
5548	184	1987	120F	5	2	CCQZ	NC	SFP	1.7
5701	184	5221	120F5	1	3	CCQZ	NC	SFP	2.9
6587	184	2399	120F5	6	1	CCQZ	NC	SFP	0.9
5542	184	942	120G	1	2	CCQZ	NC	SFP	1.6
5929	184	1023	125D	3	2	CCQZ	NC	SFP	3.2
5478	184	431	125E5	3	1	CCQZ	NC	SFP	0.3
6313	184	4838	125G5	3	1	CCQZ	NC	SFP	1.7
5975	184	5047	140I	1	1	CCQZ	NC	SFP	1.1
5457	184	6372	160I	1	1	CCQZ	NC	SFP	0.3
6030	184	2764	160I	2	1	CCQZ	NC	SFP	4.6
5662	184	6408	160J5	1	3	CCQZ	NC	SFP	3.7
6550	184	1161	160J5	2	1	CCQZ	NC	SFP	1.6
5433	184	4998	160J5	3	1	CCQZ	NC	SFP	0.6
5740	184	6090	160K	1	2	CCQZ	NC	SFP	2.1

2011.28	SBCM	Cat. #	Unit	Level	Qty	MTRL	DEB TYPE	PLAT	WT/g
5939	184	569	165H	1	4	CCQZ	NC	SFP	4
5943	184	569	165H	1	1	CCQZ	NC	SFP	0.8
5604	184	554	165H5	1	2	CCQZ	NC	SFP	2
6189	184	2237	170H	2	1	CCQZ	NC	SFP	1
5556	184	2239	170H	2	2	CCQZ	NC	SFP	1.3
5419	184	1880	170H5	1	4	CCQZ	NC	SFP	1.9
6000	184	2775	170I5	2	1	CCQZ	NC	SFP	0.8
6230	184	2894	170J	2	2	CCQZ	NC	SFP	4
6177	184	5547	175I5	2	1	CCQZ	NC	SFP	1.8
6014	184	3225	175J	2	4	CCQZ	NC	SFP	2.2
5596	184	4477	30J5	1	1	CCQZ	NC	SFP	1
6240	184	5679	35I	3	1	CCQZ	NC	SFP	1.3
5563	184	6356	40H5	1	1	CCQZ	NC	SFP	1.1
5841	184	1493	40H5	2	1	CCQZ	NC	SFP	1.1
6022	184	1573	40I	3	2	CCQZ	NC	SFP	1.8
5754	184	1187	45I	4	1	CCQZ	NC	SFP	0.5
5507	184	2051	55I	1	2	CCQZ	NC	SFP	4.2
5961	184	2004	55I	2	1	CCQZ	NC	SFP	0.7
5446	184	655	55I	3	1	CCQZ	NC	SFP	0.5
5681	184	2747	55I5	2	4	CCQZ	NC	SFP	4.1
5470	184	2709	55I5	3	3	CCQZ	NC	SFP	0.9
5674	184	2819	55I5	4	4	CCQZ	NC	SFP	4.7

2011.28	SBCM	Cat. #	Unit	Level	Qty	MTRL	DEB TYPE	PLAT	WT/g
5569	184	2809	55I5	5	1	CCQZ	NC	SFP	2.1
6325	184	4717	55J5	4	1	CCQZ	NC	SFP	2
6199	184	4438	55J5	5	1	CCQZ	NC	SFP	2.7
5884	184	1408	55K	3	1	CCQZ	NC	SFP	0.6
5698	184	1383	55K	4	1	CCQZ	NC	SFP	3.7
5831	184	1589	55K5	1	1	CCQZ	NC	SFP	0.5
5749	184	2028	60H5	4	1	CCQZ	NC	SFP	1.1
5713	184	5975	60I5	3	1	CCQZ	NC	SFP	1
6250	184	372	60J5	2	4	CCQZ	NC	SFP	2.1
6289	184	6182	65I	1	3	CCQZ	NC	SFP	4
5628	184	6137	65I	3	3	CCQZ	NC	SFP	3.1
5978	184	6320	65I	4	2	CCQZ	NC	SFP	0.9
6597	184	6395	65I	5	1	CCQZ	NC	SFP	1.9
6004	184	574	70-5	2	2	CCQZ	NC	SFP	1.6
6008	184	574	70-5	2	1	CCQZ	NC	SFP	2.6
6332	184	1697	70C	3	1	CCQZ	NC	SFP	2.3
6344	184	1843	70C5	1	1	CCQZ	NC	SFP	1.7
6149	184	3902	70C5	2	1	CCQZ	NC	SFP	2.9
6557	184	3900	70C5	2	2	CCQZ	NC	SFP	1.3
6193	184	2734	70E5	3	1	CCQZ	NC	SFP	0.7
5520	184	2688	70E5	5	2	CCQZ	NC	SFP	4.3
5708	184	1446	70I	1	1	CCQZ	NC	SFP	4.7

2011.28	SBCM	Cat. #	Unit	Level	Qty	MTRL	DEB TYPE	PLAT	WT/g
5826	184	2727	70I	2	1	CCQZ	NC	SFP	0.7
5753	184	87	70J	1	4	CCQZ	NC	SFP	2.2
5641	184	88	70J	1	1	CCQZ	NC	SFP	0.6
5431	184	648	70J	1	1	CCQZ	NC	SFP	0.5
5921	184	389	70J5	1	1	CCQZ	NC	SFP	0.7
6170	184	28	70J5	2	4	CCQZ	NC	SFP	5.7
5530	184	194	75I	3	1	CCQZ	NC	SFP	0.9
5710	184	5600	75J	1	4	CCQZ	NC	SFP	5.2
6218	184	805	80D5	2	1	CCQZ	NC	SFP	0.7
5863	184	5358	80E	1	2	CCQZ	NC	SFP	1.9
5633	184	4046	80E	2	1	CCQZ	NC	SFP	1.1
5593	184	596	80H	3	2	CCQZ	NC	SFP	4.5
5705	184	106	85E	1	1	CCQZ	NC	SFP	0.9
6160	184	145	85E	4	1	CCQZ	NC	SFP	1.6
5934	184	886	85F	2	2	CCQZ	NC	SFP	1
5726	184	4973	85F5	5	2	CCQZ	NC	SFP	1.2
5950	184	4806	85G	4	1	CCQZ	NC	SFP	0.6
5728	184	61	85G5	4	3	CCQZ	NC	SFP	3
6272	184	483	85H	3	2	CCQZ	NC	SFP	0.8
6577	184	3527	90D	4	1	CCQZ	NC	SFP	1.2
6185	184	3273	90E	2	1	CCQZ	NC	SFP	2.6
6310	184	2320	90E5	3	1	CCQZ	NC	SFP	0.8

2011.28	SBCM	Cat. #	Unit	Level	Qty	MTRL	DEB TYPE	PLAT	WT/g
6590	184	4639	90G	3	1	CCQZ	NC	SFP	0.8
5516	184	4522	90H	3	1	CCQZ	NC	SFP	2.3
6567	184	1814	90I	3	1	CCQZ	NC	SFP	0.7
6615	184	2150	95E	4	1	CCQZ	NC	SFP	0.9
6299	184	2149	95E	4	1	CCQZ	NC	SFP	0.6
5822	184	3047	95E5	2	1	CCQZ	NC	SFP	0.7
6259	184	1238	95G	3	1	CCQZ	NC	SFP	2.1
6048	184	1114	95I	2	1	CCQZ	NC	SFP	1
6214	184	4078	80E	4	2	CCQZ	NC/ALT	PA	2.6
6595	184	2928	100D5	3	1	CCQZ	NC/ALT	SFP	0.9
5614	184	769	100F5	8	1	CCQZ	NC/ALT	SFP	2
5469	184	2709	55I5	3	2	CCQZ	NC/ALT	SFP	2.6
5882	184	1408	55K	3	1	CCQZ	NC/ALT	SFP	4
6584	184	3851	70C	2	1	CCQZ	NC/ALT	SFP	1.7
6330	184	1697	70C	3	1	CCQZ	NC/ALT	SFP	1.4
5449	184	2695	100D	1	1	CCQZ	NC/ALT		2.2
5536	184	4058	115F	2	2	CCQZ	NC/ALT		1.5
6554	184	2103	170H	1	1	CCQZ	NC/ALT		3
6227	184	1886	170H5	2	1	CCQZ	NC/ALT		1.3
6205	184	2589	170I5	1	1	CCQZ	NC/ALT		2.2
5549	184	3253	175H5	1	1	CCQZ	NC/ALT		2.3
6015	184	3225	175J	2	1	CCQZ	NC/ALT		0.6

2011.28	SBCM	Cat. #	Unit	Level	Qty	MTRL	DEB TYPE	PLAT	WT/g
5655	184	4742	30J5	1	1	CCQZ	NC/ALT		0.9
6023	184	1573	40I	3	2	CCQZ	NC/ALT		2
6221	184	2483	55I	4	1	CCQZ	NC/ALT		0.7
5685	184	2747	55I5	2	2	CCQZ	NC/ALT		2.7
5568	184	2809	55I5	5	1	CCQZ	NC/ALT		2.7
6039	184	1951	60H5	1	2	CCQZ	NC/ALT		1.6
5630	184	6137	65I	3	1	CCQZ	NC/ALT		3.3
6006	184	574	70-5	2	3	CCQZ	NC/ALT		3
5946	184	2661	70I5	4	12	CCQZ	NC/ALT		2.3
5839	184	1079	80D5	2	1	CCQZ	NC/ALT		1.3
5865	184	4541	90G	2	1	CCQZ	NC/ALT		1.1
5625	184	3233	95E	5	1	CCQZ	NC/ALT		0.9
6169	184	28	70J5	2	1	CCQZ	NC/BULB	PA	2.9
6134	184	398	115F	1	1	CCQZ	NC/BULB		1.7
5924	184	152	165I5	1	1	CCQZ	NC/EDGE	PA	0.6
5955	184	6443	160J	1	1	CCQZ	NC/EDGE	SFP	0.6
5926	184	152	165I5	1	1	CCQZ	NC/EDGE	SFP	0.6
5688	184	4733	20J5	2	1	CCQZ	NC/EDGE	SFP	0.5
5461	184	5	65H5	1	2	CCQZ	NC/EDGE		0.3
6244	184	1040	100E5	3	1	CCQZ	NC/MARG	SFP	0.9
5953	184	5758	105E	3	1	CCQZ	NC/MARG		0.7
5619	184	1654	115F5	3	1	CCQZ	NC/MARG		2.45

2011.28	SBCM	Cat. #	Unit	Level	Qty	MTRL	DEB TYPE	PLAT	WT/g
5997	184	2985	175I	1	1	CCQZ	NC/MARG		0.9
5518	184	5115	80E5	1	1	CCQZ	NC/MARG		1.4
5850	184	3287	95E	5	2	CCQZ	NC/MARG		1.6
5571	184	2809	55I5	5	1	CCQZ	NC/outré		3.8
5656	184	4551	65E	1	1	CCQZ	NC/outré		5.6
5517	184	4522	90H	3	1	CCQZ	NC/outré		2
5580	184	6067	160I5	1	1	CCQZ	NC	SFP	2.5
5582	184	3570	85F5	3	1	CCQZ	NC	SFP	0.5
5416	184	2993	85D	3	2	CCQZ	NC	SFP	1.5
5846	184	4919	85F5	1	1	CCQZ	PC	MFP	1.1
5647	184	3013	100E5	2	11	CCQZ	PC	NP	1
6255	184	1540	110I5	1	2	CCQZ	PC	NP	9.5
6298	184	1491	120F5	3	1	CCQZ	PC	NP	0.6
5547	184	450	165H	2	1	CCQZ	PC	NP	0.5
5418	184	1880	170H5	1	2	CCQZ	PC	NP	0.9
6228	184	1886	170H5	2	1	CCQZ	PC	NP	1.4
6208	184	2589	170I5	1	1	CCQZ	PC	NP	3
5722	184	2429	170J	1	4	CCQZ	PC	NP	3.4
5553	184	242	170J5	1	1	CCQZ	PC	NP	1.1
5741	184	3111	175J	3	1	CCQZ	PC	NP	1.6
5598	184	4477	30J5	1	1	CCQZ	PC	NP	1
6304	184	6412	30M	1	2	CCQZ	PC	NP	1.2

2011.28	SBCM	Cat. #	Unit	Level	Qty	MTRL	DEB TYPE	PLAT	WT/g
5916	184	2087	60H5	3	2	CCQZ	PC	NP	1.7
5751	184	2028	60H5	4	1	CCQZ	PC	NP	1.1
5466	184	5951	70C	2	2	CCQZ	PC	NP	0.1
6346	184	1843	70C5	1	1	CCQZ	PC	NP	0.8
5947	184	2661	70I5	4	3	CCQZ	PC	NP	2.3
5485	184	2507	70J5	1	1	CCQZ	PC	NP	0.3
5965	184	423	84-85H	6	1	CCQZ	PC	NP	0.8
5611	184	3277	90E	2	1	CCQZ	PC	NP	0.6
5413	184	4484	90G	1	1	CCQZ	PC	NP	2.1
6273	184	2031	95E	3	1	CCQZ	PC	NP	2
5757	184	2216	95E	7	1	CCQZ	PC	NP	4.6
5821	184	3047	95E5	2	2	CCQZ	PC	NP	2.8
5747	184	4497	95E5	4	1	CCQZ	PC	NP	0.5
6049	184	1114	95I	2	1	CCQZ	PC	NP	3.7
6245	184	1040	100E5	3	2	CCQZ	PC	PA	2
6154	184	1010	105E5	3	1	CCQZ	PC	PA	2.2
6269	184	6215	110H5	1	1	CCQZ	PC	PA	2.3
6044	184	4007	115-E	1	1	CCQZ	PC	PA	2.1
5587	184	6168	115F5	5	1	CCQZ	PC	PA	1.3
5544	184	450	165H	2	2	CCQZ	PC	PA	3.4
6263	184	583	55I	4	1	CCQZ	PC	PA	1.5
5657	184	4551	65E	1	1	CCQZ	PC	PA	1.5

2011.28	SBCM	Cat. #	Unit	Level	Qty	MTRL	DEB TYPE	PLAT	WT/g
6290	184	6182	65I	1	1	CCQZ	PC	PA	0.8
5827	184	2727	70I	2	1	CCQZ	PC	PA	1.1
6204	184	5024	80E5	3	1	CCQZ	PC	PA	1.8
5694	184	205	85E5	4	2	CCQZ	PC	PA	3.4
5440	184	59	85G5	4	1	CCQZ	PC	PA	0.6
6591	184	4639	90G	3	1	CCQZ	PC	PA	0.6
6258	184	1238	95G	3	1	CCQZ	PC	PA	0.5
6317	184	956	105D5	1	1	CCQZ	PC	SFP	2.6
5818	184	862	105F5	4	1	CCQZ	PC	SFP	1.5
5668	184	1096	110E5	4	1	CCQZ	PC	SFP	1.8
5464	184	5992	110I	4	1	CCQZ	PC	SFP	5.3
5958	184	5556	110I5	2	1	CCQZ	PC	SFP	1.2
5441	184	5319	110J5	3	2	CCQZ	PC	SFP	1.6
5493	184	2331	120D	7	1	CCQZ	PC	SFP	1.1
6034	184	4606	125G	2	1	CCQZ	PC	SFP	0.5
5861	184	4700	125G5	1	1	CCQZ	PC	SFP	1.6
5956	184	6443	160J	1	1	CCQZ	PC	SFP	1.9
6549	184	1161	160J5	2	2	CCQZ	PC	SFP	3
5995	184	2985	175I	1	1	CCQZ	PC	SFP	2.3
5913	184	3348	175I	2	1	CCQZ	PC	SFP	1.5
5522	184	1669	175J5	2	1	CCQZ	PC	SFP	2.7
5717	184	5704	30I	2	1	CCQZ	PC	SFP	1.3

2011.28	SBCM	Cat. #	Unit	Level	Qty	MTRL	DEB TYPE	PLAT	WT/g
5653	184	4742	30J5	1	1	CCQZ	PC	SFP	2.2
5858	184	1905	40I	1	1	CCQZ	PC	SFP	3.3
5574	184	1716	55J	1	2	CCQZ	PC	SFP	1.6
5661	184	4551	65E	1	2	CCQZ	PC	SFP	3.7
5515	184	5989	70D	1	1	CCQZ	PC	SFP	6.2
5945	184	2661	70I5	4	2	CCQZ	PC	SFP	3
5450	184	5575	75I	1	4	CCQZ	PC	SFP	2
5635	184	4046	80E	2	1	CCQZ	PC	SFP	0.9
5868	184	6120	80E5	3	1	CCQZ	PC	SFP	1.6
5873	184	2312	95D	2	1	CCQZ	PC	SFP	4.8
5819	184	3047	95E5	2	2	CCQZ	PC	SFP	9.8
6293	184	6182	65I	1	1	CCQZ	PC/ALT	SFP	2.2
5919	184	389	70J5	1	1	CCQZ	PC/ALT	SFP	1.1
5937	184	886	85F	2	1	CCQZ	PC/ALT	SFP	2.9
6036	184	3159	90E	3	1	CCQZ	PC/ALT	SFP	1.6
6270	184	6215	110H5	1	1	CCQZ	PC/ALT		0.9
5463	184	1740	115F5	4	2	CCQZ	PC/ALT		0.8
5558	184	2239	170H	2	1	CCQZ	PC/ALT		2.1
5999	184	2775	170I5	2	2	CCQZ	PC/ALT		1.8
5584	184	3570	85F5	3	1	CCQZ	PC/ALT		1.9
6186	184	3273	90E	2	1	CCQZ	PC/ALT		2.2
5525	184	2536	100D5	1	1	CCQZ	PC/EDGE	SFP	18.9

2011.28	SBCM	Cat. #	Unit	Level	Qty	MTRL	DEB TYPE	PLAT	WT/g
5454	184	2949	85F	1	1	CCQZ	PC/PA		3
5484	184	2507	70J5	1	2	CCQZ	PC/PS		0.8
6320	184	166	100D5	3	1	CCQZ	SHT		1.2
5473	184	5433	110D	6	1	CCQZ	SHT		0.6
5942	184	569	165H	1	1	CCQZ	SHT		1.3
5546	184	450	165H	2	1	CCQZ	SHT		0.7
6319	184	2519	170J	1	2	CCQZ	SHT		2.3
5998	184	2985	175I	1	4	CCQZ	SHT		2.7
5742	184	3111	175J	3	2	CCQZ	SHT		0.8
6026	184	1573	40I	3	2	CCQZ	SHT		1
6264	184	583	55I	4	2	CCQZ	SHT		8.2
5481	184	1390	55J5	3	1	CCQZ	SHT		0.1
6593	184	1655	55K5	2	22	CCQZ	SHT		25.6
5896	184	15	65H5	2	3	CCQZ	SHT		6.6
5828	184	2727	70I	2	1	CCQZ	SHT		2.9
5964	184	423	84-85H	6	4	CCQZ	SHT		4.8
5695	184	205	85E5	4	2	CCQZ	SHT		4.5
5453	184	2949	85F	1	2	CCQZ	SHT		3.5
5848	184	4919	85F5	1	1	CCQZ	SHT		1.4
6274	184	5906	85F5	3	4	CCQZ	SHT		3.2
6343	184	4657	TEST	N/A	2	CCQZ	SHT		5.4
5914	184	3348	175I	2	4	CCQZ	SHT/C		1.5

2011.28	SBCM	Cat. #	Unit	Level	Qty	MTRL	DEB TYPE	PLAT	WT/g
6340	184	3066	100D5	1	2	CCQZ	SHT/C		4
6585	184	669	100F5	3	1	CCQZ	SHT/C		2.6
5731	184	440	110E5	3	1	CCQZ	SHT/C		1
5669	184	1096	110E5	4	1	CCQZ	SHT/C		0.7
6611	184	1797	110H5	5	1	CCQZ	SHT/C		4.1
6043	184	4007	115-E	1	2	CCQZ	SHT/C		1.4
5590	184	4873	115E5	8	1	CCQZ	SHT/C		1.4
6168	184	398	115F	1	3	CCQZ	SHT/C		6.6
5586	184	6168	115F5	5	2	CCQZ	SHT/C		4
5415	184	3329	120G	2	2	CCQZ	SHT/C		1.6
6028	184	2764	160I	2	1	CCQZ	SHT/C		1.6
5957	184	6443	160J	1	2	CCQZ	SHT/C		1.6
5432	184	4998	160J5	3	1	CCQZ	SHT/C		1.1
5987	184	505	165H	3	2	CCQZ	SHT/C		2.6
5925	184	152	165I5	1	1	CCQZ	SHT/C		2.2
5877	184	38	165J5	2	1	CCQZ	SHT/C		1.2
6002	184	2775	170I5	2	1	CCQZ	SHT/C		0.8
5594	184	4477	30J5	1	1	CCQZ	SHT/C		1
5654	184	4742	30J5	1	2	CCQZ	SHT/C		0.8
6239	184	5679	35I	3	1	CCQZ	SHT/C		4
5608	184	1176	45I	4	3	CCQZ	SHT/C		1.3
6196	184	2054	60H5	6	2	CCQZ	SHT/C		1.5

2011.28	SBCM	Cat. #	Unit	Level	Qty	MTRL	DEB TYPE	PLAT	WT/g
5660	184	4551	65E	1	3	CCQZ	SHT/C		5.1
5980	184	6320	65I	4	3	CCQZ	SHT/C		5.5
5948	184	2661	70I5	4	9	CCQZ	SHT/C		2.6
6173	184	28	70J5	2	2	CCQZ	SHT/C		7.6
5451	184	5575	75I	1	4	CCQZ	SHT/C		0.7
5709	184	5600	75J	1	1	CCQZ	SHT/C		10.2
5837	184	1079	80D5	2	1	CCQZ	SHT/C		1.6
5634	184	4046	80E	2	3	CCQZ	SHT/C		1.7
6212	184	4078	80E	4	3	CCQZ	SHT/C		4.4
6161	184	145	85E	4	1	CCQZ	SHT/C		1
5935	184	886	85F	2	1	CCQZ	SHT/C		3.5
5725	184	4973	85F5	5	2	CCQZ	SHT/C		2.9
5949	184	4806	85G	4	3	CCQZ	SHT/C		2.6
5938	184	4670	85G5	4	1	CCQZ	SHT/C		1.8
6271	184	483	85H	3	1	CCQZ	SHT/C		1.4
5496	184	3301	90E	1	1	CCQZ	SHT/C		2
6592	184	4639	90G	3	2	CCQZ	SHT/C		6.3
5931	184	5408	90I	1	2	CCQZ	SHT/C		2.8
5874	184	2312	95D	2	2	CCQZ	SHT/C		1.6
5720	184	2127	95D5	2	1	CCQZ	SHT/C		3.3
5427	184	1978	95E	3	1	CCQZ	SHT/C		0.6
6614	184	2150	95E	4	1	CCQZ	SHT/C		1.6

2011.28	SBCM	Cat. #	Unit	Level	Qty	MTRL	DEB TYPE	PLAT	WT/g
5626	184	3233	95E	5	1	CCQZ	SHT/C		0.8
5853	184	3287	95E	5	3	CCQZ	SHT/C		1.2
5503	184	2533	100D5	1	1	CCQZ	SHT/NC		0.4
6596	184	2928	100D5	3	2	CCQZ	SHT/NC		3.6
5646	184	3013	100E5	3	11	CCQZ	SHT/NC		2.2
5577	184	700	100E5	9	1	CCQZ	SHT/NC		1.5
5601	184	819	100E5	6,7	2	CCQZ	SHT/NC		3.7
6146	184	180	100F	1	1	CCQZ	SHT/NC		1.1
5489	184	784	100F5	1	2	CCQZ	SHT/NC		2.7
5560	184	2682	100F5	5	1	CCQZ	SHT/NC		2.9
5952	184	5758	105E	3	2	CCQZ	SHT/NC		0.8
6285	184	1091	105E	4	1	CCQZ	SHT/NC		1.5
6013	184	824	105E5	1	2	CCQZ	SHT/NC		3.5
6153	184	1010	105E5	3	3	CCQZ	SHT/NC		2.3
5969	184	4580	105E5	5	3	CCQZ	SHT/NC		9.2
5743	184	880	105F	4	1	CCQZ	SHT/NC		2.3
6201	184	5340	110D	3	1	CCQZ	SHT/NC		1.4
5513	184	5727	110E5	2	3	CCQZ	SHT/NC		2.4
6175	184	4993	110E5	7	1	CCQZ	SHT/NC		0.6
6589	184	5040	110E5	7	3	CCQZ	SHT/NC		2.6
6202	184	4954	110E5	8	2	CCQZ	SHT/NC		1.7
5887	184	5060	110G	1	1	CCQZ	SHT/NC		1.8

2011.28	SBCM	Cat. #	Unit	Level	Qty	MTRL	DEB TYPE	PLAT	WT/g
6619	184	5715	110I	1	1	CCQZ	SHT/NC		1
5592	184	1527	110I5	4	1	CCQZ	SHT/NC		0.4
5622	184	3001	110I5	4	1	CCQZ	SHT/NC		0.9
6334	184	1566	115D5	2	1	CCQZ	SHT/NC		3.2
5425	184	4885	115E	6	1	CCQZ	SHT/NC		0.4
6184	184	5143	115E5	7	3	CCQZ	SHT/NC		3.4
6166	184	398	115F	1	1	CCQZ	SHT/NC		1.3
5651	184	3180	115F	2	2	CCQZ	SHT/NC		2.8
5639	184	2957	115F	4	1	CCQZ	SHT/NC		0.8
5618	184	1654	115F5	3	1	CCQZ	SHT/NC		0.6
5462	184	1740	115F5	4	3	CCQZ	SHT/NC		4.4
5932	184	269	120-5E	3	1	CCQZ	SHT/NC		4.8
6143	184	5292	120F	1	1	CCQZ	SHT/NC		0.4
5702	184	5221	120F5	1	1	CCQZ	SHT/NC		0.6
6586	184	2399	120F5	6	1	CCQZ	SHT/NC		0.7
6267	184	5135	140H5	3	2	CCQZ	SHT/NC		1
5974	184	5047	140I	1	2	CCQZ	SHT/NC		2
6276	184	6525	140I5	1	1	CCQZ	SHT/NC		2.3
5456	184	6372	160I	1	2	CCQZ	SHT/NC		2.4
5581	184	6067	160I5	1	3	CCQZ	SHT/NC		1.4
5738	184	6090	160K	1	2	CCQZ	SHT/NC		2.8
5606	184	554	165H5	1	2	CCQZ	SHT/NC		3.2

2011.28	SBCM	Cat. #	Unit	Level	Qty	MTRL	DEB TYPE	PLAT	WT/g
6046	184	2835	165J	3	1	CCQZ	SHT/NC		1.7
6552	184	2103	170H	1	5	CCQZ	SHT/NC		5.7
6191	184	2237	170H	2	1	CCQZ	SHT/NC		0.5
5559	184	2239	170H	2	3	CCQZ	SHT/NC		5.8
5417	184	1880	170H5	1	3	CCQZ	SHT/NC		5.4
6206	184	2589	170I5	1	2	CCQZ	SHT/NC		1.9
5724	184	2429	170J	1	2	CCQZ	SHT/NC		6.4
5504	184	2670	170J	2	3	CCQZ	SHT/NC		2.8
5538	184	2676	175H	2	1	CCQZ	SHT/NC		0.9
5550	184	3253	175H5	1	1	CCQZ	SHT/NC		1.9
6016	184	3225	175J	2	3	CCQZ	SHT/NC		2.8
5524	184	1669	175J5	2	1	CCQZ	SHT/NC		0.5
5890	184	5695	175K	1	1	CCQZ	SHT/NC		1.7
6305	184	6412	30M	1	1	CCQZ	SHT/NC		1.7
6020	184	1573	40I	3	3	CCQZ	SHT/NC		8
6024	184	1573	40I	3	4	CCQZ	SHT/NC		4.1
5532	184	2176	55H5	2	2	CCQZ	SHT/NC		4.2
5408	184	6052	55H5	3	10	CCQZ	SHT/NC		15
5511	184	2051	55I	1	1	CCQZ	SHT/NC		2
5962	184	2004	55I	2	2	CCQZ	SHT/NC		1.4
5447	184	655	55I	3	3	CCQZ	SHT/NC		1.6
5983	184	525	55I	4	2	CCQZ	SHT/NC		2.9

2011.28	SBCM	Cat. #	Unit	Level	Qty	MTRL	DEB TYPE	PLAT	WT/g
5682	184	2747	55I5	2	4	CCQZ	SHT/NC		2.6
5472	184	2709	55I5	3	2	CCQZ	SHT/NC		0.8
5672	184	2819	55I5	4	3	CCQZ	SHT/NC		3.2
5567	184	2809	55I5	5	5	CCQZ	SHT/NC		6.9
6326	184	4717	55J5	4	1	CCQZ	SHT/NC		2.2
5885	184	1408	55K	3	2	CCQZ	SHT/NC		4.4
5700	184	1383	55K	4	2	CCQZ	SHT/NC		1.9
5833	184	1589	55K5	1	2	CCQZ	SHT/NC		1.6
6040	184	1951	60H5	1	2	CCQZ	SHT/NC		1.7
5714	184	5975	60I5	3	2	CCQZ	SHT/NC		1.8
6253	184	372	60J5	2	1	CCQZ	SHT/NC		1.7
5991	184	92	65H5	5	1	CCQZ	SHT/NC		0.5
6292	184	6182	65I	1	4	CCQZ	SHT/NC		3
5690	184	6105	65I	2	1	CCQZ	SHT/NC		0.7
5629	184	6137	65I	3	2	CCQZ	SHT/NC		1
6005	184	574	70-5	2	7	CCQZ	SHT/NC		4.7
5465	184	5951	70C	2	2	CCQZ	SHT/NC		0.5
6331	184	1697	70C	3	3	CCQZ	SHT/NC		1.6
6347	184	1843	70C5	1	2	CCQZ	SHT/NC		3.1
6558	184	3900	70C5	2	2	CCQZ	SHT/NC		1.2
6281	184	2866	70E5	2	1	CCQZ	SHT/NC		2.3
6194	184	2734	70E5	3	2	CCQZ	SHT/NC		

2011.28	SBCM	Cat. #	Unit	Level	Qty	MTRL	DEB TYPE	PLAT	WT/g
5707	184	1446	70I	1	1	CCQZ	SHT/NC		0.6
6613	184	2581	70I	1	2	CCQZ	SHT/NC		3.2
5644	184	88	70J	1	6	CCQZ	SHT/NC		6.2
5922	184	389	70J5	1	1	CCQZ	SHT/NC		0.9
5483	184	2507	70J5	1	2	CCQZ	SHT/NC		4.6
5878	184	3202	75D	5	3	CCQZ	SHT/NC		3.2
5711	184	5600	75J	1	2	CCQZ	SHT/NC		3
5609	184	6222	80E	7	3	CCQZ	SHT/NC		1.9
5678	184	318	85D5	4	1	CCQZ	SHT/NC		1.6
6296	184	274	85E	3	2	CCQZ	SHT/NC		2
5666	184	6432	85G	3	1	CCQZ	SHT/NC		1.2
5497	184	4692	85G	5	1	CCQZ	SHT/NC		1.1
5406	184	1772	85G5	3	2	CCQZ	SHT/NC		8.1
5439	184	59	85G5	4	3	CCQZ	SHT/NC		0.4
6216	184	3356	90D	2	3	CCQZ	SHT/NC		2.5
6578	184	3527	90D	4	2	CCQZ	SHT/NC		2.8
5527	184	68	90D5	4	1	CCQZ	SHT/NC		0.7
6035	184	3159	90E	3	1	CCQZ	SHT/NC		3.2
5735	184	3218	90E	4	1	CCQZ	SHT/NC		1.7
6309	184	2320	90E5	3	1	CCQZ	SHT/NC		1.9
6575	184	4411	90H	4	1	CCQZ	SHT/NC		1.1
6302	184	2149	95E	4	3	CCQZ	SHT/NC		2

2011.28	SBCM	Cat. #	Unit	Level	Qty	MTRL	DEB TYPE	PLAT	WT/g
5745	184	4497	95E5	4	1	CCQZ	SHT/NC		1
Crytocrystalline Quartz Debitage Notation Key									
2011.28: Pechanga Cultural Resource catalogue number									
SBCM: San Bernardino Catalogue collection number									
CAT #: Catalog number									
UNIT: Location									
	According to excavation map								
	TEST: Test Hole								
LEVEL: Depth									
	SURF: Surface								
	Levels 1-10 (Increments of 6 inches each level)								
	N/A: Not applicable								
QTY: Quantity									
MTRL: Material									
	CCQZ: Cryptocrystalline quartz								
DEB TYPE: Debitage Type									
	BF/ALT: Biface alternate flake								
	BF: EPERC: Biface early percussion flake								
	BF/EDGE: Biface edge modified flake								
	BF/EPRES: Biface early pressure flake								
	BF/LPERC: Biface late percussion flake								

	BF/MARG: Biface margin removal flake							
	Burin spall							
	CC: Completely Cortical							
	FF/C: Flake fragment cortical							
	FF/NC: Flake Fragment no cortex							
	NC: No Cortex							
	NC/ALT: No Cortex alternate flake							
	NC/BULB: No Cortex bulb removal flake							
	NC/EDGE: No cortex edge modified flake							
	NC/MARG: No Cortex margin removal flake							
	NC/outré: No cortex outré passé							
	PC: Partially Cortical							
	PC/ALT: Partically cortical alternate flake							
	PC/EDGE: Partially cortical edge modified flake							
	PC/MARG: Partially cortical margin removal flake							
	SHT: Shatter							
	SHT/C: Shatter Cortical							
	SHT/NC: Shatter No Cortex							
PLAT: Platform								
	PA: Platform absent							
	NP: Natural Platform							
	MFP: Multi-faceted platform							
	SFP: Single faceted platform							

WT/g: Weight measured in grams						

APPENDIX E

METAVOLCANIC AND METASEDIMENTRY DEBITAGE

Appendix E: Metavolcanic and Metasedimentary Debitage									
2011.28	**SBCM**	**Cat. #**	**Unit**	**Level**	**Qty**	**MTRL**	**DEB TYPE**	**PLAT**	**WT/g**
7692	184	3064	100D5	1	2	MTSD	PC	PA	4.6
7692	184	3064	100D5	1	2	MTSD	SHT		
5697	184	205	85E5	4	1	MTSD	PC	PC	2.8
7635	184	4760	75H5	1	1	MTVC	BF/EDGE		1.7
7673	184	5622	90I	2	1	MTVC	CC	NP	22
5500	184	5074	75C5	5	1	MTVC	NC	PA	0.4
5526	184	68	90D5	4	1	MTVC	NC/ALT		2.8
7693	184	976	105D5	2	1	MTVC	PC	NP	0.2
7645	184	1541	110I5	1	1	MTVC	PC	NP	3.8
7690	184	1731	140I	2	2	MTVC	PC	NP	
7717	184	2833	165J	3	10	MTVC	PC	NP	
7664	184	2244	170H	2	1	MTVC	PC	NP	1.3
7719	184	6409	30M	1	1	MTVC	PC	NP	14.4
7707	184	1574	40I	3	4	MTVC	PC	NP	2.1
7722	184	2713	55I5	3	1	MTVC	PC	NP	0.4
7630	184	6132	65I	3	1	MTVC	PC	NP	
7643	184	1829	70C5	5	1	MTVC	PC	NP	5.2
5912	184	4786	75H5	2	1	MTVC	PC	NP	6
7627	184	5571	75I	1	3	MTVC	PC	NP	
7731	184	3744	80D	5	4	MTVC	PC	NP	6.1
7675	184	600	80E	3	2	MTVC	PC	NP	

2011.28	SBCM	Cat. #	Unit	Level	Qty	MTRL	DEB TYPE	PLAT	WT/g
7674	184	2806	90D5	2	3	MTVC	PC	NP	
7725	184	2018	90E5	4	2	MTVC	PC	NP	1.7
7651	184	2147	95E	4	5	MTVC	PC	NP	4
7720	184	3237	95E	5	1	MTVC	PC	NP	0.7
7684	184	2215	95E	7	2	MTVC	PC	NP	2.2
7709	184	1112	95I	2	1	MTVC	PC	NP	4
7711	184	962	100E	2	3	MTVC	PC	PA	3.8
7624	184	702	100E5	9	4	MTVC	PC	PA	7.1
7713	184	1853	105E	1	1	MTVC	PC	PA	0.9
7729	184	1001	105F	1	1	MTVC	PC	PA	2.9
7629	184	3186	110F5	4	1	MTVC	PC	PA	2.1
7723	184	1422	110I	2	1	MTVC	PC	PA	1.7
7628	184	4055	115F	2	1	MTVC	PC	PA	
7662	184	726	120F	2	1	MTVC	PC	PA	1.2
7702	184	1988	120F	5	1	MTVC	PC	PA	1.1
7718	184	692	120G	1	4	MTVC	PC	PA	8.3
7690	184	1731	140I	2	2	MTVC	PC	PA	6.4
7714	184	2567	160H	1	1	MTVC	PC	PA	11.8
7689	184	6447	160J	1	1	MTVC	PC	PA	2
7656	184	2597	175H	3	1	MTVC	PC	PA	1
7706	184	4630	20J5	4	8	MTVC	PC	PA	
7696	184	6354	40H5	1	4	MTVC	PC	PA	

APPENDIX E

2011.28	SBCM	Cat. #	Unit	Level	Qty	MTRL	DEB TYPE	PLAT	WT/g
7655	184	1903	40I	1	2	MTVC	PC	PA	2.1
7707	184	1574	40I	3	4	MTVC	PC	PA	
7716	184	4444	55	2	8	MTVC	PC	PA	
7730	184	2049	55I	1	1	MTVC	PC	PA	1.1
7637	184	2821	55I5	4	4	MTVC	PC	PA	9
7715	184	2810	55I5	5	4	MTVC	PC	PA	13.5
7658	184	1389	55J5	3	1	MTVC	PC	PA	0.3
7728	184	2059	60H5	6	1	MTVC	PC	PA	1.5
7630	184	6132	65I	3	1	MTVC	PC	PA	
7697	184	6134	65I	3	2	MTVC	PC	PA	
7654	184	3856	70C	2	1	MTVC	PC	PA	0.5
7643	184	1829	70C5	5	1	MTVC	PC	PA	
7698	184	760	70I5	2	1	MTVC	PC	PA	3.8
7708	184	2660	70I5	4	1	MTVC	PC	PA	10.3
7678	184	3263	75D5	5	1	MTVC	PC	PA	3.4
7663	184	4532	75E5	3	1	MTVC	PC	PA	6
7627	184	5571	75I	1	4	MTVC	PC	PA	
7680	184	1081	80D5	2	2	MTVC	PC	PA	1.5
7675	184	600	80E	3	2	MTVC	PC	PA	1.5
7683	184	4082	80E	4	1	MTVC	PC	PA	1
7622	184	4130	80I	2	1	MTVC	PC	PA	2.4
7691	184	510	85F	4	2	MTVC	PC	PA	2

2011.28	SBCM	Cat. #	Unit	Level	Qty	MTRL	DEB TYPE	PLAT	WT/g
7668	184	1771	85G5	3	1	MTVC	PC	PA	5.3
7674	184	2806	90D5	2	3	MTVC	PC	PA	
7695	184	5302	90H	2	1	MTVC	PC	PA	4.4
7710	184	1973	95E	3	1	MTVC	PC	PA	1.1
7640	184	3270	95E5	7	1	MTVC	PC	PA	1.3
7638	184	3555	95E5	9	2	MTVC	PC	PA	1.1
7646	184	6232	120D5	2	1	MTVC	PC/EDGE		0.5
7641	184	5976	60I5	3	1	MTVC	PC/EDGE		3
7649	184	2534	100D5	1	1	MTVC	SHT		3.6
7657	184	2642	100D5	2	1	MTVC	SHT		1
7670	184	2930	100D5	3	1	MTVC	SHT		1.2
7703	184	2293	100D5	6	1	MTVC	SHT		0.5
7671	184	2918	100E5	4	3	MTVC	SHT		1.6
7677	184	3010	100E5	5	1	MTVC	SHT		0.9
7631	184	4634	105D	1	2	MTVC	SHT		0.7
7727	184	1062	105F5	7	1	MTVC	SHT		2.3
7700	184	3003	110I5	4	1	MTVC	SHT		1.4
7699	184	5823	110J5	1	3	MTVC	SHT		16
7628	184	4055	115F	2	3	MTVC	SHT		5.8
7623	184	2839	120E	2	1	MTVC	SHT		5
7718	184	692	120G	1	4	MTVC	SHT		
7714	184	2567	160H	1	1	MTVC	SHT		

2011.28	SBCM	Cat. #	Unit	Level	Qty	MTRL	DEB TYPE	PLAT	WT/g
7687	184	5001	160J5	3	2	MTVC	SHT		1.6
5545	184	450	165H	2	1	MTVC	SHT		1.8
7717	184	2833	165J	3	10	MTVC	SHT		26
7666	184	2980	175I	1	2	MTVC	SHT		4.9
7681	184	5209	175I5	1	1	MTVC	SHT		
7706	184	4630	20J5	4	8	MTVC	SHT		46.9
7652	184	5437	35I	2	1	MTVC	SHT		1.6
7648	184	5690	35I	3	1	MTVC	SHT		1
7696	184	6354	40H5	1	4	MTVC	SHT		2
7636	184	1513	40K	1	3	MTVC	SHT		4
7621	184	1472	40K	3	2	MTVC	SHT		4.8
7686	184	1186	45I	4	1	MTVC	SHT		0.7
7716	184	4444	55	2	8	MTVC	SHT		23.2
7650	184	6055	55H5	3	3	MTVC	SHT		1.6
7634	184	4718	55J5	4	2	MTVC	SHT		4.5
7630	184	6132	65I	3	5	MTVC	SHT		7.4
7697	184	6134	65I	3	2	MTVC	SHT		9.7
7633	184	3898	70C5	2	3	MTVC	SHT		4.7
7639	184	2576	70I	1	1	MTVC	SHT		1.4
7665	184	2509	70J5	1	1	MTVC	SHT		0.6
7701	184	4797	75E5	2	2	MTVC	SHT		0.5
7627	184	5571	75I	1	8	MTVC	SHT		36.4

2011.28	SBCM	Cat. #	Unit	Level	Qty	MTRL	DEB TYPE	PLAT	WT/g
7669	184	3617	80D	6	1	MTVC	SHT		1.1
7721	184	806	80D5	2	1	MTVC	SHT		1.7
7724	184	4048	80E	2	2	MTVC	SHT		1.3
7676	184	5270	80E	5	1	MTVC	SHT		1.5
5696	184	205	85E5	4	2	MTVC	SHT		10.5
7667	184	892	85F	2	1	MTVC	SHT		0.8
7644	184	3128	85F	5	1	MTVC	SHT		3.9
7674	184	2806	90D5	2	3	MTVC	SHT		3.9
3157	184	3157	90E	3	1	MTVC	SHT		1.8
7704	184	4681	90F5	1	7	MTVC	SHT		46.1
7684	184	2215	95E	7	2	MTVC	SHT		
7659	184	3143	95E5	3	1	MTVC	SHT		1.3
7712	184	1209	95H5	3	1	MTVC	SHT		8.7
7642	184	3624	95I	1	3	MTVC	SHT		18.9
7694	184	917	100E5	1	3	MTVC	SHT/C		10.7
MTSD and MTVC Debitage Notation Key									
2011.28: Pechanga Cultural Resource catalogue number									
SBCM: San Bernardino Catalogue collection number									
CAT #: Catalog number									
UNIT: Location									
	According to excavation map								

APPENDIX E

LEVEL: Depth						
	SURF: Surface					
	Levels 1-10 (Increments of 6 inches each level)					
QTY: Quantity						
MTRL: Material						
	MTVC: Metavolcanic					
	MTSD: Metasedimentry					
DEB TYPE: Debitage Type						
	BF: EPERC: Biface early percussion flake					
	BF/EDGE: Biface edge modified flake					
	BF/EPRES: Biface early pressure flake					
	BF/LPERC: Biface late percussion flake					
	BF/MARG: Biface margin removal flake					
	CC: Completely Cortical					
	CC/outré: Completely cortical outré passé					
	FF/C: Flake fragment cortical					
	FF/NC: Flake Fragment no cortex					
	NC: No Cortex					
	NC/ALT: No Cortex alternate flake					
	NC/BULB: No Cortex bulb removal flake					
	NC/EDGE: No cortex edge modified flake					
	NC/MARG: No Cortex margin removal flake					
	NC/UNDI: No Cortex undulation removal flake					

	PC: Partially Cortical					
	PC/ALT: Partically cortical alternate flake					
	PC/EDGE: Partially cortical edge modified flake					
	PC/MARG: Partially cortical margin removal flake					
	SHT: Shatter					
	SHT/C: Shatter Cortical					
	SHT/NC: Shatter No Cortex					
PLAT: Platform						
	PA: Platform absent					
	NP: Natural Platform					
	MFP: Multi-faceted platform					
	SFP: Single faceted platform					
WT/g: Weight measured in grams						

APPENDIX F

METAQUARTZITE DEBITAGE

Appendix F: Metaquartzite Debitage									
2011.28	SBCM	Cat. #	Unit	Level	Qty	MTRL	DEB TYPE	PLAT	WT/g
8005	184	5942	85E	4	1	MQZT	BF/EDGE	MFP	
8028	184	1232	105E	2	3	MQZT	BF/EDGE		
8011	184	2290	100D5	6	1	MQZT	BF/EPERC	MFP	
8028	184	1232	105E	2	2	MQZT	BF/EPERC	MFP	
8061	184	906	105F5	3	1	MQZT	BF/EPERC	MFP	
8023	184	5054	110G	1	1	MQZT	BF/EPERC	MFP	
8039	184	1741	115F5	4	2	MQZT	BF/EPERC	MFP	
8014	184	6401	160J5	1	4	MQZT	BF/EPERC	MFP	
8017	184	5950	70C	2	1	MQZT	BF/EPERC	MFP	
8005	184	5942	85E	4	1	MQZT	BF/EPERC	MFP	8.2
8051	184	2415	90E5	5	2	MQZT	BF/EPERC	MFP	
8049	184	1907	40I	1	1	MQZT	BF/EPERC	PA	
8017	184	5950	70C	2	2	MQZT	BF/EPERC	SFP	
7992	184	617	165H	2	1	MQZT	BF/EPERC		
8026	184	3141	95E5	3	3	MQZT	BF/EPERC		
8028	184	1232	105E	2	1	MQZT	BF/EPRES		
8053	184	2867	70E5	2	1	MQZT	BF/EPRES		
8018	184	3365	40K	4	2	MQZT	BF/LPERC	MFP	
8016	184	5597	75J	1	1	MQZT	BF/LPERC	MFP	
8026	184	3141	95E5	3	1	MQZT	BF/LPERC	MFP	
7993	184	854	100F5	7	1	MQZT	BF/LPERC		

2011.28	SBCM	Cat. #	Unit	Level	Qty	MTRL	DEB TYPE	PLAT	WT/g
8009	184	6270	85F5	4	1	MQZT	BF/LPERC		
7992	184	617	165H	2	1	MQZT	BF/LPRES		
8036	184	1409	55K	3	1	MQZT	BF/MARG	MFP	
8046	184	1556	80E	6	1	MQZT	BF/MARG		
8030	184	4686	85G	5	1	MQZT	BF/outré		
8039	184	1741	115F5	4	1	MQZT	FF/C		
8021	184	946	120G	1	1	MQZT	FF/C		
8030	184	4686	85G	5	2	MQZT	FF/C		
8041	184	2699	100D	1	1	MQZT	FF/NC		
8028	184	1232	105E	2	13	MQZT	FF/NC		
8023	184	5054	110G	1	1	MQZT	FF/NC		
8042	184	1799	110H5	5	4	MQZT	FF/NC		5.5
8008	184	3179	115F	2	5	MQZT	FF/NC		
8039	184	1741	115F5	4	4	MQZT	FF/NC		
7994	184	1984	120F	5	2	MQZT	FF/NC		
8043	184	1489	120F5	3	4	MQZT	FF/NC		
8021	184	946	120G	1	4	MQZT	FF/NC		
8010	184	5132	140H5	3	6	MQZT	FF/NC		
8032	184	2766	160I	2	1	MQZT	FF/NC		6.4
8014	184	6401	160J5	1	4	MQZT	FF/NC		
7992	184	617	165H	2	4	MQZT	FF/NC		
8048	184	504	165H	3	3	MQZT	FF/NC		

2011.28	SBCM	Cat. #	Unit	Level	Qty	MTRL	DEB TYPE	PLAT	WT/g
8001	184	2669	170J	2	5	MQZT	FF/NC		
8049	184	1907	40I	1	4	MQZT	FF/NC		
8038	184	2749	55I5	2	1	MQZT	FF/NC		
8002	184	2710	55I5	3	4	MQZT	FF/NC		
8036	184	1409	55K	3	5	MQZT	FF/NC		
8037	184	2421	60J5	5	3	MQZT	FF/NC		
8024	184	93	65H5	5	2	MQZT	FF/NC		
8012	184	3852	70C	2	2	MQZT	FF/NC		4.5
8017	184	5950	70C	2	1	MQZT	FF/NC		
8022	184	3903	70C5	2	2	MQZT	FF/NC		
8069	184	2739	70E5	3	3	MQZT	FF/NC		1.8
8016	184	5597	75J	1	2	MQZT	FF/NC		
8046	184	1556	80E	6	1	MQZT	FF/NC		
8045	184	5114	80E5	1	2	MQZT	FF/NC		
8068	184	129	85E	3	3	MQZT	FF/NC		18.7
8009	184	6270	85F5	4	3	MQZT	FF/NC		17.7
8070	184	6282	85F5	6	1	MQZT	FF/NC		0.7
8013	184	4706	85G	1	1	MQZT	FF/NC		
8030	184	4686	85G	5	3	MQZT	FF/NC		
8033	184	2805	90D5	2	3	MQZT	FF/NC		
8000	184	3540	90E	6	2	MQZT	FF/NC		
8044	184	3279	90E	7	2	MQZT	FF/NC		

2011.28	SBCM	Cat. #	Unit	Level	Qty	MTRL	DEB TYPE	PLAT	WT/g
7995	184	4521	90H	3	1	MQZT	FF/NC		3.7
8004	184	121	95D	1	2	MQZT	FF/NC		
8006	184	2310	95D	2	5	MQZT	FF/NC		
7991	184	3544	95E5	1	1	MQZT	FF/NC		
8026	184	3141	95E5	3	5	MQZT	FF/NC		
8007	184	3056	95E5	8	2	MQZT	FF/NC		
8071	184	1819	95F	9	2	MQZT	FF/NC		3.4
8031	184	3106	95G	3	1	MQZT	FF/NC		1.5
7989	184	4471	110G5	4	5	MQZT	NC	MFP	
8039	184	1741	115F5	4	4	MQZT	NC	MFP	28.6
8021	184	946	120G	1	1	MQZT	NC	MFP	
8052	184	4476	30J5	1	4	MQZT	NC	MFP	
7990	184	4712	55J5	4	5	MQZT	NC	MFP	37.5
8016	184	5597	75J	1	2	MQZT	NC	MFP	
8005	184	5942	85E	4	1	MQZT	NC	MFP	
8013	184	4706	85G	1	1	MQZT	NC	MFP	
8000	184	3540	90E	6	1	MQZT	NC	MFP	10.2
8026	184	3141	95E5	3	2	MQZT	NC	MFP	41.3
8031	184	3106	95G	3	1	MQZT	NC	MFP	
8035	184	771	100F5	8	1	MQZT	NC	PA	1.1
8028	184	1232	105E	2	2	MQZT	NC	PA	74.7
8008	184	3179	115F	2	1	MQZT	NC	PA	

2011.28	SBCM	Cat. #	Unit	Level	Qty	MTRL	DEB TYPE	PLAT	WT/g
8021	184	946	120G	1	1	MQZT	NC	PA	
8050	184	6438	160J	1	1	MQZT	NC	PA	22.4
7992	184	617	165H	2	2	MQZT	NC	PA	24.4
8001	184	2669	170J	2	2	MQZT	NC	PA	
8052	184	4476	30J5	1	2	MQZT	NC	PA	11.2
8036	184	1409	55K	3	1	MQZT	NC	PA	
8022	184	3903	70C5	2	4	MQZT	NC	PA	
8025	184	4594	75C	1	2	MQZT	NC	PA	5.3
8016	184	5597	75J	1	2	MQZT	NC	PA	41.3
8019	184	4075	80E	4	2	MQZT	NC	PA	
8045	184	5114	80E5	1	1	MQZT	NC	PA	9.4
8030	184	4686	85G	5	2	MQZT	NC	PA	
8041	184	2699	100D	1	1	MQZT	NC	SFP	
8059	184	2537	100D5	1	4	MQZT	NC	SFP	3
8011	184	2290	100D5	6	2	MQZT	NC	SFP	8.6
8028	184	1232	105E	2	1	MQZT	NC	SFP	
8061	184	906	105F5	3	1	MQZT	NC	SFP	7.2
8027	184	6126	110E	2	1	MQZT	NC	SFP	
8023	184	5054	110G	1	3	MQZT	NC	SFP	33.2
7989	184	4471	110G5	4	5	MQZT	NC	SFP	43.7
8057	184	1878	110H	3	4	MQZT	NC	SFP	16.2
8065	184	410	115D5	3	1	MQZT	NC	SFP	2.8

2011.28	SBCM	Cat. #	Unit	Level	Qty	MTRL	DEB TYPE	PLAT	WT/g
8008	184	3179	115F	2	4	MQZT	NC	SFP	14.7
8039	184	1741	115F5	4	3	MQZT	NC	SFP	
7994	184	1984	120F	5	3	MQZT	NC	SFP	10.4
8021	184	946	120G	1	2	MQZT	NC	SFP	26.9
8010	184	5132	140H5	3	5	MQZT	NC	SFP	
7996	184	4934	140I5	3	1	MQZT	NC	SFP	2.9
8014	184	6401	160J5	1	2	MQZT	NC	SFP	67.5
7992	184	617	165H	2	3	MQZT	NC	SFP	
8048	184	504	165H	3	4	MQZT	NC	SFP	9.3
8020	184	2756	165J	2	2	MQZT	NC	SFP	15.8
8001	184	2669	170J	2	3	MQZT	NC	SFP	29.1
8029	184	5536	175J5	1	2	MQZT	NC	SFP	8.4
8054	184	2301	20J5	1	2	MQZT	NC	SFP	5.8
8052	184	4476	30J5	1	2	MQZT	NC	SFP	
8049	184	1907	40I	1	3	MQZT	NC	SFP	14.6
8038	184	2749	55I5	2	2	MQZT	NC	SFP	3.3
8036	184	1409	55K	3	1	MQZT	NC	SFP	
8037	184	2421	60J5	5	1	MQZT	NC	SFP	
8024	184	93	65H5	5	2	MQZT	NC	SFP	
8022	184	3903	70C5	2	5	MQZT	NC	SFP	55.6
7999	184	1827	70C5	5	3	MQZT	NC	SFP	5.7
8053	184	2867	70E5	2	4	MQZT	NC	SFP	

2011.28	SBCM	Cat. #	Unit	Level	Qty	MTRL	DEB TYPE	PLAT	WT/g
8016	184	5597	75J	1	1	MQZT	NC	SFP	
8019	184	4075	80E	4	5	MQZT	NC	SFP	21.1
8046	184	1556	80E	6	3	MQZT	NC	SFP	16
8045	184	5114	80E5	1	1	MQZT	NC	SFP	
8040	184	4120	80I	2	1	MQZT	NC	SFP	12.8
8009	184	6270	85F5	4	6	MQZT	NC	SFP	
8030	184	4686	85G	5	2	MQZT	NC	SFP	32.3
7997	184	3272	90E	2	1	MQZT	NC	SFP	16.6
8000	184	3540	90E	6	1	MQZT	NC	SFP	
8044	184	3279	90E	7	1	MQZT	NC	SFP	
8051	184	2415	90E5	5	2	MQZT	NC	SFP	7.1
8004	184	121	95D	1	1	MQZT	NC	SFP	5.8
8006	184	2310	95D	2	1	MQZT	NC	SFP	
7991	184	3544	95E5	1	1	MQZT	NC	SFP	8.8
8007	184	3056	95E5	8	1	MQZT	NC	SFP	2.8
8014	184	6401	160J5	1	3	MQZT	NC/ALT		
8020	184	2756	165J	2	3	MQZT	NC/ALT		
8053	184	2867	70E5	2	1	MQZT	NC/ALT		
8069	184	2739	70E5	3	3	MQZT	NC/ALT		
8002	184	2710	55I5	3	1	MQZT	NC/EDGE		
8053	184	2867	70E5	2	2	MQZT	NC/EDGE		
8015	184	4783	75H5	2	3	MQZT	NC/EDGE		

APPENDIX F

2011.28	SBCM	Cat. #	Unit	Level	Qty	MTRL	DEB TYPE	PLAT	WT/g
8009	184	6270	85F5	4	3	MQZT	NC/EPERC	MFP	
8008	184	3179	115F	2	1	MQZT	NC/MARG		
8018	184	3365	40K	4	2	MQZT	NC/MARG		19.7
8013	184	4706	85G	1	1	MQZT	NC/MARG		
8027	184	6126	110E	2	1	MQZT	PC	MFP	2.2
8023	184	5054	110G	1	1	MQZT	PC	NP	
8058	184	5991	110I	4	1	MQZT	PC	NP	6.6
8010	184	5132	140H5	3	1	MQZT	PC	NP	26.7
8050	184	6438	160J	1	1	MQZT	PC	NP	
8014	184	6401	160J5	1	1	MQZT	PC	NP	
7992	184	617	165H	2	1	MQZT	PC	NP	
7672	184	1883	170H5	1	7	MQZT	PC	NP	
8001	184	2669	170J	2	2	MQZT	PC	NP	
8049	184	1907	40I	1	3	MQZT	PC	NP	
8017	184	5950	70C	2	1	MQZT	PC	NP	16
8022	184	3903	70C5	2	3	MQZT	PC	NP	
8053	184	2867	70E5	2	1	MQZT	PC	NP	22.4
8015	184	4783	75H5	2	1	MQZT	PC	NP	24
8013	184	4706	85G	1	2	MQZT	PC	NP	24.3
8033	184	2805	90D5	2	1	MQZT	PC	NP	20.9
8000	184	3540	90E	6	1	MQZT	PC	NP	
8006	184	2310	95D	2	1	MQZT	PC	NP	

2011.28	SBCM	Cat. #	Unit	Level	Qty	MTRL	DEB TYPE	PLAT	WT/g
8026	184	3141	95E5	3	1	MQZT	PC	NP	
8032	184	2766	160I	2	1	MQZT	PC	PA	
8036	184	1409	55K	3	1	MQZT	PC	PA	26.1
8037	184	2421	60J5	5	1	MQZT	PC	PA	21.2
8017	184	5950	70C	2	1	MQZT	PC	PA	
8013	184	4706	85G	1	2	MQZT	PC	PA	
8044	184	3279	90E	7	1	MQZT	PC	PA	5.6
8041	184	2699	100D	1	1	MQZT	PC	SFP	24.6
8060	184	3308	120F	4	1	MQZT	PC	SFP	5.1
8024	184	93	65H5	5	1	MQZT	PC/ALT		16.8
8015	184	4783	75H5	2	1	MQZT	PC/ALT		
8030	184	4686	85G	5	1	MQZT	PC/ALT		
8026	184	3141	95E5	3	1	MQZT	PC/ALT		
8040	184	4120	80I	2	1	MQZT	PC/MARG		
7626	184	6172	115F5	5	1	MQZT	SHT		1
7672	184	1883	170H5	1	7	MQZT	SHT		11.5
7632	184	6323	85G	6	2	MQZT	SHT		3
8047	184	1236	95G	3	1	MQZT	SHT		0.01
8028	184	1232	105E	2	4	MQZT	SHT/C		
8062	184	6085	110E	3	1	MQZT	SHT/C		0.6
8023	184	5054	110G	1	2	MQZT	SHT/C		
7989	184	4471	110G5	4	5	MQZT	SHT/C		

2011.28	SBCM	Cat. #	Unit	Level	Qty	MTRL	DEB TYPE	PLAT	WT/g
8043	184	1489	120F5	3	1	MQZT	SHT/C		3.1
8016	184	5597	75J	1	1	MQZT	SHT/C		
8006	184	2310	95D	2	3	MQZT	SHT/C		75.4
7991	184	3544	95E5	1	2	MQZT	SHT/C		
8034	184	4897	100D	8	1	MQZT	SHT/NC		3.4
7993	184	854	100F5	7	1	MQZT	SHT/NC		7.1
8035	184	771	100F5	8	3	MQZT	SHT/NC		
7998	184	4803	105D5	5	1	MQZT	SHT/NC		2
8008	184	3179	115F	2	3	MQZT	SHT/NC		
8039	184	1741	115F5	4	4	MQZT	SHT/NC		
8021	184	946	120G	1	2	MQZT	SHT/NC		
8063	184	3330	120G	2	1	MQZT	SHT/NC		1.3
8010	184	5132	140H5	3	3	MQZT	SHT/NC		
8032	184	2766	160I	2	3	MQZT	SHT/NC		
8050	184	6438	160J	1	1	MQZT	SHT/NC		
7992	184	617	165H	2	4	MQZT	SHT/NC		
8048	184	504	165H	3	4	MQZT	SHT/NC		
8020	184	2756	165J	2	2	MQZT	SHT/NC		
8001	184	2669	170J	2	6	MQZT	SHT/NC		
8052	184	4476	30J5	1	4	MQZT	SHT/NC		
8049	184	1907	40I	1	1	MQZT	SHT/NC		
8067	184	1581	40K	5	1	MQZT	SHT/NC		0.9

2011.28	SBCM	Cat. #	Unit	Level	Qty	MTRL	DEB TYPE	PLAT	WT/g
8002	184	2710	55I5	3	3	MQZT	SHT/NC		12.2
8036	184	1409	55K	3	3	MQZT	SHT/NC		
8037	184	2421	60J5	5	2	MQZT	SHT/NC		
8012	184	3852	70C	2	4	MQZT	SHT/NC		
8017	184	5950	70C	2	1	MQZT	SHT/NC		
8022	184	3903	70C5	2	9	MQZT	SHT/NC		
8053	184	2867	70E5	2	3	MQZT	SHT/NC		
8025	184	4594	75C	1	4	MQZT	SHT/NC		
8016	184	5597	75J	1	3	MQZT	SHT/NC		
8019	184	4075	80E	4	3	MQZT	SHT/NC		
8045	184	5114	80E5	1	1	MQZT	SHT/NC		
8040	184	4120	80I	2	3	MQZT	SHT/NC		
8005	184	5942	85E	4	2	MQZT	SHT/NC		
8009	184	6270	85F5	4	2	MQZT	SHT/NC		
8030	184	4686	85G	5	3	MQZT	SHT/NC		
8003	184	490	85H	3	1	MQZT	SHT/NC		0.01
8072	184	360	90D5	1	1	MQZT	SHT/NC		2.1
8033	184	2805	90D5	2	3	MQZT	SHT/NC		
8000	184	3540	90E	6	1	MQZT	SHT/NC		
8044	184	3279	90E	7	5	MQZT	SHT/NC		
8051	184	2415	90E5	5	3	MQZT	SHT/NC		
8064	184	2609	90F	3	1	MQZT	SHT/NC		0.3

2011.28	SBCM	Cat. #	Unit	Level	Qty	MTRL	DEB TYPE	PLAT	WT/g
8006	184	2310	95D	2	6	MQZT	SHT/NC		
8026	184	3141	95E5	3	5	MQZT	SHT/NC		
Metaquartzite Debitage Notation Key									
2011.28: Pechanga Cultural Resource catalogue number									
SBCM: San Bernardino Catalogue collection number									
CAT #: Catalog number									
UNIT: Location									
	According to excavation map								
LEVEL: Depth									
	SURF: Surface								
	Levels 1-10 (Increments of 6 inches each level)								
QTY: Quantity									
MTRL: Material									
	MTQZ: Metaquartzite								
DEB TYPE: Debitage Type									
	BF/ EPERC: Biface early percussion flake								
	BF/EDGE: Biface edge modified flake								
	BF/EPRES: Biface early pressure flake								
	BF/LPERC: Biface late percussion flake								
	BF/MARG: Biface margin removal flake								
	BF/outré: Biface outré passé								

	CC: Completely Cortical				
	CC/outré: Completely cortical outré passé				
	FF/C: Flake fragment cortical				
	FF/NC: Flake Fragment no cortex				
	NC: No Cortex				
	NC/ALT: No Cortex alternate flake				
	NC/BULB: No Cortex bulb removal flake				
	NC/EDGE: No cortex edge modified flake				
	NC/MARG: No Cortex margin removal flake				
	NC/outré: No cortex outré passé				
	NC/UNDI: No Cortex undulation removal flake				
	PC: Partially Cortical				
	PC/ALT: Partically cortical alternate flake				
	PC/EDGE: Partially cortical edge modified flake				
	PC/MARG: Partially cortical margin removal flake				
	SHT: Shatter				
	SHT/C: Shatter Cortical				
	SHT/NC: Shatter No Cortex				
PLAT: Platform					
	PA: Platform absent				
	NP: Natural Platform				
	MFP: Multi-faceted platform				
	SFP: Single faceted platform				

WT/g: Weight measured in grams

APPENDIX G

OBSIDIAN DEBITAGE

Appendix G: Obsidian Debitage									
2011.28	**SBCM**	**Cat. #**	**Unit**	**Level**	**Qty**	**MTRL**	**DEB TYPE**	**PLAT**	**WT/g**
7824	184	3457	60H5	4	1	OBSN	BF/EDGE		0.8
7845	184	3441	85F5	2	1	OBSN	BF/EDGE		0.6
7780	184	3470	110E5	1	1	OBSN	BF/EPERC	MFP	0.3
7793	184	3426	155J	1	1	OBSN	BF/EPERC	MFP	0.5
7771	184	3472	100D5	6	1	OBSN	BF/EPERC		0.5
7779	184	3399	110D5	4	1	OBSN	BF/EPERC		0.3
7796	184	3403	160J5	1	1	OBSN	BF/EPERC		0.8
7804	184	3502	175J	1	1	OBSN	BF/EPERC		
7808	184	3425	35I	3	1	OBSN	BF/EPERC		2
7812	184	3516	40H5	3	1	OBSN	BF/EPERC		0.6
7822	184	3449	60H5	1	1	OBSN	BF/EPERC		0.8
7846	184	3512	85F5	4	1	OBSN	BF/EPERC		0.5
7800	184	3445	165I	1	1	OBSN	BF/EPREC		0.5
7805	184	3430	175J	2	1	OBSN	BF/EPREC		
7817	184	3448	55H5	4	1	OBSN	BF/EPRES		0.5
7800	184	3445	165I	1	1	OBSN	BF/FRAG		0.7
7831	184	3454	70I5	4	1	OBSN	BF/FRAG		
7855	184	3407	95E	4	1	OBSN	BF/FRAG		1.9
7855	184	3407	95E	4	1	OBSN	BF/FRAG		
7847	184	3491	90D	1	1	OBSN	BF/LPERC	MFP	1.4
7773	184	3504	100E5	4	2	OBSN	BF/LPERC		0.9

2011.28	SBCM	Cat. #	Unit	Level	Qty	MTRL	DEB TYPE	PLAT	WT/g
7821	184	3509	55K5	1	2	OBSN	BF/LPERC		1.2
7843	184	3409	85F5	1	1	OBSN	BF/LPERC		0.7
7813	184	3390	40I	1	1	OBSN	BF/LPREC	MFP	0.5
7839	184	3465	80E	1	1	OBSN	BF/MARG		1.1
7831	184	3454	70I5	4	1	OBSN	FF/NC		2.3
7834	184	3482	75C5	2	1	OBSN	FF/NC		0.7
8211	184	3452	110I5	3	1	OBSN	NC	PA	1
8212	184	3492	95E	7	1	OBSN	NC	PA	1
8213	184	3415	95E	5	1	OBSN	NC	PA	1
7807	184	3396	35H5	1	1	OBSN	NC	PA	3
7814	184	3446	40I	1	1	OBSN	NC	PA	1.1
7804	184	3502	175J	1	1	OBSN	NC	SFP	2.7
7811	184	3511	40H5	2	1	OBSN	NC	SFP	0.3
7859	184	3492	95E5	7	2	OBSN	NC	SFP	1.9
7862	184	3462	TEST	N/A	2	OBSN	NC	SFP	
7838	184	3450	80E	1	1	OBSN	NC/ALT		0.4
7776	184	3459	105F	1	1	OBSN	NC/EDGE		0.9
7782	184	3404	110G	1	1	OBSN	NC/EDGE		0.9
7810	184	3496	40H5	1	1	OBSN	PC	NP	1.8
7831	184	3454	70I5	4	1	OBSN	PC	NP	
7775	184	3418	105E5	3	1	OBSN	PC	PA	0.3
7786	184	3495	110J5	3	1	OBSN	PC	PA	0.4

2011.28	SBCM	Cat. #	Unit	Level	Qty	MTRL	DEB TYPE	PLAT	WT/g
7788	184	3460	115F	6	2	OBSN	PC	PA	0.7
7825	184	3417	60J	2	1	OBSN	PC	PA	0.7
7851	184	2319	90E5	3	1	OBSN	PC	PA	3.4
7857	184	3478	95E5	4	1	OBSN	PC	PA	0.8
7785	184	3391	110I	4	1	OBSN	PC	SFP	0.4
7784	184	3428	110G	2	1	OBSN	PC/ALT		0.7
7844	184	3414	85F5	1	1	OBSN	PC/ALT		
7774	184	3012	100E5	5	1	OBSN	SHT		0.2
7781	184	3436	110F5	5	1	OBSN	SHT		1.5
7794	184	3427	160H	1	1	OBSN	SHT		0.8
7795	184	3397	160I	1	1	OBSN	SHT		0.5
7797	184	3401	165H	1	1	OBSN	SHT		0.3
7798	184	3485	165H	3	2	OBSN	SHT		2.4
7799	184	3408	165H5	1	1	OBSN	SHT		1.1
7802	184	3413	170H	2	2	OBSN	SHT		0.9
7807	184	3396	35H5	1	2	OBSN	SHT		
7808	184	3425	35I	3	3	OBSN	SHT		
7809	184	3453	40H5	1	1	OBSN	SHT		0.3
7810	184	3496	40H5	1	2	OBSN	SHT		
7816	184	3473	55H5	1	1	OBSN	SHT		0.4
7818	184	3458	55I	2	2	OBSN	SHT		1.5
7821	184	3509	55K5	1	1	OBSN	SHT		

2011.28	SBCM	Cat. #	Unit	Level	Qty	MTRL	DEB TYPE	PLAT	WT/g
7823	184	3515	60H5	3	1	OBSN	SHT		0.3
7831	184	3454	70I5	4	4	OBSN	SHT		
7841	184	3455	85D5	2	2	OBSN	SHT		0.3
7844	184	3414	85F5	1	1	OBSN	SHT		2.7
7848	184	3508	90E	3	1	OBSN	SHT		0.5
7849	184	3393	90E	7	1	OBSN	SHT		0.6
7850	184	3421	90E5	2	1	OBSN	SHT		1.8
7855	184	3407	95E	4	1	OBSN	SHT		
7862	184	3462	TEST	N/A	2	OBSN	SHT		0.9
7857	184	3478	95E5	4	1	OBSN	SHT/C		
7777	184	3477	105F5	6	1	OBSN	SHT/C		1.4
7778	184	4214	110D	2	1	OBSN	SHT/C		0.1
7792	184	3432	150H	1	2	OBSN	SHT/C		2.6
7801	184	3394	165I	2	1	OBSN	SHT/C		0.8
7803	184	3481	175H5	1	2	OBSN	SHT/C		0.4
7815	184	3476	40I	4	2	OBSN	SHT/C		2
7820	184	3422	55K	1	1	OBSN	SHT/C		1.3
7829	184	3475	70D	1	1	OBSN	SHT/C		0.8
7832	184	2505	70J5	1	1	OBSN	SHT/C		0.4
7842	184	3402	85F	2	1	OBSN	SHT/C		1.3
7860	184	3398	95G5	1	1	OBSN	SHT/C		1.1
7772	184	3510	100E5	3	1	OBSN	SHT/NC		0.8

2011.28	SBCM	Cat. #	Unit	Level	Qty	MTRL	DEB TYPE	PLAT	WT/g
7783	184	3400	110G	2	2	OBSN	SHT/NC		2
7787	184	382	115E5	9	1	OBSN	SHT/NC		0.9
7789	184	3447	120F	5	1	OBSN	SHT/NC		1
7790	184	3513	120F5	1	1	OBSN	SHT/NC		0.6
7791	184	3514	150F5	1	1	OBSN	SHT/NC		1.4
7805	184	3430	175J	2	1	OBSN	SHT/NC		0.5
7806	184	3395	30J	1	1	OBSN	SHT/NC		0.8
7819	184	1620	55J	2	1	OBSN	SHT/NC		0.6
7826	184	3451	60J5	2	1	OBSN	SHT/NC		0.4
7827	184	3486	60J5	5	4	OBSN	SHT/NC		4
7828	184	3416	65I	4	1	OBSN	SHT/NC		0.3
7830	184	3443	70I5	2	1	OBSN	SHT/NC		0.2
7833	184	3419	70J5	2	1	OBSN	SHT/NC		0.5
7835	184	3507	75C5	4	1	OBSN	SHT/NC		0.4
7836	184	3406	75H	1	1	OBSN	SHT/NC		2.5
7837	184	3405	80D5	5	1	OBSN	SHT/NC		0.4
7840	184	3412	80E5	4	1	OBSN	SHT/NC		1.8
7852	184	3411	90I	3	1	OBSN	SHT/NC		0.8
7853	184	4176	90I5	1	1	OBSN	SHT/NC		1.1
7854	184	3410	95D5	1	1	OBSN	SHT/NC		0.8
7856	184	3438	95E	4	2	OBSN	SHT/NC		1.6
7858	184	3415	95E5	5	3	OBSN	SHT/NC		2.7

2011.28	SBCM	Cat. #	Unit	Level	Qty	MTRL	DEB TYPE	PLAT	WT/g
7863	184	3463	TEST	N/A	1	OBSN	SHT/NC		0.7
7864	184	4661	TEST	N/A	1	OBSN	SHT/NC		0.2

Obsidian Debitage Notation Key					
2011.28: Pechanga Cultural Resource catalogue number					
SBCM: San Bernardino Catalogue collection number					
CAT #: Catalog number					
UNIT: Location					
	According to excavation map				
	TEST:Test Hole				
LEVEL: Depth					
	SURF: Surface				
	Levels 1-10 (Increments of 6 inches each level)				
	N/A: Not applicable				
QTY: Quantity					
MTRL: Material					
	OBSN: Obsidian				
DEB TYPE: Debitage Type					
	BF: EPERC: Biface early percussion flake				
	BF/EDGE: Biface edge modified flake				
	BF/EPRES: Biface early pressure flake				
	BF/LPERC: Biface late percussion flake				

	BF/MARG: Biface margin removal flake				
	CC: Completely Cortical				
	CC/outré: Completely cortical outré passé				
	FF/C: Flake fragment cortical				
	FF/NC: Flake Fragment no cortex				
	NC: No Cortex				
	NC/ALT: No Cortex alternate flake				
	NC/BULB: No Cortex bulb removal flake				
	NC/EDGE: No cortex edge modified flake				
	NC/MARG: No Cortex margin removal flake				
	NC/outré: No cortex outré passé				
	NC/UNDI: No Cortex undulation removal flake				
	PC: Partially Cortical				
	PC/ALT: Partically cortical alternate flake				
	PC/EDGE: Partially cortical edge modified flake				
	PC/MARG: Partially cortical margin removal flake				
	SHT: Shatter				
	SHT/C: Shatter Cortical				
	SHT/NC: Shatter No Cortex				
PLAT: Platform					
	PA: Platform absent				
	NP: Natural platform				
	MFP: Multi-faceted platform				

	SFP: Single faceted platform				
WT/g: Weight measured in grams					

APPENDIX H

QUARTZ DEBITAGE

Appendix H: Quartz Debitage									
2011.28	**SBCM**	**Cat. #**	**Unit**	**Level**	**Qty**	**MTRL**	**DEB TYPE**	**PLAT**	**WT/g**
4345	184	2840	120E	2	1	QRTZ	BF/EDGE		
4399	184	5627	70E	5	1	QRTZ	BF/EDGE		45.5
4357	184	915	100E5	1	1	QRTZ	BF/EPERC	MFP	
4272	184	3171	115F	5	1	QRTZ	BF/EPERC	MFP	
4345	184	2840	120E	2	2	QRTZ	BF/EPERC	MFP	
4464	184	41	165K	1	1	QRTZ	BF/EPERC	MFP	
4400	184	1656	55K5	2	2	QRTZ	BF/EPERC	MFP	
4322	184	2685	70E5	5	1	QRTZ	BF/EPERC	MFP	
4393	184	1012	105E5	3	2	QRTZ	BF/EPERC		
4246	184	3060	95E5	8	1	QRTZ	BF/EPERC		
4345	184	2840	120E	2	1	QRTZ	BF/LPRES		
4643	184	6414	30M	1	3	QRTZ	BF/MARG		
4223	184	3361	40K	4	1	QRTZ	CC	NP	
4275	184	881	105F	4	3	QRTZ	FF/C		9.6
4464	184	41	165K	1	2	QRTZ	FF/C		
4217	184	1959	100D5	5	1	QRTZ	FF/NC		
4357	184	915	100E5	1	2	QRTZ	FF/NC		16.5
4386	184	4416	105B	2	1	QRTZ	FF/NC		7.5
4254	184	4632	105D	1	2	QRTZ	FF/NC		1.5
4393	184	1012	105E5	3	8	QRTZ	FF/NC		
4275	184	881	105F	4	1	QRTZ	FF/NC		

2011.28	SBCM	Cat. #	Unit	Level	Qty	MTRL	DEB TYPE	PLAT	WT/g
4272	184	3171	115F	5	3	QRTZ	FF/NC		
4345	184	2840	120E	2	8	QRTZ	FF/NC		
4445	184	22	160H	2	6	QRTZ	FF/NC		
4464	184	41	165K	1	2	QRTZ	FF/NC		
4409	184	2521	170J	1	2	QRTZ	FF/NC		2
4643	184	6414	30M	1	2	QRTZ	FF/NC		2.5
4643	184	6414	30M	1	2	QRTZ	FF/NC		
4400	184	1656	55K5	2	24	QRTZ	FF/NC		
4221	184	1786	70C5	3	1	QRTZ	FF/NC		15.6
4399	184	5627	70E	5	17	QRTZ	FF/NC		
4211	184	1080	80D5	2	6	QRTZ	FF/NC		
4227	184	4687	85G	5	4	QRTZ	FF/NC		11.1
4249	184	3297	90E	1	3	QRTZ	FF/NC		2
4423	184	2210	95E	6	1	QRTZ	FF/NC		2
4246	184	3060	95E5	8	2	QRTZ	FF/NC		
4393	184	1012	105E5	3	3	QRTZ	NC	MFP	
4445	184	22	160H	2	1	QRTZ	NC	MFP	
4357	184	915	100E5	1	4	QRTZ	NC	PA	
4393	184	1012	105E5	3	2	QRTZ	NC	PA	
4272	184	3171	115F	5	1	QRTZ	NC	PA	16.6
4345	184	2840	120E	2	2	QRTZ	NC	PA	8
4400	184	1656	55K5	2	9	QRTZ	NC	PA	195

2011.28	SBCM	Cat. #	Unit	Level	Qty	MTRL	DEB TYPE	PLAT	WT/g
4399	184	5627	70E	5	8	QRTZ	NC	PA	
4322	184	2685	70E5	5	2	QRTZ	NC	PA	5
4234	184	4593	75C	1	1	QRTZ	NC	PA	
4250	184	6237	90H5	5	2	QRTZ	NC	PA	4
4357	184	915	100E5	1	5	QRTZ	NC	SFP	
4393	184	1012	105E5	3	3	QRTZ	NC	SFP	
4272	184	3171	115F	5	2	QRTZ	NC	SFP	
4445	184	22	160H	2	7	QRTZ	NC	SFP	
4400	184	1656	55K5	2	14	QRTZ	NC	SFP	
4221	184	1786	70C5	3	3	QRTZ	NC	SFP	
4399	184	5627	70E	5	13	QRTZ	NC	SFP	
4211	184	1080	80D5	2	4	QRTZ	NC	SFP	
4423	184	2210	95E	6	1	QRTZ	NC	SFP	
4246	184	3060	95E5	8	3	QRTZ	NC	SFP	5.5
4234	184	4593	75C	1	1	QRTZ	NC	MFP	
4223	184	3361	40K	4	2	QRTZ	NC/ALT	SFP	
4234	184	4593	75C	1	2	QRTZ	NC/ALT	SFP	25.1
4341	184	1244	110D	2	1	QRTZ	NC/ALT		0.4
4445	184	22	160H	2	2	QRTZ	NC/ALT		
4464	184	41	165K	1	1	QRTZ	NC/ALT		31.1
4223	184	3361	40K	4	1	QRTZ	NC/ALT		25.3
4348	184	1935	110H	4	2	QRTZ	NC/UNDI		1

2011.28	SBCM	Cat. #	Unit	Level	Qty	MTRL	DEB TYPE	PLAT	WT/g
4400	184	1656	55K5	2	1	QRTZ	NC/UNDI		
4393	184	1012	105E5	3	1	QRTZ	PC	NP	
4445	184	22	160H	2	1	QRTZ	PC	NP	
4400	184	1656	55K5	2	3	QRTZ	PC	NP	
4221	184	1786	70C5	3	2	QRTZ	PC	NP	
4240	184	4399	75C	2	4	QRTZ	PC	NP	3
4260	184	6231	120D5	2	1	QRTZ	PC	PA	8
4345	184	2840	120E	2	1	QRTZ	PC	SFP	
4400	184	1656	55K5	2	1	QRTZ	PC	SFP	
4357	184	915	100E5	1	1	QRTZ	SHT/C		
4345	184	2840	120E	2	2	QRTZ	SHT/C		
4485	184	2546	120E5	2	1	QRTZ	SHT/C		4
4400	184	1656	55K5	2	2	QRTZ	SHT/C		
4399	184	5627	70E	5	5	QRTZ	SHT/C		
4328	184	388	70J5	1	1	QRTZ	SHT/C		3
4308	184	259	90F	1	2	QRTZ	SHT/C		2
4357	184	915	100E5	1	8	QRTZ	SHT/NC		
4393	184	1012	105E5	3	19	QRTZ	SHT/NC		
4272	184	3171	115F	5	3	QRTZ	SHT/NC		
4345	184	2840	120E	2	10	QRTZ	SHT/NC		
4485	184	2546	120E5	2	4	QRTZ	SHT/NC		
4445	184	22	160H	2	7	QRTZ	SHT/NC		6

2011.28	SBCM	Cat. #	Unit	Level	Qty	MTRL	DEB TYPE	PLAT	WT/g
4464	184	41	165K	1	6	QRTZ	SHT/NC		
4223	184	3361	40K	4	1	QRTZ	SHT/NC		
4400	184	1656	55K5	2	24	QRTZ	SHT/NC		
4399	184	5627	70E	5	37	QRTZ	SHT/NC		
4322	184	2685	70E5	5	1	QRTZ	SHT/NC		
4234	184	4593	75C	1	5	QRTZ	SHT/NC		
4211	184	1080	80D5	2	8	QRTZ	SHT/NC		12
4227	184	4687	85G	5	8	QRTZ	SHT/NC		
4250	184	6237	90H5	5	1	QRTZ	SHT/NC		
Quartz Debitage Notation Key									
2011.28: Pechanga Cultural Resource catalogue number									
SBCM: San Bernardino Catalogue collection number									
CAT #: Catalog number									
UNIT: Location									
	According to excavation map								
	TEST:Test Hole								
LEVEL: Depth									
	SURF: Surface								
	Levels 1-10 (Increments of 6 inches each level)								
	N/A: Not applicable								
QTY: Quantity									

APPENDIX H

MTRL: Material					
	QRTZ: Quartz				
DEB TYPE: Debitage Type					
	BF: EPERC: Biface early percussion flake				
	BF/EDGE: Biface edge modified flake				
	BF/EPRES: Biface early pressure flake				
	BF/LPERC: Biface late percussion flake				
	BF/MARG: Biface margin removal flake				
	CC: Completely Cortical				
	CC/outré: Completely cortical outré passé				
	FF/C: Flake fragment cortical				
	FF/NC: Flake Fragment no cortex				
	NC: No Cortex				
	NC/ALT: No Cortex alternate flake				
	NC/BULB: No Cortex bulb removal flake				
	NC/EDGE: No cortex edge modified flake				
	NC/MARG: No Cortex margin removal flake				
	NC/UNDI: No Cortex undulation removal flake				
	PC: Partially Cortical				
	PC/ALT: Partically cortical alternate flake				
	PC/EDGE: Partially cortical edge modified flake				
	PC/MARG: Partially cortical margin removal flake				
	SHT: Shatter				

	SHT/C: Shatter Cortical				
	SHT/NC: Shatter No Cortex				
PLAT: Platform					
	PA: Platform absent				
	NP: Natural Platform				
	MFP: Multi-faceted platform				
	SFP: Single faceted platform				
WT/g: Weight measured in grams					

APPENDIX I

RYOLITE, SANTIGO PEAK METAVOLANIC, AND WONDERSTONE DEBITAGE

Appendix I: Ryolite, Santigo Peak Metavolcanic, and Wonderstone Debitage									
2011.28	**SBCM**	**Cat. #**	**Unit**	**Level**	**Qty**	**MTRL**	**DEB TYPE**	**PLAT**	**WT/g**
5911	184	1476	40K	3	1	RYLT	SHT		1.1
7653	184	2050	55I	1	1	RYLT	CC	PA	3.5
7609	184	3197	75C5	6	1	SPMV	BF/EDGE		0.4
5194	184	3067	100D5	1	1	SPMV	BF/EPERC		1.2
5204	184	3600	175H5	3	1	SPMV	BF/EPERC		3.7
5227	184	6195	65I	1	2	SPMV	BF/EPERC		1.7
5221	184	4992	110E5	7	1	SPMV	BF/LPRC		0.5
5183	184	2299	20J5	1	1	SPMV	BF/MARG		1.1
5188	184	6501	35H5	1	1	SPMV	BF/MARG		0.7
5179	184	4891	100D	8	1	SPMV	CC	NP	6.8
5178	184	4956	110E5	8	1	SPMV	NC	SFP	1
5181	184	4890	115E	6	1	SPMV	NC	PA	0.5
5197	184	400	115F	1	1	SPMV	NC	MFP	0.9
5170	184	6233	120D5	2	1	SPMV	NC	SFP	4.7
5205	184	3254	175H5	1	1	SPMV	NC	SFP	1
5203	184	6351	40H5	1	1	SPMV	NC	PA	0.5
5175	184	2812	55I5	5	2	SPMV	NC	MFP	2
5174	184	599	80E	3	1	SPMV	NC	PA	0.3
5185	184	3290	95E	5	1	SPMV	NC	SFP	0.3
5213	184	6411	30M	1	1	SPMV	NC/ALT		2.3
5189	184	5069	110G	3	1	SPMV	PC	NP	3.3

2011.28	SBCM	Cat. #	Unit	Level	Qty	MTRL	DEB TYPE	PLAT	WT/g
5193	184	1922	110H5	5	1	SPMV	PC	NP	2.6
5172	184	2449	120D	6	1	SPMV	PC	PA	0.7
5182	184	6451	160J	1	1	SPMV	PC	NP	3.9
5190	184	2240	170H	2	1	SPMV	PC	PA	0.3
5201	184	1188	45I	4	1	SPMV	PC	SFP	2.5
5200	184	4546	90G	4	1	SPMV	PC	NP	3.4
5215	184	2314	95D	2	1	SPMV	PC	PA	6.3
5199	184	1974	95E	3	3	SPMV	PC	PA	2.7
5183	184	5209	175I5	1	1	SPMV	PC/NP		0.9
5196	184	400	115F	1	1	SPMV	SHT		0.1
5173	184	2449	120D	6	1	SPMV	SHT		1.1
5171	184	6233	120D5	2	1	SPMV	SHT		0.4
5180	184	5567	35I	4	2	SPMV	SHT		6.8
5198	184	1619	55J	2	1	SPMV	SHT	N/A	1.1
5207	184	3125	85F	5	1	SPMV	SHT		0.7
5186	184	6436	85G	3	1	SPMV	SHT		0.4
5195	184	3236	95E	5	1	SPMV	SHT		2.2
5184	184	3290	95E	5	1	SPMV	SHT		0.2
5177	184	4956	110E5	8	1	SPMV	SHT/C		6.8
5176	184	2983	175I	1	2	SPMV	SHT/C		4.6
5214	184	6411	30M	1	1	SPMV	SHT/C		7.1
5208	184	5053	110G	1	1	SPMV	SHT/NC		0.9

2011.28	SBCM	Cat. #	Unit	Level	Qty	MTRL	DEB TYPE	PLAT	WT/g
5202	184	5953	120D	1	1	SPMV	SHT/NC		0.5
5206	184	2564	160H	1	1	SPMV	SHT/NC		3.4
5187	184	6501	35H5	1	1	SPMV	SHT/NC		3.2
5191	184	2423	60J5	5	1	SPMV	SHT/NC		0.8
5226	184	6195	65I	1	1	SPMV	SHT/NC		1.2
5192	184	5607	75J	1	1	SPMV	SHT/NC		4.4
8373	184	4378	55J5	4	3	WOND	BF/EDGE		11.1
8372	184	181	100F	1	1	WOND	BF/LPERC		0.4
5498	184	4086	105F5	6	1	WOND	BIF/FRAG		3.6
8369	184	151	165I5	1	2	WOND	FF/NC		
8367	184	524	55I	4	2	WOND	FF/NC		4.9
6249	184	372	60J5	2	1	WOND	FF/NC		0.6
8370	184	4397	75C	2	2	WOND	FF/NC		3.5
8369	184	151	165I5	1	2	WOND	NC	NP	1.9
8366	184	1510	40K	1	4	WOND	NC	SFP	12.5
6248	184	372	60J5	2	1	WOND	NC	SFP	0.5
8368	184	262	120E	3	1	WOND	PC	NP	0.2
8366	184	1510	40K	1	1	WOND	PC	NP	
8374	184	558	165H5	1	2	WOND	PC/ALT		3.4
8366	184	1510	40K	1	1	WOND	SHT/C		
8367	184	524	55I	4	1	WOND	SHT/C		
6247	184	372	60J5	2	1	WOND	SHT/NC		0.8

APPENDIX I

RYLT, SPMV and WOND Debitage Notation Key					
2011.28: Pechanga Cultural Resource catalogue number					
SBCM: San Bernardino Catalogue collection number					
CAT #: Catalog number					
UNIT: Location					
	According to excavation map				
LEVEL: Depth					
	SURF: Surface				
	Levels 1-10 (Increments of 6 inches each level)				
QTY: Quantity					
MTRL: Material					
	RYLT: Ryolite				
	SPMV: Santigo Peck Metavolanic				
	WOND: Wonderstone				
DEB TYPE: Debitage Type					
	BF: EPERC: Biface early percussion flake				
	BF/EDGE: Biface edge modified flake				
	BF/EPRES: Biface early pressure flake				
	BF/LPERC: Biface late percussion flake				
	BF/MARG: Biface margin removal flake				
	CC: Completely Cortical				
	CC/outré: Completely cortical outré passé				
	FF/C: Flake fragment cortical				

	FF/NC: Flake Fragment no cortex				
	NC: No Cortex				
	NC/ALT: No Cortex alternate flake				
	NC/BULB: No Cortex bulb removal flake				
	NC/EDGE: No cortex edge modified flake				
	NC/MARG: No Cortex margin removal flake				
	NC/UNDI: No Cortex undulation removal flake				
	PC: Partially Cortical				
	PC/ALT: Partically cortical alternate flake				
	PC/EDGE: Partially cortical edge modified flake				
	PC/MARG: Partially cortical margin removal flake				
	SHT: Shatter				
	SHT/C: Shatter Cortical				
	SHT/NC: Shatter No Cortex				
PLAT: Platform					
	PA: Platform absent				
	NP: Natural Platform				
	MFP: Multi-faceted platform				
	SFP: Single faceted platform				
WT/g: Weight measured in grams					

APPENDIX J

BIFACES

Appendix J: Bifaces														
2011.3	SBCM	Cat #	Unit	Level	Qty	MTRL	COND	PORT	FLMD	L/MM	W/MM	T/MM	W/g	Comments
6545	184	UNKN	UNKN	UNKN	1	BLST	FRAG	ENSF	BOTH	15	15	2	1	
6518	184	5589	115B	3,4	1	BSLT	NRCP	N/A	BOTH	40.5	30.6	9	18	
6426	184	2207	120D	5	1	BSLT	WHLE	N/A	PRCS	27	17	5	2	PREFORM
6454	184	2966	120G	3	1	BSLT	FRAG	N/A	PERC	22	20	9	4	
6386	184	1025	125D	3	1	BSLT	WHLE	N/A	BOTH	22.9	14.1	7.2	1.6	
6516	184	5519	160I5	2	1	BSLT	FRAG	ENSF	PRES	15.6	13.8	4.1	0.9	
6360	184	241	170J5	1	1	BSLT	FRAG	MEDF	PERC	35	14	15	8	
6503	184	4731	20J5	2	1	BSLT	FRAG	ENSF	BOTH	30	20	8	4	
6532	184	6058	55H5	3	1	BSLT	WHLE	N/A	BOTH	29	15.9	5.2	2.7	
6400	184	1590	55K5	1	1	BSLT	FRAG	N/A	BOTH	38	42	12	8	
6362	184	391	70J5	1	1	BSLT	NRCP	N/A	BOTH	27	20	10	4.1	
6495	184	4405	75C	2	1	BSLT	FRAG	N/A	BOTH	25	18	4	3	
6456	184	2994	85D	5	1	BSLT	WHLE	N/A	BOTH	29	20	6	4	
6415	184	2016	90E	4	2	BSLT	FRAG	N/A	BOTH	27	21	10	6	
6416	184	2016	90E	4	2	BSLT	FRAG	N/A	BOTH	21	20	5	4	

2011.3	SBCM	Cat #	Unit	Level	Qty	MTRL	COND	PORT	FLMD	L/MM	W/MM	T/MM	W/g	Comments
6441	184	2697	100D	1	1	CCQZ	FRAG	ENSF	BOTH	14	14	6	1	
6383	184	964	100E	2	1	CCQZ	FRAG	ENSF	BOTH	11	15	4	0.5	EAR
6389	184	1040	100E5	3	1	CCQZ	FRAG	N/A	BOTH	19	11	6	2	
6378	184	856	100F5	7	1	CCQZ	NRCP	N/A	BOTH	21.5	14.2	7.6	1.6	
6384	184	977	105D5	2	1	CCQZ	FRAG	N/A	BOTH	12.2	28.6	7.8	2.6	
6377	184	824	105E5	1	1	CCQZ	FRAG	ENSF	BOTH	11	10	2	0.4	EAR
6500	184	4580	105E5	5	1	CCQZ	FRAG	ENSF	BOTH	17	11	4	0.8	
6381	184	901	105F5	3	1	CCQZ	FRAG	N/A	BOTH	19	15	6	3	tabular
6382	184	905	105F5	3	1	CCQZ	NRCP	N/A	BOTH	18.6	17.2	7.3	3.2	
6191	184	4212	110D	2	1	CCQZ	FRAG	MEDF	BOTH	15	15	10	2	
6455	184	2990	110D5	5	1	CCQZ	FRAG	MEDF	BOTH	14	13	5	1	
6474	184	3550	110E	1	1	CCQZ	FRAG	MEDF	BOTH	23	15	7	1	
6364	184	440	110E	3	1	CCQZ	FRAG	ENSF	BOTH	16	15	5	2	Ear/trug
6367	184	589	110E5	2	1	CCQZ	FRAG	ENSF	BOTH	22.9	19.2	8.5	3.2	
6457	184	3001	110I5	4	1	CCQZ	WHLE	N/A	BOTH	21	23	6	2	
6489	184	3987	115-E	3	1	CCQZ	FRAG	ENSF	BOTH	15	24	6	1	

2011.3	SBCM	Cat #	Unit	Level	Qty	MTRL	COND	PORT	FLMD	L/MM	W/MM	T/MM	W/g	Comments
6363	184	404	115F	1	1	CCQZ	FRAG	ENSF	PRES	17.8	13.9	4.8	0.6	
6422	184	2165	115F	1	1	CCQZ	FRAG	N/A	BOTH	11	15	5	0.8	EAR
6414	184	1987	120F	5	1	CCQZ	FRAG	ENSF	BOTH	21	15	5	1	
6376	184	744	125D5	1	1	CCQZ	WHLE	N/A	BOTH	24	18	8	2	
6404	184	1726	140I	2	1	CCQZ	FRAG	MEDF	BOTH	28	14	5	1.5	
6405	184	1726	140I	2	1	CCQZ	FRAG	MEDF	BOTH	10	22	8	1	
6434	184	2473	160H5	1	1	CCQZ	FRAG	N/A	BOTH	22	10	5	0.8	
6509	184	4998	160J5	3	1	CCQZ	FRAG	N/A	BOTH	24	10	5	1	
6387	184	1036	160K	2	1	CCQZ	FRAG	ENSF	BOTH	20	17	7	1.5	
6472	184	3484	165H	3	1	CCQZ	WHLE	N/A	BOTH	17.7	12.7	4.4	1	
6420	184	2103	170H	1	1	CCQZ	FRAG	ENSF	BOTH	12	34	10	4	
6419	184	2103	170H	1	1	CCQZ	FRAG	N/A	BOTH	15	10	4	0.5	
6428	184	2239	170H	2	1	CCQZ	FRAG	N/A	BOTH	18	14	4	2	
6453	184	2894	170J	2	1	CCQZ	FRAG	N/A	BOTH	15	5	4	0.8	
6517	184	5547	175I5	2	1	CCQZ	FRAG	N/A	PERC	26	13	8	2	
6467	184	3225	175J	2	1	CCQZ	FRAG	ENSF	BOTH	33	23	7	6	

2011.3	SBCM	Cat #	Unit	Level	Qty	MTRL	COND	PORT	FLMD	L/MM	W/MM	T/MM	W/g	Comments
6504	184	4733	20J5	2	1	CCQZ	FRAG	ENSF	BOTH	19	10	5	0.8	
6393	184	1176	45I	4	1	CCQZ	FRAG	ENSF	BOTH	25	15	6	2	
6425	184	2176	55H5	2	1	CCQZ	FRAG	ENSF	BOTH	29	23	10	6	
6423	184	2176	55H5	2	1	CCQZ	FRAG	MEDF	BOTH	20	12	10	1	
6424	184	2176	55H5	2	1	CCQZ	FRAG	MEDF	BOTH	25	15	8	2	
6365	184	524	55I	4	1	CCQZ	FRAG	N/A	BOTH	17	13	3	1	
6677	184	525	55I	4	1	CCQZ	NRCP	N/A	PRES	22	10	5	1	Drill
6436	184	2483	55I	4	1	CCQZ	WHLE	N/A	BOTH	22	20	8	4	
6442	184	2747	55I5	2	1	CCQZ	FRAG	ENSF	BOTH	11	16	5	0.5	EAR/TUNG
6388	181	1037	55I5	2	1	CCQZ	FRAG	ENSF	PRES	17.1	18.7	3.2	1.1	
6401	184	1621	55J	2	1	CCQZ	FRAG	ENSF	BOTH	24.2	23.8	7.6	4.8	
6395	184	1390	55J5	3	1	CCQZ	NRCP	N/A	BOTH	28	13	7	2	
6493	184	4389	55J5	4	1	CCQZ	NRCP	N/A	BOTH	15	14	5	2	
6397	184	1408	55K	3	1	CCQZ	FRAG	ENSF	BOTH	25	22	9	4	
6396	184	1408	55K	3	1	CCQZ	FRAG	N/A	BOTH	25	15	10	1	
6399	184	1589	55K5	1	1	CCQZ	FRAG	ENSF	BOTH	14	17	6	1	

2011.3	SBCM	Cat #	Unit	Level	Qty	MTRL	COND	PORT	FLMD	L/MM	W/MM	T/MM	W/g	Comments
6417	184	2028	60H5	4	1	CCQZ	FRAG	MEDF	BOTH	22	14	5	2	
6418	184	2028	60H5	4	1	CCQZ	FRAG	MEDF	BOTH	33	18	8	6	
6479	184	3855	70C	2	1	CCQZ	FRAG	MEDF	BOTH	20	13	5	2	
6530	184	5951	70C	2	1	CCQZ	FRAG	N/A	BOTH	27	26	14	8	exhausted
6487	184	3905	70C5	2	1	CCQZ	FRAG	ENSF	PRES	10.9	19.1	4.1	0.8	
6485	184	3900	70C5	2	1	CCQZ	FRAG	N/A	BOTH	19	14	4	0.8	
6486	184	3900	70C5	2	1	CCQZ	FRAG	N/A	BOTH	24	14	3	1	
6521	184	5653	75E5	1	1	CCQZ	FRAG	N/A	BOTH	22	15	9	2.5	
6505	184	4763	75H5	1	1	CCQZ	FRAG	MEDF	BOTH	22	18	5	4	
6476	184	3620	80D	6	1	CCQZ	FRAG	MEDF	BOTH	16	9	6	1	
6477	184	3620	80D	6	1	CCQZ	FRAG	MEDF	BOTH	24	11	6	2	
6369	184	596	80H	3	1	CCQZ	FRAG	ENSF	BOTH	24	15	10	4	
6359	184	240	85D	3	1	CCQZ	FRAG	ENSF	PRES	26	21	7	2	
6358	184	240	85D	3	1	CCQZ	FRAG	MEDF	BOTH	34	24	11	10	
6380	184	886	85F	2	1	CCQZ	FRAG	ENSF	BOTH	15	12	3	0.5	EAR
6507	184	4806	85G	4	1	CCQZ	FRAG	ENSF	BOTH	24	11	5	2	

2011.3	SBCM	Cat #	Unit	Level	Qty	MTRL	COND	PORT	FLMD	L/MM	W/MM	T/MM	W/g	Comments
6407	184	1772	85G5	3	1	CCQZ	FRAG	ENSF	BOTH	17	15	5	2	
6408	184	1772	85G5	3	1	CCQZ	FRAG	MEDF	BOTH	25	9	7	2	
6460	184	3159	90E	3	1	CCQZ	FRAG	ENSF	BOTH	15	8	4	0.8	Ear
6498	184	4541	90G	2	1	CCQZ	FRAG	ENSF	BOTH	26	28	10	6	
6499	184	4547	90G	4	1	CCQZ	NRCP	N/A	BOTH	30	18	7	4	
6514	184	5408	90I	1	1	CCQZ	FRAG	ENSF	BOTH	18	14	4	0.8	EAR
6421	184	2127	95D5	2	1	CCQZ	FRAG	ENSF	BOTH	16	13	4	1	EAR
6413	184	1978	95E	3	1	CCQZ	FRAG	N/A	BOTH	19	11	5	1	
6469	184	3233	95E	5	1	CCQZ	FRAG	N/A	BOTH	34	15	11	6	
6538	184	6157	UNKN	UNKN	1	CCQZ	FRAG	N/A	BOTH	25.7	20.3	7.4	4.4	
6539	184	6205	UNKN	UNKN	1	CCQZ	WHLE	N/A	BOTH	29.5	22.1	3.7	1.9	
6410	184	1878	110H	3	1	MQZT	FRAG	MEDF	BOTH	36	12	9	3	
6366	184	569	165H	1	1	MQZT	FRAG	ENSF	BOTH	21	15	5	1	
6429	184	2421	60J5	5	1	MQZT	FRAG	MEDF	BOTH	17	10	5	0.8	
6501	184	4594	75C	1	1	MQZT	FRAG	ENSF	BOTH	14	20	4	4	
6529	184	5942	85E	4	1	MQZT	FRAG	ENSF	BOTH	21	20	4	3	

2011.3	SBCM	Cat #	Unit	Level	Qty	MTRL	COND	PORT	FLMD	L/MM	W/MM	T/MM	W/g	Comments
6496	184	4481	90G	1	1	MQZT	FRAG	ENSF	BOTH	32	30	10	5	
6459	184	3141	95E5	3	1	MQZT	FRAG	MEDF	BOTH	20	40	11	10	
6440	184	2583	70I	1	1	MTSD	FRAG	MEDF	BOTH	12.2	23.5	8.3	2.9	
6513	184	5399	UNKN	UNKN	1	MTSD	FRAG	ENSF	BOTH	22.4	13	5.7	1.1	
6427	184	2208	120D	5	1	MTVC	NRCP	N/A	BOTH	22	27	7	6	
6531	184	5989	70D	1	1	MTVC	FRAG	N/A	BOTH	26	18	11	6	
6473	184	3498	120G	1	1	OBSN	FRAG	ENSF	BOTH	10.2	17.8	2.6	0.8	
7906	184	3420	130E	1	1	OBSN	FRAG	ENSF	BOTH	10	15	3	1	
7907	184	3501	65E	1	1	OBSN	FRAG	ENSF	PRES	11.8	7.1	3.4	0.5	
6492	184	4272	UNKN	UNKN	1	OBSN	FRAG	N/A	BOTH	44.3	40.1	7.4	13	
4698	184	2683	100F5	5	1	QRTZ	FRAG	MEDF	BOTH	26	22	11	4	
6385	184	1012	105E5	3	1	QRTZ	FRAG	ENSF	BOTH	27	20	7	3	
6534	184	6084	110E	3	1	QRTZ	WHLE	N/A	BOTH	21.5	16.6	5.2	1.7	
6461	184	3187	110F5	4	1	QRTZ	FRAG	ENSF	BOTH	21	19	7	2	
6488	184	3986	115-E	3	1	QRTZ	FRAG	MEDF	BOTH	11	12	2	0.5	
6458	184	3025	115F	3	1	QRTZ	NRCP	N/A	BOTH	14	9	4	0.5	

2011.3	SBCM	Cat #	Unit	Level	Qty	MTRL	COND	PORT	FLMD	L/MM	W/MM	T/MM	W/g	Comments
6406	184	1739	115F5	4	1	QRTZ	FRAG	ENSF	BOTH	14	9	5	0.8	
6512	184	5325	115F5	6	1	QRTZ	FRAG	ENSF	BOTH	29	22	14	6	
6439	184	2546	120E5	2	1	QRTZ	FRAG	ENSF	BOTH	28	20	10	4	
6470	184	3332	120G	2	1	QRTZ	FRAG	ENSF	BOTH	15	11	5	2	EAR
4491	184	1071	125D	2	1	QRTZ	FRAG	MEDF	BOTH	61	18	11	11	learning
6402	184	1722	140I	2	1	QRTZ	FRAG	ENSF	BOTH	28	16	7	2.3	
6403	184	1722	140I	2	1	QRTZ	FRAG	MEDF	BOTH	37	22	9	6	
6391	184	1146	140I5	2	1	QRTZ	WHLE	N/A	BOTH	30	15	8	4	
6392	184	1149	140I5	2	1	QRTZ	WHLE	N/A	BOTH	26.6	13.7	8	2.1	
6435	184	2474	160H5	1	1	QRTZ	FRAG	MEDF	BOTH	24	18	6	3	
6533	184	6064	160I5	1	1	QRTZ	FRAG	N/A	PRES	17.5	9.5	3.8	0.3	
6508	184	4997	160J5	3	1	QRTZ	FRAG	MEDF	PRES	12.5	18.5	4.6	1.3	
6510	184	5007	160J5	3	1	QRTZ	FRAG	N/A	PRES	17	12	4	1	
6536	184	6092	160K	1	1	QRTZ	FRAG	ENSF	BOTH	23	18	6	2	
6537	184	6092	160K	1	1	QRTZ	FRAG	ENSF	BOTH	23	20	6	2	
6535	184	6092	160K	1	1	QRTZ	FRAG	N/A	BOTH	14	13	3	0.8	

2011.3	SBCM	Cat #	Unit	Level	Qty	MTRL	COND	PORT	FLMD	L/MM	W/MM	T/MM	W/g	Comments
6357	184	156	165I5	1	1	QRTZ	FRAG	N/A	BOTH	16.6	14.3	5.5	1.5	
6353	184	41	165K	1	1	QRTZ	FRAG	MEDF	BOTH	30	28	10	10	
6411	184	1882	170H5	1	1	QRTZ	FRAG	N/A	BOTH	25	16	8	2	
6412	184	1882	170H5	1	1	QRTZ	FRAG	N/A	BOTH	15	7	4	1	
6432	184	2432	170J	1	1	QRTZ	FRAG	ENSF	BOTH	16	10	4	1	
6433	184	2432	170J	1	1	QRTZ	FRAG	ENSF	BOTH	44	25	13	12	
6431	184	2432	170J	1	1	QRTZ	FRAG	ENSF	PRES	12	10	3	0.5	
6430	184	2432	170J	1	1	QRTZ	FRAG	N/A	PRES	14	15	7	1	
6448	184	2853	170J	2	1	QRTZ	FRAG	ENSF	BOTH	26	18	7	2	
6447	184	2853	170J	2	1	QRTZ	FRAG	MEDF	PRES	13	10	3	0.5	
6443	184	2836	175H	1	1	QRTZ	FRAG	N/A	BOTH	27	16	6	2	
6444	184	2836	175H	1	1	QRTZ	FRAG	N/A	BOTH	30	14	9	4	
6445	184	2836	175H	1	1	QRTZ	FRAG	N/A	BOTH	27	12	14	4	
6446	184	2836	175H	1	1	QRTZ	FRAG	N/A	BOTH	20	15	6	2	
6449	184	2882	175H	1	1	QRTZ	FRAG	N/A	BOTH	22	19	7	2	
6450	184	2882	175H	1	1	QRTZ	FRAG	N/A	BOTH	17	16	8	2	

2011.3	SBCM	Cat #	Unit	Level	Qty	MTRL	COND	PORT	FLMD	L/MM	W/MM	T/MM	W/g	Comments
6451	184	2882	175H	1	1	QRTZ	FRAG	N/A	BOTH	35	15	8	4	
6452	184	2882	175H	1	1	QRTZ	FRAG	N/A	BOTH	19	15	7	2	
6462	184	3222	175J	2	1	QRTZ	FRAG	ENSF	BOTH	20	11	6	1	EAR
6463	184	3222	175J	2	1	QRTZ	FRAG	MEDF	BOTH	25	21	11	4	
6464	184	3222	175J	2	1	QRTZ	FRAG	MEDF	BOTH	24	17	7	4	
6465	184	3222	175J	2	1	QRTZ	FRAG	MEDF	BOTH	25	15	8	2	
6466	184	3222	175J	2	1	QRTZ	FRAG	MEDF	BOTH	28	17	7	4	
6468	184	3226	175J	2	1	QRTZ	WHLE	N/A	BOTH	38.8	25.3	6	6.7	
6544	184	6491	35H5	1	1	QRTZ	FRAG	N/A	BOTH	15	22	6	2	
6471	184	3363	40K	4	1	QRTZ	FRAG	N/A	BOTH	28.3	9.6	4.5	1.5	
6372	184	653	55I	3	1	QRTZ	FRAG	N/A	BOTH	30	20	8	4	
6373	184	653	55I	3	1	QRTZ	FRAG	N/A	BOTH	20	13	9	2	
6494	184	4394	55J5	4	1	QRTZ	FRAG	N/A	BOTH	16	13	3	2	
6361	184	376	60J5	2	1	QRTZ	FRAG	MEDF	BOTH	24.1	7.2	5.1	0.9	
6541	184	6316	65I	4	1	QRTZ	FRAG	N/A	BOTH	23	15	10	4	
6542	184	6316	65I	4	1	QRTZ	FRAG	N/A	BOTH	27	16	7	2	

2011.3	SBCM	Cat #	Unit	Level	Qty	MTRL	COND	PORT	FLMD	L/MM	W/MM	T/MM	W/g	Comments
6368	184	595	70C	2	1	QRTZ	FRAG	ENSF	BOTH	27	15	5	2	
6481	184	3899	70C5	2	1	QRTZ	FRAG	MEDF	BOTH	34	15	10	4	
6482	184	3899	70C5	2	1	QRTZ	FRAG	MEDF	BOTH	34	12	8	6	
6484	184	3899	70C5	2	1	QRTZ	FRAG	MEDF	BOTH	18	11	5	1	EAR
6483	184	3899	70C5	2	1	QRTZ	FRAG	MEDF	PRES	14	13	5	0.5	EAR
6409	184	1786	70C5	3	1	QRTZ	FRAG	ENSF	BOTH	20	10	10	2	
6374	184	695	70E5	1	1	QRTZ	FRAG	ENSF	BOTH	24	15	6	2	
6375	184	695	70E5	1	1	QRTZ	FRAG	ENSF	BOTH	22	16	7	2	
6438	184	2513	70J5	1	1	QRTZ	FRAG	ENSF	BOTH	13.4	16	4.8	1	
6437	184	2512	70J5	1	1	QRTZ	NRCP	N/A	BOTH	22	11.7	7.3	2.2	
6351	184	34	70J5	2	1	QRTZ	FRAG	N/A	BOTH	17.4	11.2	4.8	1	
6350	184	33	70J5	2	1	QRTZ	NRCP	N/A	BOTH	24.2	14.9	7	2.4	
6352	184	35	70J5	2	1	QRTZ	WHLE	N/A	BOTH	16	11	3	0.8	
6475	184	3564	75D	1	1	QRTZ	FRAG	MEDF	BOTH	30	15	6	3	
6506	184	4767	75H5	1	1	QRTZ	FRAG	ENSF	BOTH	20.2	14.7	7.6	2.1	
6520	184	5612	75J	1	1	QRTZ	FRAG	N/A	BOTH	18	9.6	6.7	1.2	

2011.3	SBCM	Cat #	Unit	Level	Qty	MTRL	COND	PORT	FLMD	L/MM	W/MM	T/MM	W/g	Comments
6519	184	5603	75J	1	1	QRTZ	FRAG	N/A	PRES	11.9	18.7	6.8	1.9	
6478	184	3841	80D	2	1	QRTZ	NRCP	N/A	BOTH	16.5	16.4	5.3	1.5	
4540	184	5304	80E	2	1	QRTZ	FRAG	ENSF	BOTH	22	16	7	2.7	
6370	184	603	80E	3	1	QRTZ	FRAG	MEDF	BOTH	42	22	10	12	
6371	184	603	80E	3	1	QRTZ	FRAG	MEDF	BOTH	49	25	15	24	
6490	184	4081	80E	4	1	QRTZ	FRAG	ENSF	BOTH	25	15	5	2	
6511	184	5028	80E5	3	1	QRTZ	NRCP	N/A	PRES	15.9	10.7	3.9	0.9	
6356	184	117	85D5	UNKN	1	QRTZ	FRAG	ENSF	BOTH	13.4	7.6	3.3	0.3	
6379	184	883	85F	2	1	QRTZ	FRAG	ENSF	BOTH	18	15	5	1	
6527	184	5894	85F5	3	1	QRTZ	NRCP	N/A	BOTH	20	18	5	2	
6540	184	6284	85F5	6	1	QRTZ	FRAG	N/A	BOTH	21.1	10.3	4.8	0.9	
6502	184	4694	85G	5	1	QRTZ	FRAG	N/A	BOTH	21	11	5	1	
6354	184	67	90D5	4	1	QRTZ	FRAG	ENSF	PRES	19	8	6	0.8	
6355	184	67	90D5	4	1	QRTZ	FRAG	ENSF	PRES	17	15	6	2	EAR
4610	184	4804	90F5	2	1	QRTZ	FRAG	ENSF	BOTH	28	26	8	8	
6497	184	4482	90G	1	1	QRTZ	WHLE	N/A	BOTH	26.6	22.9	6.2	3.7	

2011.3	SBCM	Cat #	Unit	Level	Qty	MTRL	COND	PORT	FLMD	L/MM	W/MM	T/MM	W/g	Comments
4674	184	4543	90G	4	1	QRTZ	FRAG	ENSF	BOTH	20.1	20	7	2	
6398	184	1497	95G5	3	1	QRTZ	WHLE	N/A	BOTH	23.6	16.3	7.4	2.5	
241	184	5335	95I	3	1	QRTZ	FRAG	ENSF	BOTH	11	7	2	0.4	
6522	184	5776	95I5	3	1	QRTZ	NRCP	N/A	BOTH	14.9	16.8	6.5	1.8	
6523	184	5777	95I5	3	1	QRTZ	NRCP	N/A	BOTH	25.5	17.8	7.1	3	
6525	184	5815	UNKN	2	1	QRTZ	FRAG	ENSF	BOTH	19	13	5	1	EAR
6526	184	5815	UNKN	2	1	QRTZ	FRAG	ENSF	BOTH	25	12	6	1	EAR
6524	184	5815	UNKN	2	1	QRTZ	NRCP	N/A	PRES	12	10	3	0.5	
6394	184	1258	UNKN	UNKN	1	QRTZ	FRAG	ENSF	BOTH	14.5	12.5	2	0.4	
6390	184	1139	UNKN	UNKN	1	QRTZ	FRAG	MEDF	BOTH	25	10	6	2	
6480	184	3875	UNKN	UNKN	1	QRTZ	FRAG	N/A	BOTH	18.6	18.2	6.9	2.8	
6543	184	6366	UNKN	UNKN	1	QRTZ	FRAG	N/A	BOTH	12.7	16.5	4.9	1.1	
6528	184	5910	UNKN	UNKN	1	QRTZ	NRCP	N/A	PRES	21	15	8	2	
6515	184	5478	UNKN	UNKN	1	QRTZ	WHLE	N/A	PRES	20.9	7.5	5.2	1.2	
6546	184	6105	65I	2	1	WOND	FRAG	N/A	BOTH	33	18	13	2.5	

Biface Notation Key									
2011.28: Pechanga Cultural Resource catalogue number									
SBCM: San Bernardino Catalogue collection number									
CAT #: Catalog number									
UNIT: Location									
	According to excavation map								
LEVEL: Depth									
	SURF: Surface								
	Levels 1-10 (Increments of 6 inches each level)								
QTY: Quantity									
MTRL: Material									
	BSLT: Basalt								
	CCQZ: Cryptocrystalline quartz								
	MTVC: Metavolcanic								
	MTSD: Metasedimentry								
	MTQZ: Metaquartzite								
	OBSN: Obsidian								

	QRTZ: Quartz								
COND: Condition									
	WHLE: Whole								
	FRAG: Fragment								
	NRCP: Nearly Complete								
PORT: Portion									
	MEDF: Medial Section Fragment								
	ENSF: End Section Fragment								
	N/A: Not Applicable								
FLMD: Flaking Method									
	PERC: Percussion								
	PRES: Pressure								
	BOTH: Both Percussion and Pressure								
L/mm: Length measured in mm from end to edge									
W/mm: Width measured in mm from edge to edge									
T/mm: Thickness measured in mm from top to bottom									
WT/g: Weight measured in grams									

Comments:									
	Additional location								
	Other number								
	learning: evidence of a learning projectile point/ crude/ developing point								
	Tabular								
	Ear								
	Exhausted								

APPENDIX K

PROJECTILE POINTS

Appendix K:Projectile Points

2011.3	SBCM	Cat #	Unit	Level	Qty	MTRL	COND	FLMD	FKPT	SHPE	L/MM	W/MM	T/MM	W/g	Comments
6136	184	5469	UNKN	UNKN	1	MTVC	NRCP	BOTH	RNDM	ESCB	38.7	34	7.8	12.6	
6134	184	5470	UNKN	UNKN	1	MTVC	NRCP	BOTH	RNDM	ESCB	29.9	29.6	8.7	10	
6135	184	5453	UNKN	UNKN	1	CCQZ	NRCP	BOTH	RNDM	ESSB	25.6	20.6	5.3	3.6	
6094	184	2931	100D5	3	1	QRTZ	WHLE	BOTH	RNDM	INDT	14	13	4	0.6	
6074	184	1045	100E	3	1	QRTZ	WHLE	BOTH	RNDM	INDT	17.8	12.7	3.2	0.7	
6119	184	876	100E	10,11	1	QRTZ	FRAG	BOTH	RNDM	INDT	10.7	8.5	3	0.01	
6121	184	1856	105E	1	1	QRTZ	FRAG	BOTH	RNDM	INDT	16.4	11.2	3	0.7	
6112	184	1014	105E	3	1	CCQZ	FRAG	BOTH	RNDM	INDT	21.6	18.9	7.9	1.4	
6113	184	5284	120F	1	1	CCQZ	FRAG	BOTH	RNDM	INDT	13.3	13.1	2.1	0.6	
6115	184	3327	120G	2	1	WOND	FRAG	BOTH	RNDM	INDT	20	10.2	5.3	2.5	
6122	184	1162	160J5	2	1	QRTZ	FRAG	BOTH	RNDM	INDT	10.8	18.1	3.5	0.7	
6106	184	4566	20G5	2	1	QRTZ	FRAG	BOTH	RNDM	INDT	18.8	6.4	2.1	0.4	
6062	184	2939	34F4	UNKN	1	CCQZ	NRCP	BOTH	RNDM	INDT	19.3	13	3.9	0.8	
6101	184	6513	35H5	1	1	CCQZ	NRCP	BOTH	RNDM	INDT	14.6	11.1	2.2	0.5	
6050	184	6348	40H5	1	1	MTVC	NRCP	BOTH	RNDM	INDT	22	19	5	1.8	

2011.3	SBCM	Cat #	Unit	Level	Qty	MTRL	COND	FLMD	FKPT	SHPE	L/MM	W/MM	T/MM	W/g	Comments
6059	184	2025	60H5	4	1	BSLT	NRCP	BOTH	RNDM	INDT	15.2	9.8	2.6	0.5	
6109	184	395	70J5	1	1	CCQZ	FRAG	BOTH	RNDM	INDT	10.2	5.7	3.8	0.6	
6065	184	4761	75H5	1	1	CCQZ	NRCP	BOTH	RNDM	INDT	18	13.5	2.9	0.8	
6138	184	1600	85G5	2	1	CCQZ	NRCP	BOTH	RNDM	INDT	20.5	15	5	1.5	
6055	184	3541	95E	1	1	QRTZ	NRCP	BOTH	RNDM	INDT	22.1	15.2	4.7	1.6	
6129	184	3293	95E	5	1	QRTZ	NRCP	BOTH	RNDM	INDT	17.3	9	4.7	1	
6053	184	5375	UNKN	3,4	1	BSLT	NRCP	BOTH	RNDM	INDT	27.8	18.1	5.2	3	
6104	184	5791	UNKN	UNKN	1	BSLT	NRCP	BOTH	RNDM	INDT	31	17	6	1.5	
6125	184	4193	UNKN	UNKN	1	CCQZ	FRAG	BOTH	TVPL	INDT	35.8	33.5	7.3	10.2	SPEAR
6137	184	3723	UNKN	UNKN	1	OBSN	FRAG	BOTH	RNDM	INDT	25	24	8	3.8	
6123	184	231	100D	5	1	QRTZ	FRAG	PRES	RNDM	INDT	10.9	8	2.6	0.1	
6079	184	4894	100D	8	1	CCQZ	FRAG	PRES	RNDM	INDT	18	13	4	0.9	
6141	184	4581	105E	5	1	QRTZ	FRAG	PRES	RNDM	INDT	10	5	2	0.3	
6099	184	5732	1.10E+07	2	1	CCQZ	FRAG	PRES	RNDM	INDT	10.7	10	3	0.3	
6107	184	4952	1.10E+07	8	1	QRTZ	FRAG	PRES	RNDM	INDT	9.5	10.3	3	0.3	
6142	184	6245	110I5	3	1	QRTZ	FRAG	PRES	RNDM	INDT	17	8	3	0.5	

2011.3	SBCM	Cat #	Unit	Level	Qty	MTRL	COND	FLMD	FKPT	SHPE	L/MM	W/MM	T/MM	W/g	Comments
6051	184	2562	160H	1	1	QRTZ	NRCP	PRES	RNDM	INDT	12.6	10.9	3	0.5	
6117	184	5839	160K	UNKN	1	QRTZ	FRAG	PRES	RNDM	INDT	9	7	3	0.1	
6097	184	555	165H5	1	1	QRTZ	FRAG	PRES	RNDM	INDT	12.5	10.6	3.3	0.3	
6073	184	4562	20G5	2	1	MTVC	NRCP	PRES	COLT	INDT	21.3	8.5	2.7	0.6	
6082	184	4564	20G5	2	1	QRTZ	NRCP	PRES	RNDM	INDT	29.3	16.1	5.1	2.3	
6118	184	4565	20G5	2	1	QRTZ	NRCP	PRES	RNDM	INDT	12.7	15.2	4	0.8	
6110	184	6512	35H5	1	1	QRTZ	FRAG	PRES	RNDM	INDT	8.2	9.5	2.7	0.3	
6124	184	5681	35I	3	1	CCQZ	FRAG	PRES	RNDM	INDT	11.6	18.5	3.8	0.7	
6111	184	5689	35I	3	1	CCQZ	FRAG	PRES	RNDM	INDT	11.8	12.3	4.3	0.5	
6116	184	1584	55K5	1	1	CCQZ	FRAG	PRES	RNDM	INDT	12.7	7	2.3	0.01	
6100	184	1844	70C5	1	1	QRTZ	FRAG	PRES	RNDM	INDT	9.6	10.6	3	0.3	
6114	184	759	70I5	2	1	QRTZ	FRAG	PRES	RNDM	INDT	9.8	14.5	3.9	0.7	
6086	184	737	70J	3,4	1	CCQZ	FRAG	PRES	RNDM	INDT	6	15	2	0.3	
6120	184	4791	75H5	2	1	QRTZ	FRAG	PRES	RNDM	INDT	13	11	4	0.6	
6064	184	4790	75H5	2	1	QRTZ	NRCP	PRES	RNDM	INDT	19	7.5	3	0.6	
6057	184	118	85D5	UNKN	1	MQTZ	NRCP	PRES	RNDM	INDT	16	10	4.1	0.8	

2011.3	SBCM	Cat #	Unit	Level	Qty	MTRL	COND	FLMD	FKPT	SHPE	L/MM	W/MM	T/MM	W/g	Comments
6108	184	4810	85G	4	1	QRTZ	FRAG	PRES	RNDM	INDT	13.5	12	4	0.8	
6054	184	3051	9.50E+06	2	1	QRTZ	NRCP	PRES	RNDM	INDT	21.6	10.1	3.6	0.8	
6058	184	2926	100D5	3	1	MTVC	WHLE	BOTH	RNDM	TRCB	31	17.1	8.7	3.4	LEARNING
6060	184	5742	105E	3	1	QRTZ	NRCP	BOTH	RNDM	TRCB	13.3	11.9	3.9	0.6	
6126	184	2152	95E	4	1	CCQZ	WHLE	BOTH	RNDM	TRCB	15.6	9.2	3.5	0.5	
6063	184	5480	UNKN	UNKN	1	BSLT	WHLE	BOTH	RNDM	TRCB	18.7	16.7	4.1	1.1	
6089	184	5481	UNKN	UNKN	1	CCQZ	WHLE	BOTH	RNDM	TRCB	17.7	15.3	4.9	1.4	
6139	184	2677	175H	2	1	QRTZ	FRAG	PRES	RNDM	TRCB	7	12	4	0.5	
6098	184	32	70J5	2	1	CCQZ	NRCP	PRES	RNDM	TRCB	13.6	9.2	2.9	0.5	
6072	184	196	75I	3	1	CCQZ	NRCP	PRES	TVPL	TRCB	23.7	16.1	4.4	1.9	
6095	184	197	75I	3	1	QRTZ	NRCP	PRES	RNDM	TRCB	15.7	9.6	4	0.5	
6087	184	3077	95E	1	1	CCQZ	WHLE	PRES	RNDM	TRCB	23.2	11.6	3.8	1	
6070	184	5473	UNKN	UNKN	1	BSLT	NRCP	PRES	RNDM	TRCB	26.1	14.1	3.1	1.3	
6102	184	5471	UNKN	UNKN	1	BSLT	WHLE	PRES	RNDM	TRCB	20	11	3.8	0.7	
6078	184	5913	UNKN	UNKN	1	CCQZ	NRCP	PRES	RNDM	TRCB	15.5	10.5	2.5	0.4	
6052	184	5914	UNKN	UNKN	1	CCQZ	NRCP	PRES	RNDM	TRCB	21.5	12.5	4	1.1	

2011.3	SBCM	Cat #	Unit	Level	Qty	MTRL	COND	FLMD	FKPT	SHPE	L/MM	W/MM	T/MM	W/g	Comments
6103	184	5455	UNKN	UNKN	1	CCQZ	WHLE	PRES	COLT	TRCB	21.7	7.7	2.9	0.9	
6133	184	5474	UNKN	UNKN	1	OBSN	NRCP	PRES	RNDM	TRCB	17.2	10.5	4.2	0.9	
6090	184	5459	UNKN	UNKN	1	QRTZ	WHLE	PRES	RNDM	TRCB	21.3	11.1	4.3	0.4	
6105	184	4765	75H5	1	1	OBSN	FRAG	PRES	RNDM	TRCB	12.9	14.7	2.9	0.5	
6068	184	1870	110H	1	1	MTSD	NRCP	BOTH	RNDM	TRSB	28.9	15.1	6.3	2.8	LEARNING
6140	184	3045	95E	2	1	BSLT	NRCP	BOTH	RNDM	TRSB	15	17	5	1	
6085	184	5472	UNKN	UNKN	1	BSLT	WHLE	BOTH	RNDM	TRSB	21.5	14	3.3	0.9	
5476	184	5476	UNKN	UNKN	1	CCQZ	WHLE	PRES	RNDM	TRSB	25.6	10.8	4.8	1.3	
6081	184	4556	65E	1	1	QRTZ	WHLE	BOTH	RNDM	TRXB	20.8	11.9	3.3	0.6	
6067	184	198	75I	3	1	MQTZ	WHLE	BOTH	RNDM	TRXB	28.2	16.1	6.1	2.1	
6056	184	5458	UNKN	UNKN	1	QRTZ	NRCP	BOTH	RNDM	TRXB	20.2	13.5	5	1.3	
6066	184	5463	UNKN	UNKN	1	CCQZ	WHLE	PRES	COLT	TSCB	16.9	14.6	3.7	1	
6093	184	5475	UNKN	UNKN	1	CCQZ	WHLE	PRES	COLT	TSCB	24.3	7.1	3.1	0.5	
6092	184	5468	UNKN	UNKN	1	CCQZ	WHLE	PRES	RNDM	TSCB	31.8	14.1	4.6	2	
6128	184	5457	UNKN	UNKN	1	QRTZ	WHLE	PRES	RNDM	TSCB	20.9	8.4	3.3	0.7	
6083	184	5464	UNKN	UNKN	1	QRTZ	WHLE	PRES	RNDM	TSCM	14.3	13	2.9	0.8	

2011.3	SBCM	Cat #	Unit	Level	Qty	MTRL	COND	FLMD	FKPT	SHPE	L/MM	W/MM	T/MM	W/g	Comments
6071	184	5467	UNKN	UNKN	1	QRTZ	NRCP	PRES	RNDM	TSNC	25.1	17.5	6.8	3.2	
6088	184	5454	UNKN	UNKN	1	QRTZ	WHLE	PRES	COLT	TSNC	17.5	10.9	3.1	0.6	
6091	184	5456	UNKN	UNKN	1	QRTZ	WHLE	PRES	RNDM	TSNC	21.1	15.8	6.8	2.2	
6131	184	5479	UNKN	UNKN	1	QRTZ	WHLE	PRES	RNDM	TSNC	21.8	14.2	6.1	2	
6132	184	5461	UNKN	UNKN	1	QRTZ	NRCP	BOTH	RNDM	TSNS	17.9	16	6.1	1.8	
6077	184	5460	UNKN	UNKN	1	CCQZ	NRCP	PRES	RNDM	TSSB	18.1	12.4	4.1	1	
6061	184	4792	75H5	2	1	BSLT	NRCP	BOTH	RNDM	TSXB	15	15	3	0.9	
6130	184	5815	60J	2	1	QRTZ	NRCP	PRES	RNDM	TTCB	13	14	2	0.5	
6076	184	4766	75H5	1	1	BSLT	NRCP	PRES	RNDM	TTCB	16.3	12.1	3	0.6	
6096	184	3082	95E	1	1	QRTZ	NRCP	PRES	RNDM	TTCB	12.1	14.7	4.1	0.8	
6084	184	5452	UNKN	UNKN	1	CCQZ	WHLE	PRES	RNDM	TTCB	25.8	12.7	3.3	0.8	
6075	184	5466	UNKN	UNKN	1	CCQZ	WHLE	PRES	RNDM	TTCB	18.7	10.9	2.4	0.4	
6080	184	5462	UNKN	UNKN	1	QRTZ	WHLE	PRES	COLT	TTCB	16.8	12.2	3.9	0.9	
6069	184	5465	UNKN	UNKN	1	BSLT	WHLE	PRES	RNDM	TTCB	19.5	11.5	2.5	0.5	
Projectile Point Notation Key															

APPENDIX K

2011.28: Pechanga Cultural Resource catalogue number									
SBCM: San Bernardino Catalogue collection number									
CAT #: Catalog number									
UNIT: Location									
	According to excavation map								
LEVEL: Depth									
	SURF: Surface								
	Levels 1-10 (Increments of 6 inches each level)								
QTY: Quantity									
MTRL: Material									
	BSLT: Basalt								
	CCQZ: Cryptocrystalline quartz								
	MTVC: Metavolcanic								
	MTSD: Metasedimentry								
	MTQZ: Metaquartzite								
	OBSN: Obsidian								
	QRTZ: Quartz								

	WOND: Wonderstone								
COND: Condition									
	WHLE: Whole								
	FRAG: Fragment								
	NRCP: Nearly Complete								
FLMD: Flaking Method									
	PRES: Pressure								
	BOTH: Pressure and percussion								
FKPT: Flaking Pattern									
	COLT: Collateral								
	RNDM: Random								
	TVPL: Transverse parallel								
SHPE: Shape									
	ESCB: Elko eared, side notch, concave base								
	ESSB: Elko eared side notch, straight base								
	TRCB: Triangle, round, concave base								
	TRSB: Triangle, straight base								

	TRXB: Triangle, convex base								
	TSCB: Triangle, serrated, concave base								
	TSNC: Triangle, side notch, concave base								
	TSSB: Triangle, serrated, straight base								
	TSXB: Triangle, serrated, convex base								
	TTCB: Triangle, triangle concave base								
	INDT: Indeterminate								
L/mm: Length measured in mm from end to edge									
W/mm: Width measured in mm from edge to edge									
T/mm: Thickness measured in mm from top to bottom									
WT/g: Weight measured in grams									
Comments:									
	Spear type point								
	learning: evidence of a learning projectile point/ crude/ developing point								

APPENDIX L

FLAKE TOOLS

Appendix L: Flake Tools													
2011.28	SBCM	Cat #	Unit	Level	QTY	MTRL	EDG	TYP MOD	L/MM	W/MM	T/MM	W/g	Comments
2359	184	2289	100D5	6	1	BSLT	1	BIFC	43.3	29.1	18	24	
2296	184	1046	100E5	3	1	BSLT	1	UNFC	40	68.1	30	70.1	
2376	184	812	100F5	4	1	BSLT	3	UNFC	35.4	26	9.4	8.9	
2295	184	1482	105F5	1	1	MQTZ	1	UNFC	35.9	22.1	8.1	5.2	
6672	184	1778	110D5	3	1	CCQZ	2	BIFC	24	38	10	8	Marging
6673	184	1778	110D5	3	1	SPMV	1	UNFC	30	19	9	4	thumbnail
6691	184	5715	110I	1	1	CCQZ	1	UNFC	32	25	11	12	
2162	184	1539	110I5	1	1	MQTZ	2	UNFC	43.5	43.2	14.3	26.7	
2155	184	3002	110I5	4	1	BSLT	2	UNFC	51.7	49.3	21.1	49.4	
2159	184	3992	115E	3	1	MTQZ	3	BIFC	28.7	27.2	13.2	11.1	
2147	184	5248	115E	3,4	1	BSLT	2	UNFC	40.6	30.1	0.7	20.6	
2168	184	5293	120F	1	1	BSLT	2	UNFC	41.2	36.7	13.2	24.6	
6667	184	249	120F5	2	1	BSLT	1	UNFC	22	16	4	2	
6669	184	1491	120F5	3	1	CCQZ	2	UNFC	21	20	6	2	
2298	184	433	125E5	3	1	BSLT	3	UNFC	56.1	45.8	13.9	31.7	

2011.28	SBCM	Cat #	Unit	Level	QTY	MTRL	EDG	TYP MOD	L/MM	W/MM	T/MM	W/g	Comments
2286	184	1150	140I5	2	1	QRTZ	1	UNFC	45.8	30.6	15.6	19.2	
2292	184	1151	140I5	2	1	QRTZ	1	UNFC	49.9	41.3	21.4	38.3	
6671	184	1704	150E5	1,2,3,4	1	QRTZ	1	UNFC	41.9	37.3	17.4	26.7	
2156	184	2604	170H	3	1	MTSD	1	UNFC	27.7	24.2	8.5	8.9	
2143	184	5550	175I5	2	1	MQTZ	1	UNFC	94.1	50	19.9	72	
6690	184	5536	175J5	1	1	MQTZ	1	BIFC	34	19	10	6	
6670	184	1669	175J5	2	1	CCQZ	1	UNFC	20	15	4	2	
6675	184	2302	20J5	1	1	CCQZ	2	UNFC	27	25	4	2	
6696	184	5865	30H5	1,2,3	1	MQTZ	3	BIFC	94	62.5	34.7	250	
2294	184	5676	35I	3	1	WOND	1	BIFC	19.5	30.7	12.1	7	
2303	184	6349	40H5	1	1	SPMV	3	UNFC	27	15	4	1	
2164	184	1906	40I	1	1	BSLT	2	BIFC	30.7	26.9	11.5	8.2	
6679	184	3364	40K	4	1	BSLT	2	UNFC	38	30	7	10	
2957	184	2278	55H5	4,5	1	BSLT	3	BIFC	32.8	25.7	10.2	7.4	
6685	184	4395	55J5	4	1	QRTZ	2	BIFC	94	62.5	34.7	250	
6684	184	4393	55J5	5	1	BSLT	2	UNFC	32	25	4	4	

2011.28	SBCM	Cat #	Unit	Level	QTY	MTRL	EDG	TYP MOD	L/MM	W/MM	T/MM	W/g	Comments
2358	184	1660	55K5	2	1	BSLT	2	BIFC	22.4	24.8	5.5	3.2	
6678	184	2661	70I5	4	1	CCQZ	1	UNFC	22	12	7	2	
6676	184	2507	70J5	1	1	CCQZ	1	UNFC	22	21	10	4	
6683	184	4372	75D5	4	1	BSLT	2	BIFC	54	20	8	10	
6682	184	4371	75D5	4	1	MQTZ	3	BIFC	63.9	53.7	20.5	79.1	
6698	184	5927	75E5	7	1	CCQZ	1	UNFC	34.3	15.2	10.9	5.5	
2300	184	5928	75E5	7	1	MTVC	1	UNFC	27.9	20.9	6	3.3	
2404	184	280	85E	1	1	MTVC	3	BIFC	31	27.8	9.8	10.7	
2403	184	891	85F	2	1	MTVC	1	UNFC	28.7	16.2	10.4	5.6	
6686	184	4806	85G	4	1	CCQZ	1	UNFC	42	18	9	6	
2146	184	370	85H	2	1	CCQZ	1	UNFC	27.5	23.4	10.1	5.1	
2153	184	5923	90E5	8	1	BSLT	2	BIFC	29.6	31.6	5.3	5.1	
6697	184	5918	90E5	8	1	MQTZ	4	BIFC	34.1	26.7	4.8	5.1	
6681	184	4150	90J5	1	1	BSLT	2	UNFC	30	26	8	6	
2170	184	2194	95D	3,4	1	BSLT	3	UNFC	74.3	35.7	11.3	26.6	
6674	184	2216	95E	7	1	SPMV	2	BIFC	32	17	5	2	

2011.28	SBCM	Cat #	Unit	Level	QTY	MTRL	EDG	TYP MOD	L/MM	W/MM	T/MM	W/g	Comments
2169	184	3091	95E	1	1	MQTZ	3	UNFC	41.2	33.5	9.7	17.5	
6668	184	1211	95H5	3	1	CCQZ	1	BIFC	19.4	10.3	3.2	0.7	
2150	184	5093	UNKN	UNKN	1	BSLT	1	BIFC	47.3	32.9	17.4	36	
6680	184	3724	UNKN	UNKN	1	BSLT	2	UNFC	32	49	9	12	
2163	184	4986	UNKN	UNKN	1	BSLT	2	UNFC	52	41.1	16.7	39.3	
6695	184	5800	UNKN	UNKN	1	BSLT	3	BIFC	94	62.5	34.7	250	
2302	184	6295	UNKN	UNKN	1	BSLT	3	UNFC	33.6	18	10.3	6	thumbnail
2301	184	5096	UNKN	UNKN	1	CCQZ	1	BIFC	32.4	27.5	11.9	11.5	
2214	184	4318	UNKN	UNKN	1	CCQZ	2	UNFC	61.8	52.5	20	76.7	
2299	184	4982	UNKN	UNKN	1	CCQZ	2	UNFC	45.6	37.3	15.4	31.2	
2151	184	5103	UNKN	UNKN	1	CCQZ	3	UNFC	46.4	22.9	6.7	6.7	
2145	184	5641	UNKN	UNKN	1	GRNT	1	UNFC	62.3	53.7	24.3	90.3	
2288	184	5101	UNKN	UNKN	1	MQTZ	1	UNFC	35.8	34	10	10.6	
2305	184	5105	UNKN	UNKN	1	MQTZ	1	UNFC	44.1	44.8	15.5	32.6	
2154	184	5111	UNKN	UNKN	1	MQTZ	1	UNFC	50.8	37.7	16.3	27.4	
2290	184	5094	UNKN	UNKN	1	MQTZ	2	UNFC	34.9	32.7	9.4	11.4	

2011.28	SBCM	Cat #	Unit	Level	QTY	MTRL	EDG	TYP MOD	L/MM	W/MM	T/MM	W/g	Comments
2144	184	5107	UNKN	UNKN	1	MQTZ	2	UNFC	44.7	33.4	7.6	13.2	
2304	184	5109	UNKN	UNKN	1	MQTZ	2	UNFC	67.4	45.4	13.7	42.1	
2166	184	5177	UNKN	UNKN	1	MQTZ	2	UNFC	70	49.3	13.4	53.8	
2157	184	6074	UNKN	UNKN	1	MQTZ	2	UNFC	34.9	30.3	8.5	9.5	
6699	184	6335	UNKN	UNKN	1	MQTZ	2	UNFC	52	45	15	62	
2161	184	5099	UNKN	UNKN	1	MQTZ	3	BIFC	47.3	38.9	14.5	32.4	
6689	184	5197	UNKN	UNKN	1	MQTZ	3	BIFC	70.6	50.7	10.7	106	
6693	184	5788	UNKN	UNKN	1	MQTZ	3	BIFC	86.2	78.9	23.1	181	
2149	184	5182	UNKN	UNKN	1	MQTZ	3	UNFC	50.8	33.1	13.1	25.2	
2160	184	6076	UNKN	UNKN	1	MQTZ	4	BIFC	30	22.3	6.1	5	
2165	184	4190	UNKN	UNKN	1	MTSD	1	BIFC	42.8	46.7	15.2	34.8	
2148	184	6076	UNKN	UNKN	1	MTSD	1	UNFC	35.8	27.2	10.9	14.4	
2293	184	6075	UNKN	UNKN	1	MTSD	2	BIFC	47	20.7	12.6	16.5	
2167	184	5448	UNKN	UNKN	1	MTSD	3	UNFC	25.5	23.3	6	4.3	
2158	184	5106	UNKN	UNKN	1	MTVC	1	UNFC	46.3	35.5	12.8	18.4	
2287	184	6077	UNKN	UNKN	1	MTVC	1	UNFC	42.5	39	14.1	20	

2011.28	SBCM	Cat #	Unit	Level	QTY	MTRL	EDG	TYP MOD	L/MM	W/MM	T/MM	W/g	Comments
6688	184	5098	UNKN	UNKN	1	MTVC	2	BIFC	32.2	29.5	11.5	10.4	
2289	184	5801	UNKN	UNKN	1	MTVC	2	UNFC	72.9	60.7	11.8	97.5	
2215	184	6290	UNKN	UNKN	1	MTVC	2	UNFC	43	38.9	12.2	20.3	
6692	184	5780	UNKN	UNKN	1	MTVC	3	BIFC	109.9	75.9	27.1	223	
2291	184	6294	UNKN	UNKN	1	MTVC	3	UNFC	40.8	27.1	7	7.9	
6694	184	5799	UNKN	UNKN	1	QRTZ	1	BIFC	47.4	39.5	20	46.1	
2297	184	5147	UNKN	UNKN	1	QRZT	1	UNFC	54	34.5	14.8	27	
6687	184	5091	UNKN	UNKN	1	SPMV	2	UNFC	42	27	13	16	
2152	184	5108	UNKN	UNKN	1	SPMV	2	UNFC	24.5	17	10.3	5.7	
Flake Tool Notation Key:													
2011.28: Pechanga Cultural Resource catalogue number													
SBCM: San Bernardino Catalogue collection number													
CAT #: Catalog number													
UNIT: Location													
	According to excavation map												

LEVEL: Depth								
	SURF: Surface							
	Levels 1-10 (Increments of 6 inches each level)							
QTY: Quantity								
MTRL: Material								
	BSLT: Basalt							
	CCQZ: Cryptocrystalline Quartz							
	SPMV: Santigo Peak Metavolcanic							
	MTVC: Metavolcanic							
	MTSD: Metasedimentry							
	MQTZ: Metaquartzite							
	QRTZ: Quartzite							
EDG: Edge								
	Number of modified edges							
TYP MOD: Type Modification								
	BIFC: Biface							
	UNFC: Uniface							

<table>
<tr><td colspan="9">L/mm: Length measured in mm from end to edge</td></tr>
<tr><td colspan="9">W/mm: Width measured in mm from edge to edge</td></tr>
<tr><td colspan="9">T/mm: Thickness measured in mm from top to bottom</td></tr>
<tr><td colspan="9">WT/g: Weight measured in grams</td></tr>
<tr><td colspan="9">Comments: Any additional data (fire-affected, etc.)</td></tr>
<tr><td></td><td>Margining</td><td></td><td></td><td></td><td></td><td></td><td></td><td></td></tr>
<tr><td></td><td>Thumbnail</td><td></td><td></td><td></td><td></td><td></td><td></td><td></td></tr>
</table>

APPENDIX M

CORES

Appendix M: Cores																
2011.8	**SBCM**	**Cat #**	**Unit**	**Level**	**Qty**	**MTRL**	**Type**	**Form**	**NFSC**	**STFL**	**EDGE**	**L/MM**	**W/MM**	**T/MM**	**Wt/g**	**Comments**
6728	184	2452	120D	6	1	BSLT	MUDC	COBL	MULT	HMST	3+	55.5	48.4	40.2	95.6	
6764	184	4715	55J5	4	1	BSLT	MUDC	COBL	MULT	HMST	3+	45	37	27	42	
6782	184	6078	UNKN	UNKN	1	BSLT	MUDC	COBL	MULT	HMST	3+	39.7	19.2	16.5	15.5	
6753	184	4326	UNKN	UNKN	1	CCQZ	MUDC	COBL	MULT	HMST	3+	72.6	70.3	63.7	324.1	
6754	184	4348	UNKN	UNKN	1	CCQZ	MUDC	COBL	MULT	HMST	3+	57.4	40.9	44.6	125.5	
6726	184	2418	60J5	5	1	MQTZ	MUDC	COBL	MULT	HMST	3+	54.3	54.3	47.7	218.5	
6759	184	4406	75C	2	1	MQTZ	MUDC	COBL	MULT	HMST	3+	88.4	63	41.4	273.3	
6786	184	6288	UNKN	UNKN	1	MQTZ	MUDC	COBL	MULT	HMST	3+	49.8	44	31.7	76.6	
6755	184	4349	UNKN	UNKN	1	MQTZ	MUDC	COBL	MULT	HMST	3+	73.8	68.9	29.7	194	
6785	184	6287	UNKN	UNKN	1	MTVC	MUDC	COBL	MULT	HMST	3+	42.7	36.2	31.4	61.6	
6734	184	2882	175H	1	1	QRTZ	MUDC	COBL	MULT	N/A	1	37	39	28	40	
6768	184	4937	70J	1	1	QRTZ	MUDC	COBL	MULT	N/A	2	77.5	81	44	228.6	
6702	184	129	85E	3	1	MQTZ	MUDC	COBL	MULT	N/A	3+	46	30	11	16	
6729	184	2546	120E5	2	1	QRTZ	MUDC	COBL	MULT	N/A	3+	40	38	20	30	
6709	184	723	120F	2	1	QRTZ	MUDC	COBL	MULT	N/A	3+	43	35	25	30	

2011.8	SBCM	Cat #	Unit	Level	Qty	MTRL	Type	Form	NFSC	STFL	EDGE	L/MM	W/MM	T/MM	Wt/g	Com-ments
4606	184	1644	95H	1	1	QRTZ	MUDC	COBL	MULT	N/A	3+	39	32	15	22	
6740	184	3622	95I	1	1	CCQZ	MUDC	COBL	MULT	N/A	N/A	29	20	10	6	EX
6790	184	6293	UNKN	UNKN	1	BSLT	MUDC	COBL	MULT	SCRP	3+	42.6	28.6	17.8	24.5	
6779	184	5771	UNKN	UNKN	1	BSLT	MUDC	FLKE	MULT	HMST	1	91	82	24	242	
6719	184	1656	55K5	2	1	QRTZ	MUDC	FLKE	MULT	HMST	2	56	40	35	56	
6701	184	109	85D5	UNKN	1	SPMV	MUDC	FLKE	MULT	HMST	2	35	25	25	16	
6788	184	6291	UNKN	UNKN	1	MTVC	MUDC	FLKE	MULT	HMST	3	46.1	42.4	28.5	57.2	
6766	184	4784	75H5	2	1	BSLT	MUDC	FLKE	MULT	HMST	3+	55	45	21	62	
6733	184	2878	UNKN	2	1	BSLT	MUDC	FLKE	MULT	HMST	3+	68	40	20	62	
6760	184	1492	UNKN	UNKN	1	CCQZ	MUDC	FLKE	MULT	HMST	3+	41.2	39.5	22.8	45.5	
6769	184	4988	UNKN	UNKN	1	CCQZ	MUDC	FLKE	MULT	HMST	3+	49.6	37.7	19.8	47.5	
6765	184	4763	75H5	1	1	CCQZ	MUDC	FLKE	MULT	N/A	1	34	20	10	6	EX
6784	184	6183	65I	1	1	MTSD	MUDC	FLKE	MULT	N/A	1	37.7	29.6	12.4	3.1	
6741	184	3724	UNKN	UNKN	1	MTVC	MUDC	FLKE	MULT	N/A	1	58	55	18	60	
6781	184	5993	110I	4	1	QRTZ	MUDC	FLKE	MULT	N/A	1	53.6	40.9	29.8	62.5	
6708	184	603	80E	3	1	QRTZ	MUDC	FLKE	MULT	N/A	1	35	25	15	16	

2011.8	SBCM	Cat #	Unit	Level	Qty	MTRL	Type	Form	NFSC	STFL	EDGE	L/MM	W/MM	T/MM	Wt/g	Comments
4507	184	1813	90I	3	1	QRTZ	MUDC	FLKE	MULT	N/A	1	19	20	7	4	
6776	184	5577	75I	1	1	BSLT	MUDC	FLKE	MULT	N/A	2	46	40	20	30	
6747	184	4019	UNKN	UNKN	1	BSLT	MUDC	FLKE	MULT	N/A	2	20.7	35.4	24.9	33.6	
6707	184	587	110E	2	1	CCQZ	MUDC	FLKE	MULT	N/A	2	40	21	15	12	EX
6770	184	5060	110G	1	1	CCQZ	MUDC	FLKE	MULT	N/A	2	35	18	14	8	EX
6720	184	1510	40K	1	1	CCQZ	MUDC	FLKE	MULT	N/A	2	30	15	10	4	
6721	184	2054	60H5	6	1	CCQZ	MUDC	FLKE	MULT	N/A	2	29	19	14	6	EX
6796	184	6182	65I	1	1	CCQZ	MUDC	FLKE	MULT	N/A	2	27	25	15	8	EX
6767	184	4901	80D5	1	1	CCQZ	MUDC	FLKE	MULT	N/A	2	35	17	15	10	EX
6700	184	106	85E	1	1	CCQZ	MUDC	FLKE	MULT	N/A	2	32	29	17	18	
6762	184	4639	90G	3	1	CCQZ	MUDC	FLKE	MULT	N/A	2	24	14	10	4	
6742	184	3724	UNKN	UNKN	1	MTVC	MUDC	FLKE	MULT	N/A	2	54	45	22	56	
6703	184	168	100D5	3	1	QRTZ	MUDC	FLKE	MULT	N/A	2	32	19	15	8	
6792	184	6316	65I	4	1	QRTZ	MUDC	FLKE	MULT	N/A	2	37	29	15	20	
6738	184	3213	90E	5	1	QRTZ	MUDC	FLKE	MULT	N/A	2	72	58	34	168	
6732	184	2818	55I5	4	1	QRTZ	MUDC	FLKE	MULT	N/A	3	49	32	15	16	

2011.8	SBCM	Cat #	Unit	Level	Qty	MTRL	Type	Form	NFSC	STFL	EDGE	L/MM	W/MM	T/MM	Wt/g	Comments
6722	184	2091	55I	1	1	BSLT	MUDC	FLKE	MULT	N/A	3+	43.3	36.9	27.5	40.7	
6711	184	978	105D5	2	1	CCQZ	MUDC	FLKE	MULT	N/A	3+	43	41	15	20	
6775	184	5547	175I5	2	1	CCQZ	MUDC	FLKE	MULT	N/A	3+	22	17	10	6	EX
6712	184	1152	UNKN	UNKN	1	CCQZ	MUDC	FLKE	MULT	N/A	3+	69.3	23.1	19.4	29.6	
6761	184	4543	90G	4	1	CYSL	MUDC	FLKE	MULT	N/A	3+	20	19	10	2	
4551	184	3771	95I5	1	1	CYSL	MUDC	FLKE	MULT	N/A	3+	20	17	9	4	
6780	184	5597	75J	1	1	MQTZ	MUDC	FLKE	MULT	N/A	3+	38	25	10	8	
6724	184	2310	95D	2	1	MQTZ	MUDC	FLKE	MULT	N/A	3+	48	35	13	24	
6746	184	4011	115E	1	1	QRTZ	MUDC	FLKE	MULT	N/A	3+	23.2	36.8	36.3	62.2	
6727	184	2450	120D	6	1	QRTZ	MUDC	FLKE	MULT	N/A	3+	34	34	24	18	EX
6797	184	1146	140I5	2	1	QRTZ	MUDC	FLKE	MULT	N/A	3+	37	27	18	16	
6777	184	5599	75J	1	1	QRTZ	MUDC	FLKE	MULT	N/A	3+	27	25	20	12	
6748	184	4194	UNKN	UNKN	1	QRTZ	MUDC	FLKE	MULT	N/A	3+	48.2	44.2	22.5	43.9	
6791	184	6296	UNKN	UNKN	1	SPMV	MUDC	FLKE	MULT	N/A	3+	36.3	31.3	14.9	19.6	
6756	184	4378	55J5	4	1	WOND	MUDC	FLKE	MULT	N/A	3+	36	30	10	10	
6736	184	3066	100D5	1	1	CCQZ	MUDC	FLKE	MULT	N/A	N/A	15	14	13	2	EX

2011.8	SBCM	Cat #	Unit	Level	Qty	MTRL	Type	Form	NFSC	STFL	EDGE	L/MM	W/MM	T/MM	Wt/g	Com-ments
6735	184	2990	110D5	2	1	CCQZ	MUDC	FLKE	MULT	N/A	N/A	20	12	10	2	EX
6794	184	6525	140I5	1	1	CCQZ	MUDC	FLKE	MULT	N/A	N/A	24	16	12	2	EX
6713	184	1176	45I	4	1	CCQZ	MUDC	FLKE	MULT	N/A	N/A	15	14	12	4	EX
6773	184	5408	90I	1	1	CCQZ	MUDC	FLKE	MULT	N/A	N/A	24	21	10	4	EX
6706	18	584	55I	4	1	MQTZ	MUDC	FLKE	MULT	N/A	N/A	29	24	9	4	
6744	184	3866	UNKN	UNKN	1	OBSN	MUDC	FLKE	MULT	N/A	N/A	108.4	29.3	39.6	121.5	
6749	184	4269	UNKN	UNKN	1	OBSN	MUDC	FLKE	MULT	N/A	N/A	44.9	25.3	9.2	11.7	
6750	184	4270	UNKN	UNKN	1	OBSN	MUDC	FLKE	MULT	N/A	N/A	59.2	30.8	16.1	23.4	
6751	184	4271	UNKN	UNKN	1	OBSN	MUDC	FLKE	MULT	N/A	N/A	58.3	36.4	12.3	24.4	
6758	184	4394	55J5	4	1	QRTZ	MUDC	FLKE	MULT	N/A	N/A	36	30	20	18	
6716	184	1605	55K	1	1	QRTZ	MUDC	FLKE	MULT	N/A	N/A	24	14	12	4	EX
6783	184	6102	65I	2	1	QRTZ	MUDC	FLKE	MULT	N/A	N/A	49.8	26.1	24.2	37.4	
6793	184	6318	65I	4	1	QRTZ	MUDC	FLKE	MULT	N/A	N/A	32.8	21.3	21.1	17.5	
6710	184	757	70I5	2	1	QRTZ	MUDC	FLKE	MULT	N/A	N/A	27	23	12	10	
6739	184	3257	75D5	5	1	QRTZ	MUDC	FLKE	MULT	N/A	N/A	43.9	34.2	30.2	36.6	
6778	184	5656	75E5	1	1	QRTZ	MUDC	FLKE	MULT	N/A	N/A	55	40	22	54	

2011.8	SBCM	Cat #	Unit	Level	Qty	MTRL	Type	Form	NFSC	STFL	EDGE	L/MM	W/MM	T/MM	Wt/g	Com-ments
6714	184	1440	75N	1	1	QRTZ	MUDC	FLKE	MULT	N/A	N/A	29	17	15	10	EX
6743	184	3798	80D	4	1	QRTZ	MUDC	FLKE	MULT	N/A	N/A	30	10	15	6	EX
6718	184	1644	95H	1	1	QRTZ	MUDC	FLKE	MULT	N/A	N/A	23	20	10	6	EX
6795	184	UNKN	UNKN	UNKN	1	QRTZ	MUDC	FLKE	MULT	N/A	N/A	20	12	20	6	EX
6737	184	3142	95E5	3	1	BSLT	MUDC	FLKE	MULT	SCRP	1	40	35	18	20	
6723	184	2202	120D5	UNKN	1	BSLT	MUDC	FLKE	MULT	SCRP	3+	21.1	37.5	14.3	12	
6752	184	4320	UNKN	UNKN	1	BSLT	MUDC	FLKE	MULT	SCRP	3+	77.1	48.8	14.4	68.2	
6730	184	2613	100D	4	1	CCQZ	MUDC	FLKE	MULT	SCRP	3+	40	30	13	14	
6774	184	5477	UNKN	UNKN	1	CCQZ	MUDC	FLKE	MULT	SCRP	3+	60	35	14	22	
6787	184	6289	UNKN	UNKN	1	MTVC	MUDC	FLKE	MULT	SCRP	3+	44.9	33.8	12.5	19.7	
4538	184	6419	110F	3	1	QRTZ	MUDC	FLKE	MULT	SCRP	3+	29	12	10	2	
6717	184	1640	95J	1	1	QRTZ	MUDC	FLKE	MULT	SCRP	3+	57	47	15	38	
6789	184	6292	UNKN	UNKN	1	QRTZ	MUDC	FLKE	MULT	SCRP	3+	32.6	24.4	11.5	9.3	
6715	184	1492	40H5	2	1	QRTZ	MUDC	FLKE	UNDC	N/A	N/A	29	22	12	6	
6725	184	2417	60J5	5	1	MQTZ	MUDC	TBLR	MULT	HMST	2	59.6	47	31.6	124.5	
6745	184	3904	70C5	2	1	BSLT	MUDC	TBLR	MULT	HMST	3+	57.8	38.7	30.8	75	

2011.8	SBCM	Cat #	Unit	Level	Qty	MTRL	Type	Form	NFSC	STFL	EDGE	L/MM	W/MM	T/MM	Wt/g	Com-ments
6731	184	2721	UNKN	1	1	CCQZ	MUDC	TBLR	MULT	HMST	3+	64.9	20.3	16.8	35.5	
6705	184	398	115F	1	1	CCQZ	MUDC	TBLR	MULT	N/A	2	33	24	15	10	
6772	184	5286	120F	1	1	CCQZ	MUDC	TBLR	MULT	N/A	2	30	25	12	8	
6763	184	4681	140I5	2	1	QRTZ	MUDC	TBLR	MULT	N/A	3+	36	27	19	18	
6771	184	5133	140H5	3	1	QRTZ	MUDC	TBLR	MULT	N/A	N/A	42	18	13	10	EX
6757	184	4390	55J5	4	1	QRTZ	MUDC	TBLR	MULT	N/A	N/A	50.2	24.4	25.7	50.3	
6704	184	191	75I	3	1	QRTZ	MUDC	TBLR	MULT	N/A	N/A	18.7	19.5	24.5	14.9	
Core Notation Key																
2011.28: Pechanga Cultural Resource catalogue number																
SBCM: San Bernardino Catalogue collection number																
CAT #: Catalog number																
UNIT: Location																
	According to excavation map															
LEVEL: Depth																
	SURF: Surface															

	Levels 1-10 (Increments of 6 inches each level)										
QTY: Quantity											
MTRL: Material											
	BSLT: Basalt										
	CCQZ: Cryptocrystalline quartz										
	CYSL: Crystal, Quartz										
	SPMV: Santigo Peak Metavolcanic										
	MTVC: Metavolcanic										
	MTSD: Metasedimentry										
	MQTZ: Metaquartzite										
	OBSN: Obsidian										
	QRTZ: Quartz										
	WOND: Wonderstone										
Type:											
	MUDC: Multidirectional										
Form:											
	COBL: Cobble										

	FLKE: Flake										
	TBLR: Tabular										
NFSC: Negative Flake Scar											
	MULT: 3+ Flake scars										
	N/A: Not Applicable										
STLF: Secondary tool function											
	HMST: Hammerstone										
	SCRP: Scraper										
	N/A: Not Applicable										
EDGE: Number of modified edges											
	1, 2 or 3+										
L/mm: Length measured in mm from end to edge											
W/mm: Width measured in mm from edge to edge											
T/mm: Thickness measured in mm from top to bottom											
WT/g: Weight measured in grams											
Comments:											
	EX:Exhausted										

APPENDIX N

HAMMERSTONES

Appendix N: Hammerstones

2011.28	SBCM	Cat. #	Unit	Level	Qty	MTRL	Form	EDGE	STLF	L/MM	W/MM	T/MM	Wt/g
6803	184	3783	100F5	6	1	MTQZ	COBL	MULT	N/A	59	63	41.5	164
6804	184	3787	100F5	6	1	QRTZ	COBL	MULT	N/A	33.6	51.5	47.4	104.3
6813	184	4880	115E5	8	1	GRNT	COBL	MULT	N/A	71.6	68.3	42.9	208.4
6805	184	4027	80I	2	1	BSLT	COBL	MULT	N/A	64	50	23	88
6802	184	2036	90E5	6	1	QRTZ	COBL	MULT	N/A	67.1	49.3	28.7	148.3
6799	184	1373	UNKN	UNKN	1	BSLT	COBL	MULT	N/A	55.5	60.7	43.5	186.4
6809	184	4331	UNKN	UNKN	1	BSLT	COBL	MULT	N/A	86.1	63.7	57.6	503.6
6810	184	4344	UNKN	UNKN	1	BSLT	COBL	MULT	N/A	73.4	64	40.9	304.5
6815	184	5778	UNKN	UNKN	1	BSLT	COBL	MULT	N/A	69.8	61.3	29.8	166.3
6801	184	1457	UNKN	UNKN	1	BSLT	TBLR	MULT	N/A	63.3	40.7	39.6	136.5
6814	184	5104	UNKN	UNKN	1	CCQZ	COBL	MULT	N/A	59	49.2	33.5	154.9
6812	184	4351	UNKN	UNKN	1	CCQZ	COBL	MULT	SCRP	102	86.2	28.8	320.9
6806	184	4306	UNKN	UNKN	1	GRNT	COBL	MULT	N/A	130	90	65	1104
6807	184	4327	UNKN	UNKN	1	MTQZ	COBL	MULT	N/A	82.6	48	37.9	233
6817	184	5784	UNKN	UNKN	1	MTQZ	COBL	MULT	N/A	78.2	72.5	30.2	233.1

2011.28	SBCM	Cat. #	Unit	Level	Qty	MTRL	Form	EDGE	STLF	L/MM	W/MM	T/MM	Wt/g
6811	184	4346	UNKN	UNKN	1	MTQZ	TBLR	MULT	N/A	74.1	67.6	32.6	186.3
6800	184	1374	UNKN	UNKN	1	MTSD	COBL	MULT	N/A	68.7	56.7	62.7	342.8
6808	184	4329	UNKN	UNKN	1	QRTZ	COBL	MULT	N/A	94.7	72.3	64.6	544.7
6816	184	5782	UNKN	UNKN	1	QRTZ	COBL	MULT	N/A	53.3	56	34.9	115.5
6798	184	1372	UNKN	UNKN	1	RYLT	COBL	MULT	N/A	76.9	58	81.1	463.7
Hammerstone Notation Key													
2011.28: Pechanga Cultural Resource catalogue number													
SBCM: San Bernardino Catalogue collection number													
CAT #: Catalog number													
UNIT: Location													
	According to excavation map												
LEVEL: Depth													
	SURF: Surface												
	Levels 1-10 (Increments of 6 inches each level)												
QTY: Quantity													

MTRL: Material								
	BSLT: Basalt							
	CCQZ: Cryptocrystalline quartz							
	GRNT: Granitic							
	MTSD: Metasedimentry							
	MTQZ: Metaquartzite							
	QRTZ: Quartzite							
Form:								
	COBL: Cobble							
	TBLR: TBLRular							
EDGE: Edge								
	MULT: 3+ modified edges							
STLF: Secondary tool function								
	SCRP: Scraper							
	N/A: Not Applicable							
L/mm: Length measured in mm from end to edge								
W/mm: Width measured in mm from edge to edge								

T/mm: Thickness measured in mm from top to bottom
WT/g: Weight measured in grams

APPENDIX O

MANOS

Appendix O: Manos																		
2011.28	SBCM	Cat #	Unit	Level	Qty	MTRL	SURF	FORM	SHAPE	SRFP	COND	PTLF	STLF	L/ mm	W/ mm	T/ mm	Wt/ g	Com-ments
5804	184	5769	UNKN	UNKN	1	BSLT	BIFC	MDFD	UNKN	MILL	FRAG	MLST	PSTL	48.4	56.5	27.4	120.6	
5767	184	2934	34F4	UNKN	1	GRNT	BIFC	MDFD	UNKN	MILL	FRAG	MLST	N/A	66.5	38.9	39.1	147.3	Burned
5787	184	4347	UNKN	UNKN	1	GRNT	UNFC	MDFD	UNKN	MILL	FRAG	MLST	N/A	88.2	66.7	58.4	450.2	
5774	184	4338	55J5	4	1	GRNT	BIFC	MDFD	OVID	MILL	FRAG	MLST	N/A	31.4	75.3	37.6	140.7	
5816	184	1377	UNKN	UNKN	1	GRNT	BIFC	NATL	OVID	MILL	FRAG	MLST	N/A	116.1	79	58.8	810.7	
5790	184	4325	UNKN	UNKN	1	GRNT	BIFC	MDFD	OVID	MILL	FRAG	MLST	ANVL	44.4	82	26.1	141	
5785	184	4328	UNKN	UNKN	1	GRNT	BIFC	MDFD	OVID	MILL	FRAG	MLST	HMST	50.5	84.6	53.2	312.2	
5770	184	4198	UNKN	UNKN	1	SHST	BIFC	MDFD	OVID	MILL	FRAG	MLST	N/A	48.6	69.8	36.2	212	
5782	184	5596	75J	1	1	BSLT	BIFC	UNKN	UNKN	MILL	FRAG	MLST	N/A	76	60.7	41.9	243.2	
5296	184	3977	UNKN	UNKN	1	GRNT	BIFC	UNKN	UNKN	MILL	FRAG	MLST	N/A	73.5	92.4	52.1	542.2	
5797	184	4359	UNKN	UNKN	1	BSLT	BIFC	MDFD	UNKN	MILL	FRAG	MLST	N/A	51.5	94.4	43.4	387.5	
5303	184	420	115D	2	1	GRNT	BIFC	MDFD	UNKN	MILL	FRAG	MLST	N/A	72.6	27.9	38.1	114.5	
5799	184	5633	70E	5	1	GRNT	BIFC	MDFD	UNKN	MILL	FRAG	MLST	N/A	62	39.6	48.7	132	
5292	184	4667	85G5	4	1	GRNT	BIFC	MDFD	UNKN	MILL	FRAG	MLST	N/A	86.8	56.8	42.9	392.2	
5777	184	1266	UNKN	UNKN	1	GRNT	BIFC	MDFD	UNKN	MILL	FRAG	MLST	N/A	88.5	58.8	52	440	

2011.28	SBCM	Cat #	Unit	Level	Qty	MTRL	SURF	FORM	SHAPE	SRFP	COND	PTLF	STLF	L/ mm	W/ mm	T/ mm	Wt/ g	Com-ments
5780	184	3973	UNKN	UNKN	1	GRNT	BIFC	MDFD	UNKN	MILL	FRAG	MLST	N/A	70.1	69.3	41.9	335.8	
5808	184	4338	UNKN	UNKN	1	GRNT	BIFC	MDFD	UNKN	MILL	FRAG	MLST	N/A	31.4	75.3	37.6	140.7	
5297	184	4342	UNKN	UNKN	1	GRNT	BIFC	MDFD	UNKN	MILL	FRAG	MLST	N/A	61.3	87.4	41.1	320.8	
5773	184	4358	UNKN	UNKN	1	GRNT	BIFC	MDFD	UNKN	MILL	FRAG	MLST	N/A	87.1	45.1	37	229.3	hole drilled
5798	184	3993	115-E	3	1	QRTZ	BIFC	MDFD	UNKN	MILL	FRAG	MLST	N/A	35	44.3	40	95.5	
5287	184	4931	140H5	1,2	1	VBAS	BIFC	MDFD	UNKN	MILL	FRAG	MLST	N/A	65	52.5	46	229.2	
5294	184	3813	UNKN	UNKN	1	VBAS	BIFC	MDFD	UNKN	MILL	FRAG	MLST	N/A	91.5	51.1	51.9	410.2	
7405	184	5618	UNKN	UNKN	1	VBAS	BIFC	MDFD	UNKN	MILL	FRAG	MLST	HMST	79.7	54.9	37.8	257.9	
5812	184	4333	UNKN	UNKN	1	GRNT	UNFC	MDFD	UNKN	MILL	FRAG	MLST	N/A	57.3	79.3	41	290	
5806	184	4340	UNKN	UNKN	1	GRNT	UNFC	MDFD	UNKN	MILL	FRAG	MLST	ANVL	49.6	92.1	37.8	306.2	
5763	184	4970	UNKN	UNKN	1	GRNT	UNFC	MDFD	UNKN	MILL	FRAG	MLST	N/A	58	75.5	41	265	
5805	184	2683	100F5	5	1	QRTZ	UNFC	MDFD	UNKN	MILL	FRAG	MLST	N/A	68.3	46.4	18.2	72	
5779	184	3251	175H5	1	1	QRTZ	UNFC	MDFD	UNKN	MILL	FRAG	MLST	N/A	55.3	35.1	26.6	59.6	
5811	184	1707	80D5	5	1	GRNT	BIFC	NATL	UNKN	MILL	FRAG	MLST	ANVL	79.2	61.2	28.7	219.3	
5293	184	73	90D5	4	1	GRNT	BIFC	NATL	UNKN	MILL	FRAG	MLST	N/A	77.4	59.9	514	255.4	Burned
5302	184	1261	UNKN	UNKN	1	GRNT	BIFC	NATL	UNKN	MILL	FRAG	MLST	PSTL	97.2	35	62.7	309.7	

2011.28	SBCM	Cat #	Unit	Level	Qty	MTRL	SURF	FORM	SHAPE	SRFP	COND	PTLF	STLF	L/ mm	W/ mm	T/ mm	Wt/ g	Com-ments
5794	184	1375	UNKN	UNKN	1	GRNT	BIFC	NATL	UNKN	MILL	FRAG	MLST	N/A	78.5	56.5	47.6	328.3	Burned
5298	184	3978	UNKN	UNKN	1	GRNT	BIFC	NATL	UNKN	MILL	FRAG	MLST	N/A	41.7	70.5	71.8	433.4	
5792	184	4341	UNKN	UNKN	1	GRNT	BIFC	NATL	UNKN	MILL	FRAG	MLST	N/A	57.9	88.1	35.5	257.6	Burned
5760	184	3018	115F	3	1	GRNT	UNFC	NATL	UNKN	MILL	FRAG	MLST	N/A	56.6	65.5	42.6	211.3	Burned
5769	184	321	85D5	4	1	GRNT	UNFC	NATL	UNKN	MILL	FRAG	MLST	N/A	53.5	39.7	39.4	88.2	
5791	184	74	90D5	4	1	GRNT	UNFC	NATL	UNKN	MILL	FRAG	MLST	N/A	93.7	71.1	51.7	339.6	
5289	184	293	UNKN	UNKN	1	GRNT	UNFC	NATL	UNKN	MILL	FRAG	MLST	N/A	39.7	72.4	35.4	139.9	
5261	184	1260	UNKN	UNKN	1	GRNT	UNFC	NATL	UNKN	MILL	FRAG	MLST	N/A	86	89.3	70.1	601.3	Burned
5802	184	1267	UNKN	UNKN	1	GRNT	UNFC	NATL	UNKN	MILL	FRAG	MLST	N/A	71.8	44.9	41.6	189.1	
5778	184	1376	UNKN	UNKN	1	GRNT	UNFC	NATL	UNKN	MILL	FRAG	MLST	N/A	86.2	73.8	69.1	515.8	
5810	184	4336	UNKN	UNKN	1	GRNT	UNFC	NATL	UNKN	MILL	FRAG	MLST	ANVL	80.3	104.6	30.2	437.6	
5283	184	4343	UNKN	UNKN	1	GRNT	UNFC	NATL	UNKN	MILL	FRAG	MLST	N/A	58.4	109.7	53	609.2	
5776	184	5640	UNKN	UNKN	1	GRNT	UNFC	NATL	UNKN	MILL	FRAG	MLST	N/A	82.7	61.8	44.6	286.4	
5282	184	2460	UNKN	UNKN	1	GRNT	BIFC	NATL	OVID	MILL	NRCP	MLST	N/A	98.4	85.8	48	569.7	
5762	184	1265	UNKN	UNKN	1	GRNT	UNFC	UNKN	OVID	MILL	NRCP	MLST	HMST	87.2	70.9	49	352.5	
5764	184	4315	UNKN	UNKN	1	GRNT	BIFC	MDFD	OVID	MILL	NRCP	MLST	ANVL	79.6	90.8	48.9	818	

2011.28	SBCM	Cat #	Unit	Level	Qty	MTRL	SURF	FORM	SHAPE	SRFP	COND	PTLF	STLF	L/ mm	W/ mm	T/ mm	Wt/ g	Com-ments
5795	184	5639	UNKN	UNKN	1	GRNT	BIFC	MDFD	OVID	MILL	NRCP	MLST	N/A	74.6	68.2	34.1	288.4	
5814	184	4313	UNKN	UNKN	1	GRNT	MLPL	MDFD	OVID	MILL	NRCP	MLST	PSTL	105	90	50	856	
5768	184	4314	UNKN	UNKN	1	GRNT	UNFC	MDFD	OVID	MILL	NRCP	MLST	HMST	115	90	50	828	
5761	184	1155	UNKN	UNKN	1	GRNT	UNFC	NATL	OVID	MILL	NRCP	MLST	PEKG	110.4	82.7	43.3	568	Burned
5796	184	4356	UNKN	UNKN	1	GRNT	MLFC	MDFD	RCTL	MILL	NRCP	MLST	PEKG	85.8	52.6	33.6	298.3	
7404	184	5196	UNKN	UNKN	1	VBAS	UNFC	MDFD	RUND	MILL	NRCP	MLST	N/A	90.6	90.3	50.7	734	
5290	184	4345	UNKN	UNKN	1	GRNT	BIFC	MDFD	UNKN	MILL	NRCP	MLST	HMST	96.9	92.8	44.4	573.1	
5803	184	4330	UNKN	UNKN	1	GRNT	BIFC	NATL	UNKN	MILL	NRCP	MLST	N/A	107.4	83.9	48.3	562.8	
5807	184	3976	UNKN	UNKN	1	GRBR	UNFC	MDFD	IRRG	MILL	WHLE	MLST	N/A	66.7	70.2	58.9	464.8	
5813	184	6234	UNKN	UNKN	1	GRNT	BIFC	NATL	IRRG	MILL	WHLE	MLST	PEKG	110.8	79.5	59.8	839.6	
5759	184	4353	UNKN	UNKN	1	GRNT	UNFC	NATL	IRRG	MILL	WHLE	MLST	HMST	103.7	88.8	49	656.8	
5299	184	4312	UNKN	UNKN	1	GRNT	BIFC	MDFD	OVID	MILL	WHLE	MLST	HMST	110	105	50.5	1194	
5800	184	6286	UNKN	UNKN	1	GRNT	BIFC	MDFD	OVID	MILL	WHLE	MLST	N/A	103.1	98.9	43.2	780	
5788	184	UNKN	UNKN	UNKN	1	GRNT	UNFC	MDFD	OVID	MILL	WHLE	MLST	ANVL	115	95	45	852	
5784	184	5194	120E	4	1	GRNT	UNFC	NATL	OVID	MILL	WHLE	MLST	N/A	100.7	70.4	30.2	426	
5793	184	3797	80D5	4	1	GRNT	UNFC	NATL	OVID	MILL	WHLE	MLST	N/A	37	30	26.1	41.2	

2011.28	SBCM	Cat #	Unit	Level	Qty	MTRL	SURF	FORM	SHAPE	SRFP	COND	PTLF	STLF	L/ mm	W/ mm	T/ mm	Wt/ g	Com-ments
5783	184	3908	UNKN	UNKN	1	GRBR	BIFC	MDFD	OVID	MILL	WHLE	MLST	PSTL	109.5	84.9	56	970.9	
5285	184	2461	UNKN	UNKN	1	GRNT	BIFC	MDFD	OVID	MILL	WHLE	MLST	ANVL	140.1	108.4	61.7	1598.2	
5801	184	2465	UNKN	UNKN	1	GRNT	BIFC	MDFD	OVID	MILL	WHLE	MLST	HMST	124.7	92	43.6	918.9	
5789	184	2466	UNKN	UNKN	1	GRNT	BIFC	MDFD	OVID	MILL	WHLE	MLST	N/A	113.5	94	51	889.2	
5766	184	3909	UNKN	UNKN	1	GRNT	BIFC	MDFD	OVID	MILL	WHLE	MLST	HMST	125.7	109.1	50.4	1225.8	
5300	184	4354	UNKN	UNKN	1	GRNT	BIFC	MDFD	OVID	MILL	WHLE	MLST	HMST	77.8	68.2	43.9	382.5	
5781	184	6235	UNKN	UNKN	1	GRNT	BIFC	MDFD	OVID	MILL	WHLE	MLST	HMST	97	87.8	32.4	529.2	
5775	184	6276	UNKN	UNKN	1	QRTZ	BIFC	MDFD	OVID	MILL	WHLE	MLST	HMST	108.5	91	42.3	79.6	
5295	184	2463	UNKN	UNKN	1	VBAS	BIFC	MDFD	OVID	MILL	WHLE	MLST	HMST	115.5	96.2	35.9	644	
6893	184	4352	UNKN	UNKN	1	VBAS	BIFC	MDFD	OVID	MILL	WHLE	MLST	HMST	81	74.9	42.9	354	
5765	184	4370	75D5	4	1	GRNT	UNFC	MDFD	OVID	MILL	WHLE	MLST	HMST	69.8	58.2	41.7	255.8	
5771	184	3842	UNKN	UNKN	1	GRNT	UNFC	MDFD	OVID	MILL	WHLE	MLST	ANVL	109.4	93	60.9	991.4	
5288	184	2462	UNKN	UNKN	1	GRNT	BIFC	NATL	OVID	MILL	WHLE	MLST	N/A	114.6	85.3	56.8	861.7	
5786	184	3865	UNKN	UNKN	1	GRNT	BIFC	NATL	OVID	MILL	WHLE	MLST	PEKG	72.1	57.5	38.3	235.9	
5809	184	2458	UNKN	UNKN	1	GRNT	UNFC	NATL	OVID	MILL	WHLE	MLST	N/A	111.7	99.7	71.9	1322.7	
5772	184	5789	UNKN	UNKN	1	GRNT	UNFC	NATL	OVID	MILL	WHLE	MLST	N/A	63.05	56.4	40.39	188	

2011.28	SBCM	Cat #	Unit	Level	Qty	MTRL	SURF	FORM	SHAPE	SRFP	COND	PTLF	STLF	L/ mm	W/ mm	T/ mm	Wt/ g	Com-ments
5286	184	5786	UNKN	UNKN	1	SHST	UNFC	NATL	OVID	MILL	WHLE	MLST	PSTL	118.4	70.9	29.6	394.1	
5301	184	2459	UNKN	UNKN	1	GRNT	BIFC	MDFD	TRGL	MILL	WHLE	MLST	HMST	115.1	101.1	47.6	950.8	
5284	184	4200	UNKN	UNKN	1	QRTZ	BIFC	NATL	UNKN	MILL	WHLE	MLST	N/A	44.9	92.8	39.4	316	
Mano Notation Key																		
2011.28: Pechanga Cultural Resource catalogue number																		
SBCM: San Bernardino Catalogue collection number																		
CAT #: Catalog number																		
UNIT: Location																		
	According to excavation map																	
LEVEL: Depth																		
	SURF: Surface																	
	Levels 1-10 (Increments of 6 inches each level)																	
QTY: Quantity																		
MTRL: Material																		
	BSLT: Basalt																	

	GRNT: Granitic												
	GRBR: Gabbro												
	QRTZ: Quartzite												
	SHST: Schist												
	VBSL: Vesicular Basalt												
SURF: Surface													
	BIFC: Biface												
	UNFC: Uniface												
	MLPL: Multiple												
FORM: Form													
	NATL: Natural												
	MDFD: Modified												
	UNKN: Inderminate												
SHAPE:													
	OVID: Ovoid												
	RCTL: Rectangular												
	TRGL: Triangle												

	IRRG: Irregular												
	RUND: Round												
	UNKN: Unknown												
SFRP: Surface use pattern													
	MILL: Milling												
COND: Condition													
	WHLE: Whole												
	FRAG: Fragment												
	NRCP: Nearly Complete												
PTLF: Primary tool function													
	MLST: Milling stone												
STLF: Secondary tool function													
	ANVI: Anvil												
	HMST: Hammerstone												
	PEKG: Pecking												
	PSLT: Pestle												
	N/A: Not Applicable												

L/mm: Length measured in mm from end to edge
W/mm: Width measured in mm from edge to edge
T/mm: Thickness measured in mm from top to bottom
WT/g: Weight measured in grams
Comments: Any additional data (fire-affected)

APPENDIX P

PESTLES

Appendix P: Pestles

2011.28	SBCM	Cat #	Unit	Level	Qty	MTRL	SHAPE	COND	PORT	PTLF	STLF	SURF	L/ mm	W/ mm	T/ mm	Wt/g	Com- ments
5388	184	1031	100F5	4	1	GRNT	CYDL	WHLE	N/A	CRML	N/A	INDT	61.1	21.2	14	32.2	
5387	184	1727	140I	2	1	GRNT	CYDL	WHLE	N/A	CRML	N/A	INDT	34.9	21.3	20.3	21.8	
5386	184	1072	152D	2	1	GRNT	CYDL	WHLE	N/A	CRML	N/A	INDT	50.4	21.2	19.2	32.3	
5389	184	2154	20J5	4	1	GRNT	CYDL	WHLE	N/A	CRML	N/A	INDT	41.6	22.8	19.4	34	
5385	184	656	55I	3	1	GRNT	CYDL	WHLE	N/A	CRML	N/A	INDT	47.3	19.9	17.1	25.6	
5384	184	5785	UNKN	UNKN	1	MTVC	CYDL	WHLE	N/A	CRML	N/A	INDT	70.6	38.1	27.8	107.2	
5399	184	5180	UNKN	UNKN	1	BSLT	CYDL	FRAG	NEND	PSTL	N/A	NEND	65.9	39.6	44.6	145.8	
5390	184	4305	UNKN	UNKN	1	GRBR	RCTL	WHLE	N/A	PSTL	N/A	NEND	150	95	55	1342	
5383	184	4189	UNKN	UNKN	1	GRNT	CNCL	NRCP	NEND	PSTL	ANVL	NEND	225	90	90	2746	
5400	184	4339	UNKN	UNKN	1	GRNT	CNCL	FRAG	NEND	PSTL	N/A	MLTI	73.7	40.6	63.8	277.6	
5397	184	4335	UNKN	UNKN	1	GRNT	CYDL	WHLE	BTHE	PSTL	ANVL	NATL	99.2	61.9	62.6	556	
5396	184	85	UNKN	UNKN	1	GRNT	INDT	FRAG	MEDL	PSTL	N/A	INDT	62.6	55	60.5	330.6	
5394	184	1212	UNKN	UNKN	1	GRNT	INDT	FRAG	N/A	PSTL	MANO	MLTI	98.2	72.8	67.4	723.9	
5402	184	1264	UNKN	UNKN	1	GRNT	INDT	FRAG	NEND	PSTL	N/A	NEND	47.5	59.8	37	173.5	Burned
5398	184	3974	UNKN	UNKN	1	GRNT	NATL	FRAG	NEND	PSTL	ANVL	NEND	53.4	61.7	52.8	297	

2011.28	SBCM	Cat #	Unit	Level	Qty	MTRL	SHAPE	COND	PORT	PTLF	STLF	SURF	L/ mm	W/ mm	T/ mm	Wt/g	Com- ments
5401	184	3975	UNKN	UNKN	1	GRNT	NATL	FRAG	NEND	PSTL	MANO	NEND	55.4	87.8	46.2	343.2	
5392	184	4310	UNKN	UNKN	1	GRNT	NATL	WHLE	BTHE	PSTL	N/A	NATL	140	90	83.1	2144	
5396	184	4286	UNKN	UNKN	1	GRNT	RCTL	NRCP	NEND	PSTL	N/A	NEND	100	95	60	1406	
5391	184	4307	UNKN	UNKN	1	GRNT	RCTL	NRCP	NEND	PSTL	N/A	NEND	110.5	100	21.3	1038	
5395	184	4311	UNKN	UNKN	1	GRNT	RCTL	NRCP	NEND	PSTL	MANO	NEND	80.2	74.2	53.4	776	
7606	184	4308	UNKN	UNKN	1	GRANT	NATL	WHLE	N/A	CRML	N/A	N/A	160.5	150	70	4602	flat, spher- ical

Pestle Notion Key
2011.28: Pechanga Cultural Resource catalogue number
SBCM: San Bernardino Catalogue collection number
CAT #: Catalog number
UNIT: Location
According to excavation map
LEVEL: Depth
SURF: Surface
Levels 1-10 (Increments of 6 inches each level)

QTY: Quantity												
MTRL: Material												
	GRNT: Granitic											
	GRBR: Gabbro											
	BSLT: Basalt											
	MTVC: Metavolcanic											
SHAPE:												
	NATL: Natural											
	RCTL: Rectangular											
	CYDL: Cylindrical											
	CNCL: Conical											
	INDT: Inderminate											
COND: Condition												
	WHLE: Whole											
	FRAG: Fragment											
	NRCP: Nearly Complete											
PORT: Portion												

	NEND: Neither end											
	BTHE: Both ends											
	MEDL: Medial											
	N/A: Not Applicable											
PTLF: Primary tool function												
	PSTL: Pestle, food and/or material processing											
	CRML: Ceremonial Pestle											
STLF: Secondary tool function												
	ANVL: Anvil											
	MANO: Mano											
	N/A: Not Applicable											
SURF: Surface												
	MLTI: Multi											
	NEND: Neither end											
	NATL: Natural											
	INDT: Inderminate											
	N/A: Not Applicable											

L/mm: Length measured in mm from end to edge
W/mm: Width measured in mm from edge to edge
T/mm: Thickness measured in mm from top to bottom
WT/g: Weight measured in grams
Comments: Any additional data (fire-affected)

APPENDIX Q

HEATING STONES

Appendix Q: Heating Stones

2011.28	SBCM	Cat #	Unit	Level	Qty	MTRL	COND	PORT	L/mm	W/mm	T/mm	Wt/g	Comments
7174	184	3718	UNKN	UNKN	1	STET	FRAG	MEDF	86.9	63.7	54	348.6	Hole-Conical
7175	184	5971	UNKN	UNKN	1	SOAP	FRAG	ENSF	25	26.5	10	7.9	Hole-Conical
7176	184	5972	UNKN	UNKN	1	STET	FRAG	ENSF	21.5	14	12.5	4.1	fits with 184-5973
7177	184	5973	UNKN	UNKN	1	STET	FRAG	ENSF	26.5	14	9	4.1	fits with 184-5972
7178	184	6202	UNKN	UNKN	1	STET	FRAG	MEDF	55.4	41.1	29.2	82.5	
7179	184	6279	UNKN	UNKN	1	STET	FRAG	UNKN	36.9	30	2	26.1	

Heating Stone Notation Key

2011.28: Pechanga Cultural Resource catalogue number

SBCM: San Bernardino Catalogue collection number

CAT #: Catalog number

UNIT: Location

According to excavation map

LEVEL: Depth

SURF: Surface

Levels 1-10 (Increments of 6 inches each level)							
QTY: Quantity							
MTRL: Material							
STET: Steatite							
SOAP: Soapstone							
COND: Condition							
FRAG: Fragment							
PORT: Portion							
MEDF: Medial Section Fragment							
ENSF: End Section Fragment							
UNKN: Unknown							
L/mm: Length measured in mm from end to edge							
W/mm: Width measured in mm from edge to edge							
T/mm: Thickness measured in mm from top to bottom							
WT/g: Weight measured in grams							
Comments: Any additional data							
Hole-Conically drilled							

							Fits with another #	

APPENDIX R

PIPES

Appendix R: Pipes

2011.28	SBCM	Cat #	Unit	Level	Qty	MTRL	COND	L/mm	W/mm	T/mm	Wt/g	Comments
7474	184	4703	85G	1	1	BONE	FRAG	42	16.2	4.3	3.7	POLISHED, BURNED
7475	184	6115	80E5	3	1	BONE	FRAG	33.2	17.3	8.3	4	POLISHED, BURNED
7476	184	6162	UNKN	UNKN	1	BONE	FRAG	13.1	12.3	6.1	0.9	POLISHED, BURNED
7478	184	4026	UNKN	UNKN	1	BONE	FRAG	20	7	5	1.1	BURNED
7479	184	2909	100E5	4	1	BONE	FRAG	37	12	5	3	
7480	184	4951	110E5	8	1	BONE	FRAG	15	14	4	2	BURNED
7482	184	3057	95E5	8	1	BONE	FRAG	24	17	5	4	BURNED
7483	184	791	110F5	6	1	BONE	FRAG	19	15	5	3	BURNED
7509	184	5722	110E5	5	1	BONE	FRAG	25	14	5	2	BURNED
7477	184	1051	100E5	3	1	CLAY	FRAG	13.3	13.2	3	0.6	POLISHED, BURNED
7481	184	1030	125D	3	1	CLAY	FRAG	16	10	4	2	BURNED
7484	184	2125	95D5	2	1	CLAY	FRAG	44	23	8	8	BURNED
7485	184	4739	90F5	2	1	CLAY	FRAG	11.4	8.5	4.1	0.5	BURNED
7486	184	4519	90H	3	1	CLAY	FRAG	24	13	5	2	BURNED
7487	184	6253	UNKN	UNKN	1	CLAY	FRAG	42.8	29.5	18	19.5	BURNED

2011.28	SBCM	Cat #	Unit	Level	Qty	MTRL	COND	L/mm	W/mm	T/mm	Wt/g	Comments
7488	184	355	95E	1	1	CLAY	FRAG	17	9	5	3	BURNED
7489	184	6260	UNKN	UNKN	1	CLAY	FRAG	31.9	15.5	15.1	7.1	
7490	184	6256	UNKN	UNKN	1	CLAY	FRAG	28.6	15.7	7.8	3.6	BURNED
7491	184	1368	UNKN	UNKN	1	CLAY	FRAG	32.8	21.1	7.6	4.3	BURNED
7492	184	3352	90D	2	1	CLAY	FRAG	17.2	19.2	11.9	2.6	BURNED
7493	184	3962	UNKN	UNKN	1	CLAY	FRAG	24	11	5	4	BURNED
7494	184	3963	UNKN	UNKN	1	CLAY	FRAG	13	11	3	0.03	
7495	184	3964	UNKN	UNKN	1	CLAY	FRAG	20	10	5	0.07	
7497	184	4502	95E5	4	4	CLAY	FRAG	35	16	12	6.1	BURNED
7498	184	4577	105E5	5	1	CLAY	FRAG	22.8	14.1	3.8	1	BURNED
7499	184	6254	UNKN	UNKN	1	CLAY	FRAG	26.6	12.4	12.8	3.8	BURNED
7500	184	6255	UNKN	UNKN	1	CLAY	FRAG	39.9	17.4	12.6	6.3	
7501	184	6257	UNKN	UNKN	1	CLAY	FRAG	26	13.5	12.4	3.9	BURNED
7502	184	6258	UNKN	UNKN	1	CLAY	FRAG	22.9	25.6	11.1	4.6	BURNED
7503	184	6259	UNKN	UNKN	1	CLAY	FRAG	46.6	23.4	14.6	10	BURNED
7504	184	6538	70C	1	1	CLAY	FRAG	11.3	10.5	3.8	0.3	BURNED

2011.28	SBCM	Cat #	Unit	Level	Qty	MTRL	COND	L/mm	W/mm	T/mm	Wt/g	Comments
7510	184	581	105D5	1	1	CLAY	FRAG	22	14	5	2	BURNED
7511	184	114	85D5	UNKN	2	CLAY	FRAG	15	10	4	1	BURNED
7496	184	4360	UNKN	UNKN	1	STET	WHLE	86.3	25	58.9	52.9	BURNED, ETCHED
7505	184	4367	UNKN	UNKN	1	STET	WHLE	178	37	38	459.1	Riverside Co. Temecula, G.S., etched, sucking tube
7506	184	4368	UNKN	UNKN	1	STET	WHLE	188	37	37	406.7	etched, POLISHED, sucking tube
7507	184	4369	UNKN	UNKN	1	STET	WHLE	106.7	49.7	46.9	388.7	etched, Riverside Co., Temecula, G.S. sucking tube
7508	184	6331	UNKN	UNKN	1	STET	FRAG	62.4	42.8	17	55.5	sucking tube, BURNED
Pipe Notation Key												
2011.28: Pechanga Cultural Resource catalogue number												
SBCM: San Bernardino Catalogue collection number												
CAT #: Catalog number												
UNIT: Location												
	According to excavation map											
LEVEL: Depth												
	SURF: Surface											

	Levels 1-10 (Increments of 6 inches each level)						
QTY: Quantity							
MTRL: Material							
	STET: Steatite						
	BONE: Faunal bone						
	CLAY: Clay						
COND: Condition							
	WHLE: Whole						
	FRAG: Fragment						
L/mm: Length measured in mm from end to edge							
W/mm: Width measured in mm from edge to edge							
T/mm: Thickness measured in mm from top to bottom							
WT/g: Weight measured in grams							
Comments: Any additional data (fire-affected, etc.)							
	Sucking tube						
	Polished						
	Burned						

	Etched						
	Location						

APPENDIX S

METATES AND MORTARS

Appendix S: Metates and Mortars

2011.3	SBCM	Cat #	Unit	Level	Qty	Object	MTRL	COND	L/mm	W/mm	T/mm	Wt/g	Comments
7512	184	4289	110G	5,6	1	MORT	VBSL	FRAG	67.5	43.7	19.1	90	attaches to 4290
7513	184	4290	110G	5,6	1	MORT	VBSL	FRAG	110	90	100	1132	attaches to 4289
7514	184	4291	110G	5,6	1	MORT	VBSL	FRAG	65.5	39.9	84	498	
7515	184	4292	110G	5,6	1	MORT	VBSL	FRAG	65	60	70	410	
7516	184	4293	110G	5,6	1	MORT	VBSL	FRAG	49.3	60.9	34.2	246	
7517	184	4294	110G	5,6	1	MORT	VBSL	FRAG	38.2	39.3	63.7	240	
7518	184	4295	110G	5,6	1	MORT	VBSL	FRAG	43.1	42.9	31.8	108	rim
7519	184	4296	110G	5,6	1	MORT	VBSL	FRAG	48.6	50.9	51.5	196	rim
7520	184	4350	UNKN	UNKN	1	MORT	VBSL	FRAG	131.1	66.9	40.6	441.8	
7521	184	173	120E5	4	1	MORT	VBSL	FRAG	44.4	64.4	34.4	131.6	
7522	184	174	120E5	4	1	MORT	VBSL	FRAG	27.1	69.9	19.1	39.4	
7523	184	175	120E5	4	1	MORT	VBSL	FRAG	26.2	58.6	15.7	40.2	
7524	184	959	105D5	1	1	MORT	VBSL	FRAG	49	29.3	27.3	40.5	
7525	184	1026	125D	3	1	MORT	VBSL	FRAG	70.2	101.2	48.2	481.5	
7526	184	1463	65I	4	1	MORT	GRNT	FRAG	88.6	62.2	29.6	141.9	

2011.3	SBCM	Cat #	Unit	Level	Qty	Object	MTRL	COND	L/mm	W/mm	T/mm	Wt/g	Comments
7527	184	1587	55K5	1	1	MORT	GRNT	FRAG	32	24.6	15.4	12.8	
7528	184	1932	110H	4	1	MORT	VBSL	FRAG	139	68.6	77.5	753	
7529	184	2457	UNKN	UNKN	1	MORT	VBSL	FRAG	141.3	132.5	74.3	1419.1	
7530	184	2464	UNKN	UNKN	1	MORT	VBSL	FRAG	84.9	127.5	55	737.4	
7531	184	3786	100F5	6	1	MORT	BSLT	FRAG	60.5	50.5	43.2	176.1	
7532	184	4407	75C	2	1	MORT	GRNT	FRAG	88.5	70.1	35.6	236.9	
7533	184	4578	105E5	5	1	MORT	VBSL	FRAG	68.8	49.8	40.1	157.8	
7534	184	5674	35I	3	1	MORT	GRNT	FRAG	62.3	45.8	31.6	124.8	RIM
7535	184	5770	UNKN	UNKN	1	MORT	VBSL	FRAG	116.8	73.2	62.2	842	
7536	184	5781	UNKN	UNKN	1	MORT	VBSL	FRAG	37.4	39	24.1	50.7	
7537	184	5787	UNKN	UNKN	1	MORT	GRNT	FRAG	159.6	124.3	40	1160	
7538	184	5805	UNKN	UNKN	1	MORT	GRNT	FRAG	83.2	53	40.2	150.5	
7539	184	6184	65I	1	1	MORT	GRNT	FRAG	28.6	37.5	20.8	38.1	
7540	184	4287	110G	5,6	1	MORT	GRNT	FRAG	75	55	110	624	BURNED
7541	184	2863	70E5	2	1	MORT	BSLT	FRAG	28	37	29	42.5	RIM
7542	184	4932	140H5	1,2	1	MORT	GRNT	FRAG	50	49	37.5	91	

2011.3	SBCM	Cat #	Unit	Level	Qty	Object	MTRL	COND	L/mm	W/mm	T/mm	Wt/g	Comments
7543	184	5442	35I	2	1	MORT	GRNT	FRAG	55.1	58.5	38.9	111.4	
7544	184	5100	UNKN	UNKN	1	MORT	GRNT	FRAG	72.1	36.6	38.6	115.3	
7545	184	5779	UNKN	UNKN	1	MORT	VBSL	FRAG	66	56.6	53.2	278.6	
7546	184	4288	110G	5,6	1	MORT	GRNT	FRAG	40	55	60	198	
7547	184	5791	UNKN	UNKN	1	MORT	BSLT	FRAG	25	30	25	8.2	
7548	184	2824	55I5	4	1	MORT	GRNT	FRAG	100	68	53	521	
7549	184	3188	110F5	4	1	MORT	VBSL	FRAG	50	55	28	102	BURNED
7550	184	4299	110G	5,6	1	MORT	GRNT	FRAG	43.8	48.3	47	147.5	BURNED
7551	184	2454	UNKN	UNKN	1	META	GRNT	FRAG	179.6	146.2	76.5	2110+	ANVIL
7552	184	1795	110H5	5	1	META	GRNT	FRAG	80	73.2	15.1	120	
7553	184	2456	UNKN	UNKN	1	META	GRNT	FRAG	139.7	113.9	67.4	1408.4	Burned
7554	184	2862	70E5	2	1	META	VBSL	FRAG	29	40	32	85.5	
7555	184	4357	UNKN	UNKN	1	META	GRNT	FRAG	105.6	81.1	75.6	845.4	
7556	184	5365	UNKN	UNKN	1	META	SLAT	FRAG	155	115	10.3	286	
7557	184	1611	95H5	2	1	META	GRNT	FRAG	141	126.5	39.7	1253.2	
7558	184	4856	75E5	6	1	META	GRNT	FRAG	67	62	44.5	261.8	

2011.3	SBCM	Cat #	Unit	Level	Qty	Object	MTRL	COND	L/mm	W/mm	T/mm	Wt/g	Comments
7559	184	4282	UNKN	UNKN	1	META	GRNT	FRAG	150	100	80	2648	ANVIL

Motar and Metate Notation Key	
2011.28: Pechanga Cultural Resource catalogue number	
SBCM: San Bernardino Catalogue collection number	
CAT#: Catalog number	
UNIT: Location	
	According to excavation map
LEVEL: Depth	
	SURF: Surface
	Levels 1-10 (Increments of 6 inches each level)
QTY: Quantity	
MTRL: Material	
	GRNT: Granitic
	VBSL: Vesicular Basalt
	UNKN: Unknown

	BSLT: Basalt							
	SLAT: Slate							
COND: Condition								
	WHLE: Whole							
	FRAG: Fragment							
L/mm: Length measured in mm from end to edge								
W/mm: Width measured in mm from edge to edge								
T/mm: Thickness measured in mm from top to bottom								
WT/g: Weight measured in grams								
Comments: Any additional data (fire-affected, etc.)								
	Secondary tool usc: anvil							

APPENDIX T

PENDANTS AND STONE BEADS

Appendix T: Pendants and Stone Beads													
2011.3	**SBCM**	**Cat #**	**Unit**	**Level**	**Qty**	**MTRL**	**COND**	**HOLE**	**L/mm**	**W/mm**	**T/mm**	**Wt/g**	**Comments**
7416	184	230	100D	5	1	SLAT	FRAG	N/A	39.1	27	5.2	8.6	BURNED
7448	184	920	100E5	1	1	SLAT	NRCP	N/A	16.8	11.1	2.4	0.6	BURNED
7417	184	1089	105E	4	1	SLAT	NRCP	BCOL	31.2	22.6	4.7	3.5	BURNED
7428	184	5347	110D	3	1	BONE	FRAG	CONL	16.8	9.8	1.4	0.2	
7418	184	1537	110I5	1	1	SLAT	FRAG	N/A	24	21	7.4	5.3	BURNED
7426	184	5586	115B	3,4	1	SLAT	FRAG	N/A	20.4	10	5	2	BURNED
7414	184	5364	115E	3,4	1	GNAL	FRAG	CONL	11	9	0.3	0.2	
7410	184	2964	120G	3	1	CLAY	FRAG	CONL	16.5	29.2	5.8	3.2	BURNED
7146	184	5840	160K	UNKN	1	CLAY	FRAG	BCOL	29	20	5	3.4	BURNED
7413	184	1887	170H5	2	1	SLAT	NRCP	N/A	17.6	9.1	1.5	0.5	
7422	184	3227	175J	2	1	SLAT	FRAG	CONL	23.8	21.2	3.7	2.8	BURNED
7420	184	1634	40	2	1	SLAT	NRCP	N/A	14.1	15	2.8	1	BURNED
7419	184	1609	55K	1	1	STET	FRAG	N/A	21.6	12.7	7.7	2.5	BURNED
7407	184	1695	70C	3	1	STET	NRCP	N/A	17.5	9.1	4.8	1.4	BURNED
7421	184	1791	70C5	3	1	SLAT	FRAG	N/A	30.8	23	4.6	4.7	BURNED

2011.3	SBCM	Cat #	Unit	Level	Qty	MTRL	COND	HOLE	L/mm	W/mm	T/mm	Wt/g	Comments
7409	184	1832	70C5	5	1	SLAT	FRAG	N/A	19.5	12.7	2.4	1.1	BURNED
7445	184	5664	75E5	1	1	CLAY	FRAG	BCOL	13.8	15.5	6.7	1.6	
7415	184	199	75I	3	1	SLAT	NRCP	N/A	33	17.9	5.4	6.6	BURNED
7450	184	1438	75N	1	1	SLAT	NRCP	N/A	28.6	15.7	2.5	1.8	BURNED, Scalloped edges
7453	184	5267	80E	5	1	STET	NRCP	N/A	40	29	5	8.6	BURNED
7427	184	6274	85F5	4	1	SLAT	FRAG	N/A	26.9	10.5	2.1	1.5	BURNED
7447	184	6433	85G	3	1	CLAY	NRCP	CONL	16.3	19.6	4.3	1.6	BURNED
7423	184	3534	90E	6	1	SLAT	NRCP	N/A	18	21.6	3.8	1.8	BURNED
2106	184	5379	95D	3,4	1	STON	WHLE	BCOL	3	3	1.5	2	Bead
7429	184	5378	95D	3,4	2	BONE	FRAG	N/A	15.1	4.1	0.9	0.1	BURNED
7430	184	5381	95D	3,4	1	BONE	FRAG	BCOL	17.6	12.6	2.4	0.3	BURNED
7431	184	5382	95D	3,4	1	TURT	FRAG	CONL	21.5	14.2	0.7	0.3	BURNED
7433	184	5384	95D	3,4	1	TURT	FRAG	CONL	18.9	17.8	5.1	0.7	BURNED
7436	184	5388	95D	3,4	1	TURT	FRAG	BCOL	15.9	13	2.9	0.4	BURNED
7437	184	5389	95D	3,4	2	TURT	FRAG	BCOL	25.2	10.3	2.5	0.5	BURNED
7438	184	5391	95D	3,4	1	TURT	FRAG	BCOL	15.1	14.4	2.4	0.4	BURNED

2011.3	SBCM	Cat #	Unit	Level	Qty	MTRL	COND	HOLE	L/mm	W/mm	T/mm	Wt/g	Comments
7439	184	5392	95D	3,4	1	TURT	FRAG	BCOL	12.4	12.4	4.8	0.4	BURNED
7434	184	5386	95D	3,4	1	TURT	FRAG	BOTH	22.9	19.9	3.1	0.7	BURNED, 2 HOLES
7432	184	5383	95D	3,4	1	TURT	FRAG	CONL	12.7	7.9	2	0.2	
7435	184	5387	95D	3,4	1	TURT	FRAG	CONL	17.2	14	1.7	0.3	
7440	184	2440	95D5	3	1	CLAY	FRAG	CONL	24.3	23.3	7.5	5.2	BURNED
7441	184	2441	95D5	3	1	CLAY	FRAG	BCOL	16.9	27.2	5.2	2.9	BURNED
7408	184	1752	95H	2,3	1	SLAT	NRCP	N/A	51.4	21.1	10.7	17.8	BURNED
2107	184	6035	UNKN	UNKN	1	SOAP	WHLE	BCOL	3.3	3.3	2	2	Bead, BURNED
7443	184	4453	UNKN	UNKN	1	CLAY	FRAG	BCOL	22.2	44	5.5	6.4	BURNED
7444	184	4454	UNKN	UNKN	1	CLAY	NRCP	CONL	20.3	33.8	5.7	5.8	BURNED
7442	184	3915	UNKN	UNKN	1	CLAY	FRAG	N/A	26.2	36.6	5.1	8.9	
7411	184	4362	UNKN	UNKN	1	GNAL	NRCP	CONL	15.4	10.4	2.1	0.3	
7412	184	4363	UNKN	UNKN	1	GNAL	WHLE	CONL	9.6	7.7	1.7	0.1	
7452	184	4365	UNKN	UNKN	1	PECT	WHLE	BCOL	29.3	27.5	1.3	1.7	
7406	184	1689	UNKN	UNKN	1	SLAT	NRCP	N/A	20.3	28.2	2.6	2.4	BURNED
7425	184	4324	UNKN	UNKN	1	SLAT	NRCP	N/A	26.9	16.2	5.1	2.9	BURNED

2011.3	SBCM	Cat #	Unit	Level	Qty	MTRL	COND	HOLE	L/mm	W/mm	T/mm	Wt/g	Comments
7449	184	1370	UNKN	UNKN	1	SLAT	FRAG	N/A	36	6	2.5	1.2	BURNED
7424	184	4255	UNKN	UNKN	1	SLAT	NRCP	N/A	33.1	19.5	6.1	4.7	BURNED, ETCHED
7451	184	5970	UNKN	UNKN	1	SOAP	NRCP	N/A	5.5	19.5	4	2.8	BURNED

Pendant and Stone Bead Notation Key	
2011.28: Pechanga Cultural Resource catalogue number	
SBCM: San Bernardino Catalogue collection number	
CAT# : Catalog number	
UNIT: Location	
	According to excavation map
LEVEL: Depth	
	SURF: Surface
	Levels 1-10 (Increments of 6 inches each level)
QTY: Quantity	
MTRL: Material	
	STET: Steatite

	SOAP: Soapstone						
	BONE: Fanual bone						
	TURT: Turtle, Western Pond						
	SLAT: Slate						
	CLAY: Clay						
	GNAL: Green Abalone						
	PECT: Pecten						
	STON: Unidentified stone						
COND: Condition							
	WHLE: Whole						
	FRAG: Fragment						
	NRCP: Nearly Complete						
HOLE: Hole Drilled							
	CONL: Conical						
	BCOL: Biconical						
	PUCH: Punched						
	BOTH: Conical and Biconial holes						

	N/A: Not Applicable						
L/mm: Length measured in mm from end to edge							
W/mm: Width measured in mm from edge to edge							
T/mm: Thickness measured in mm from top to bottom							
WT/g: Weight measured in grams							
Comments: Any additional data (fire-affected, etc.)							
	2 Holes						
	Bead						
	Etched						
	Scalloped edges						

APPENDIX U

FAUNAL

Appendix U: Faunal											
2011.28	SBCM	Cat #	Unit	Level	Qty	Size Cat	Species	Bone Type	COND	Wt/g	Comments
3022	184	4089	85	6	1	UNKN	MAML	UNKN	FRAG	0.7	
3030	184	1059	100 5	7	10	UNKN	MAML	UNKN	FRAG	9.2	
3040	184	6266	100A-20	1	2	UNKN	MAML	UNKN	FRAG	5.3	
6268	184	6268	100A-20	1	1	UNKN	MAML	UNKN	FRAG	0.4	
3043	184	2262	100A40	UNKN	22	UNKN	MAML	UNKN	FRAG	34.3	
3617	184	2860	100D	3	1	XSM	CTRBB	mandible	FRAG	1	
3639	184	638	100D	4	1	XSM	BHRB	mandible	FRAG	0.6	
2950	184	638	100D	4	1	XSM	CTRB	humerus	WHLE	0.4	distal end
2951	184	638	100D	4	1	XSM	CTRB	tibia	WHLE	0.7	
2859	184	638	100D	4	276	UNKN	MAML	UNKN	FRAG	71.4	
3065	184	638	100D	4	1	XSM	RAT	ulna	WHLE	0.5	
2923	184	2923	100D	5	1	XSM	CTRB	humerus	WHLE	2	
3664	184	233	100D	5	1	SM	SKUK	Rt mandible	WHLE	2	w/teeth
3050	184	2923	100D	5	1	SM	SKUK	Ulna	FRAG	4	
3146	184	932	100D	6	3	XSM	CTRB	skull	FRAG	0.8	
2834	184	5085	100D	7	1	UNKN	MAML	UNKN	FRAG	0.3	
4128	184	5080	100D	7	1	UNKN	MAML	UNKN	FRAG	0.6	
3629	184	4898	100D	8	1	XSM	CTRB	Lt mandible	WHLE	3	
3647	184	4898	100D	8	1	XSM	CTRB	mandible	FRAG	2	
4129	184	4893	100D	8	1	UNKN	MAML	UNKN	FRAG	0.2	
3676	184	3129	100D	SURF	1	MED	BCAT	mandible	FRAG	4	w/teeth

2011.28	SBCM	Cat #	Unit	Level	Qty	Size Cat	Species	Bone Type	COND	Wt/g	Comments
3680	184	3074	100D5	1	1	MED	MAML	incisor	FRAG	1	
3127	184	2924	100D5	3	1	MED	BCAT	Ulna	FRAG	6	
2943	184	2924	100D5	3	1	MED	COYT	humerus	FRAG	2.2	distal end
3062	184	164	100D5	3	1	XSM	CTRB	femur	WHLE	1	
3631	184	2924	100D5	3	1	XSM	CTRB	Lt mandi-ble	WHLE	3	
3129	184	2924	100D5	3	1	MED	DEER	tibia	WHLE	10	
3624	184	2924	100D5	3	1	XSM	GRSQL	Rt mandi-ble	WHLE	2	
3658	184	2924	100D5	3	1	XSM	MAML	incisor	WHLE	1	
3158	184	2924	100D5	3	2	MED	MAML	long	FRAG	8	
2854	184	2924	100D5	3	89	MED/LG	MAML	UNKN	FRAG	173.1	
2934	184	894	100D5	8	1	LG	MAML	skull	FRAG	3.8	
2814	184	894	100D5	8	4	UNKN	MAML	UNKN	FRAG	9.1	
3121	184	969	100E	2	1	SM	MAML	femur	FRAG	0.8	
3633	184	3005	100E 5	5	1	XSM	GRSQ	Maxillary	FRAG	1	
2798	184	3005	100E 5	5	200+	MED/LG	MAML	UNKN	FRAG	383.9	
3640	184	4951	100E 5	8	1	XSM	GRSQ	mandible	FRAG	0.8	
4145	184	4939	100E 5	8	1	UNKN	MAML	UNKN	FRAG	0.5	
3175	184	4939	100E 5	8	1	XSM	TURT	shell	FRAG	1	
3645	184	873	100E 5	10, 11	1	XSM	BHRB	Lt mandi-ble	WHLE	2	
3638	184	873	100E 5	10, 11	1	XSM	CTRB	maxillary	FRAG	2	
3643	184	873	100E 5	10, 11	1	XSM	RAT	mandible	FRAG	0.9	
3644	184	873	100E 5	10, 11	1	XSM	RAT	Rt mandi-ble	WHLE	0.6	

2011.28	SBCM	Cat #	Unit	Level	Qty	Size Cat	Species	Bone Type	COND	Wt/g	Comments
3657	184	873	100E 5	10, 11	1	XSM	RAT	Rt mandible	WHLE	0.8	
3641	184	873	100E 5	10,11	1	XSM	RAT	Lt mandible	WHLE	1	
2825	184	914	100E5	1	26	UNKN	MAML	UNKN	FRAG	27.8	
3156	184	989	100E5	3	3	SM	MAML	UNKN	FRAG	1.4	
3076	184	2909	100E5	4	1	XSM	CTRB	long	WHLE	0.8	
3143	184	935	100E5	4	2	XSM	CTRB	maxillary	FRAG	0.5	
3649	184	2909	100E5	4	1	XSM	CTRB	Rt mandible	WHLE	3	w/teeth
3678	184	2909	100E5	4	1	MED	MAML	mandible	FRAG	1	
3690	184	2909	100E5	4	2	UNKN	MAML	teeth	FRAG	2	
3677	184	2909	100E5	4	1	MED	MAML	tooth	WHLE	1	
2862	184	3613	100E5	4	1	LG	MAML	UNKN	FRAG	8.6	
2909	184	2909	100E5	4	8	MED	MAML	UNKN	FRAG	7.9	
3124	184	6474	100E5	6	1	SM	BADG	Metacarpal	WHLE	0.4	
3616	184	626	100E5	9	4	XSM	GOPH	Mandible/skull	FRAG	0.6	
2784	184	873	100E5	10,11	12	ALL	MAML	UNKN	FRAG	24.7	
2851	184	818	100E5	6,7	26	ALL	MAML	UNKN	FRAG	21.6	
2790	184	179	100F	1	29	ALL	MAML	UNKN	FRAG	24.3	
2665	184	2679	100F5	5	4	SM/MED	MAML	long	FRAG	6.8	
2694	184	3785	100F5	6	10	SM/MED	MAML	long	FRAG	1.6	
2806	184	853	100F5	7	3	UNKN	MAML	UNKN	FRAG	3.7	
3627	184	766	100F5	8	1	XSM	CTRBB	Lt mandible	FRAG	0.9	
3154	184	766	100F5	8	1	SM	MAML	metacarpal	WHLE	1	

2011.28	SBCM	Cat #	Unit	Level	Qty	Size Cat	Species	Bone Type	COND	Wt/g	Comments
2802	184	766	100F5	8	10	UNKN	MAML	UNKN	FRAG	10	
3032	184	1021	100O5	9	4	UNKN	MAML	UNKN	FRAG	5.3	
3047	184	4518	105B	1	1	XSM	MOUS	skull	WHLE	1	
3135	184	495	105D5	3	1	XSM	GRSQ	humerus	FRAG	2	
3162	184	495	105D5	3	1	LG	MAML	long	FRAG	18	
2756	184	718	105D5	4	4	UNKN	MAML	UNKN	FRAG	3	
2912	184	4801	105D5	5	2	UNKN	MAML	UNKN	FRAG	0.6	
5749	184	5749	105E	3	1	UNKN	MAML	UNKN	FRAG	1	
4097	184	5753	105E	3	1	UNKN	MAML	UNKN	FRAG	2	
4106	184	5759	105E	3	1	UNKN	MAML	UNKN	FRAG	0.8	
2853	184	1084	105E	4	69+	LG	MAML	UNKN	FRAG	147	
2920	184	1084	105E	4	1	LG	MAML	UNKN	WHLE	10.8	
2879	184	1016	105E5	3	50+	UNKN	MAML	UNKN	FRAG	25.3	
4711	184	4584	105E5	5	1	SM	MAML	femur	FRAG	1.4	
4705	184	4588	105E5	5	1	XSM	MAML	humerus	FRAG	0.35	
2776	184	4590	105E5	5	200+	LG	MAML	UNKN	FRAG	221.2	
4147	184	4583	105E5	5	1	UNKN	MAML	UNKN	FRAG	1.3	
4139	184	4587	105E5	5	1	UNKN	MAML	UNKN	FRAG	0.4	
2689	184	1944	105E5	5	14+	LG	MAML	vert	FRAG	31.1	
794	184	794	105F	1	4	LG	MAML	UNKN	FRAG	24.9	
3141	184	934	105F	2	2	XSM	FISH	vert	FRAG	0.6	
2650	184	866	105F	3	7	LG	MAML	long/rib	FRAG	19.7	

2011.28	SBCM	Cat #	Unit	Level	Qty	Size Cat	Species	Bone Type	COND	Wt/g	Comments
2800	184	625	105F	5	2	MED	MAML	UNKN	FRAG	5.6	
2824	184	709	105F5	2	6	UNKN	MAML	UNKN	FRAG	15.8	
3097	184	899	105F5	3	1	XSM	GRSQ	femur	FRAG	0.8	
2781	184	899	105F5	3	17	MED/LG	MAML	UNKN	FRAG	10	
2902	184	860	105F5	4	11	UNKN	MAML	UNKN	FRAG	6.7	
3621	184	1060	105F5	7	1	XSM	JKRBB	Lt mandible	WHLE	2	
3049	184	1060	105F5	7	3	UNKN	MAML	UNKN	FRAG	1.9	
2836	184	2571	105F-PA	1	5	UNKN	MAML	UNKN	FRAG	0.6	
4047	184	5253	10G5	3	1	UNKN	MAML	UNKN	FRAG	0.8	
3034	184	2132	1105	1	37	UNKN	MAML	UNKN	FRAG	29.4	
3026	184	1547	110-5	1	50+	UNKN	MAML	UNKN	FRAG	14.8	
3024	184	5374	110-5?	2	4	UNKN	MAML	UNKN	FRAG	10	
2864	184	5362	110D	1	4	LG	MAML	UNKN	FRAG	5.4	
4709	184	4222	110D	2	1	SM	MAML	Tibia	FRAG	0.9	
4703	184	4218	110D	2	1	MED	MAML	UNKN	FRAG	6.3	
4702	184	4228	110D	2	1	MED	MAML	UNKN	FRAG	1.2	
4706	184	4231	110D	2	1	SM	MAML	UNKN	FRAG	0.75	
4104	184	4226	110D	2	1	UNKN	MAML	UNKN	FRAG	0.2	
4123	184	4229	110D	2	1	UNKN	MAML	UNKN	FRAG	4.3	
4096	184	4232	110D	2	1	UNKN	MAML	UNKN	FRAG	0.9	
4134	184	4233	110D	2	1	UNKN	MAML	UNKN	FRAG	0.3	
4117	184	4234	110D	2	1	UNKN	MAML	UNKN	FRAG	1.6	

2011.28	SBCM	Cat #	Unit	Level	Qty	Size Cat	Species	Bone Type	COND	Wt/g	Comments
3670	184	4131	110D	3	1	SM	MAML	incisor	WHLE	0.5	
3059	184	5339	110D	3	1	SM	MAML	tibia	FRAG	1.5	
2858	184	4131	110D	3	35+	LG	MAML	UNKN	FRAG	34	
4125	184	5344	110D	3	1	UNKN	MAML	UNKN	FRAG	1	
3611	184	4131	110D	3	1	XSM	RAT	mandible frag	WHLE	0.4	
3661	184	1552	110D	4	1	XSM	CTRB	Rt mandi-ble	WHLE	2.5	w/teeth
2700	184	1552	110D	4	15	SM/MED	MAML	long/rib	FRAG	8.7	
2741	184	6095	110D	5	52+	MED	MAML	UNKN	FRAG	39	
3620	184	632	110D	6	3	XSM	CTRBB	mandible/ skull	FRAG	1.3	
2933	184	5434	110D	6	1	LG	MAML	metacar-pal	WHLE	15.5	
3052	184	5434	110D	6	1	SM	SKUK	femur	FRAG	3	
3126	184	6082	110D5	1	1	MED	BCAT	Metacar-pal	WHLE	0.4	TB-3
2680	184	3147	110D5	1	1	MED	MAML	skull	FRAG	5.1	
3051	184	1775	110D5	3	3	UNKN	MAML	UNKN	FRAG	4	
3682	184	2107	110D5	4	2	MED	DEER	mandible	FRAG	8	teeth
3100	184	2107	110D5	4	1	XSM	GRSQ	femur	FRAG	0.9	
2687	184	2107	110D5	4	1	MED/LG	MAML	long/rib	FRAG	18.5	
3686	184	2107	110D5	4	3	MED	MAML	teeth	FRAG	1	
3202	184	2107	110D5	4	1	XSM	TURT	shell	FRAG	0.8	
2929	184	2987	110D5	5	7	SM/LG	MAML	long/rib	FRAG	83.1	cut marks
2672	184	6083	110E	3	7	MED/LG	MAML	long	FRAG	20.4	
2946	184	5277	110E	5	1	MED	DEER	tibia epiphsis	WHLE	7.9	

2011.28	SBCM	Cat #	Unit	Level	Qty	Size Cat	Species	Bone Type	COND	Wt/g	Comments
3120	184	5277	110E	5	1	SM	MAML	pelvic	FRAG	0.5	
2922	184	5277	110E	5	1	MED	MAML	rib	FRAG	6.8	
2777	184	5277	110E	5	49	UNKN	MAML	UNKN	FRAG	49	
4110	184	5485	110E	5	1	UNKN	MAML	UNKN	FRAG	0.3	
4144	184	5486	110E	5	1	UNKN	MAML	UNKN	FRAG	0.1	
4141	184	5487	110E	5	1	UNKN	MAML	UNKN	FRAG	0.35	
4108	184	5489	110E	5	1	UNKN	MAML	UNKN	FRAG	1	
4146	184	5489	110E	5	1	UNKN	MAML	UNKN	FRAG	0.3	
2679	184	593	110E5	2	1	MED	MAML	long	FRAG	4.6	
4130	184	5729	110E5	2	1	UNKN	MAML	UNKN	FRAG	0.2	
4150	184	5730	110E5	2	1	UNKN	MAML	UNKN	FRAG	0.3	
3681	184	436	110E5	3	2	MED	MAML	teeth	FRAG	2	
3079	184	1092	110E5	4	2	XSM	CTRB	femur	FRAG	1.8	
3080	184	1092	110E5	4	2	XSM	CTRB	tibia	FRAG	1.9	
3082	184	1092	110E5	4	4	XSM	MAML	long, tooth	FRAG	2.8	
2772	184	1092	110E5	4	103+	MED/LG	MAML	UNKN	FRAG	118.4	
3077	184	1092	110E5	4	2	XSM	RAT	humerus	FRAG	2	
3078	184	1092	110E5	4	1	XSM	RAT	tibia	WHLE	0.8	
3061	184	5021	110E5	7	1	XSM	CTRB	Lt mandible	FRAG	1	
3650	184	5021	110E5	7	1	XSM	MAML	incisor	WHLE	0.9	
4708	184	4945	110E5	8	1	XSM	MAML	femur	FRAG	0.2	
4132	184	4940	110E5	8	1	UNKN	MAML	UNKN	FRAG	0.4	

2011.28	SBCM	Cat #	Unit	Level	Qty	Size Cat	Species	Bone Type	COND	Wt/g	Comments
4099	184	4941	110E5	8	1	UNKN	MAML	UNKN	FRAG	0.2	
4116	184	4944	110E5	8	1	UNKN	MAML	UNKN	FRAG	0.3	
4126	184	4946	110E5	8	1	UNKN	MAML	UNKN	FRAG	0.5	
4133	184	4947	110E5	8	1	UNKN	MAML	UNKN	FRAG	0.2	
4155	184	4949	110E5	8	1	UNKN	MAML	UNKN	FRAG	1.1	
4142	184	4950	110E5	8	1	UNKN	MAML	UNKN	FRAG	0.5	
3142	184	938	110E5	9,10	1	XSM	CTRB	maxillary	WHLE	0.01	
2931	184	6418	110F	3	1	MED	MAML	rib	FRAG	1.4	
3669	184	6418	110F	3	1	SM	MAML	tooth	FRAG	0.7	
2849	184	6418	110F	3	58+	All	MAML	UNKN	FRAG	14.1	
4143	184	6421	110F	3	1	UNKN	MAML	UNKN	FRAG	0.1	
4152	184	6423	110F	3	1	UNKN	MAML	UNKN	FRAG	0.3	
3089	184	6148	110F	4	1	XSM	CTRB	femur	FRAG	0.1	
3090	184	6148	110F	4	1	XSM	CTRB	tibia	FRAG	0.8	
3093	184	6148	110F	4	1	XSM	CTRB	ulna	FRAG	0.4	
3656	184	6148	110F	4	1	XSM	GOPH	incisor	WHLE	0.6	
3668	184	6148	110F	4	1	SM	MAML	tooth	WHLE	2	two root
2822	184	6148	110F	4	49+	UNKN	MAML	UNKN	FRAG	5.2	
2794	184	1219	110F	6	49+	LG	MAML	UNKN	FRAG	111	
2932	184	1219	110F	6	1	LG	MAML	UNKN	FRAG	26.2	
4710	184	5967	110F	7	1	XSM	MAML	femur	FRAG	0.35	
2891	184	5966	110F	7	20+	SM/LG	MAML	UNKN	FRAG	2.5	

2011.28	SBCM	Cat #	Unit	Level	Qty	Size Cat	Species	Bone Type	COND	Wt/g	Comments
2897	184	3556	110F5	5	1	UNKN	MAML	UNKN	FRAG	0.5	
3614	184	791	110F5	6	1	XSM	CHPM	Rt mandible	WHLE	2	
3118	184	117	110F5	6	12	XSM	GOPH	mandible	FRAG	1.6	
3073	184	791	110F5	6	1	XSM	GRSQ	long	WHLE	2	
3332	184	5058	110G	1	1	MED	DEER	tooth	FRAG	2.4	
2419	184	5058	110G	1	2	MED	MAML	rib	FRAG	5.6	
3318	184	5228	110G	2	1	XSM	CTRBB	Rt mandible	FRAG	1	w/teeth
2383	184	4781	110G	5	9	MED	MAML	rib	FRAG	10	
2469	184	4781	110G	5	9	XSM	RD	skull	FRAG	0.2	
2408	184	5808	110G5	1	1	UNKN	MAML	long	FRAG	1.8	
2480	184	1914	110H	2	1	MED	MAML	metapodial	WHLE	1.3	
2481	184	1879	110H	3	1	MED	MAML	rib	FRAG	9.8	
2428	184	1933	110H	4	1	UNKN	MAML	long	FRAG	2.5	
4040	184	6213	110H5	1	1	UNKN	MAML	UNKN	FRAG	3	
3393	184	5984	110H5	2	1	LG	COW	tooth	FRAG	0.6	
2434	184	5984	110H5	2	4+	MED	MAML	long	FRAG	11	
2446	184	1460	110H5	4	1	UNKN	MAML	rib	WHLE	2.7	cut marks
3391	184	1793	110H5	5	1	LG	COW	tooth	FRAG	0.8	
3346	184	5714	110I	1	1	LG	HORS	tooth	FRAG	0.1	
2371	184	1417	110I	2	3	LG	MAML	long	FRAG	13.9	
2386	184	5994	110I	4	2	UNKN	MAML	rib	FRAG	1.1	burned
3337	184	1531	110I5	1	2	MED	DEER	teeth	FRAG	2.7	

2011.28	SBCM	Cat #	Unit	Level	Qty	Size Cat	Species	Bone Type	COND	Wt/g	Comments
2482	184	6247	110I5	3	1	MED	MAML	Metacarpal	FRAG	9.6	
2473	184	2995	110I5	4	1	XSM	CTRB	tibia	FRAG	0.5	
3339	184	2995	110I5	4	1	XSM	GRSQ	Lt mandible	FRAG	0.6	
3350	184	2995	110I5	4	1	LG	HORS	tooth	FRAG	2.7	
2381	184	1521	110I5	4	4	MED	MAML	long	FRAG	1.9	
4041	184	1521	110I5	4	1	UNKN	MAML	UNKN	FRAG	0.3	
2388	184	5829	110J5	1	15+	MED	MAML	long	FRAG	4	
4712	184	5323	110J5	3	1	XSM	RAT	tibia	FRAG	0.2	
2441	184	679	115	1	1	UNKN	MAML	skull	FRAG	9.5	cut marks
3029	184	1194	115B	3,4	1	UNKN	MAML	UNKN	FRAG	2.1	
3028	184	1193	115B	3,4	190+	UNKN	MAML	UNKN	FRAG	213.8	
3037	184	5594	115B	3,4	2	UNKN	MAML	UNKN	FRAG	0.7	
3684	184	532	115D	1	1	LG	HORS	tooth	FRAG	0.8	
2778	184	536	115D	1	2	UNKN	MAML	UNKN	FRAG	1.1	
2817	184	418	115D	2	1	UNKN	MAML	UNKN	FRAG	3.7	
3161	184	406	115D5	3	8	LG	MAML	long	FRAG	28	
3108	184	4887	115E	6	1	XSM	GRSQ	femur	FRAG	1	
3107	184	4887	115E	6	1	XSM	GRSQ	femur	WHLE	2	
3106	184	4887	115E	6	1	XSM	GRSQ	tibia	WHLE	1	
3099	184	4887	115E	6	1	XSM	RAT	humerus	WHLE	0.9	
2821	184	5672	115E	3,4	3	UNKN	MAML	UNKN	FRAG	0.4	
4102	184	5245	115E	3,4	1	UNKN	MAML	UNKN	FRAG	0.9	

2011.28	SBCM	Cat #	Unit	Level	Qty	Size Cat	Species	Bone Type	COND	Wt/g	Comments
3667	184	3994	115-E	3	1	SM	MAML	tooth	WHLE	2	two root
2944	184	5139	115E5	7	1	MED	MTLIn	vert	FRAG	6.3	
3137	184	846	115E5	8	3	XSM	CTRB	maxillary	FRAG	1	
2789	184	4874	115E5	8	103+	ALL	MAML	UNKN	FRAG	48	
4098	184	4876	115E5	8	1	UNKN	MAML	UNKN	FRAG	0.2	
2813	184	401	115F	1	33	ALL	MAML	UNKN	FRAG	22.9	
3072	184	4051	115F	2	1	XSM	GRSQ	humerus	WHLE	1	
3623	184	4051	115F	2	1	XSM	GRSQL	mandible	FRAG	1	
2872	184	3173	115F	2	14	MED/LG	MAML	burned	FRAG	6.8	
3687	184	4051	115F	2	1	LG	MAML	tooth	FRAG	1	
2816	184	4051	115F	2	28	MED/LG	MAML	UNKN	FRAG	31.7	
2945	184	4051	115F	2	1	MED	SHEP	scapula	FRAG	13.4	
3634	184	3021	115F	3	1	XSM	CTRBB	mandible	FRAG	0.8	
2948	184	3016	115F	3	1	SM	MAML	skull	FRAG	0.3	
2780	184	3016	115F	3	41+	ALL	MAML	UNKN	FRAG	22.3	
3642	184	3016	115F	3	1	XSM	WRAT	Lt mandible	WHLE	2	w/tooth
2742	184	2955	115F	4	50+	UNKN	MAML	long	FRAG	32.2	
2743	184	2955	115F	4	6	UNKN	MAML	long	FRAG	6	
3167	184	3167	115F	5	2	LG	HORS	teeth	FRAG	2	
3610	184	3167	115F	5	1	XSM	MAML	Rt mandible	WHLE	2	
2876	184	3167	115F	5	35+	MED/LG	MAML	UNKN	FRAG	33.4	
3628	184	1957	115F	7	1	XSM	CTRB	Lt mandible	WHLE	2	

2011.28	SBCM	Cat #	Unit	Level	Qty	Size Cat	Species	Bone Type	COND	Wt/g	Comments
3116	184	1737	115F5	4	1	XSM	GRSQ	femur	FRAG	0.6	distal end
3115	184	1737	115F5	4	1	XSM	GRSQ	humerus	FRAG	0.5	distal end
3117	184	1737	115F5	4	1	XSM	GRSQ	pelvis	WHLE	2	
2766	184	1737	115F5	4	61	ALL	MAML	UNKN	FRAG	57.6	
3662	184	1737	115F5	4	1	XSM	WRAT	Rt mandible	WHLE	0.8	
3159	184	6164	115F5	5	1	LG	MAML	long	FRAG	34	cut marks
2758	184	6164	115F5	5	52	UNKN	MAML	UNKN	FRAG	105.4	
2925	184	6164	115F5	5	1	LG	MAML	UNKN	WHLE	1	cut marks
3652	184	6164	115F5	5	1	XSM	RAT	Lt mandible	WHLE	1	
3675	184	5332	115F5	6	1	MED	BCAT	Lt mandible	WHLE	4	w/tooth
3145	184	5332	115F5	6	1	XSM	CTRB	humerus	WHLE	0.3	
3136	184	5332	115F5	6	1	XSM	CTRB	tibia	FRAG	1.8	
3679	184	5332	115F5	6	1	MED	DEER	tooth	WHLE	2	two root
3153	184	5332	115F5	6	3	SM	MAML	long	FRAG	8	
3122	184	5332	115F5	6	1	SM	120E5+ A299:L315	pelvic	FRAG	1	
4127	184	5326	115F5	6	1	UNKN	MAML	UNKN	FRAG	0.1	
3674	184	268	120-5E	3	1	MED	MAML	tooth	FRAG	1	
2739	184	5961	120D	1	11+	MED	MAML	long	FRAG	14.2	
4101	184	5958	120D	1	1	UNKN	MAML	UNKN	FRAG	1.7	
2779	184	1142	120D	2	45+	MED/LG	MAML	UNKN	FRAG	122.4	
2693	184	1982	120D	2	1	UNKN	MAML	UNKN	WHLE	0.5	
3070	184	1123	120D	4	1	XSM	CTRB	metacarpal	WHLE	2	

2011.28	SBCM	Cat #	Unit	Level	Qty	Size Cat	Species	Bone Type	COND	Wt/g	Comments
2767	184	1190	120D	4	29+	LG	MAML	UNKN	FRAG	121.2	
2936	184	2204	120D	5	1	MED	MAML	skull	FRAG	3.3	
3630	184	2443	120D	6	1	XSM	GRSQ	Lt mandible	WHLE	1	w/teeth
3084	184	2443	120D	6	1	XSM	MAML	long	FRAG	0.9	
2880	184	2328	120D	7	10	SM/MED	MAML	UNKN	FRAG	8.5	
3058	184	2328	120D	7	1	UNKN	MAML	UNKN	FRAG	1	
2838	184	330	120E	1	1	LG	MAML	UNKN	FRAG	19.8	
2791	184	263	120E	3	1	UNKN	MAML	UNKN	FRAG	0.3	
2750	184	2542	120E5	2	3	MED	MAML	long	FRAG	7.6	
4120	184	5281	120F	1	1	UNKN	MAML	UNKN	FRAG	2.3	
4704	184	5283	120F	1	1	XSM	RAT	femur	FRAG	0.1	
2688	184	722	120F	2	42	MED/LG	MAML	long/rib	FRAG	45	
2447	184	2014	120F	3	1	SM	MAML	rib	WHLE	0.2	
3134	184	2065	120F	7	1	MED	DEER	humerus	FRAG	2	
2874	184	2065	120F	7	5	SM/LG	MAML	UNKN	FRAG	4	
3053	184	5222	120F5	1	1	SM	MAML	tibia	FRAG	3	
2860	184	5222	120F5	1	53	LG	MAML	UNKN	FRAG	47.8	
4153	184	5223	120F5	1	1	UNKN	MAML	UNKN	FRAG	0.3	
4103	184	5224	120F5	1	1	UNKN	MAML	UNKN	FRAG	0.3	
2763	184	1490	120F5	3	10	MED	MAML	UNKN	FRAG	4.7	
3104	184	5306	120F5	6	1	XSM	CTRB	humerus	WHLE	1	
3648	184	5306	120F5	6	1	XSM	CTRB	Rt mandible	WHLE	2	

2011.28	SBCM	Cat #	Unit	Level	Qty	Size Cat	Species	Bone Type	COND	Wt/g	Comments
3618	184	730	120F5	6	4	XSM	CTRBB	mandible	FRAG	1.3	
3626	184	730	120F5	6	1	XSM	CTRBB	Rt Maxil-lary	FRAG	0.8	
3625	184	5306	120F5	6	1+	XSM	JKRBB	Lt mandi-ble	FRAG	2	
2749	184	2396	120F5	6	14	UNKN	MAML	long	FRAG	11.6	
2764	184	5306	120F5	6	59+	SM/MED	MAML	UNKN	FRAG	17.8	
2597	184	687	120G	1	1	XSM	CTRB	femur	FRAG	0.5	
2592	184	687	120G	1	1	XSM	CTRB	ulna	FRAG	0.2	
2478	184	941	120G	1	1	MED	MAML	rib	WHLE	9.2	
2471	184	941	120G	1	1	XSM	RAT	raidus	WHLE	0.3	
3325	184	468	120G	2	1	XSM	RAT	Lt mandi-ble	FRAG	0.2	
3341	184	2962	120G	3	4	LG	HORS	teeth	FRAG	13.5	
3205	184	2962	120G	3	1	XSM	TURT	shell	FRAG	1.2	
3636	184	461	120G	1,2,3	1	XSM	CTRB	mandible	FRAG	0.8	
2782	184	1067	125D	2	30	LG	MAML	UNKN	FRAG	147.6	
2801	184	634	125D	3	19	LG	MAML	UNKN	FRAG	99.8	
2740	184	1030	125D	3	28	LG	MAML	UNKN	FRAG	101.4	
2805	184	741	125D5	1	3	UNKN	MAML	UNKN	FRAG	15.1	
2783	184	4834	125E	1	6	SM/MED	MAML	UNKN	FRAG	6	
3637	184	427	125E 5	3	1	XSM	CTRB	Lt mandi-ble	WHLE	2	
2809	184	427	125E5	3	16	MED/LG	MAML	UNKN	FRAG	33.6	
3317	184	4616	125G	2	1	XSM	CTRB	rt mandi-ble	FRAG	0.6	
3296	184	4616	125G	2	1	UNKN	MAML	tooth	FRAG	2.6	

2011.28	SBCM	Cat #	Unit	Level	Qty	Size Cat	Species	Bone Type	COND	Wt/g	Comments
4086	184	4607	125G	2	1	LG	MAML	UNKN	FRAG	38.2	
4093	184	4612	125G	2	1	UNKN	MAML	UNKN	FRAG	1.9	
4091	184	4613	125G	2	1	UNKN	MAML	UNKN	FRAG	1	
4092	184	4615	125G	2	1	UNKN	MAML	UNKN	FRAG	1.5	
3336	184	2076	125G	1,2,3	1	MED	DEER	tooth	FRAG	0.4	
3348	184	2076	125G	1,2,3	7	LG	HORS	teeth	FRAG	64.4	
2440	184	2076	125G	1,2,3	72+	SM/MED	MAML	long/skull	FRAG	139.3	
3298	184	2076	125G	1,2,3	2	UNKN	MAML	teeth	FRAG	1.3	
3392	184	4696	125G5	1	1	LG	COW	tooth	FRAG	0.1	
4466	184	4466	125G5	1	1	XSM	CTRB	mandible	FRAG	0.2	
2519	184	4466	125G5	1	6	MED/LG	MAML	rib	FRAG	8.4	
4087	184	4467	125G5	1	1	UNKN	MAML	UNKN	FRAG	0.1	
3333	184	3615	125G5	4	1	MED	DEER	tooth	FRAG	0.3	
3349	184	3615	125G5	4	1	LG	HORS	tooth	FRAG	0.2	
3418	184	5129	140H5	3	1	XSM	GRSQL	mandible	FRAG	0.4	
2589	184	5121	140H5	1, 2	1	XSM	CTRB	pelvic	FRAG	0.4	
2598	184	5121	140H5	1,2	1	XSM	CTRB	scapula	FRAG	0.6	
2582	184	5121	140H5	1,2	1	MED	MAML	humerus	FRAG	5.2	
2573	184	5121	140H5	1,2	1	MED	MAML	rib	FRAG	12	
2587	184	5121	140H5	1,2	1	SM	RACC	metacar-pal	FRAG	0.4	
2599	184	1729	140I	2	1	XSM	CTRB	femur	FRAG	0.3	
2578	184	1729	140I	2	1	MED	MAML	humerus	FRAG	2.9	

2011.28	SBCM	Cat #	Unit	Level	Qty	Size Cat	Species	Bone Type	COND	Wt/g	Comments
2603	184	1729	140I	2	1	SM	RACC	humerus	WHLE	0.3	
3407	184	1801	140I	3	1	XSM	JKRBB	mandible	FRAG	0.4	
2565	184	1801	140I	3	1	SM	MAML	scapula	FRAG	0.3	
3402	184	6519	140I5	1	1	UNKN	MAML	teeth	FRAG	0.7	
4088	184	6531	140I5	1	1	UNKN	MAML	UNKN	FRAG	0.4	
2572	184	1143	140I5	2	5	MED	MAML	vert	FRAG	21.9	
2576	184	4936	140I5	3	3	LG	MAML	metacar-pal	FRAG	15.9	
2571	184	4458	150H	1,2	1	UNKN	MAML	metacar-pal	FRAG	10.8	cut marks
2555	184	4003	155-H	3	1	UNKN	MAML	UNKN	WHLE	0.05	
2601	184	2470	160H5	1	1	XSM	CTRB	femur	FRAG	0.2	
2470	184	2470	160H5	1	1	XSM	CTRB	metacar-pal	FRAG	0.1	
3416	184	2470	160H5	1	1	XSM	WRAT	mandible	FRAG	0.4	
2577	184	2761	160I	2	1	MED	Shep	metacar-pal	FRAG	0.2	
4095	184	6066	160I5	1	1	UNKN	MAML	UNKN	FRAG	0.2	
2521	184	5518	160I5	2	8	UNKN	MAML	long/skull	FRAG	16.4	
4089	184	5517	160I5	2	1	UNKN	MAML	UNKN	FRAG	0.5	
3400	184	6439	160J	1	1	UNKN	MAML	tooth	FRAG	0.1	
3398	184	6400	160J5	1	1	UNKN	MAML	teeth	FRAG	1.5	
3422	184	1164	160J5	2	2	MED	DEER	teeth	FRAG	4.4	
3403	184	1164	160J5	2	3	UNKN	MAML	teeth	FRAG	1.7	
3439	184	1164	160J5	2	9+	UNKN	MAML	UNKN	FRAG	5	
2591	184	5008	160J5	3	1	XSM	CTRB	pelvic	FRAG	0.7	

2011.28	SBCM	Cat #	Unit	Level	Qty	Size Cat	Species	Bone Type	COND	Wt/g	Comments
3420	184	5008	160J5	3	1	XSM	GRSQL	mandible	FRAG	0.2	
2496	184	5008	160J5	3	6	MED	MAML	rib	FRAG	2.7	
3424	184	5842	160K	UNKN	1	MED	DEER	tooth	WHLE	3.3	
2586	184	571	165H	1	1	XSM	CTRB	femur	WHLE	0.3	
2583	184	931	165H	2	1	XSM	CTRB	skull	FRAG	0.01	
2528	184	3376	165H	2	1	UNKN	MAML	skull	FRAG	0.9	
3404	184	443	165H	2	2	SM	MAML	teeth	FRAG	0.1	
3412	184	503	165H	3	1	XSM	CTRB	mandible	FRAG	0.6	
3408	184	503	165H	3	1	XSM	CTRB	mandible	FRAG	0.1	
2584	184	503	165H	3	1	XSM	CTRB	radius/ ulna	WHLE	0.3	
2570	184	1458	165H	3	1	MED	Shep	phalange	WHLE	2.5	
2600	184	2617	165I	2	1	XSM	CTRB	femur	FRAG	0.3	
2568	184	2617	165I	2	1	MED	MTLIn	vert	FRAG	11.4	
3406	184	2644	165I	UNKN	2	SM	MAML	UNKN	FRAG	0.5	
2644	184	2644	165I	UNKN	1	SM	MAML	UNKN	WHLE	0.5	
2569	184	2644	165I	UNKN	2	MED	MTLIn	vert	FRAG	213	
2596	184	2644	165I	UNKN	1	SM	RACC	metacar-pal	FRAG	0.3	
2558	184	157	165I5	1	59	SM/MED	MAML	rib/long/ vert	FRAG	45	
3421	184	549	165J	1	1	XSM	GRSQ	mandible	FRAG	0.6	
3044	184	4143	165S5	2	2	UNKN	MAML	UNKN	FRAG	1.1	
2567	184	2092	170H	1	2	LG	MAML	rib/scap-ula	FRAG	19.3	
3413	184	2234	170H	2	1	XSM	CTRB	mandible	FRAG	0.3	

2011.28	SBCM	Cat #	Unit	Level	Qty	Size Cat	Species	Bone Type	COND	Wt/g	Comments
3423	184	2234	170H	2	1	MED	DEER	mandible	FRAG	3.8	
2602	184	2234	170H	2	1	XSM	GRSQ	humerus	FRAG	0.1	
2234	184	2234	170H	2	1	XSM	WRAT	mandible	FRAG	0.5	
3414	184	1896	170H5	1	1	XSM	CTRBB	mandible	FRAG	0.4	
3405	184	1896	170H5	1	2	SM	MAML	teeth	FRAG	0.1	
2606	184	1892	170H5	2	1	XSM	CTRB	phalange	WHLE	0.1	
3410	184	1892	170H5	2	1	XSM	CTRB	tooth	WHLE	0.3	
2593	184	1892	170H5	2	1	XSM	MAML	radius/ ulna	WHLE	0.6	
2770	184	2770	170I5	2	1	XSM	CTRB	humerus	WHLE	0.3	
2506	184	2770	170I5	2	50+	SM/MED	MAML	long/rib	FRAG	14.5	
3397	184	3388	170I5	2	1	UNKN	MAML	teeth	FRAG	0.6	
2580	184	2854	170J	2	6	MED	MAML	skull	FRAG	5.5	
3438	184	2854	170J	2	5	UNKN	MAML	UNKN	FRAG	3	
2591	184	2825	170J	UNKN	1	XSM	CTRB	pelvic	FRAG	1.3	
3415	184	2825	170J	UNKN	1	XSM	CTRBB	mandible	FRAG	0.9	
3409	184	2672	175H	2	1	XSM	CTRB	mandible	WHLE	1	w/tooth
2595	184	2595	175H	2	1	SM	MAML	radius/ ulna	WHLE	0.9	
2581	184	2672	175H	2	2	MED	MAML	skull	FRAG	20	
2566	184	2566	175H	2	3	UNKN	MAML	skull	FRAG	8.1	
2594	184	3596	175H5	3	1	XSM	CTRB	radius/ ulna	WHLE	0.5	fused
2604	184	3596	175H5	3	1	XSM	CTRB	scapula	FRAG	1.2	
2605	184	3596	175H5	3	1	XSM	RAT	phalange	WHLE	0.1	

2011.28	SBCM	Cat #	Unit	Level	Qty	Size Cat	Species	Bone Type	COND	Wt/g	Comments
3419	184	2973	175I	1	1	XSM	GRSQL	mandible	FRAG	0.2	
2532	184	3387	175I	1	20+	UNKN	MAML	UNKN	FRAG	0.9	
2575	184	3343	175I	2	3	UNKN	MAML	vert	FRAG	5.9	
3335	184	5555	175I5	2	1	MED	DEER	tooth	FRAG	1.4	
4090	184	5542	175I5	2	1	UNKN	MAML	UNKN	FRAG	0.2	
3399	184	3220	175J	2	1	UNKN	MAML	teeth	FRAG	0.3	
3401	184	3108	175J	3	1	UNKN	MAML	teeth	FRAG	0.3	
3035	184	4567	20G5	2	3	UNKN	MAML	UNKN	FRAG	27.3	SW 1/4
2179	184	4629	20J5	4	1	SM	MAML	UNKN	WHLE	0.01	
2249	184	2009	20J5	6	3	UNKN	MAML	UNKN	FRAG	0.6	
3168	184	5866	30H5	1,2,3	1	LG	HORS	tooth	FRAG	2.9	
3951	184	5700	30I	2	1	UNKN	MAML	UNKN	FRAG	0.7	
2347	184	840	30I5	2	1	XSM	GRSQ	scapula	FRAG	0.1	
2346	184	840	30I5	2	2	XSM	RD	humerus	FRAG	0.5	
3282	184	4479	30J5	1	2	LG	HORS	teeth	FRAG	0.7	
2319	184	1410	30J5	3	2	MED	DEER	tibia	FRAG	11.8	proximal end
3249	184	1410	30J5	3	1	LG	HORS	tooth	FRAG	1.1	
2200	184	5740	30J5	4	10	UNKN	MAML	long	FRAG	66.9	
3251	184	3835	30K5	1	1	LG	HORS	tooth	FRAG	0.4	
2183	184	3835	30K5	1	2	LG	MAML	rib	FRAG	5.3	
3039	184	2941	34F4	UNKN	8	UNKN	MAML	UNKN	FRAG	25	
4714	184	6504	35H5	1	1	LG	MAML	femur	FRAG	12	

2011.28	SBCM	Cat #	Unit	Level	Qty	Size Cat	Species	Bone Type	COND	Wt/g	Comments
3946	184	6490	35H5	1	1	UNKN	MAML	UNKN	FRAG	0.4	
6497	184	6497	35H5	1	1	UNKN	MAML	UNKN	FRAG	0.2	
3948	184	6509	35H5	1	1	UNKN	MAML	UNKN	FRAG	0.5	
3971	184	6514	35H5	1	1	UNKN	MAML	UNKN	FRAG	1.3	
3956	184	6518	35H5	1	2	UNKN	MAML	UNKN	FRAG	0.4	
2224	184	6242	35H5	3	1	UNKN	MAML	UNKN	FRAG	0.1	
3953	184	5439	35I	2	1	UNKN	MAML	UNKN	FRAG	3.4	
3954	184	5688	35I	3	1	UNKN	MAML	UNKN	FRAG	0.5	
3950	184	5683	35I	3	1	UNKN	MAML	UNKN	FRAG	0.6	
3955	184	5685	35I	3	1	UNKN	MAML	UNKN	FRAG	0.3	
3025	184	1636	40	2	41	UNKN	MAML	UNKN	FRAG	31	
3189	184	6357	40H5	1	1	MED	DEER	tooth	FRAG	1.3	
3281	184	6357	40H5	1	1	LG	HORS	tooth	FRAG	8.5	
3193	184	6357	40H5	1	1	SM	MAML	mandible	FRAG	0.5	
2350	184	1213	40H5	3	1	XSM	CTRB	humerus	WHLE	0.4	
2354	184	1213	40H5	3	1	XSM	CTRB	tibia	FRAG	0.5	
3226	184	1213	40H5	3	1	XSM	GRSQ	Lt mandible	FRAG	0.5	
2332	184	1213	40H5	3	1	SM	MAML	condyle	WHLE	0.4	
3192	184	1213	40H5	3	1	SM	MAML	mandible	FRAG	0.4	
3170	184	1568	40I	3	1	MED	COYT	tooth	WHLE	0.3	
3210	184	1578	40I	3	1	XSM	CTRB	mandible	FRAG	0.4	
2284	184	1122	40K	2	3	LG	COW	UNKN	FRAG	45.1	

2011.28	SBCM	Cat #	Unit	Level	Qty	Size Cat	Species	Bone Type	COND	Wt/g	Comments
3196	184	1122	40K	2	13	LG	COW	UNKN	FRAG	26.9	
2243	184	1122	40K	2	44+	UNKN	MAML	UNKN	FRAG	88.4	
3290	184	1477	40K	3	3	LG	HORS	teeth	FRAG	4	
2333	184	1477	40K	3	1	SM	MAML	ulna	WHLE	0.6	
3240	184	3359	40K	4	1	XSM	GRSQ	Rt mandi-ble	FRAG	0.5	
3254	184	3359	40K	4	2	LG	HORS	teeth	FRAG	11.7	
2351	184	1175	45I	4	1	XSM	CTRB	humerus	WHLE	0.5	
2349	184	1175	45I	4	1	XSM	GRSQ	femur	WHLE	0.1	
3227	184	1175	45I	4	1	XSM	GRSQ	Rt mandi-ble	FRAG	0.3	
1175	184	1175	45I	4	1	XSM	GYSQL	Lt mandi-ble	FRAG	0.5	
3284	184	1175	45I	4	3	LG	HORS	teeth	FRAG	3.9	
2322	184	1175	45I	4	1	MED	MAML	skull	FRAG	0.7	
2337	184	994	45I	4	1	XSM	RAT	skull	FRAG	0.3	
2317	184	1206	4H5	22	1	MED	DEER	Rt mandi-ble	WHLE	13.6	
3250	184	1206	4H5	22	2	LG	HORS	teeth	FRAG	4.4	
3283	184	1206	4H5	22	1	LG	HORS	tooth	FRAG	4.7	
2338	184	1206	4H5	22	1	XSM	RAT	calanus	WHLE	0.3	
2341	184	1206	4H5	22	1	XSM	RAT	femur	WHLE	0.1	
2314	184	1206	4H5	UNKN	1	MED	MAML	rib	FRAG	4.6	cut marks
2281	184	2173	55H5	2	1	LG	MAML	skull	FRAG	12.2	
2186	184	2044	55I	1	1	MED	MAML	tibia	WHLE	1.6	Proximal end
2276	184	1241	55I	2	1+	LG	COW	metapo-dial	FRAG	48.3	

2011.28	SBCM	Cat #	Unit	Level	Qty	Size Cat	Species	Bone Type	COND	Wt/g	Comments
2195	184	2001	55I	2	1	MED	DEER	metatarsal	WHLE	13.6	Distal
2329	184	2478	55I	4	1	XSM	CTRB	scapula	FRAG	0.8	
3191	184	528	55I	4	1	MED	DEER	mandible	WHLE	2.1	w/teeth
3219	184	528	55I	4	1	XSM	GOPH	Rt mandible	FRAG	0.8	
3280	184	614	55I	4	2	LG	HORS	teeth	FRAG	1.3	
3288	184	528	55I	4	1	LG	HORS	tooth	FRAG	6.3	
2334	184	528	55I	4	1	SM	MAML	humerus	WHLE	0.1	
2331	184	528	55I	4	1	SM	MAML	long	WHLE	0.4	
2283	184	614	55I	4	1	LG	MAML	metapodial	WHLE	15.7	distal end
2192	184	528	55I	4	1	SM	MAML	rib	WHLE	0.5	
3171	184	528	55I	4	1	UNKN	MAML	tooth	FRAG	0.1	
3195	184	528	55I	4	1	MED	MAML	UNKN	FRAG	1.4	
2285	184	528	55I	4	1	LG	MAML	UNKN	WHLE	12.1	
2191	184	528	55I	4	1	SM	RACC	skull	FRAG	1.4	
2340	184	528	55I	4	1	XSM	RAT	humerus	WHLE	0.1	
2318	184	2707	55I5	3	3	MED	DEER	long	FRAG	9.2	
3166	184	1715	55J	1	1	XSM	FISH	vert	WHLE	0.2	
3173	184	1715	55J	1	1	UNKN	MAML	tooth	FRAG	0.7	
2320	184	1623	55J	2	2	MED	DEER	radius/tibia	FRAG	15.5	
3213	184	1394	55J5	3	1	XSM	CTRBB	Lt mandible	FRAG	0.4	
2316	184	1394	55J5	3	1	MED	DEER	radius/tibia	WHLE	7.3	
3222	184	1394	55J5	3	1	XSM	GRSQ	Rt mandible	FRAG	0.8	

2011.28	SBCM	Cat #	Unit	Level	Qty	Size Cat	Species	Bone Type	COND	Wt/g	Comments
3292	184	1394	55J5	3	1	LG	HORS	tooth	FRAG	0.9	
4715	184	4381	55J5	4	1	XSM	CTRB	mandible	FRAG	0.3	
3212	184	4720	55J5	4	1	XSM	CTRBB	mandible	FRAG	0.7	
3253	184	4387	55J5	4	3	LG	HORS	teeth	FRAG	2.9	fireplace
3247	184	4720	55J5	4	3	LG	HORS	teeth	FRAG	5.2	
3216	184	4383	55J5	4	4	XSM	KRAT	Rt mandible	FRAG	0.2	fire place, frag w/teeth
4716	184	4386	55J5	4	1	MED	MAML	tibia	FRAG	5.1	
3172	184	4387	55J5	4	1	UNKN	MAML	tooth	FRAG	0.6	fireplace
3950	184	4380	55J5	4	1	UNKN	MAML	UNKN	FRAG	0.4	fireplace
3944	184	4382	55J5	4	1	UNKN	MAML	UNKN	FRAG	0.8	fireplace
3947	184	4384	55J5	4	1	UNKN	MAML	UNKN	FRAG	0.8	fireplace
3194	184	4443	55J5	5	1	SM	MAML	mandible	FRAG	0.4	
3943	184	1378	55K	1	1	UNKN	MAML	UNKN	FRAG	0.6	
2219	184	1397	55K	2	6	XSM	RD	long	FRAG	2.4	
2348	184	4099	55K	3	3	XSM	RAT	metatarsal	FRAG	0.5	
2328	184	6080	55K	4	1	MED	BCAT	phalange	WHLE	0.4	
3169	184	1379	55K	4	3	LG	HORS	teeth	FRAG	1.5	
3188	184	1585	55K5	1	1	LG	HORS	tooth	FRAG	1.2	
3291	184	1658	55K5	2	30	LG	HORS	teeth	FRAG	52.5	
3689	184	2346	58E 5	UNKN	1	LG	MAML	tooth	FRAG	0.5	
3027	184	2347	58E5	UNKN	92	UNKN	MAML	UNKN	FRAG	47.3	
2312	184	1946	60H5	1	2	MED	DEER	radius	FRAG	9.7	

2011.28	SBCM	Cat #	Unit	Level	Qty	Size Cat	Species	Bone Type	COND	Wt/g	Comments
2278	184	1946	60H5	1	3	LG	MAML	UNKN	FRAG	15	
2310	184	2090	60H5	3	1	MED	DEER	long	WHLE	14.2	
3197	184	2024	60H5	4	3	LG	COW	teeth	FRAG	1.8	
2307	184	2024	60H5	4	1	LG	COW	UNKN	WHLE	25.6	
2352	184	2024	60H5	4	1	XSM	CTRB	humerus	WHLE	0.2	
2353	184	2024	60H5	4	1	XSM	CTRB	tibia	FRAG	0.5	
2327	184	2024	60H5	4	1	SM	MAML	pelvis	FRAG	0.3	
2279	184	2024	60H5	4	1	MED	MAML	skull	FRAG	0.69	
3186	184	2024	60H5	4	1	UNKN	MAML	tooth	FRAG	0.4	
2345	184	2024	60H5	4	1	XSM	MAML	UNKN	WHLE	0.2	poss bird
3217	184	2063	60H5	6	1	XSM	KRAT	Rt mandible	FRAG	1	w/teeth
2336	184	6387	60I	UNKN	1	XSM	CTRB	humerus	WHLE	0.2	
3287	184	6387	60I	UNKN	10	LG	HORS	teeth	FRAG	11.5	
2342	184	6387	60I	UNKN	1	XSM	MAML	vert	WHLE	0.6	
3221	184	5821	60J	2	1	XSM	GRSQL	Rt mandible	FRAG	0.4	
2315	184	2419	60J5	5	1	MED	DEER	metapodial	WHLE	3.3	
2344	184	2419	60J5	5	1	XSM	RAT	long	WHLE	0.3	
3038	184	5164	60M8	1,2	3	UNKN	MAML	UNKN	FRAG	0.9	test hole by the rocks
3036	184	4820	65E5	2	50	UNKN	MAML	UNKN	FRAG	38	
2326	184	7	65H5	1	1	MED	DEER	tibia	WHLE	2.3	epipysis of juvenile
3225	184	7	65H5	1	1	XSM	GRSQ	Lt mandible	FRAG	0.4	
3224	184	7	65H5	1	1	XSM	GRSQ	Lt mandible	FRAG	0.1	

2011.28	SBCM	Cat #	Unit	Level	Qty	Size Cat	Species	Bone Type	COND	Wt/g	Comments
3279	184	7	65H5	1	1	LG	HORS	tooth	FRAG	0.6	
3248	184	9	65H5	2	1	LG	HORS	tooth	FRAG	0.8	
2228	184	3374	65I	1	1	UNKN	MAML	UNKN	FRAG	1	
3952	184	6197	65I	1	1	UNKN	MAML	UNKN	FRAG	1	
3214	184	6107	65I	2	1	XSM	CTRBB	Lt mandible	FRAG	0.3	
2330	184	1246	65I	4	1	XSM	GRSQ	scapula	FRAG	0.2	
2335	184	1246	65I	4	1	SM	MAML	femur	WHLE	0.6	
3198	184	1246	65I	4	1	XSM	TURT	shell	FRAG	2.4	
3021	184	572	70-5	2	71	UNKN	MAML	UNKN	FRAG	89.1	
3932	184	6543	70C	1	1	UNKN	MAML	UNKN	FRAG	3.1	
3940	184	3882	70C5	2	1	UNKN	MAML	UNKN	FRAG	0.6	
3939	184	3885	70C5	2	1	UNKN	MAML	UNKN	FRAG	0.8	
2628	184	1782	70C5	3	4	MED/LG	MAML	rib	FRAG	1.9	
3609	184	1782	70C5	3	1	UNKN	MAML	tooth	FRAG	0.8	
2611	184	5988	70D	1	2	UNKN	MAML	long	FRAG	0.8	
3688	184	5630	70E	5	1	UNKN	MAML	UNKN	FRAG	0.8	
2652	184	696	70E5	1	1	MED	MAML	UNKN	FRAG	1.5	
2913	184	2703	70E5	4	3	MED	MAML	UNKN	FRAG	4.2	
3069	184	2684	70E5	5	1	XSM	GRSQ	long	FRAG	0.5	
2915	184	2792	70E5	7	1	UNKN	MAML	UNKN	WHLE	0.9	
3187	184	1443	70I	1	1	LG	HORS	tooth	FRAG	1.6	
3440	184	1443	70I	1	19	UNKN	MAML	UNKN	FRAG	16.4	

2011.28	SBCM	Cat #	Unit	Level	Qty	Size Cat	Species	Bone Type	COND	Wt/g	Comments
2256	184	2578	70I	1	22	UNKN	MAML	UNKN	FRAG	18.1	
2308	184	2723	70I	2	3	LG	MAML	UNKN	FRAG	17.3	
3322	184	103	70I	3	1	XSM	GRSQ	Lt mandi-ble	FRAG	0.2	
2465	184	103	70I	3	1	UNKN	MAML	skull	FRAG	0.1	
3327	184	103	70I	3	1	XSM	RAT	incisor	FRAG	0.1	
3220	184	758	70I5	2	1	XSM	GOPH	Rt mandi-ble	FRAG	0.4	w/teeth
2309	184	1115	70I5	4	17+	LG	COW	UNKN	FRAG	25.7	
2311	184	1115	70I5	4	4	MED	DEER	Rt humer-us	FRAG	21.6	distal end
3242	184	2651	70I5	4	1	XSM	GRSQ	Lt mandi-ble	FRAG	0.4	
2306	184	2651	70I5	4	3	LG	MAML	UNKN	FRAG	3	
4035	184	2653	70I5	4	1	UNKN	MAML	UNKN	FRAG	0.6	
3285	184	90	70J	1	4	LG	HORS	teeth	FRAG	2.5	
2313	184	90	70J	1	1	MED	MAML	long	FRAG	13	
3245	184	647	70J	1	1	MED	PIG	teeth	WHLE	1.1	
2339	184	999	70J	3	1	XSM	MAML	UNKN	WHLE	0.4	vert
2324	184	733	70J	3,4	1	LG	MAML	long	FRAG	6.6	
387	184	387	70J5	1	1	XSM	GRSQ	Lt mandi-ble	FRAG	0.5	
3244	184	387	70J5	1	1	XSM	GYSQL	Rt mandi-ble	FRAG	0.3	
3246	184	387	70J5	1	1	LG	HORS	tooth	FRAG	1.2	
3223	184	24	70J5	2	1	XSM	GRSQ	Rt mandi-ble	FRAG	1	w/teeth
3211	184	24	70J5	2	1	XSM	JKRBB	Rt mandi-ble	FRAG	1	frag w/teeth
3941	184	4403	75C	2	1	UNKN	MAML	UNKN	FRAG	0.4	burned

2011.28	SBCM	Cat #	Unit	Level	Qty	Size Cat	Species	Bone Type	COND	Wt/g	Comments
3928	184	4404	75C	2	1	UNKN	MAML	UNKN	WHLE	0.9	
3579	184	3579	75C5	3	1	LG	COW	tooth	FRAG	20	
3603	184	3569	75D	1	1	SM	MAML	Rt mandible	WHLE	2	
2771	184	3209	75D	6	6	UNKN	MAML	UNKN	FRAG	11.8	
3132	184	5659	75E 5	1	1	MED	DEER	femur	FRAG	7	
2867	184	5659	75E 5	1	13	MED/LG	MAML	UNKN	FRAG	18	
3942	184	5666	75E 5	1	1	UNKN	MAML	UNKN	FRAG	0.7	
4121	184	5662	75E5	1	1	UNKN	MAML	UNKN	FRAG	0.1	
4113	184	5665	75E5	1	1	UNKN	MAML	UNKN	FRAG	0.5	
4115	184	4800	75E5	2	1	UNKN	MAML	UNKN	FRAG	0.2	
4107	184	4852	75E5	6	1	UNKN	MAML	UNKN	FRAG	1.2	
2466	184	4787	75H5	2	2	UNKN	MAML	skull	FRAG	0.9	
3328	184	4787	75H5	2	2	SM	RACC	tooth	FRAG	0.4	
3286	184	5580	75I	1	1	LG	HORS	tooth	FRAG	0.4	
3293	184	201	75I	3	26	LG	HORS	teeth	FRAG	45.3	
3190	184	5601	75J	1	1	MED	DEER	tooth	FRAG	0.8	juvenile
3252	184	5601	75J	1	2	LG	HORS	teeth	FRAG	20.1	
2280	184	5601	75J	1	1	LG	MAML	UNKN	WHLE	13.5	
3019	184	1435	75N	1	8	UNKN	MAML	UNKN	FRAG	14.1	
3601	184	3619	80D	6	1	MED	DEER	tooth	WHLE	2	
2626	184	3859	80D	6,7	5	SM/MED	MAML	long/skull/rib	FRAG	6.1	
2753	184	1467	80D5	1	1	UNKN	MAML	long	WHLE	1.1	

2011.28	SBCM	Cat #	Unit	Level	Qty	Size Cat	Species	Bone Type	COND	Wt/g	Comments
2631	184	4900	80D5	1	2	UNKN	MAML	rib	FRAG	1	burned
3606	184	1075	80D5	2	20+	LG	HORS	teeth	FRAG	34	
2647	184	1075	80D5	2	2	LG	MAML	Femur/ humerus	FRAG	19.7	
2649	184	1075	80D5	2	2	MED	MAML	metacar-pal	FRAG	2.1	
2646	184	1075	80D5	2	1	LG	MAML	metapo-dial	WHLE	72.6	cut marks
2648	184	1075	80D5	2	1	MED	MAML	skull	FRAG	1.7	
3612	184	1710	80D5	5	1	XSM	CTRBB	mandible	WHLE	0.3	
3615	184	1710	80D5	5	1	XSM	JKRBB	Lt mandi-ble	WHLE	2	
2878	184	4050	80E	2	6	UNKN	MAML	UNKN	FRAG	7	burned
2774	184	4031	80E	2	18	ALL	MAML	UNKN	FRAG	26.3	
2941	184	4067	80E	4	1	MED	DEER	Rib	FRAG	15.1	
2940	184	4067	80E	4	1	MED	MAML	metapo-dial	FRAG	2.1	
4775	184	4071	80E	4	1	UNKN	MAML	UNKN	FRAG	0.9	cut marks
2949	184	4067	80E	4	1	MED	MAML	UNKN	FRAG	1.4	
4109	184	4072	80E	4	1	UNKN	MAML	UNKN	FRAG	0.5	
3663	184	5268	80E	5	1	SM	MAML	mandible	WHLE	0.9	
4105	184	5272	80E	5	1	UNKN	MAML	UNKN	FRAG	0.2	
3102	184	5268	80E	5	1	XSM	RAT	femur	FRAG	0.8	
3138	184	995	80E	5	1	XSM	RAT	pelvic	WHLE	0.8	
2833	184	1554	80E	6	4	SM/MED	MAML	UNKN	FRAG	2.4	
3066	184	1554	80E	6	1	XSM	RAT	femur	WHLE	3	
3067	184	1554	80E	6	1	XSM	RAT	skull	WHLE	3	

2011.28	SBCM	Cat #	Unit	Level	Qty	Size Cat	Species	Bone Type	COND	Wt/g	Comments
2752	184	6220	80E	7	12	UNKN	MAML	long	FRAG	7.5	
4707	184	6225	80E	7	1	MED	MAML	rib	FRAG	3.2	
4122	184	6226	80E	7	1	UNKN	MAML	UNKN	FRAG	0.5	
4149	184	6227	80E	7	1	UNKN	MAML	UNKN	FRAG	0.5	
2830	184	5112	80E5	1	2	LG	MAML	UNKN	FRAG	2.8	
4148	184	6119	80E5	3	1	UNKN	MAML	UNKN	FRAG	1.2	
2747	184	5236	80E5	5	19	UNKN	MAML	UNKN	FRAG	29	
3315	184	749	80H	2	1	UNKN	MAML	tooth	FRAG	0.8	
2420	184	598	80H	3	1	MED	MAML	long	FRAG	3.7	
2468	184	1505	80H5	1,2	3	MED	DEER	femur	FRAG	2.1	
3289	184	1858	80I	1	2	LG	HORS	teeth	FRAG	4.3	
2474	184	996	80I	2	1	XSM	FISH	vert	WHLE	0.3	
2197	184	4029	80I	2	5	UNKN	MAML	long	FRAG	1.6	
4713	184	4126	80I	2	1	SM	MAML	pelvic gridle	FRAG	0.55	
3112	184	2991	85D	3	1	XSM	CTRB	femur	WHLE	1	
3114	184	2991	85D	3	1	XSM	CTRB	Pelvic	WHLE	1	
3113	184	2991	85D	3	1	XSM	CTRB	Ulna	WHLE	1	
3123	184	2991	85D	3	1	SM	RACC	humerus	FRAG	2.5	
4118	184	3862	85D	7	1	UNKN	MAML	UNKN	FRAG	5.3	
3149	184	990	85D5	1	1	SM	MAML	UNKN	WHLE	1	
3148	184	990	85D5	1	1	XSM	RAT	maxillary	WHLE	0.7	
3147	184	990	85D5	1	2	XSM	RAT	scapula	FRAG	1.1	

2011.28	SBCM	Cat #	Unit	Level	Qty	Size Cat	Species	Bone Type	COND	Wt/g	Comments
3608	184	112	85D5	UNKN	1	XSM	CTRB	Lt mandible	WHLE	1	
3607	184	112	85D5	UNKN	2	LG	HORS	teeth	FRAG	10	
3605	184	112	85D5	UNKN	1	MED	MAML	tooth	FRAG	1	
3683	184	108	85E	1	1	MED	DEER	tooth	WHLE	4	three root
2871	184	1528	85E	1	3	MED	MAML	long	FRAG	2.5	
2799	184	108	85E	1	15	UNKN	MAML	UNKN	FRAG	8.1	
3140	184	992	85E	2	1	XSM	MAML	UNKN	WHLE	0.5	
3151	184	992	85E	2	1	SM	MAML	vert	WHLE	0.8	
3139	184	936	85E	3	1	XSM	GRSQ	mandible	WHLE	0.3	
2900	184	276	85E	3	20	MED/LG	MAML	UNKN	FRAG	11.6	
3125	184	5964	85E	4	1	MED	BCAT	femur	WHLE	2.3	
3672	184	143	85E	4	1	MED	MAML	tooth	WHLE	2	three root
2786	184	5939	85E	4	13	UNKN	MAML	UNKN	FRAG	18.2	
4114	184	5944	85E	4	1	UNKN	MAML	UNKN	FRAG	1.4	
3133	184	143	85E	4	1	MED	SHEP	metapodial	WHLE	32	
2690	184	1064	85E	6	6+	SM/MED	MAML	long/scapula	FRAG	3.7	
2937	184	3740	85E5	4	2	MED	MAML	rib	FRAG	11.8	
2812	184	210	85E5	4	10	UNKN	MAML	UNKN	FRAG	3.3	
3654	184	324	85E5	2,3	1	XSM	GRSQL	Lt mandible	WHLE	1	
3673	184	324	85E5	2,3	1	MED	MAML	tooth	FRAG	1.2	
3344	184	2943	85F	1	4	LG	HORS	teeth	FRAG	11.1	
3215	184	884	85F	2	1	XSM	CTRBB	Rt mandible	FRAG	0.3	

2011.28	SBCM	Cat #	Unit	Level	Qty	Size Cat	Species	Bone Type	COND	Wt/g	Comments
2804	184	4918	85F5	1	24	UNKN	MAML	UNKN	FRAG	16.4	
4157	184	4911	85F5	1	1	UNKN	MAML	UNKN	FRAG	0.2	
4136	184	4920	85F5	1	1	UNKN	MAML	UNKN	FRAG	0.45	
3632	184	3576	85F5	3	1	XSM	CTRB	Rt mandible	WHLE	2	
2757	184	5900	85F5	3	4	UNKN	MAML	UNKN	FRAG	8.6	
4156	184	5904	85F5	3	1	UNKN	MAML	UNKN	FRAG	0.2	
3635	184	6272	85F5	4	1	XSM	JKRBB	Mandible	FRAG	1	
2923	184	4971	85F5	5	1	MED	MAML	rib	FRAG	10.7	cut marks
2819	184	6280	85F5	6	5	UNKN	MAML	UNKN	FRAG	4	
4094	184	4704	85G	1	1	UNKN	MAML	UNKN	FRAG	5.3	
2476	184	4749	85G	2	1	MED	DEER	femur	WHLE	5.1	
3321	184	4749	85G	2	1	XSM	GRSQ	Rt mandible	FRAG	0.3	
3343	184	3369	85G	2	3	LG	HORS	teeth	FRAG	0.6	
3347	184	4749	85G	2	1	LG	HORS	tooth	FRAG	0.8	
2367	184	6427	85G	3	28+	SM/MED	MAML	long/tibia	FRAG	23.1	
3316	184	6427	85G	3	1	XSM	MAML	tooth	FRAG	0.1	
4030	184	6434	85G	3	1	UNKN	MAML	UNKN	FRAG	0.3	
4033	184	6435	85G	3	1	UNKN	MAML	UNKN	FRAG	0.6	
2470	184	6427	85G	3	1	XSM	RAT	femur	WHLE	0.2	
3324	184	6427	85G	3	1	XSM	WRAT	Rt mandible	FRAG	0.4	
3323	184	6427	85G	3	1	XSM	WRAT	Rt mandible	FRAG	0.3	
2489	184	4807	85G	4	1	SM	MAML	femur	FRAG	0.3	

2011.28	SBCM	Cat #	Unit	Level	Qty	Size Cat	Species	Bone Type	COND	Wt/g	Comments
4042	184	4807	85G	4	1	UNKN	MAML	UNKN	FRAG	0.65	
4693	184	4693	85G	5	1	MED	DEER	tooth	FRAG	0.6	
2475	184	933	85G	5	4	XSM	FISH	vert	FRAG	0.5	
2487	184	4693	85G	5	1	SM	MAML	radius/ ulna	WHLE	0.7	
2484	184	4693	85G	5	1	MED	MAML	tibia	FRAG	4.3	
4693	184	4693	85G	5	1	SM	MAML	tibia	WHLE	0.7	
4038	184	4690	85G	5	1	UNKN	MAML	UNKN	FRAG	4.6	
2442	184	6325	85G	6	1	UNKN	MAML	UNKN	FRAG	0.7	
4032	184	6324	85G	6	1	UNKN	MAML	UNKN	FRAG	0.1	
3295	184	1766	85G5	3	2	UNKN	MAML	teeth	FRAG	0.7	
2472	184	62	85G5	4	1	XSM	GRSQ	pelvic girdle	FRAG	0.3	
4029	184	4672	85G5	4	1	UNKN	MAML	UNKN	FRAG	0.8	
4039	184	4673	85G5	4	1	UNKN	MAML	UNKN	FRAG	0.3	
2432	184	367	85H	2	1	UNKN	MAML	UNKN	WHLE	1	
3297	184	485	85H	3	1	UNKN	MAML	tooth	FRAG	0.9	root
3150	184	937	90D	2	2	XSM	FISH	vert	FRAG	0.4	
2746	184	3192	90D	4	1	UNKN	MAML	UNKN	FRAG	2.7	
3094	184	3520	90D	4	1	XSM	RAT	femur	FRAG	0.8	
3095	184	3520	90D	4	1	XSM	RAT	Ulna	WHLE	0.2	
2820	184	2798	90D5	1	6	UNKN	MAML	UNKN	FRAG	3.7	
2744	184	2804	90D5	2	10	UNKN	MAML	long	FRAG	9.8	
3660	184	2082	90D5	3	1	XSM	GOPH	incisor	WHLE	0.4	

2011.28	SBCM	Cat #	Unit	Level	Qty	Size Cat	Species	Bone Type	COND	Wt/g	Comments
3068	184	2082	90D5	3	1	XSM	GRSQ	scapula	WHLE	2.5	
3671	184	71	90D5	4	1	SM	MAML	tooth	FRAG	0.1	
3074	184	71	90D5	4	1	XSM	RAT	scapula	WHLE	0.4	
2927	184	3152	90E	3	1	LG	MAML	long	FRAG	12.4	
2938	184	3152	90E	3	1	MED	MAML	vert	FRAG	8.2	
2654	184	3538	90E	6	1	MED	MAML	skull	FRAG	1.6	
2751	184	3536	90E	6	8	UNKN	MAML	UNKN	FRAG	1.5	
2935	184	3280	90E	7	1	MED	SHEP	femur	FRAG	7.1	
3666	184	2022	90E 5	4	1	SM	MAML	tooth	WHLE	2	two root
3619	184	2022	90E 5	4	1	XSM	WRAT	Lt mandible	WHLE	2	
2803	184	4465	90E5	1	4	UNKN	MAML	UNKN	FRAG	2.4	
2768	184	2316	90E5	3	4	MED/LG	MAML	long	FRAG	6	
2734	184	5924	90E5	8	10+	SM	MAML	long	FRAG	1.8	
4151	184	5921	90E5	8	1	UNKN	MAML	UNKN	FRAG	0.4	
2670	184	2157	90E5	9	19	SM/MED	MAML	Long/rib	FRAG	4.8	
2659	184	2099	90E5	10	4	UNKN	MAML	long	FRAG	3.2	
2835	184	260	90F	1	2	MED	MAML	UNKN	FRAG	4.8	
2677	184	2895	90F	2	3	MED	MAML	long/rib	FRAG	5.5	
2671	184	2605	90F	3	1	LG	MAML	UNKN	FRAG	3.4	
2737	184	4685	90F5	1	4	SM/MED	MAML	long/skull	FRAG	2.5	
2792	184	4738	90F5	2	12	MED/LG	MAML	UNKN	FRAG	30	
2807	184	4666	90F5	3	2	UNKN	MAML	UNKN	FRAG	3.3	

2011.28	SBCM	Cat #	Unit	Level	Qty	Size Cat	Species	Bone Type	COND	Wt/g	Comments
4031	184	4641	90F5	5,6	1	UNKN	MAML	UNKN	FRAG	0.6	
2422	184	4489	90G	1	1	UNKN	MAML	long	FRAG	0.7	
4043	184	4487	90G	1	1	UNKN	MAML	UNKN	FRAG	0.3	
3342	184	4534	90G	2	3	LG	HORS	teeth	FRAG	0.5	
3394	184	4637	90G	3	1	LG	COW	tooth	FRAG	2.8	
4044	184	4638	90G	3	1	UNKN	MAML	UNKN	FRAG	1.9	
3320	184	4542	90G	4	1	XSM	CTRBB	Lt mandi-ble	FRAG	1.8	
3299	184	4542	90G	4	8	UNKN	MAML	teeth	FRAG	0.4	
2460	184	4004	90G5	3	2	LG	MAML	epiphysis	FRAG	6.9	
4046	184	5651	90H	1	1	UNKN	MAML	UNKN	FRAG	1.8	
2415	184	4410	90H	4	8	UNKN	MAML	long	FRAG	6.8	
2453	184	6330	90H5	4	2	UNKN	MAML	UNKN	FRAG	1.9	
2462	184	1118	90H5	5	1	UNKN	FISH	vert	WHLE	0.3	
3340	184	6236	90H5	5	1	LG	HORS	tooth	FRAG	23.6	
4037	184	5417	90I	1	1	UNKN	MAML	UNKN	FRAG	0.1	
4045	184	5418	90I	1	1	UNKN	MAML	UNKN	FRAG	2	
4034	184	5421	90I	1	1	UNKN	MAML	UNKN	FRAG	1.3	
2391	184	1808	90I	3	14+	LG	MAML	UNKN	FRAG	8.3	
4012	184	4169/71	90I5	1	2	UNKN	MAML	UNKN	FRAG	0.9	fit together
3338	184	4157	90I5	2	1	MED	DEER	tooth	FRAG	1.9	
2363	184	4179	90I5	2	2	LG	MAML	vert	FRAG	7.2	fireplace
4036	184	4146	90J	2	2	UNKN	MAML	UNKN	FRAG	2.9	

2011.28	SBCM	Cat #	Unit	Level	Qty	Size Cat	Species	Bone Type	COND	Wt/g	Comments
2865	184	1000	95D	1	1	SM	MAML	UNKN	FRAG	1.8	
2773	184	2306	95D	2	45	ALL	MAML	UNKN	FRAG	49.6	
2930	184	1999	95D	5	1	LG	MAML	skull	FRAG	8.9	
3685	184	1999	95D	5	3	MED	MAML	teeth	FRAG	0.5	
3096	184	2186	95D	3,4	1	XSM	CTRB	tibia	FRAG	1	
3165	184	2186	95D	3,4	3	LG	MAML	long	FRAG	68	
3164	184	2186	95D	3,4	1	LG	MAML	long	FRAG	44	
4112	184	5380	95D	3,4	1	UNKN	MAML	UNKN	FRAG	0.3	
3177	184	2186	95D	3,4	1	XSM	TURT	shell	FRAG	1	
2745	184	2125	95D5	2	4	UNKN	MAML	long	FRAG	9.8	
4154	184	2125	95D5	2	2	UNKN	MAML	UNKN	FRAG	3	
2928	184	2435	95D5	3	1	LG	COW	UNKN	FRAG	42	
3131	184	2435	95D5	3	1	MED	DEER	tibia	FRAG	8	
3128	184	1135	95D5	4	1	MED	BCAT	long	FRAG	14	
3130	184	1135	95D5	4	1	MED	DEER	vert-thoracic	WHLE	3	
2735	184	1135	95D5	4	2	SM	MAML	long	FRAG	103.5	
3160	184	1135	95D5	4	1	LG	MAML	long	WHLE	40	
2885	184	2117	95D5	4	10	MED/LG	MAML	UNKN	FRAG	6.4	
3060	184	343	95D5	5	1	XSM	CTRB	femur	FRAG	3	
2868	184	343	95D5	5	56	MED/LG	MAML	UNKN	FRAG	49.1	
2653	184	355	95E	1	1	UNKN	MAML	skull	FRAG	0.3	
2748	184	2245	95E	2	18+	SM/MED	MAML	UNKN	FRAG	23.3	

2011.28	SBCM	Cat #	Unit	Level	Qty	Size Cat	Species	Bone Type	COND	Wt/g	Comments
4137	184	1981	95E	3	1	UNKN	MAML	UNKN	FRAG	1	
2924	184	3907	95E	3	1	MED	SHEP	vert	FRAG	10.1	
3157	184	997	95E	4	1	SM	MAML	vert-cer-vical	WHLE	0.1	
3646	184	3228	95E	5	1	XSM	CTRB	Rt mandi-ble	WHLE	2	
3111	184	3228	95E	5	1	XSM	RAT	humerus	WHLE	1	
3110	184	3228	95E	5	1	XSM	RAT	pelvic	WHLE	1	
3622	184	2218	95E	7	1	XSM	CTRBB	Lt mandi-ble	WHLE	2	
2907	184	6050	95E	8	6	SM/MED	MAML	UNKN	FRAG	3.5	
3085	184	2335	95E	UNKN	1	XSM	CTRB	fibula	FRAG	0.9	
3086	184	2335	95E	UNKN	1	XSM	CTRB	Rt mandi-ble	FRAG	0.8	
2939	184	2335	95E	UNKN	1	MED	MAML	metapo-dial	FRAG	1.7	
2926	184	2335	95E	UNKN	1	MED	MAML	scapula	FRAG	4.6	
3056	184	2335	95E	UNKN	1	MED	MAML	skull	FRAG	3	
3665	184	2335	95E	UNKN	1	SM	MAML	tooth	WHLE	0.2	three root
3048	184	2335	95E	UNKN	1	MED	MAML	UNKN	FRAG	2	
3054	184	2335	95E	UNKN	1	SM	RACC	metacar-pal	FRAG	2	
3064	184	2335	95E	UNKN	1	XSM	RAT	femur	WHLE	0.5	
3063	184	2335	95E	UNKN	1	XSM	RAT	tibia	FRAG	0.5	
3055	184	2335	95E	UNKN	1	SM	SKUK	pelvic gridle	FRAG	4	
3071	184	3028	95E 5	2	1	XSM	CTRB	femur	WHLE	2.5	
3651	184	3028	95E 5	2	1	XSM	GRSQ	Lt mandi-ble	WHLE	2	w/teeth
3613	184	3028	95E 5	2	1	XSM	GRSQ	Lt mandi-ble	WHLE	2	

2011.28	SBCM	Cat #	Unit	Level	Qty	Size Cat	Species	Bone Type	COND	Wt/g	Comments
2755	184	3547	95E5	1	20	MED/LG	MAML	long	FRAG	27	
2870	184	3028	95E5	2	78	LG	MAML	UNKN	FRAG	46.1	
3155	184	3134	95E5	3	1	SM	MAML	humerus	FRAG	2	
3152	184	3134	95E5	3	1	SM	MAML	ulna	FRAG	2	
3098	184	4503	95E5	4	1	XSM	CTRB	humerus	FRAG	1	
2785	184	3333	95E5	6	26	SM/MED	MAML	UNKN	FRAG	28.8	
2942	184	1156	95E5	7	1	MED	COYT	metatarsal	WHLE	11.5	
3057	184	3265	95E5	7	1	UNKN	MAML	UNKN	FRAG	1	
2754	184	3057	95E5	8	20	SM/MED	MAML	UNKN	FRAG	12.8	
3103	184	3552	95E5	9	1	XSM	CTRB	pelvic	WHLE	3	
3655	184	3552	95E5	9	1	XSM	GRSQ	Rt mandi-ble	WHLE	2	
3015	184	3552	95E5	9	1	XSM	RAT	humerus	WHLE	0.8	
3101	184	3189	95E5	10	1	XSM	GRSQ	vert-lum-bar	WHLE	0.7	
2682	184	3189	95E5	10	13	MED	MAML	long	FRAG	0.7	
2837	184	3079	95E5/152	1	12	ALL	MAML	UNKN	FRAG	10.2	
3319	184	1235	95G	3	1	XSM	CTRBB	Lt mandi-ble	FRAG	1.8	
3329	184	3181	95G	5	1	MED	BCAT	Lt mandi-ble	WHLE	1	w/tooth
3326	184	3181	95G	5	1	XSM	RAT	mandible	FRAG	0.6	
3396	184	1495	95G5	3	1	LG	COW	tooth	FRAG	1.4	
3331	184	1495	95G5	3	1	MED	DEER	incisor	FRAG	0.3	
3209	184	1495	95G5	3	1	XSM	TURT	shell	FRAG	1.1	
3390	184	1646	95H	1	1	LG	HORS	tooth	FRAG	0.6	

2011.28	SBCM	Cat #	Unit	Level	Qty	Size Cat	Species	Bone Type	COND	Wt/g	Comments
3345	184	1733	95H	2	10	LG	HORS	teeth	FRAG	11.5	
3395	184	1866	95H	UNKN	1	LG	COW	tooth	FRAG	6.4	
3294	184	1866	95H	UNKN	2	UNKN	MAML	mandible	FRAG	1.4	frag w/teeth
2458	184	1866	95H	UNKN	46+	LG	MAML	skull/rib	FRAG	77	cut marks
3334	184	1208	95H5	3	8	MED	DEER	mandible	FRAG	9.4	w/teeth
2413	184	5334	95I	3	2	UNKN	MAML	long	FRAG	3	
2414	184	1613	95I	4	1	UNKN	MAML	long	FRAG	3.2	
2461	184	1106	95I5	1	1	MED	SHEP	metapo-dial	WHLE	21.6	
2390	184	5404	95I5	4	5	UNKN	MAML	long	FRAG	5.4	
2235	184	1595	95J5	2	1	UNKN	MAML	UNKN	WHLE	0.6	
3031	184	3607	9D	3	22+	UNKN	MAML	UNKN	FRAG	43.1	
3003	184	5511	E5	5	47+	UNKN	MAML	UNKN	FRAG	29.1	
4100	184	5491	E5	5	1	UNKN	MAML	UNKN	FRAG	0.3	
4138	184	5492	E5	5	1	UNKN	MAML	UNKN	FRAG	0.8	
4124	184	5497	E5	5	1	UNKN	MAML	UNKN	FRAG	0.3	
4140	184	5499	E5	5	1	UNKN	MAML	UNKN	FRAG	0.5	
4131	184	5500	E5	5	1	UNKN	MAML	UNKN	FRAG	1.3	
3045	184	5804	I55	1	3	UNKN	MAML	UNKN	FRAG	0.2	
3923	184	4658	TEST	N/A	1	XSM	GRSQ	long	WHLE	0.3	
3924	184	4658	TEST	N/A	1	XSM	GRSQ	mandible frag	FRAG	0.7	
2993	184	3115	UNKN	2	40+	LG	MAML	UNKN	FRAG	49.5	
2956	184	2719	UNKN	1	1	UNKN	MAML	UNKN	WHLE	3.4	wall corner

2011.28	SBCM	Cat #	Unit	Level	Qty	Size Cat	Species	Bone Type	COND	Wt/g	Comments
3109	184	3238	UNKN	2	1	XSM	CTRB	rib	WHLE	1	
3005	184	3238	UNKN	2	35	UNKN	MAML	UNKN	FRAG	43.2	
2983	184	1098	UNKN	4	134+	·LG	MAML	UNKN	FRAG	134.2	
2958	184	752	UNKN	6	4	UNKN	MAML	UNKN	FRAG	3.4	
3016	184	2903	UNKN	3,4	860+	UNKN	MAML	UNKN	FRAG	426.7	
2982	184	3754	UNKN	3,4,5	3	UNKN	MAML	UNKN	FRAG	0.4	level 4 ash + burned
2477	184	3778	UNKN	UNKN	1	MED	DEER	metatarsal	WHLE	1.2	distal end
3925	184	3795	UNKN	UNKN	1	XSM	GRSQ	mandible	FRAG	0.7	
4804	184	1323	UNKN	UNKN	1	MED	MAML	Rib	FRAG	4.3	
4856	184	1315	UNKN	UNKN	1	MED	MAML	Tibia	FRAG	10	cut marks
4167	184	4268	UNKN	UNKN	1	UNKN	MAML	UNKN	FRAG	0.4	Pinto Point
2971	184	4512	UNKN	UNKN	14	UNKN	MAML	UNKN	FRAG	5.2	cremation pt.
4812	184	4258	UNKN	UNKN	1	UNKN	MAML	UNKN	FRAG	0.3	cut marks
2980	184	4276	UNKN	UNKN	32	UNKN	MAML	UNKN	FRAG	8.1	Pinto Point
2996	184	5931	UNKN	UNKN	9	SM/MED	MAML	UNKN	FRAG	2	
2988	184	1250	UNKN	UNKN	4	LG	MAML	UNKN	FRAG	128	
2970	184	4184	UNKN	UNKN	4	LG	MAML	UNKN	FRAG	63.1	
3023	184	287	UNKN	UNKN	1	UNKN	MAML	UNKN	FRAG	1	
2989	184	1154	UNKN	UNKN	4	UNKN	MAML	UNKN	FRAG	91.8	
3002	184	1174	UNKN	UNKN	31	UNKN	MAML	UNKN	FRAG	20.9	
3003	184	1240	UNKN	UNKN	1	UNKN	MAML	UNKN	FRAG	1.5	
2992	184	1242	UNKN	UNKN	18	UNKN	MAML	UNKN	FRAG	59.7	

2011.28	SBCM	Cat #	Unit	Level	Qty	Size Cat	Species	Bone Type	COND	Wt/g	Comments
2974	184	1250	UNKN	UNKN	10	UNKN	MAML	UNKN	FRAG	132.4	
2984	184	1365	UNKN	UNKN	26+	UNKN	MAML	UNKN	FRAG	117.2	
2990	184	1425	UNKN	UNKN	40	UNKN	MAML	UNKN	FRAG	57.6	
3006	184	1506	UNKN	UNKN	1	UNKN	MAML	UNKN	FRAG	1.1	
2961	184	1516	UNKN	UNKN	2	UNKN	MAML	UNKN	FRAG	0.7	
2977	184	1688	UNKN	UNKN	1	UNKN	MAML	UNKN	FRAG	1	
3011	184	1924	UNKN	UNKN	5	UNKN	MAML	UNKN	FRAG	12.4	
3008	184	2781	UNKN	UNKN	70	UNKN	MAML	UNKN	FRAG	31.6	
3017	184	2908	UNKN	UNKN	50+	UNKN	MAML	UNKN	FRAG	430.4	
3000	184	2942	UNKN	UNKN	21+	UNKN	MAML	UNKN	FRAG	483.1	
2955	184	3631	UNKN	UNKN	1	UNKN	MAML	UNKN	FRAG	0.2	
2999	184	3633	UNKN	UNKN	75+	UNKN	MAML	UNKN	FRAG	82.9	
2994	184	3715	UNKN	UNKN	13	UNKN	MAML	UNKN	FRAG	9.2	
2959	184	3720	UNKN	UNKN	5	UNKN	MAML	UNKN	FRAG	2.6	
3015	184	3732	UNKN	UNKN	500+	UNKN	MAML	UNKN	FRAG	393.9	
2953	184	3750	UNKN	UNKN	1	UNKN	MAML	UNKN	FRAG	1	
2962	184	3778	UNKN	UNKN	3	UNKN	MAML	UNKN	FRAG	1.7	
2998	184	3812	UNKN	UNKN	147+	UNKN	MAML	UNKN	FRAG	131.7	
2957	184	3827	UNKN	UNKN	3	UNKN	MAML	UNKN	FRAG	1.4	
3010	184	3843	UNKN	UNKN	1	UNKN	MAML	UNKN	FRAG	0.1	
3014	184	3934	UNKN	UNKN	1	UNKN	MAML	UNKN	FRAG	0.07	
2981	184	3972	UNKN	UNKN	20+	UNKN	MAML	UNKN	FRAG	18.2	

2011.28	SBCM	Cat #	Unit	Level	Qty	Size Cat	Species	Bone Type	COND	Wt/g	Comments
2997	184	4024	UNKN	UNKN	24	UNKN	MAML	UNKN	FRAG	24.8	
3007	184	4084	UNKN	UNKN	8	UNKN	MAML	UNKN	FRAG	10.5	
3012	184	4184	UNKN	UNKN	2	UNKN	MAML	UNKN	FRAG	2	
2937	184	4256	UNKN	UNKN	8	UNKN	MAML	UNKN	FRAG	3.6	
2975	184	4281	UNKN	UNKN	6	UNKN	MAML	UNKN	FRAG	13.8	
3004	184	4495	UNKN	UNKN	2	UNKN	MAML	UNKN	FRAG	3.3	
2987	184	4845	UNKN	UNKN	92+	UNKN	MAML	UNKN	FRAG	157.4	
2986	184	4964	UNKN	UNKN	11+	UNKN	MAML	UNKN	FRAG	69.4	
3013	184	5127	UNKN	UNKN	1	UNKN	MAML	UNKN	FRAG	1	
2954	184	5176	UNKN	UNKN	2	UNKN	MAML	UNKN	FRAG	2	
3001	184	5199	UNKN	UNKN	2	UNKN	MAML	UNKN	FRAG	0.8	
2985	184	5451	UNKN	UNKN	3	UNKN	MAML	UNKN	FRAG	0.8	
2976	184	6155	UNKN	UNKN	26	UNKN	MAML	UNKN	FRAG	21.6	
2952	184	6322	UNKN	UNKN	1	UNKN	MAML	UNKN	FRAG	0.4	
2995	184	6341	UNKN	UNKN	1	UNKN	MAML	UNKN	FRAG	0.01	
2979	184	6369	UNKN	UNKN	3	UNKN	MAML	UNKN	FRAG	0.1	
4168	184	6502	UNKN	UNKN	1	UNKN	MAML	UNKN	FRAG	0.6	
2978	184	UNKN	UNKN	UNKN	1	UNKN	MAML	UNKN	FRAG	0.5	
4827	184	1321	UNKN	UNKN	1	UNKN	MAML	UNKN	FRAG	1.7	
4814	184	1322	UNKN	UNKN	1	UNKN	MAML	UNKN	FRAG	0.4	
4826	184	1326	UNKN	UNKN	1	UNKN	MAML	UNKN	FRAG	1.3	
4809	184	1344	UNKN	UNKN	1	UNKN	MAML	UNKN	FRAG	0.2	

2011.28	SBCM	Cat #	Unit	Level	Qty	Size Cat	Species	Bone Type	COND	Wt/g	Comments
4823	184	1347	UNKN	UNKN	1	UNKN	MAML	UNKN	FRAG	1.2	
4817	184	1364	UNKN	UNKN	1	UNKN	MAML	UNKN	FRAG	1.2	
4878	184	1367	UNKN	UNKN	1	UNKN	MAML	UNKN	FRAG	5.8	
4818	184	3936	UNKN	UNKN	1	UNKN	MAML	UNKN	FRAG	1.4	
4820	184	4116	UNKN	UNKN	1	UNKN	MAML	UNKN	FRAG	1.9	
4813	184	4259	UNKN	UNKN	1	UNKN	MAML	UNKN	FRAG	0.1	
4810	184	4260	UNKN	UNKN	1	UNKN	MAML	UNKN	FRAG	0.1	
4816	184	4261	UNKN	UNKN	1	UNKN	MAML	UNKN	FRAG	0.3	
4828	184	4262	UNKN	UNKN	1	UNKN	MAML	UNKN	FRAG	0.2	
4822	184	4263	UNKN	UNKN	1	UNKN	MAML	UNKN	FRAG	0.5	
4815	184	4264	UNKN	UNKN	1	UNKN	MAML	UNKN	FRAG	0.9	
4821	184	4265	UNKN	UNKN	1	UNKN	MAML	UNKN	FRAG	0.3	
4808	184	4266	UNKN	UNKN	1	UNKN	MAML	UNKN	FRAG	0.3	
4811	184	4267	UNKN	UNKN	1	UNKN	MAML	UNKN	FRAG	0.9	
4824	184	4279	UNKN	UNKN	1	UNKN	MAML	UNKN	FRAG	1.5	
4717	184	5273	UNKN	UNKN	2+	UNKN	MAML	UNKN	FRAG	0.1	
4807	184	6160	UNKN	UNKN	1	UNKN	MAML	UNKN	FRAG	0.9	
4819	184	6338	UNKN	UNKN	1	UNKN	MAML	UNKN	FRAG	0.4	
4806	184	6340	UNKN	UNKN	1	UNKN	MAML	UNKN	FRAG	0.6	
2967	184	3621	UNKN	UNKN	1	UNKN	MAML	UNKN	WHLE	27.5	
2963	184	84	UNKN	UNKN	1	UNKN	MAML	UNKN	WHLE	0.7	
2964	184	2280	UNKN	UNKN	1	UNKN	MAML	UNKN	WHLE	1.2	

2011.28	SBCM	Cat #	Unit	Level	Qty	Size Cat	Species	Bone Type	COND	Wt/g	Comments
2960	184	3725	UNKN	UNKN	1	UNKN	MAML	UNKN	WHLE	1.1	
2965	184	4238	UNKN	UNKN	1	UNKN	MAML	UNKN	WHLE	1	
3926	184	3795	UNKN	UNKN	1	XSM	RAT	femur	WHLE	0.4	
3184	184	3805	UNKN	UNKN	4	XSM	TURT	shell	FRAG	20.1	
Fanual Notation Key											
2011.28: Pechanga Cultural Resource catalogue number											
SBCM: San Bernardino Catalogue collection number											
CAT #: Catalog number											
UNIT: Location											
	According to excavation map										
	TEST: Test Hole										
LEVEL: Depth											
	SURF: Surface										
	Levels 1-10 (Increments of 6 inches each level)										
QTY: Quantity											
Size Cat: Size Category											
	XSM: X-Small 10lb or less										
	SM: Small 10-30lbs										
	MED: Medium 30-200lbs										
	LG: Large 200lb +										
	UNKN: Unknown										

	ALL: all sizes mixed					
Species:						
	Common name		Scientific name			
	BADG: Badger		Taxidea taxus			
	BCAT: Bob Cat/ WildCat		Lynx rufus			
	BHRB: Brush Rabbit		Sylvilagus bachmani			
	CHPM: Chipmunk		Tamias			
	COW: Cow		Bos primigenius			
	COYT: Coyote		Canis latrans			
	CTRB: Cotton tail Rabbit		Sylvilagus			
	DEER: Deer, mule		Odocoileus hemionus			
	FISH: Fish, Rainbow Trout		Oncorhynchus mykiss			
	GOPH: Gopher, pocket		Geomyidae			
	GRSQ: Ground Squirel		Ictidomys tridecemlineatus			
	GYSQ: Grey Squirel		Sciurus carolinensis			
	HORS: Horse		Equua ferus caballus			
	JKRB: Jack Rabbit		Lepus			
	KRAT: Kangaroo Rat		Dipodys			
	MAML: Mammal		Mammalia			
	MOUS: Mouse		Mus musculus			
	MTLI: Mountain Lion		Puma concolor			
	PIG: Pig		Sus			
	RACC: Raccoon		Procyon lotor			

	RAT: Rat		Rattus					
	RD: Rodent		Rodentia					
	SHEP: Sheep		Ovis aries					
	SKUK: Skunk		Mephitidae					
	TURT: Turtle, Western Pond		Actinemys marmorata					
	WRAT: Wood Rat		Neotoma					
Bone Type:								
	Femur							
	Humerus							
	Incisors							
	Long: Long bone							
	Mandible							
	Maxillary							
	Metacarpal							
	Metapodial							
	Pelvic girdle							
	Phalange							
	Radius							
	Rib							
	Scapula							
	Shell							
	skull							
	Teeth							

	Tibia							
	Ulna							
	Vert: Vertebra							
	Vert-Cervical vertebra							
	Vert-Lumbar vertebra							
	Vert-Thoraic vertebra							
COND: Condition								
	WHLE: Whole							
	FRAG: Fragment							
WT/g: Weight measured in grams								
Comments:								
	Juvenile							
	burned							
	Cut Marks							
	Distal End							
	Proximal end							
	Root: tooth with root							
	Wall corner							
	w/tooth/teeth: a mandible/maxillary with intacted tooth/teeth							

APPENDIX V

MODIFIED FAUNAL

Appendix V: Modified Faunal										
2011.28	**SBCM**	**Cat #**	**Unit**	**Level**	**Qty**	**MODF**	**Species**	**COND**	**Wt/g**	**Comments**
4802	184	6267	100A	1	1	POSH	MAML	WHLE	2.3	
4772	184	3070	100D5	1	1	POSH	MAML	WHLE	0.9	bead, coyote canine tooth, burned
4786	184	2629	100D5	2	1	POSH	MAML	WHLE	1.2	burned
4803	184	2628	100D5	2	1	POSH	MAML	WHLE	0.5	
4797	184	5750	105E	3	1	POSH	MAML	WHLE	1.1	
4781	184	5760	105E	3	1	POSH	MAML	WHLE	1.6	
4051	184	827	105E 5	1	1	POSH	MAML	FRAG	1	burned
4789	184	4219	110D	2	1	POSH	MAML	WHLE	1.3	
4779	184	4224	110D	2	1	POSH	MAML	FRAG	0.4	
4784	184	4227	110D	2	1	POSH	MAML	WHLE	1.3	
4783	184	5342	110D	3	1	POSH	MAML	FRAG	0.6	possible pipe end
4790	184	5345	110D	3	1	POSH	MAML	WHLE	3.6	
4794	184	4943	110E5	8	1	POSH	MAML	WHLE	0.3	
4048	184	5721	110I	1	1	POSH	MAML	FRAG	1	burned
4052	184	5190	110J5	UNKN	1	POSH	MAML	FRAG	1	burned
4777	184	4777	115E	6	1	POSH	MAML	WHLE	3.7	burned
4782	184	3995	115-E	3	1	POSH	MAML	WHLE	0	
4787	184	5305	120F5	6	1	POSH	MAML	WHLE	0.3	
4062	184	4611	125G	2	1	POSH	MAML	FRAG	0.9	burned
4058	184	5124	140H5	1,2	1	POSH	MAML	FRAG	1.3	burned
4057	184	6530	140I5	1	1	GRND	MAML	FRAG	0.7	burned

2011.28	SBCM	Cat #	Unit	Level	Qty	MODF	Species	COND	Wt/g	Comments
4060	184	2076	152G	1,2,3	1	POSH	MAML	WHLE	2.3	
4063	184	6377	160I	1	1	POSH	MAML	FRAG	0.5	burned
4055	184	2762	160I	2	1	POSH	MAML	FRAG	1.3	
4064	184	5516	160I5	2	1	POSH	MAML	FRAG	1	burned
4065	184	6406	160J5	1	1	POSH	MAML	FRAG	1	burned
4059	184	5003	160J5	3	`	POSH	MAML	FRAG	0.7	
4056	184	5541	175I5	2	1	POSH	MAML	FRAG	0.3	
4000	184	5850	30H5	1,2,3	1	POSH	MAML	WHLE	0.2	
3990	184	5852	30H5	1,2,3	1	POSH	MAML	WHLE	0.8	
3999	184	5853	30H5	1,2,3	1	POSH	MAML	WHLE	0.8	
3991	184	5854	30H5	1,2,3	1	POSH	MAML	WHLE	0.3	
3993	184	6493	35H5	1	1	POSH	MAML	WHLE	0.1	
3994	184	6496	35H5	1	1	POSH	MAML	WHLE	0.3	
4002	184	6498	35H5	1	1	POSH	MAML	WHLE	0.7	
4004	184	6507	35H5	1	1	POSH	MAML	WHLE	0.6	
3995	184	6510	35H5	1	1	POSH	MAML	WHLE	0.7	
3996	184	6517	35H5	1	1	POSH	MAML	WHLE	0.1	
4001	184	5687	35I	3	1	POSH	MAML	WHLE	0.3	
3992	184	4377	55J5	4	1	POSH	MAML	WHLE	0.6	
4884	184	3886	70C5	2	1	POSH	MAML	FRAG	1.5	burned
4883	184	3887	70C5	2	1	POSH	MAML	FRAG	7.3	
4881	184	3888	70C5	2	1	POSH	MAML	FRAG	2.8	

2011.28	SBCM	Cat #	Unit	Level	Qty	MODF	Species	COND	Wt/g	Comments
4793	184	5638	70E	5	1	POSH	MAML	WHLE	0.8	burned
3998	184	2654	70I5	4	1	POSH	MAML	WHLE	1.4	
4882	184	5076	75C5	5	1	ETCH	MAML	WHLE	0.7	
4785	184	4798	75E5	2	1	POSH	MAML	WHLE	1.1	burned
3997	184	5606	75J	1	1	POSH	MAML	WHLE	0.8	
4003	184	5614	75J	1	1	POSH	MAML	WHLE	0.3	
4791	184	4073	80E	4	1	POSH	MAML	WHLE	0.3	burned
4780	184	6218	80E	7	1	POSH	MAML	FRAG	4.5	burned
4792	184	4908	85F5	1	1	POSH	MAML	WHLE	0.9	burned
4799	184	5905	85F5	3	1	POSH	MAML	WHLE	0.4	burned
4801	184	5895	85F5	3	1	POSH	MAML	FRAG	2.1	
4795	184	5899	85F5	3	1	POSH	MAML	WHLE	1.2	burned, scratches
4053	184	4750	85G	2	1	POSH	MAML	FRAG	1.1	
4007	184	5422	90I	1	1	POSH	MAML	WHLE	0.5	burned
4054	184	5405	90I	1	1	POSH	MAML	FRAG	4.7	burned
4050	184	5419	90I	1	1	POSH	MAML	FRAG	1.7	burned
4049	184	4156	90I5	3	1	POSH	MAML	WHLE	2.4	burned
4008	184	4145	90J	2	1	POSH	MAML	WHLE	0.6	burned
5977	184	2186	95D	3,4	1	POSH	MAML	FRAG	0.4	drilled
4796	184	5376	95D	3,4	1	POSH	MAML	WHLE	0.3	burned
4788	184	3027	95E5	2	1	POSH	MAML	WHLE	1.9	
4061	184	5737	G150	1	1	POSH	MAML	FRAG	4.2	

2011.28	SBCM	Cat #	Unit	Level	Qty	MODF	Species	COND	Wt/g	Comments
4005	184	4775	TEST	UNKN	1	POSH	MAML	WHLE	1	burned
4006	184	4776	TEST	UNKN	1	POSH	MAML	WHLE	0.4	burned
4871	184	1355	UNKN	UNKN	1	POSH	MAML	FRAG	1.2	stained, grooves
4862	184	1334	UNKN	UNKN	1	POSH	MAML	FRAG	0.5	burned
4858	184	1337	UNKN	UNKN	1	POSH	MAML	WHLE	1.1	burned
4863	184	1339	UNKN	UNKN	1	POSH	MAML	FRAG	0.9	burned
4874	184	1346	UNKN	UNKN	1	POSH	MAML	FRAG	1.3	burned
4859	184	1354	UNKN	UNKN	1	POSH	MAML	FRAG	1.4	burned
4870	184	1356	UNKN	UNKN	1	POSH	MAML	FRAG	0.2	burned
4841	184	1357	UNKN	UNKN	1	POSH	MAML	FRAG	0.3	burned
4848	184	UNKN	UNKN	UNKN	1	POSH	MAML	FRAG	3.6	burned
4849	184	1333	UNKN	UNKN	1	POSH	MAML	FRAG	1.2	burned
4840	184	1350	UNKN	UNKN	1	POSH	MAML	FRAG	0.2	burned
4839	184	1363	UNKN	UNKN	1	POSH	MAML	FRAG	3.7	burned
4846	184	3808	UNKN	UNKN	1	POSH	MAML	FRAG	2.6	burned
4835	184	1341	UNKN	UNKN	1	POSH	MAML	FRAG	1.2	burned, poss scratching stick
4855	184	4510	UNKN	UNKN	1	POSH	MAML	FRAG	2.7	cremation pt., 4-42"
4857	184	1360	UNKN	UNKN	1	POSH	MAML	WHLE	13	
4852	184	1330	UNKN	UNKN	1	GRND	MAML	FRAG	1.1	
4860	184	1314	UNKN	UNKN	1	POSH	MAML	FRAG	3.3	
4865	184	1316	UNKN	UNKN	1	POSH	MAML	FRAG	3.7	
4854	184	1317	UNKN	UNKN	1	POSH	MAML	FRAG	0.8	

2011.28	SBCM	Cat #	Unit	Level	Qty	MODF	Species	COND	Wt/g	Comments
4836	184	1318	UNKN	UNKN	1	POSH	MAML	WHLE	1.5	
4867	184	1319	UNKN	UNKN	1	POSH	MAML	FRAG	14	
4851	184	1320	UNKN	UNKN	1	POSH	MAML	FRAG	12	
4873	184	1328	UNKN	UNKN	1	POSH	MAML	FRAG	0.5	
4845	184	1329	UNKN	UNKN	2	POSH	MAML	WHLE	0.6	
4837	184	1338	UNKN	UNKN	1	POSH	MAML	FRAG	0.8	
4833	184	1343	UNKN	UNKN	1	POSH	MAML	FRAG	3.5	
4869	184	1348	UNKN	UNKN	1	POSH	MAML	FRAG	1.4	
4843	184	1349	UNKN	UNKN	1	POSH	MAML	FRAG	9.3	
4853	184	1351	UNKN	UNKN	1	POSH	MAML	FRAG	3.8	
4842	184	1352	UNKN	UNKN	1	POSH	MAML	FRAG	2.1	
4875	184	1359	UNKN	UNKN	1	POSH	MAML	FRAG	1.8	
4876	184	1427	UNKN	UNKN	1	POSH	MAML	FRAG	3.1	
4868	184	3933	UNKN	UNKN	1	POSH	MAML	FRAG	0.1	
4844	184	4188	UNKN	UNKN	1	POSH	MAML	FRAG	0.3	
4866	184	4494	UNKN	UNKN	1	POSH	MAML	FRAG	4.2	
4834	184	4846	UNKN	UNKN	1	POSH	MAML	FRAG	0.1	

Modified Fanual Notation Key
2011.28: Pechanga Cultural Resource catalogue number
SBCM: San Bernardino Catalogue collection number
CAT #: Catalog number

UNIT: Location					
	According to excavation map				
	TEST: Test Hole				
LEVEL: Depth					
	SURF: Surface				
	Levels 1-10 (Increments of 6 inches each level)				
QTY: Quantity					
MODF: Modification:					
	POSH: Polished				
	ETCH: Etched				
	GRND: Ground				
Species:					
	MAML: Mammal				
COND: Condition					
	FRAG: Fragment				
	WHLE: Whole				
WT/g: Weight measured in grams					
Comments:					
	Burned				
	Stained				
	Grooved				
	Cremation area				
	Drilled				

APPENDIX W

AWLS

Appendix W: Awls

2011.28	SBCM	Cat. #	Unit	Level	Qty	MTRL	COND	L/MM	W/MM	T/MM	Wt/g	Comments
4778	184	4898	100D	8	1	BONE	FRAG	28.5	3.2	17.6	1.8	burned
4773	184	4869	100G5	3	1	BONE	FRAG	49.2	6.2	7	3	burned
4776	184	1483	105F5	1	1	BONE	FRAG	10.9	3.9	11.4	1	burned
4800	184	2443	120D	6	1	BONE	FRAG	10.1	2.8	6.1	1	polished
4880	184	3881	70C5	2	1	BONE	FRAG	14.9	9.4	3.5	1	
3238	184	5963	95E	3	1	BCAT	FRAG	53.5	26	14	5.7	wildcat- lynx rufus
4798	184	3059	95E5	8	1	BONE	FRAG	12.4	4.4	7.6	0.7	burned
3260	184	1201	UNKN	UNKN	1	BONE	FRAG	37.6	22.2	12.8	5.2	burned
3236	184	1284	UNKN	UNKN	2	BONE	NRCP	147.1	17.9	8.1	13.9	fit together
3228	184	1302	UNKN	UNKN	1	DEER	FRAG	23.7	9.2	8.1	1.2	antler
3234	184	1305	UNKN	UNKN	1	DEER	FRAG	30.8	12.2	10.2	2.1	antler
3310	184	1306	UNKN	UNKN	1	DEER	FRAG	27	8.5	8.4	1.5	antler
3307	184	1307	UNKN	UNKN	1	DEER	FRAG	28.4	9.7	8.9	1.6	antler
3275	184	1308	UNKN	UNKN	1	DEER	FRAG	34.6	8.4	10.5	1.7	antler
3256	184	1309	UNKN	UNKN	1	DEER	FRAG	34.2	11.6	10	1.4	antler

2011.28	SBCM	Cat. #	Unit	Level	Qty	MTRL	COND	L/MM	W/MM	T/MM	Wt/g	Comments
3278	184	1310	UNKN	UNKN	1	DEER	FRAG	12.2	5.8	6.2	0.01	antler
3277	184	1311	UNKN	UNKN	1	DEER	FRAG	24.1	6.4	5.9	0.6	antler
3276	184	1312	UNKN	UNKN	1	DEER	FRAG	30.5	7.8	9.4	1.5	antler
3266	184	1313	UNKN	UNKN	1	DEER	FRAG	17.1	9.5	7.2	1.2	antler
4838	184	1304	UNKN	UNKN	1	DEER	FRAG	17.1	8.8	8.1	0.8	antler, awl tip
3273	184	1303	UNKN	UNKN	1	DEER	FRAG	26.5	8.7	7.1	1.6	antler, burned
3274	184	1286	UNKN	UNKN	1	BONE	FRAG	40.6	7.2	4.2	0.9	awl tip
3267	184	1294	UNKN	UNKN	1	BONE	FRAG	46.1	11.3	4.5	1.7	awl tip
3263	184	1198	UNKN	UNKN	1	BONE	FRAG	31.3	18.4	8.1	3	burned
3257	184	1270	UNKN	UNKN	1	BONE	FRAG	19.7	9.4	3.3	0.9	burned
3258	184	1275	UNKN	UNKN	1	BONE	FRAG	22.3	7.2	3.5	0.5	burned
3312	184	1280	UNKN	UNKN	1	BONE	FRAG	13.2	6.6	3.6	0.5	burned
3270	184	1289	UNKN	UNKN	1	BONE	FRAG	25.5	8.7	4.1	1.2	burned
3271	184	1289	UNKN	UNKN	1	BONE	FRAG	20.3	7.1	3.7	0.4	burned
3303	184	1291	UNKN	UNKN	1	BONE	FRAG	15	6.2	4	0.3	burned
3259	184	1296	UNKN	UNKN	1	BONE	FRAG	11.4	7.3	2.7	0.4	burned

2011.28	SBCM	Cat. #	Unit	Level	Qty	MTRL	COND	L/MM	W/MM	T/MM	Wt/g	Comments
3261	184	1300	UNKN	UNKN	1	BONE	FRAG	25.5	14.6	5.3	2.4	burned
3272	184	1301	UNKN	UNKN	1	BONE	FRAG	37.2	12.1	7.7	3	burned
4830	184	1324	UNKN	UNKN	1	BONE	FRAG	12.2	4.1	7.8	0.6	burned
4847	184	1345	UNKN	UNKN	1	BONE	FRAG	29.3	3.5	11	1.5	burned
4877	184	1331	UNKN	UNKN	1	BONE	FRAG	12.7	7.3	4.3	0.5	burned, polished
3239	184	1269	UNKN	UNKN	1	BONE	FRAG	87	29.7	21.7	27.1	drilled
3268	184	1278	UNKN	UNKN	1	BONE	FRAG	20.4	9.2	2.2	0.6	polished
4861	184	1325	UNKN	UNKN	1	BONE	FRAG	17.3	11.2	3.8	1.1	polished
3306	184	1299	UNKN	UNKN	1	BONE	FRAG	79.1	34.2	20.2	18.9	polished
4831	184	3807	UNKN	UNKN	1	BONE	FRAG	21	5.5	7.7	1	polished, coated
3269	184	1271	UNKN	UNKN	1	BONE	FRAG	12.2	5	3.4	0.2	
3255	184	1272	UNKN	UNKN	1	BONE	FRAG	29.5	12.3	3.9	0.9	
3233	184	1273	UNKN	UNKN	1	BONE	FRAG	33.5	15.7	3.8	1.8	
3235	184	1274	UNKN	UNKN	1	BONE	FRAG	62.5	22.3	13.3	7.3	
3302	184	1276	UNKN	UNKN	1	BONE	FRAG	25.9	11.1	3.9	1.1	
3308	184	1277	UNKN	UNKN	1	BONE	FRAG	18.4	5.9	5.1	0.6	

2011.28	SBCM	Cat. #	Unit	Level	Qty	MTRL	COND	L/MM	W/MM	T/MM	Wt/g	Comments
3300	184	1279	UNKN	UNKN	1	BONE	FRAG	28.1	5.2	3.7	0.7	
3311	184	1281	UNKN	UNKN	1	BONE	FRAG	16.3	3.4	3.4	0.3	
3301	184	1282	UNKN	UNKN	1	BONE	FRAG	35.8	11.4	3.1	1	
3265	184	1283	UNKN	UNKN	1	BONE	FRAG	23	9.7	4.2	1.1	
3231	184	1285	UNKN	UNKN	1	BONE	FRAG	15.9	8.1	4.5	0.6	
3229	184	1287	UNKN	UNKN	1	BONE	FRAG	21.5	5.2	4.8	0.5	
3232	184	1288	UNKN	UNKN	1	BONE	FRAG	70.6	30.2	20	16.3	
3230	184	1290	UNKN	UNKN	1	BONE	FRAG	18.4	4.8	2.5	0.3	
3305	184	1292	UNKN	UNKN	1	BONE	FRAG	40.2	6.4	2.7	0.6	
3262	184	1293	UNKN	UNKN	1	BONE	FRAG	15.9	10.7	2.3	0.8	
3309	184	1295	UNKN	UNKN	1	BONE	FRAG	20.1	9.7	3.2	0.7	
3264	184	1297	UNKN	UNKN	1	BONE	FRAG	34.2	11.4	4.5	1.7	
4864	184	1336	UNKN	UNKN	1	BONE	FRAG	30.2	9.8	4.8	1.1	
4832	184	1340	UNKN	UNKN	1	BONE	FRAG	28	4.9	9	1.4	
3304	184	1342	UNKN	UNKN	1	BONE	FRAG	19.3	6.3	4.2	0.8	
3237	184	1369	UNKN	UNKN	1	BONE	FRAG	15.5	5.1	2	0.6	

2011.28	SBCM	Cat. #	Unit	Level	Qty	MTRL	COND	L/MM	W/MM	T/MM	Wt/g	Comments
4829	184	1366	UNKN	UNKN	1	BONE	FRAG	45.4	4.6	17.4	3	
4850	184	3806	UNKN	UNKN	1	BONE	FRAG	30.6	3.9	6.2	0.7	
Awl Notation Key												
2011.28: Pechanga Cultural Resource catalogue number												
SBCM: San Bernardino Catalogue collection number												
CAT #: Catalog number												
UNIT: Location												
	According to excavation map											
LEVEL: Depth												
	SURF: Surface											
	Levels 1-10 (Increments of 6 inches each level)											
QTY: Quantity												
MTRL: Material												
	BONE: Faunal bone											
	DEER: Deer, Mule											

<table>
<tr><td></td><td>BCAT: Bob Cat/ WildCat</td><td></td><td></td><td></td><td></td><td></td><td></td></tr>
<tr><td colspan="8">L/mm: Length measured in mm from end to edge</td></tr>
<tr><td colspan="8">W/mm: Width measured in mm from edge to edge</td></tr>
<tr><td colspan="8">T/mm: Thickness measured in mm from top to bottom</td></tr>
<tr><td colspan="8">WT/g: Weight measured in grams</td></tr>
<tr><td colspan="8">Comments: Any additional data (fire-affected, etc.)</td></tr>
<tr><td></td><td>Polished</td><td></td><td></td><td></td><td></td><td></td><td></td></tr>
</table>

APPENDIX X

BURNED FAUNAL

Appendix X: Burned Faunal											
2011.28	**SBCM**	**Cat #**	**Unit**	**Level**	**Qty**	**Size Cat**	**Species**	**Bone Type (s)**	**COND**	**Wt/g**	**Comments**
3042	184	253	0-G	UNKN	2	UNKN	MAML	UNKN	FRAG	4.7	burned
2877	184	2693	100D	1	38	UNKN	MAML	UNKN	FRAG	40.5	burned
2827	184	185	100D	2	1	UNKN	MAML	UNKN	FRAG	4	burned
2811	184	188	100D	2	7	UNKN	MAML	UNKN	FRAG	20.8	burned
2724	184	2860	100D	3	16	MED/LG	MAML	rib	FRAG	23	burned
2826	184	133	100D	3	2	UNKN	MAML	UNKN	FRAG	1	burned
2664	184	2611	100D	4	25+	SM/MED	MAML	long/rib	FRAG	16.9	burned
3180	184	638	100D	4	1	XSM	TURT	shell	FRAG	0.8	burned
3204	184	643	100D	4	1	XSM	TURT	shell	FRAG	1.2	burned
2715	184	2923	100D	5	7	SM/MED	MAML	long/rib	FRAG	9.2	burned
2823	184	233	100D	5	13	UNKN	MAML	UNKN	FRAG	10.8	burned
2707	184	2923	100D	5	1	UNKN	MAML	UNKN	FRAG	0.8	burned
3206	184	233	100D	5	1	XSM	TURT	shell	FRAG	0.6	burned
3179	184	2923	100D	5	1	XSM	TURT	shell	FRAG	0.5	burned
2676	184	5086	100D	7	8	MED	MAML	long/rib	FRAG	7.1	burned
2730	184	4898	100D	8	5	MED	MAML	long/rib	FRAG	7.4	burned
2708	184	3129	100D	SURF	5	SM/MED	MAML	rib/vert/skull	FRAG	8.6	burned
2697	184	3074	100D5	1	42	All	MAML	long/rib/vert	FRAG	120.5	burned
2669	184	2531	100D5	1	21	MED	MAML	long/rib	FRAG	22.5	burned
2883	184	2630	100D5	2	57	MED/LG	MAML	UNKN	FRAG	123.7	burned
3163	184	2924	100D5	3	1	LG	COW	metapo-dial	WHLE	18	burned

2011.28	SBCM	Cat #	Unit	Level	Qty	Size Cat	Species	Bone Type (s)	COND	Wt/g	Comments
2711	184	164	100D5	3	22	SM/MED	MAML	long/rib	FRAG	27.6	burned
2721	184	135	100D5	4	5	MED	MAML	long	FRAG	5.1	burned
2888	184	2287	100D5	6	9	MED	MAML	UNKN	FRAG	5	burned
2917	184	969	100E	2	13	SM/MED	MAML	UNKN	FRAG	9.6	burned
2896	184	1049	100E5	3	113+	ALL	MAML	UNKN	FRAG	67	burned
3200	184	1049	100E5	3	1	XSM	TURT	shell	FRAG	0.8	burned
2704	184	2909	100E5	4	157+	ALL	MAML	long/rib/ skull	FRAG	247.1	burned
2810	184	699	100E5	9	22	SM/MED	MAML	UNKN	FRAG	17.1	burned
3203	184	699	100E5	9	2	XSM	TURT	shell	FRAG	1.5	burned
2832	184	778	100F5	3	1	UNKN	MAML	UNKN	FRAG	0.9	burned
4631	184	4631	105D	1	7	ALL	MAML	UNKN	FRAG	9.4	burned
2857	184	952	105D5	1	52	ALL	MAML	UNKN	FRAG	41.6	burned
2658	184	983	105D5	2	24	MED	MAML	long/rib	FRAG	26.3	burned
2797	184	498	105D5	3	9	UNKN	MAML	UNKN	FRAG	3.8	burned
2661	184	2488	105D5	5	43	SM/MED	MAML	long/rib	FRAG	40.5	burned
2727	184	1845	105E	1	32	SM/MED	MAML	long/rib	FRAG	21.8	burned
2685	184	1007	105E	1	1	UNKN	MAML	UNKN	FRAG	0.5	burned
2706	184	1225	105E	2	126+	SM/LG	MAML	long/rib/ skull	FRAG	199.5	burned
2861	184	5743	105E	3	86	LG	MAML	UNKN	FRAG	48.2	burned
2609	184	2362	105E	3	1	UNKN	MAML	rib	FRAG	1.9	burned
4160	184	5757	105E	3	1	UNKN	MAML	UNKN	FRAG	1.4	burned
2899	184	827	105E5	1	63	ALL	MAML	UNKN	FRAG	36.7	burned

2011.28	SBCM	Cat #	Unit	Level	Qty	Size Cat	Species	Bone Type (s)	COND	Wt/g	Comments
2692	184	2359	105E5	3	1	UNKN	MAML	UNKN	WHLE	1.4	burned
4161	184	4586	105E5	5	1	UNKN	MAML	UNKN	FRAG	0.3	burned
2844	184	1483	105F5	1	3	LG	MAML	UNKN	FRAG	4.4	burned
2720	184	352	110D	1	1	MED	MAML	UNKN	FRAG	2.1	burned
2673	184	1243	110D	2	27	MED	MAML	long/rib	FRAG	41.1	burned
2788	184	4237	110D	2	54	UNKN	MAML	UNKN	FRAG	54	burned
4759	184	4221	110D	2	1	UNKN	MAML	UNKN	FRAG	0.4	burned
4726	184	4223	110D	2	1	UNKN	MAML	UNKN	FRAG	0.5	burned
4754	184	4225	110D	2	1	UNKN	MAML	UNKN	FRAG	1.2	burned
4162	184	4220	110D	2	1	UNKN	MAML	UNKN	FRAG	0.5	burned
4735	184	4230	110D	2	1	UNKN	MAML	UNKN	FRAG	0.4	burned
4746	184	4235	110D	2	1	UNKN	MAML	UNKN	FRAG	2.7	burned
4745	184	4236	110D	2	1	UNKN	MAML	UNKN	FRAG	1.2	burned
2881	184	5339	110D	3	16	MED/LG	MAML	UNKN	FRAG	5.1	burned
4768	184	4132	110D	3	1	UNKN	MAML	UNKN	FRAG	1.1	burned
4756	184	4133	110D	3	1	UNKN	MAML	UNKN	FRAG	1.2	burned
4733	184	4134	110D	3	1	UNKN	MAML	UNKN	FRAG	0.9	burned
4774	184	4135	110D	3	1	UNKN	MAML	UNKN	FRAG	0.8	burned
4729	184	4136	110D	3	1	UNKN	MAML	UNKN	FRAG	0.5	burned
4166	184	5343	110D	3	1	UNKN	MAML	UNKN	FRAG	0.1	burned
4165	184	5346	110D	3	1	UNKN	MAML	UNKN	FRAG	0.1	burned
4739	184	6097	110D	5	1	UNKN	MAML	UNKN	FRAG	0.7	burned

2011.28	SBCM	Cat #	Unit	Level	Qty	Size Cat	Species	Bone Type (s)	COND	Wt/g	Comments
2916	184	5434	110D	6	25	SM/MED	MAML	UNKN	FRAG	83.8	burned
2698	184	1775	110D5	3	48	SM/MED	MAML	long/rib	FRAG	38.7	burned
2831	184	6125	110E	2	5	LG	MAML	UNKN	FRAG	6.3	burned
4751	184	6128	110E	2	1	UNKN	MAML	UNKN	FRAG	1.1	burned
4770	184	5488	110E	5	1	UNKN	MAML	UNKN	FRAG	0.2	burned
2733	184	5722	110E5	2	184	ALL	MAML	long/rib/ skull	FRAG	194	burned
2829	184	436	110E5	3	18	LG	MAML	UNKN	FRAG	42.2	burned
3081	184	1092	110E5	4	2	XSM	CTRB	humerus	FRAG	1.8	burned
2717	184	5021	110E5	7	39	SM/MED	MAML	long/rib	FRAG	19.9	burned
2840	184	5042	110E5	7	2	UNKN	MAML	UNKN	FRAG	1.7	burned
2728	184	4951	110E5	8	40+	SM/MED	MAML	long/skull	FRAG	8.2	burned
4762	184	4948	110E5	8	1	UNKN	MAML	UNKN	FRAG	1.9	burned
4748	184	6422	110F	3	1	UNKN	MAML	UNKN	FRAG	0.7	burned
4742	184	6424	110F	3	1	UNKN	MAML	UNKN	FRAG	1.7	burned
2699	184	3319	110F5	3	60+	SM/MED	MAML	long/rib	FRAG	48	burned
2765	184	791	110F5	6	25	MED	MAML	UNKN	FRAG	11.7	burned
2409	184	5228	110G	2	4	MED/LG	MAML	long	FRAG	7	burned
2357	184	5070	110G	3	4	MED	MAML	rib	FRAG	6.7	burned
2410	184	4868	110G5	3	10	SM/MED	MAML	long	FRAG	8.6	burned
2369	184	1911	110H	1	8	UNKN	MAML	long	FRAG	7.3	burned
2405	184	1914	110H	2	7	MED	MAML	rib/vert	FRAG	13.1	burned, cut marks
2431	184	1879	110H	3	25+	MED/LG	MAML	long/rib	FRAG	42.9	burned

2011.28	SBCM	Cat #	Unit	Level	Qty	Size Cat	Species	Bone Type (s)	COND	Wt/g	Comments
2451	184	6211	110H5	1	8	UNKN	MAML	long	FRAG	2.9	burned
2493	184	1793	110H5	5	1	MED	MAML	metacar-pal	FRAG	3.7	burned
2421	184	1919	110H5	5	4	UNKN	MAML	long	FRAG	0.6	burned
2412	184	1793	110H5	5	25+	UNKN	MAML	rib/long	FRAG	36.2	burned,
2375	184	5714	110I	1	19	MED/LG	MAML	long/rib	FRAG	37.4	burned
4021	184	5711	110I	1	1	UNKN	MAML	UNKN	FRAG	0.6	burned
2439	184	1531	110I5	1	14	MED	MAML	long	FRAG	22.9	burned
2374	184	6247	110I5	3	3	MED	MAML	long	FRAG	11.9	burned
3982	184	6251	110I5	3	1	UNKN	MAML	UNKN	FRAG	0.4	burned
2485	184	2995	110I5	4	1	SM	MAML	radius/ ulna	WHLE	1	burned
4019	184	5828	110J5	1	1	UNKN	MAML	UNKN	FRAG	0.3	burned
4015	184	5827	110J5	1	1	UNKN	MAML	UNKN	FRAG	1	burned
2407	184	5321	110J5	3	3	UNKN	MAML	rib	FRAG	4.3	burned
2683	184	1560	115D5	2	12	MED	MAML	long/rib	FRAG	17.2	burned
2796	184	406	115D5	3	8	LG	MAML	UNKN	FRAG	82	burned
2921	184	762	115D5	4	5	MED	MAML	long/skull	FRAG	12.9	burned
2254	184	6467	115E	2	21	UNKN	MAML	UNKN	FRAG	17.4	burned
4159	184	6472	115E	2	1	UNKN	MAML	UNKN	FRAG	0.4	burned
2695	184	4887	115E	6	47+	SM/MED	MAML	long/rib	FRAG	37.9	burned
4749	184	4888	115E	6	1	UNKN	MAML	UNKN	FRAG	0.9	burned
2843	184	5240	115E	3,4	4	UNKN	MAML	UNKN	FRAG	2.1	burned
2886	184	5351	115E	3,4	2	UNKN	MAML	UNKN	FRAG	0.5	burned

2011.28	SBCM	Cat #	Unit	Level	Qty	Size Cat	Species	Bone Type (s)	COND	Wt/g	Comments
4766	184	5244	115E	3,4	1	UNKN	MAML	UNKN	FRAG	0.2	burned
2719	184	4006	115-E	1	17	MED/LG	MAML	long/rib	FRAG	18.2	burned, cut marks
2722	184	3994	115-E	3	96	All	MAML	long/rib/ scapula	FRAG	191.9	burned
4767	184	3989	115-E	3	1	UNKN	MAML	UNKN	FRAG	0.6	burned
2892	184	5139	115E5	7	18	ALL	MAML	UNKN	FRAG	44.6	burned
4734	184	4875	115E5	8	1	UNKN	MAML	UNKN	FRAG	1.2	burned
4740	184	4877	115E5	8	1	UNKN	MAML	UNKN	FRAG	0.3	burned
4743	184	4878	115E5	8	1	UNKN	MAML	UNKN	FRAG	0.4	burned
2787	184	381	115E5	9	16	UNKN	MAML	UNKN	FRAG	10.2	burned
3174	184	381	115E5	9	2	XSM	TURT	shell	FRAG	1.4	burned
3207	184	3173	115F	2	1	XSM	TURT	shell	FRAG	1	burned
2655	184	1957	115F	7	9	SM/MED	MAML	long	FRAG	2.9	burned
2910	184	1649	115F5	3	70+	SM/MED	MAML	UNKN	FRAG	73.6	burned
4758	184	6173	115F5	5	1	UNKN	MAML	UNKN	FRAG	1.1	burned
3185	184	6174	115F5	5	1	XSM	TURT	shell	FRAG	0.01	burned
2818	184	5332	115F5	6	48+	UNKN	MAML	UNKN	FRAG	31.1	burned
3208	184	5332	115F5	6	1	XSM	TURT	shell	FRAG	1.9	burned
2828	184	268	120-5E	3	3	UNKN	MAML	UNKN	FRAG	1.2	burned
4760	184	5957	120D	1	1	UNKN	MAML	UNKN	FRAG	1.1	burned
2725	184	1123	120D	4	89+	MED/LG	MAML	long/rib	FRAG	82.7	burned, cut marks
2908	184	2204	120D	5	3	MED	MAML	UNKN	FRAG	4.6	burned
2898	184	2443	120D	6	20	ALL	MAML	UNKN	FRAG	11.3	burned

2011.28	SBCM	Cat #	Unit	Level	Qty	Size Cat	Species	Bone Type (s)	COND	Wt/g	Comments
3083	184	2443	120D	6	1	XSM	CTRB	femur	FRAG	0.3	burned
2905	184	2844	120E	2	5	MED/LG	MAML	UNKN	FRAG	11	burned
4737	184	5282	120F	1	1	UNKN	MAML	UNKN	FRAG	0.8	burned
2884	184	2014	120F	3	28	MED/LG	MAML	UNKN	FRAG	26.4	burned
2901	184	1989	120F	5	10	ALL	MAML	UNKN	FRAG	7.7	burned
3119	184	3592	120F	5	1	SM	MAML	tibia	FRAG	1	burned
2775	184	245	120F5	2	2	MED/LG	MAML	UNKN	FRAG	14.2	burned
2918	184	926	120F5	7	20	All	MAML	UNKN	FRAG	6.1	burned
2427	184	941	120G	1	22	MED	MAML	long	FRAG	31.1	burned
2502	184	687	120G	1	17	MED/LG	MAML	long	FRAG	16.3	burned
2486	184	941	120G	1	1	SM	MAML	radius/ ulna	WHLE	0.6	burned
2401	184	3323	120G	2	27	SM/LG	MAML	long	FRAG	15.8	burned
2769	184	461	120G	1,2,3	49	SM/MED	MAML	UNKN	FRAG	20.5	burned
2360	184	2962	120G/ 120F5	3	78+	LG	MAML	long	FRAG	116.4	burned,
2448	184	468	120F5	2	32	SM/MED	MAML	rib/long	FRAG	18.5	burned
2667	184	2179	120J5	UNKN	11	MED	MAML	long	FRAG	0.1	burned
2850	184	515	125D5	3	2	SM/MED	MAML	UNKN	FRAG	2.5	burned
2852	184	4823	1.25E+ 07	2	5	LG	MAML	UNKN	FRAG	15.9	burned
2438	184	4616	125G	2	36	SM/MED	MAML	long	FRAG	34.4	burned
4078	184	4610	125G	2	1	UNKN	MAML	UNKN	FRAG	1.3	burned
4071	184	4614	125G	2	1	UNKN	MAML	UNKN	FRAG	1.3	burned
4068	184	4608	125G	2	2	UNKN	MAML	UNKN	FRAG	1.8	burned, fit together

2011.28	SBCM	Cat #	Unit	Level	Qty	Size Cat	Species	Bone Type (s)	COND	Wt/g	Comments
2972	184	6013	125G	3	1	UNKN	MAML	UNKN	FRAG	2	burned
2362	184	4695	125G5	1	21+	UNKN	MAML	long	FRAG	13.9	burned
2384	184	4680	125G5	4	4	MED/LG	MAML	UNKN	FRAG	7	burned
2378	184	3615	125G5	4	14	SM/MED	MAML	long/rib	FRAG	16.3	burned
2559	184	3736	125G5	4	2	UNKN	MAML	long	FRAG	1.9	burned, cut marks
2464	184	3615	125G5	4	1	UNKN	MAML	UNKN	FRAG	0.5	burned
2534	184	5129	140H5	3	26+	SM	MAML	long	FRAG	7.7	burned
2563	184	5121	140H5	1,2	35	SM/MED	MAML	long/rib/ skull	FRAG	54.8	burned
2562	184	5045	140I	1	36	ALL	MAML	long/rib	FRAG	21.6	burned
2516	184	1729	140I	2	53	XSM	RAT	long/skull	FRAG	82.7	burned
2560	184	1801	140I	3	25	SM/MED	MAML	rib	FRAG	13.8	burned
2550	184	6519	140I5	1	42	SM/MED	MAML	long/rib	FRAG	7.3	burned
4083	184	6524	140I5	1	1	UNKN	MAML	UNKN	FRAG	0.6	burned
4066	184	6534	140I5	1	1	UNKN	MAML	UNKN	FRAG	0.2	burned
2530	184	1143	140I5	2	39	MED/LG	MAML	rib/long	FRAG	112.4	burned, cut marks
2564	184	1143	140I5	2	2	UNKN	MAML	phalange	FRAG	4.1	burned
2535	184	4936	140I5	3	50+	MED/LG	MAML	rib/long	FRAG	76.4	burned
2491	184	5429	155F5	1,2,3	1	UNKN	MAML	UNKN	FRAG	1.6	burned
2511	184	5079	155H	2	6+	UNKN	MAML	UNKN	FRAG	11.9	burned
2547	184	2558	160H	1	33	ALL	MAML	long/rib	FRAG	68.6	burned
2539	184	18	160H	2	28	SM/MED	MAML	long/rib/ skull	FRAG	33.4	burned, cut marks
2497	184	2470	160H5	1	34	SM/MED	MAML	long/rib	FRAG	44	burned

2011.28	SBCM	Cat #	Unit	Level	Qty	Size Cat	Species	Bone Type (s)	COND	Wt/g	Comments
2553	184	2522	160H5	2	6	UNKN	MAML	long	FRAG	12.6	burned, cut marks
2510	184	6371	160I	1	14	MED	MAML	long/rib	FRAG	31.9	burned
2585	184	6371	160I	1	1	MED	Shep	phalange	FRAG	1.2	burned
4073	184	6379	160I	1	1	UNKN	MAML	UNKN	FRAG	0.3	burned
4074	184	6380	160I	1	1	UNKN	MAML	UNKN	FRAG	0.4	burned
4076	184	6381	160I	1	1	UNKN	MAML	UNKN	FRAG	0.5	burned
2490	184	2761	160I	2	20	SM/MED	MAML	long	FRAG	16.4	burned
2507	184	6063	160I5	1	28+	SM/MED	MAML	long/vert	FRAG	10.4	burned
4079	184	6065	160I5	1	1	UNKN	MAML	UNKN	FRAG	0.2	burned
4075	184	6068	160I5	1	1	UNKN	MAML	UNKN	FRAG	0.4	burned
2503	184	6439	160J	1	67	MED/LG	MAML	long/skull	FRAG	81.4	burned
4081	184	6444	160J	1	1	UNKN	MAML	UNKN	FRAG	0.3	burned
4084	184	6445	160J	1	1	UNKN	MAML	UNKN	FRAG	0.5	burned
3931	184	6449	160J	1	1	UNKN	MAML	UNKN	FRAG	2	burned
2493	184	6400	160J5	1	29+	MED/LG	MAML	long	FRAG	69.6	burned
2509	184	1164	160J5	2	86	MED	MAML	long/skull	FRAG	107.7	burned, cut marks
2505	184	6087	160K	1	21+	MED/LG	MAML	long/rib	FRAG	47.5	burned
4082	184	6086	160K	1	1	UNKN	MAML	UNKN	FRAG	2.5	burned
2498	184	5842	160K	UNKN	16	LG	MAML	long	FRAG	32.9	burned
4070	184	5837	160K	UNKN	1	UNKN	MAML	UNKN	FRAG	0.8	burned
2529	184	6347	160K5	UNKN	15+	SM/MED	MAML	rib/skull	FRAG	25	burned
2501	184	571	165H	1	36	SM/MED	MAML	long	FRAG	19.3	burned

2011.28	SBCM	Cat #	Unit	Level	Qty	Size Cat	Species	Bone Type (s)	COND	Wt/g	Comments
2561	184	443	165H	2	42	ALL	MAML	skull/rib/long	FRAG	28.7	burned
2544	184	619	165H	2	19	SM/MED	MAML	long	FRAG	13.8	burned
2540	184	503	165H	3	47	SM/MED	MAML	long/rib	FRAG	19.8	burned
2531	184	561	165H5	1	48	SM/MED	MAML	long/rib	FRAG	23.2	burned
2515	184	2617	165I	2	37	SM/MED	MAML	long/skull	FRAG	27.6	burned
2574	184	2617	165I	2	1	UNKN	MAML	rib	FRAG	1.2	burned
3199	184	2617	165I	2	1	XSM	TURT	shell	FRAG	0.9	burned
2552	184	2644	165I	UNKN	34+	SM/MED	MAML	long	FRAG	43.7	burned
2554	184	160	165I5	1	1	LG	MAML	rib	FRAG	9.4	burned
2518	184	2495	165I5	2	17	SM/MED	MAML	long	FRAG	9.7	burned
2536	184	549	165J	1	20	MED	MAML	long/rib	FRAG	15.4	burned
2504	184	2753	165J	2	31+	LG	HORS	long/rib/vert	FRAG	137.5	burned
2546	184	2838	165J	3	33+	ALL	MAML	long/rib	FRAG	69.5	burned, cut marks
2520	184	40	165J5	2	9	UNKN	MAML	longskull	FRAG	7.5	burned
2513	184	45	165K	1	4	MED	MAML	long	FRAG	6.9	burned
2508	184	2092	170H	1	23	SM	MAML	long	FRAG	31.4	burned
2523	184	2234	170H	2	50	SM/MED	MAML	long/rib	FRAG	24.4	burned
2543	184	1896	170H5	1	77+	SM/MED	MAML	long/rib	FRAG	34.7	burned
2537	184	1892	170H5	2	50+	SM/MED	MAML	long/rib	FRAG	16.6	burned
2500	184	2584	170I5	1	18	SM/MED	MAML	long	FRAG	13.7	burned
2495	184	2514	170J	1	6	MED	MAML	long	FRAG	6.8	burned
2557	184	2431	170J	1	25+	SM/MED	MAML	long	FRAG	20.8	burned

2011.28	SBCM	Cat #	Unit	Level	Qty	Size Cat	Species	Bone Type (s)	COND	Wt/g	Comments
2538	184	2891	170J	2	5	UNKN	MAML	UNKN	FRAG	1.7	burned
4072	184	2664	170J	2	1	UNKN	MAML	UNKN	FRAG	1	burned
4069	184	2665	170J	2	1	UNKN	MAML	UNKN	FRAG	0.6	burned
2551	184	2825	170J	UNKN	23	MED/LG	MAML	long	FRAG	30.5	burned
2527	184	234	170J5	1	11	UNKN	MAML	long/rib	FRAG	5.6	burned, cut marks
2512	184	2547	170J5	3	4	MED	MAML	long	FRAG	31	burned
2522	184	2690	170K	1	1	UNKN	MAML	UNKN	WHLE	1.1	burned
2681	184	3378	175E	6	1	UNKN	MAML	UNKN	FRAG	1.9	burned
2492	184	2881	175H	1	23	SM/MED	MAML	long/rib/ skull	FRAG	21.4	burned
2545	184	2672	175H	2	54+	SM/LG	MAML	long/rib/ vert	FRAG	58.1	burned
2387	184	2594	175H	3	15	SM/MED	MAML	long	FRAG	10.1	burned
2526	184	3248	175H5	1	14	MED	MAML	long	FRAG	12.2	burned
2542	184	3596	175H5	3	110+	All	MAML	Rib/long/ vert	FRAG	188	burned
2514	184	2973	175I	1	44	SM/MED	MAML	long	FRAG	28.8	burned
2524	184	3343	175I	2	40+	SM/MED	MAML	long/rib/ scapula	FRAG	19.2	burned
2499	184	5211	175I5	1	73+	SM/MED	MAML	long/rib	FRAG	38	burned
2399	184	5555	175I5	2	79+	SM/LG	MAML	long/rib	FRAG	65	burned
4067	184	5549	175I5	2	1	UNKN	MAML	UNKN	FRAG	0.5	burned
4085	184	5554	175I5	2	1	UNKN	MAML	UNKN	FRAG	1.8	burned
2525	184	5553	175I5	2	1	UNKN	MAML	UNKN	WHLE	0.5	burned
2540	184	3220	175J	2	71	SM/MED	MAML	long	FRAG	30.2	burned
2549	184	3108	175J	3	141+	SM/LG	MAML	long/rib/ skull	FRAG	138.8	burned

2011.28	SBCM	Cat #	Unit	Level	Qty	Size Cat	Species	Bone Type (s)	COND	Wt/g	Comments
2556	184	5530	175J5	1	36	UNKN	MAML	rib	FRAG	16.7	burned, cut marks
4077	184	5525	175J5	1	1	UNKN	MAML	UNKN	FRAG	0.1	burned
2548	184	1672	175J5	2	84	UNKN	MAML	long/rib	FRAG	37.3	burned
2533	184	5697	175K	1	16+	UNKN	MAML	UNKN	FRAG	22.5	burned
2234	184	4734	20J5	2	3	UNKN	MAML	UNKN	FRAG	2.9	burned
2198	184	2388	20J5	3	3	UNKN	MAML	UNKN	FRAG	0.5	burned
2221	184	5866	30H5	1,2,3	26	UNKN	MAML	UNKN	FRAG	19.4	burned
3962	184	5848	30H5	1,2,3	1	UNKN	MAML	UNKN	FRAG	0.7	burned
3967	184	5851	30H5	1,2,3	1	UNKN	MAML	UNKN	FRAG	0.4	burned
3975	184	5856	30H5	1,2,3	1	UNKN	MAML	UNKN	FRAG	0.9	burned
3979	184	5860	30H5	1,2,3	1	UNKN	MAML	UNKN	FRAG	1.4	burned
3988	184	5849	30H5	1,2,3	1	UNKN	MAML	UNKN	FRAG	0.4	burned
2231	184	5699	30I	2	8	UNKN	MAML	UNKN	FRAG	3.5	burned
2201	184	4747	30J5	1	12	UNKN	MAML	long	FRAG	7.4	burned
2210	184	4479	30J5	1	5	UNKN	MAML	skull/ metacarp	FRAG	6.6	burned
2277	184	5740	30J5	4	2	LG	COW	vert	FRAG	64	burned
2255	184	3823	30K5	2	3	UNKN	MAML	UNKN	FRAG	2.1	burned
2237	184	3762	30K5	3	11+	UNKN	MAML	long	FRAG	8	burned
2259	184	6486	35H5	1	41	UNKN	MAML	long	FRAG	21.8	burned
3981	184	6511	35H5	1	1	UNKN	MAML	UNKN	FRAG	0.6	burned
3963	184	6499	35H5	1	1	UNKN	MAML	UNKN	FRAG	0.6	burned
3987	184	6495	35H5	1	1	UNKN	MAML	UNKN	FRAG	0.5	burned

2011.28	SBCM	Cat #	Unit	Level	Qty	Size Cat	Species	Bone Type (s)	COND	Wt/g	Comments
3976	184	6505	35H5	1	1	UNKN	MAML	UNKN	FRAG	0.7	burned
3959	184	6506	35H5	1	1	UNKN	MAML	UNKN	FRAG	3.8	burned
3974	184	6516	35H5	1	1	UNKN	MAML	UNKN	FRAG	0.4	burned
3958	184	6243	35H5	3	1	UNKN	MAML	UNKN	FRAG	5.8	burned
2251	184	5438	35I	2	7	XSM/ MED	MAML	long	FRAG	12.4	burned
2226	184	5684	35I	3	11	UNKN	MAML	long	FRAG	7.1	burned
3960	184	5686	35I	3	1	UNKN	MAML	UNKN	FRAG	1	burned
3983	184	5691	35I	3	1	UNKN	MAML	UNKN	FRAG	0.6	burned
2178	184	5565	35I	4	10	UNKN	MAML	UNKN	FRAG	8.2	burned
2267	184	6357	40H5	1	26+	UNKN	MAML	UNKN	FRAG	29.4	burned
2193	184	1213	40H5	3	27	SM/LG	MAML	long	FRAG	9.2	burned
2239	184	1755	40I	1	25	UNKN	MAML	long	FRAG	23.7	burned
2187	184	1902	40I	1	32+	UNKN	MAML	long/rib	FRAG	29.2	burned
2246	184	1578	40I	3	49+	XSM/LG	MAML	long/ max/etc	FRAG	28.6	burned
2248	184	1507	40K	1	12	UNKN	MAML	UNKN	FRAG	7.5	burned
2240	184	1477	40K	3	11	LG	MAML	long	FRAG	10.7	burned
2253	184	3359	40K	4	58+	LG	MAML	UNKN	FRAG	110	burned
3218	184	1579	40K	5	1	XSM	MAML	Lt mandi- ble	FRAG	0.2	burned
2274	184	1175	45I	4	37	UNKN	MAML	long/skull	FRAG	29.9	burned
2199	184	1183	45I	4	2	UNKN	MAML	UNKN	FRAG	1	burned
2207	184	1206	4H5	22	17+	UNKN	MAML	long	FRAG	10.6	burned
2343	184	1206	4H5	22	1	XSM	RD	phalange	WHLE	0.2	burned

2011.28	SBCM	Cat #	Unit	Level	Qty	Size Cat	Species	Bone Type (s)	COND	Wt/g	Comments
3020	184	4451	55	2	14	UNKN	MAML	UNKN	FRAG	19.6	burned
2257	184	2173	55H5	2	101	XSM/LG	MAML	UNKN	FRAG	99	burned
2250	184	6051	55H5	3	55	XSM/LG	MAML	long	FRAG	33.1	burned
2264	184	2271	55H5	4,5	55	UNKN	MAML	UNKN	FRAG	32.5	burned, cut marks
2185	184	2044	55I	1	24	UNKN	MAML	UNKN	FRAG	14.5	burned
2194	184	2001	55I	2	26	LG	MAML	long	FRAG	12.8	burned,
2181	184	654	55I	3	9	UNKN	MAML	UNKN	FRAG	8.4	burned
2260	184	614	55I	4	32	UNKN	MAML	UNKN	FRAG	29.4	burned
2227	184	586	55I	4	1	UNKN	MAML	UNKN	WHLE	0.3	burned
2190	184	528	55I	4	24	UNKN	MAML	long bone	FRAG	24.1	burned
2245	184	2478	55I	4	19	XSM/ MED	MAML	long, hu-merus	FRAG	12.5	burned
2209	184	2403	55I	6,7	9	UNKN	MAML	UNKN	FRAG	1.5	burned
2236	184	2744	55I5	2	29	LG	MAML	long	FRAG	17.9	burned
2325	184	2707	55I5	3	1	MED	MAML	rib	FRAG	0.5	burned
2188	184	2707	55I5	3	13	UNKN	MAML	UNKN	FRAG	14.1	burned
3972	184	2717	55I5	3	1	UNKN	MAML	UNKN	FRAG	0.8	burned
2223	184	2817	55I5	4	19	MED	MAML	long	FRAG	8.8	burned
2271	184	2808	55I5	5	13	UNKN	MAML	UNKN	FRAG	11	burned
2270	184	1715	55J	1	60	XSM/LG	MAML	UNKN	FRAG	25.8	burned
2263	184	1623	55J	2	8	UNKN	MAML	UNKN	FRAG	21.7	burned, cut marks
2212	184	1394	55J5	3	22	UNKN	MAML	UNKN	FRAG	12.4	burned
2244	184	4436	55J5	3	43	XSM/ MED	MAML	long/rib	FRAG	17.2	burned

2011.28	SBCM	Cat #	Unit	Level	Qty	Size Cat	Species	Bone Type (s)	COND	Wt/g	Comments
2242	184	4387	55J5	4	35	LG	MAML	long/rib	FRAG	27.3	burned
2211	184	4720	55J5	4	23	UNKN	MAML	long	FRAG	10.7	burned
3976	184	4385	55J5	4	1	UNKN	MAML	UNKN	FRAG	1.1	burned
3989	184	4379	55J5	4	1	UNKN	MAML	UNKN	FRAG	0.8	burned
2202	184	4443	55J5	5	15	UNKN	MAML	UNKN	FRAG	5.3	burned
2189	184	1604	55K	1	17	UNKN	MAML	long	FRAG	27.9	burned
2205	184	1404	55K	3	9	UNKN	MAML	UNKN	FRAG	2.8	burned
2208	184	1379	55K	4	28	UNKN	MAML	long/rib	FRAG	13.4	burned
2196	184	1585	55K5	1	17	UNKN	MAML	long	FRAG	8.6	burned,
2770	184	1968	60E5	1	4	MED/LG	MAML	UNKN	FRAG	6.2	burned
2760	184	2223	60E5	1	10	UNKN	MAML	long	FRAG	10.5	burned
2174	184	1946	60H5	1	48	UNKN	MAML	UNKN	FRAG	34.6	burned
2241	184	3381	60H5	3	1	UNKN	MAML	UNKN	FRAG	0.2	burned
2252	184	2090	60H5	3	42+	XSM/LG	MAML	long/rib	FRAG	87.7	burned, cut marks
2180	184	2024	60H5	4	27	UNKN	MAML	UNKN	FRAG	12.5	burned
2173	184	2063	60H5	6	49	LG	MAML	humerus	FRAG	32	burned
2232	184	6201	60I	UNKN	2	UNKN	MAML	long	FRAG	4.9	burned
2229	184	6387	60I	UNKN	27	UNKN	MAML	long	FRAG	11.5	burned
2182	184	6459	60I	UNKN	1	UNKN	MAML	UNKN	FRAG	0.2	burned
3960	184	5820	60J	2	1	UNKN	MAML	UNKN	FRAG	1.5	burned
2233	184	5821	60J	2	35	XSM/LG	MAML	long	FRAG	39.5	burned
2265	184	379	60J5	2	16	UNKN	MAML	UNKN	FRAG	15.5	burned

2011.28	SBCM	Cat #	Unit	Level	Qty	Size Cat	Species	Bone Type (s)	COND	Wt/g	Comments
2262	184	2419	60J5	5	16+	UNKN	MAML	UNKN	FRAG	27.5	burned
2738	184	4557	65E	1	36	ALL	MAML	long/rib	FRAG	40.6	burned
2268	184	7	65H5	1	38	UNKN	MAML	UNKN	FRAG	27.2	burned
2261	184	9	65H5	2	57	XSM/ MED	MAML	long/rib	FRAG	33.3	burned
2456	184	81	65H5	3, 4	299	SM/MED	MAML	skull/ long/rib	FRAG	129.3	burned
2184	184	6188	65I	1	23	UNKN	MAML	skull	FRAG	11.9	burned
3965	184	6191	65I	1	1	UNKN	MAML	UNKN	FRAG	1.4	burned
3984	184	6192	65I	1	1	UNKN	MAML	UNKN	FRAG	3.4	burned
2177	184	6107	65I	2	11	UNKN	MAML	long	FRAG	10.4	burned
3964	184	6109	65I	2	1	UNKN	MAML	UNKN	FRAG	0.5	burned
3985	184	6110	65I	2	1	UNKN	MAML	UNKN	FRAG	1.4	burned
2222	184	6133	65I	3	25	UNKN	MAML	long	FRAG	16.4	burned
2213	184	6138	65I	3	1	UNKN	MAML	UNKN	WHLE	1	burned
3970	184	6140	65I	3	1	UNKN	MAML	UNKN	FRAG	0.4	burned
3973	184	6141	65I	3	1	UNKN	MAML	UNKN	FRAG	0.2	burned
2269	184	1246	65I	4	16	XSM/LG	MAML	long	FRAG	11.5	burned
2272	184	55	65J5	UNKN	33	MED/LG	MAML	UNKN	FRAG	29.4	burned
2614	184	6542	70C	1	2	UNKN	MAML	long	FRAG	0.4	burned
3934	184	6547	70C	1	1	UNKN	MAML	UNKN	FRAG	1	burned
3933	184	6544	70C	1	1	UNKN	MAML	UNKN	FRAG	0.2	burned
3929	184	6545	70C	1	1	UNKN	MAML	UNKN	FRAG	0.3	burned
3938	184	6548	70C	1	1	UNKN	MAML	UNKN	FRAG	0.3	burned

2011.28	SBCM	Cat #	Unit	Level	Qty	Size Cat	Species	Bone Type (s)	COND	Wt/g	Comments
3927	184	6549	70C	1	1	UNKN	MAML	UNKN	FRAG	0.5	burned
3930	184	6550	70C	1	1	UNKN	MAML	UNKN	FRAG	1.4	burned
3936	184	6551	70C	1	1	UNKN	MAML	UNKN	FRAG	0.2	burned
4885	184	6546	70C	1	1	UNKN	MAML	UNKN	FRAG	0.6	burned
2635	184	5949	70C	2	31+	ALL	MAML	long/rib	FRAG	34	burned
2639	184	3847	70C	2	20	SM/MED	MAML	long/rib	FRAG	10.9	burned
2627	184	1691	70C	3	27	SM/MED	MAML	long/rib	FRAG	11.9	burned
2630	184	1833	70C5	1	11	MED	MAML	long/rib	FRAG	11.1	burned
2640	184	3880	70C5	2	36	SM/MED	MAML	long/rib	FRAG	31.5	burned
3935	184	3884	70C5	2	1	UNKN	MAML	UNKN	FRAG	0.5	burned
4884	184	3886	70C5	2	1	UNKN	MAML	UNKN	FRAG	1.5	burned
3937	184	3889	70C5	2	1	UNKN	MAML	UNKN	FRAG	1.6	burned
2617	184	1824	70C5	5	8	SM/MED	MAML	long/rib	FRAG	4.7	burned
2624	184	1666	70D	2	6	MED	MAML	rib/long	FRAG	20.9	burned
2657	184	5630	70E	5	36	MED	MAML	long/rib	FRAG	34.8	burned
2619	184	2868	70E5	2	12	SM/MED	MAML	long/rib	FRAG	10.8	burned
2637	184	2735	70E5	3	16	MED/LG	MAML	long/rib	FRAG	18.2	burned
2702	184	2550	70E5	6	4	SM	MAML	long	FRAG	1.8	burned
2204	184	2723	70I	2	53+	UNKN	MAML	long/rib	FRAG	26.8	burned
3969	184	2730	70I	2	1	UNKN	MAML	UNKN	FRAG	1.1	burned
3957	184	2731	70I	2	1	UNKN	MAML	UNKN	FRAG	1.1	burned
2417	184	103	70I	3	38	SM/MED	MAML	long/rib	FRAG	20.2	burned

2011.28	SBCM	Cat #	Unit	Level	Qty	Size Cat	Species	Bone Type (s)	COND	Wt/g	Comments
2206	184	758	70I5	2	24	LG	MAML	long	FRAG	23.3	burned
2220	184	2651	70I5	4	54+	MED	MAML	long/rib	FRAG	22	burned
3961	184	2652	70I5	4	1	UNKN	MAML	UNKN	FRAG	1.1	burned
2203	184	647	70J	1	4	UNKN	MAML	UNKN	FRAG	4.5	burned
2273	184	90	70J	1	27	XSM/LG	MAML	vert	FRAG	45	burned
2225	184	733	70J	3,4	9	UNKN	MAML	UNKN	FRAG	3.3	burned
2282	184	387	70J5	1	1	LG	MAML	UNKN	WHLE	9.8	burned
2321	184	387	70J5	1	1	MED	DEER	rib	WHLE	1.3	burned
2323	184	2503	70J5	1	2	MED	MAML	long	FRAG	7.5	burned
2176	184	2503	70J5	1	55	UNKN	MAML	long	FRAG	88.9	burned
2258	184	387	70J5	1	48	XSM/ MED	MAML	long, rib	FRAG	45.7	burned
2216	184	24	70J5	2	173+	LG	MAML	long	FRAG	180.3	burned, cut marks
2275	184	24	70J5	2	3	LG	MAML	UNKN	FRAG	72.6	burned
2623	184	4596	75C	1	9	MED	MAML	long/rib	FRAG	7	burned
2633	184	3310	75C	4	22	All	MAML	long/rib/ phalan	FRAG	13.7	burned
2616	184	4420	75C	6	12	SM/MED	MAML	long/rib/ skull	FRAG	7.8	burned
2615	184	3579	75C5	3	2	UNKN	MAML	rib	FRAG	20.1	burned
2625	184	5076	75C5	5	21	SM/MED	MAML	long/rib	FRAG	10.8	burned
2622	184	3196	75C5	6	3	SM/MED	MAML	long	FRAG	3.2	burned
2629	184	3569	75D	1	21	SM/MED	MAML	long/rib/ skull	FRAG	15.5	burned
2621	184	3199	75D	5	28	SM/MED	MAML	long/skull	FRAG	6.1	burned
4080	184	3206	75D	5	1	UNKN	MAML	UNKN	FRAG	1.5	burned

2011.28	SBCM	Cat #	Unit	Level	Qty	Size Cat	Species	Bone Type (s)	COND	Wt/g	Comments
2642	184	2469	75D5	3	350+	ALL	MAML	UNKN	FRAG	742	burned
3602	184	2469	75D5	3	1	LG	HORS	tooth	FRAG	2	burned
2643	184	2467	75D5	3	120+	LG	MAML	UNKN	FRAG	1022	burned
2848	184	4530	75D5	3	9	LG	MAML	UNKN	FRAG	13.1	burned
2644	184	2468	75D5	3	115+	MED/LG	MAML	UNKN	FRAG	958.4	burned
3922	184	3260	75D5	5	1	UNKN	MAML	UNKN	WHLE	2	burned
4763	184	5660	75E5	1	1	UNKN	MAML	UNKN	FRAG	1.4	burned
4796	184	4796	75E5	2	5	MED	MAML	long	FRAG	22	burned
2418	184	4620	75H	1,2	3	UNKN	MAML	UNKN	FRAG	0.1	burned
2361	184	4762	75H5	1	3	UNKN	MAML	long	FRAG	2.5	burned
2217	184	5580	75I	1	35	UNKN	MAML	long	FRAG	22.5	burned, cut marks
2218	184	5601	75J	1	36	UNKN	MAML	UNKN	FRAG	10.4	burned
2266	184	5601	75J	1	16	UNKN	MAML	UNKN	WHLE	12.4	burned
3968	184	5608	75J	1	1	UNKN	MAML	UNKN	FRAG	3.1	burned
3978	184	5611	75J	1	1	UNKN	MAML	UNKN	FRAG	0.4	burned
3986	184	5613	75J	1	1	UNKN	MAML	UNKN	FRAG	0.5	burned
2613	184	3763	80D	1	7	All	MAML	long/rib/skull	FRAG	30.1	burned
2618	184	3748	80D	5	17+	SM	MAML	long/rib	FRAG	5.4	burned
2632	184	3619	80D	6	24	XSM/SM	MAML	Long/skull/rib	FRAG	13.9	burned
2641	184	1075	80D5	2	200+	SM/MED	MAML	long/rib/skull	FRAG	429	burned
2612	184	1465	80D5	2	1	UNKN	MAML	rib	WHLE	1.3	burned
2841	184	809	80D5	2	6	UNKN	MAML	UNKN	FRAG	3.7	burned

2011.28	SBCM	Cat #	Unit	Level	Qty	Size Cat	Species	Bone Type (s)	COND	Wt/g	Comments
2645	184	1075	80D5	2	1	UNKN	MAML	vert	FRAG	1.7	burned
3182	184	1075	80D5	2	1	XSM	TURT	shell	FRAG	1.2	burned
2716	184	1710	80D5	5	58	ALL	MAML	long/rib	FRAG	33.5	burned
2919	184	605	80E	3	29	MED/LG	MAML	UNKN	FRAG	42.1	burned
2795	184	4067	80E	4	62	ALL	MAML	UNKN	FRAG	72.8	burned
4741	184	4068	80E	4	1	UNKN	MAML	UNKN	FRAG	0.8	burned
4163	184	4069	80E	4	1	UNKN	MAML	UNKN	FRAG	1.1	burned
4755	184	4070	80E	4	1	UNKN	MAML	UNKN	FRAG	1.4	burned
4765	184	4074	80E	4	1	UNKN	MAML	UNKN	FRAG	0.2	burned
2863	184	5268	80E	5	25	SM/MED	MAML	UNKN	FRAG	17.3	burned
4764	184	6224	80E	7	1	UNKN	MAML	UNKN	FRAG	1.2	burned
4747	184	6228	80E	7	1	UNKN	MAML	UNKN	FRAG	0.6	burned
4728	184	6229	80E	7	1	UNKN	MAML	UNKN	FRAG	0.2	burned
4732	184	6223	80E	7	1	UNKN	MAML	UNKN	FRAG	0.3	burned
2887	184	5315	80E5	2	38+	MED/LG	MAML	UNKN	FRAG	22.4	burned
2904	184	6116	80E5	3	42	All	MAML	UNKN	FRAG	22.6	burned
4771	184	6113	80E5	3	1	UNKN	MAML	UNKN	FRAG	0.7	burned
2463	184	1505	80H5	1,2	3	UNKN	MAML	long	FRAG	0.6	burned
2175	184	1858	80I	1	12	UNKN	MAML	long	FRAG	15.6	burned,
2238	184	4124	80I	2	7	UNKN	MAML	rib	FRAG	6.1	burned
4013	184	4125	80I	2	1	UNKN	MAML	UNKN	FRAG	1.7	burned
2423	184	425	84-85H	6	2	UNKN	MAML	UNKN	FRAG	0.8	burned

2011.28	SBCM	Cat #	Unit	Level	Qty	Size Cat	Species	Bone Type (s)	COND	Wt/g	Comments
2762	184	2991	85D	3	29	UNKN	MAML	UNKN	FRAG	17.8	burned
2608	184	315	85D5	4	1	UNKN	MAML	long	FRAG	0.4	burned
2610	184	114	85D5	UNKN	1	UNKN	MAML	Rib	FRAG	0.8	burned
2662	184	109	85D5	UNKN	1	UNKN	MAML	UNKN	FRAG	0.1	burned
2634	184	112	85D5	UNKN	102	XSM/SM	MAML	long/ skull/rib	FRAG	55.2	burned
2793	184	130	85E	3	27	SM/MED	MAML	UNKN	FRAG	14.3	burned
2686	184	2365	85E	3	1	UNKN	MAML	UNKN	FRAG	1.2	burned
4744	184	5946	85E	4	1	UNKN	MAML	UNKN	FRAG	1.1	burned
2732	184	324	85E5	2,3	12	MED	MAML	long/rib	FRAG	8.2	burned
2450	184	2943	85F	1	10	MED	MAML	long	FRAG	29.8	burned
4736	184	2945	85F	1	1	UNKN	MAML	UNKN	FRAG	0.9	burned
2723	184	884	85F	2	13	MED	MAML	long/rib	FRAG	15.3	burned
2691	184	511	85F	4	4	SM	MAML	mandible/ long	FRAG	2.5	burned
2668	184	3122	85F	5	14	SM/MED	MAML	long/rib	FRAG	12.2	burned
4727	184	4915	85F5	1	1	UNKN	MAML	UNKN	FRAG	0.7	burned
4730	184	4909	85F5	1	1	UNKN	MAML	UNKN	FRAG	1.1	burned
4757	184	4912	85F5	1	1	UNKN	MAML	UNKN	FRAG	0.2	burned
4761	184	4913	85F5	1	1	UNKN	MAML	UNKN	FRAG	0.7	burned
2911	184	3576	85F5	3	4	MED	MAML	UNKN	FRAG	4.1	burned
4752	184	5897	85F5	3	1	UNKN	MAML	UNKN	FRAG	0.3	burned
4731	184	5903	85F5	3	1	UNKN	MAML	UNKN	FRAG	0.6	burned
2914	184	6272	85F5	4	12+	MED/LG	MAML	UNKN	FRAG	8.6	burned, tooth

2011.28	SBCM	Cat #	Unit	Level	Qty	Size Cat	Species	Bone Type (s)	COND	Wt/g	Comments
2731	184	4971	85F5	5	5	SM/MED	MAML	long, rib	FRAG	14.3	burned
4753	184	6281	85F5	6	1	UNKN	MAML	UNKN	FRAG	0.5	burned
2435	184	4701	85G	1	4	UNKN	MAML	UNKN	FRAG	2	burned
2379	184	4749	85G	2	22	SM/MED	MAML	long/rib	FRAG	20	burned
2373	184	4807	85G	4	21	SM/MED	MAML	long/rib	FRAG	14	burned
2397	184	4693	85G	5	25	SM/MED	MAML	UNKN	FRAG	15	burned
2468	184	4693	85G	5	1	UNKN	MAML	long	WHLE	0.9	burned
1543	184	1543	85G5	1	4	MED	MAML	long	FRAG	8.6	burned
2377	184	1598	85G5	2	2	LG	MAML	long	FRAG	9.7	burned
2424	184	1766	85G5	3	4	UNKN	MAML	UNKN	FRAG	3.8	burned, poss tool
2380	184	62	85G5	4	31	SM/MED	MAML	long	FRAG	7.4	burned
2389	184	4674	85G5	4	7	UNKN	MAML	long	FRAG	3.4	burned
4016	184	4675	85G5	4	1	UNKN	MAML	UNKN	FRAG	0.4	burned
2385	184	911	85H	1	2	UNKN	MAML	UNKN	FRAG	5.8	burned
2395	184	485	85H	3	4	MED	MAML	UNKN	FRAG	3.4	burned
2382	184	2367	85H5	1	11	XSM/ MED	MAML	long, pelvic	FRAG	29.7	burned
2230	184	629	85I	1	4	LG	MAML	long	FRAG	11.8	burned, cut marks
2847	184	3351	90D	2	23	MED/LG	MAML	UNKN	FRAG	12	burned
2709	184	3520	90D	4	70+	SM/MED	MAML	long/rib/ skull	FRAG	45.8	burned
2674	184	2082	90D5	3	31	SM/LG	MAML	long/rib	FRAG	65.7	burned
2856	184	48	90D5	4	1	MED	MAML	UNKN	FRAG	3.1	burned
2703	184	71	90D5	4	123	MED/LG	MAML	long/rib	FRAG	256	burned

2011.28	SBCM	Cat #	Unit	Level	Qty	Size Cat	Species	Bone Type (s)	COND	Wt/g	Comments
2815	184	3294	90E	1	9	UNKN	MAML	UNKN	FRAG	14.6	burned
2842	184	3274	90E	2	3	UNKN	MAML	UNKN	FRAG	4	burned
2710	184	3152	90E	3	22+	MED	MAML	long/rib	FRAG	54.8	burned
2839	184	3215	90E	5	21	MED/LG	MAML	UNKN	FRAG	11.5	burned
2678	184	3280	90E	7	10	MED	MAML	long/rib	FRAG	7.5	burned
2759	184	3280	90E	7	10	UNKN	MAML	UNKN	FRAG	6.5	burned
2875	184	3586	90E	8	4	UNKN	MAML	UNKN	FRAG	2.5	burned
2906	184	2281	90E5	2	9	LG	MAML	UNKN	FRAG	15.4	burned
2761	184	2022	90E5	4	27	UNKN	MAML	UNKN	FRAG	22.8	burned
2675	184	2412	90E5	5	9	SM/MED	MAML	long/skull	FRAG	7.7	burned
2895	184	2037	90E5	6	6	SM/MED	MAML	UNKN	FRAG	5.1	burned
4750	184	5925	90E5	8	1	UNKN	MAML	UNKN	FRAG	0.6	burned
4158	184	5926	90E5	8	1	UNKN	MAML	UNKN	FRAG	0.7	burned
2808	184	284	90F	2	1	MED	MAML	UNKN	FRAG	1.2	burned
2447	184	4641	90F5	5,6	3	UNKN	MAML	long/rib	FRAG	2.5	burned
4027	184	4488	90G	1	1	UNKN	MAML	UNKN	FRAG	0.5	burned
2452	184	4637	90G	3	13	SM/MED	MAML	long	FRAG	8.1	burned
2370	184	4542	90G	4	16	UNKN	MAML	long/rib	FRAG	9.5	burned
2429	184	4428	90-G5	1	1	UNKN	MAML	rib	WHLE	2.6	burned
2454	184	4723	90GS	3	3	UNKN	MAML	long	FRAG	3.1	burned
2445	184	5643	90H	1	3	MED/LG	MAML	long	FRAG	24.9	burned
4026	184	5647	90H	1	1	UNKN	MAML	UNKN	FRAG	2.3	burned

2011.28	SBCM	Cat #	Unit	Level	Qty	Size Cat	Species	Bone Type (s)	COND	Wt/g	Comments
2356	184	6298	90H5	2	4	MED	MAML	rib	FRAG	6.1	burned
2437	184	6236	90H5	5	6	UNKN	MAML	long	FRAG	28.4	burned
2416	184	5424	90I	1	32	SM/LG	MAML	long/rib/ vert	FRAG	40.8	burned
4018	184	5420	90I	1	1	UNKN	MAML	UNKN	FRAG	0.3	burned
3980	184	5415	90I	1	1	UNKN	MAML	UNKN	FRAG	1.4	burned
4014	184	5415	90I	1	1	UNKN	MAML	UNKN	FRAG	1.4	burned
4020	184	5416	90I	1	1	UNKN	MAML	UNKN	FRAG	0.6	burned
2444	184	4166	90I5	1	20	MED/LG	MAML	long/rib	FRAG	29.7	burned
4010	184	4167	90I5	1	1	UNKN	MAML	UNKN	FRAG	2.2	burned
4028	184	4172	90I5	1	1	UNKN	MAML	UNKN	FRAG	0.3	burned
4023	184	4168	90I5	1	1	UNKN	MAML	UNKN	FRAG	1.3	burned
4024	184	4170	90I5	1	1	UNKN	MAML	UNKN	FRAG	0.7	burned
2355	184	4157	90I5	2	24+	LG	MAML	long	FRAG	38	burned
4009	184	4159	90I5	2	1	UNKN	MAML	UNKN	FRAG	2.1	burned
4017	184	4160	90I5	2	1	UNKN	MAML	UNKN	FRAG	1.9	burned
4011	184	4180	90I5	2	1	UNKN	MAML	UNKN	FRAG	0.8	burned
4022	184	4181	90I5	2	1	UNKN	MAML	UNKN	FRAG	0.7	burned
2392	184	4155	90I5	3	2	UNKN	MAML	long	FRAG	4.9	burned
2455	184	4147	90J	1	3	LG	MAML	skull/long	FRAG	6.8	burned
2893	184	123	95D	1	11	MED/LG	MAML	UNKN	FRAG	7.1	burned
2718	184	1999	95D	5	13	SM/MED	MAML	long/rib/ skull	FRAG	93.5	burned, cut marks
2705	184	2186	95D	3,4	450+	All	MAML	long/rib/ vert	FRAG	755.3	burned

2011.28	SBCM	Cat #	Unit	Level	Qty	Size Cat	Species	Bone Type (s)	COND	Wt/g	Comments
2656	184	2326	95D	3,4	4	SM/MED	MAML	UNKN	FRAG	1.1	burned
3176	184	5385	95D	3,4	1	XSM	TURT	shell	FRAG	0.2	burned
2889	184	2435	95D5	3	16	MED/LG	MAML	UNKN	FRAG	88.9	burned
2890	184	2386	95E	1	40	MED/LG	MAML	UNKN	FRAG	50.1	burned
2696	184	1980	95E	3	83	All	MAML	long/rib	FRAG	70	burned
2736	184	2035	95E	3	35	MED/LG	MAML	long/rib/vert	FRAG	79.3	burned
2882	184	2138	95E	4	103	All	MAML	UNKN	FRAG	79	burned
2729	184	3285	95E	5	13	SM/MED	MAML	long/skull	FRAG	6.8	burned
2855	184	3228	95E	5	46	UNKN	MAML	UNKN	FRAG	30.5	burned
3201	184	3285	95E	5	1	XSM	TURT	shell	FRAG	1	burned
2701	184	2218	95E	7	4	SM/MED	MAML	long/rib	FRAG	4	burned
2663	184	2230	95E	7	3	SM/MED	MAML	long/rib	FRAG	2.9	burned
2726	184	2335	95E	UNKN	102	SM/MED	MAML	long/rib/skull	FRAG	70.8	burned
3181	184	2335	95E	UNKN	1	XSM	TURT	shell	FRAG	1.7	burned
2866	184	3134	95E5	3	33+	LG	MAML	UNKN	FRAG	28.8	burned
2666	184	4503	95E5	4	72	SM/MED	MAML	long/rib	FRAG	27.2	burned
2684	184	3265	95E5	7	16	SM	MAML	long/pelvic	FRAG	6.4	burned
2651	184	3552	95E5	9	35	SM/MED	MAML	long/rib	FRAG	17	burned
2903	184	1818	95F	9	50+	UNKN	MAML	UNKN	FRAG	7.7	burned
2425	184	3098	95G	3	300+	SM/MED	MAML	rib,long,femur	FRAG	82.5	burned
2394	184	1235	95G	3	11	UNKN	MAML	UNKN	FRAG	5.4	burned
2433	184	1626	95G	4	10	MED	MAML	long	FRAG	11	burned

2011.28	SBCM	Cat #	Unit	Level	Qty	Size Cat	Species	Bone Type (s)	COND	Wt/g	Comments
2443	184	3181	95G	5	20	SM/MED	MAML	long	FRAG	24.7	burned, cut marks
2398	184	1495	95G5	3	20	MED/LG	MAML	long/rib	FRAG	16.6	burned
2411	184	1646	95H	1	6	MED/LG	MAML	long/rib	FRAG	23.1	burned
2479	184	1733	95H	2	1	MED	MAML	metapo-dial	FRAG	2.2	burned
2449	184	1733	95H	2	8	UNKN	MAML	skull/long	FRAG	21	burned
2402	184	1745	95H	2,3	28	XSM	BIRD	skull	FRAG	6.1	burned
2400	184	5263	95H5	2	27+	MED	MAML	long	FRAG	12.1	burned
2393	184	1208	95H5	3	19	SM/LG	MAML	long	FRAG	24.3	burned
2406	184	3623	95I	1	31	MED	MAML	phalange	FRAG	14.8	burned
2459	184	1108	95I	2	1	LG	MAML	skull	FRAG	6.7	burned
2396	184	1107	95I	2	19+	MED/LG	MAML	long/vert	FRAG	94.4	burned
4025	184	5333	95I	3	1	UNKN	MAML	UNKN	FRAG	1.1	burned
2436	184	3773	95I5	1	10	UNKN	MAML	long	WHLE	7.9	burned
2426	184	3782	95I5	2	8	LG	MAML	long, rib	FRAG	43.3	burned
2372	184	1641	95J	1	7	LG	MAML	long	FRAG	27.9	burned
4769	184	5495	E5	5	1	UNKN	MAML	UNKN	FRAG	0.4	burned
4738	184	5498	E5	5	1	UNKN	MAML	UNKN	FRAG	0.7	burned
4164	184	5496	E5	5	1	UNKN	MAML	UNKN	FRAG	1.2	burned
3041	184	5510	E5	5	1	XSM	TURT	shell	FRAG	0.4	burned
4879	184	278	K155	1	6	UNKN	MAML	UNKN	FRAG	15.9	burned
2991	184	658	UNKN	1	8	MED/LG	MAML	UNKN	FRAG	20	burned
2629	184	1128	UNKN	2	29	MED/LG	MAML	UNKN	FRAG	33.7	burned

2011.28	SBCM	Cat #	Unit	Level	Qty	Size Cat	Species	Bone Type (s)	COND	Wt/g	Comments
2966	184	4710	UNKN	5	6	MED/LG	MAML	UNKN	FRAG	31.4	burned
4805	184	4186	UNKN	UNKN	1	MED	MAML	Rt mandible	FRAG	2.1	burned
2968	184	291	UNKN	UNKN	20	MED/LG	MAML	UNKN	FRAG	29.2	burned
4719	184	1332	UNKN	UNKN	1	UNKN	MAML	UNKN	FRAG	0.8	burned
4721	184	1335	UNKN	UNKN	1	UNKN	MAML	UNKN	FRAG	1.25	burned
4723	184	1358	UNKN	UNKN	1	UNKN	MAML	UNKN	FRAG	3.6	burned
4725	184	1362	UNKN	UNKN	1	UNKN	MAML	UNKN	FRAG	3	burned
4825	184	4185	UNKN	UNKN	1+	UNKN	MAML	UNKN	FRAG	0.5	burned
4718	184	4187	UNKN	UNKN	1	UNKN	MAML	UNKN	FRAG	0.8	burned
4720	184	5274	UNKN	UNKN	1	UNKN	MAML	UNKN	FRAG	0.05	burned
4722	184	6158	UNKN	UNKN	1	UNKN	MAML	UNKN	FRAG	2.6	burned
4724	184	6363	UNKN	UNKN	1	UNKN	MAML	UNKN	FRAG	0.4	burned
4872	184	1361	UNKN	UNKN	1	UNKN	MAML	UNKN	FRAG	2.4	burned, cut marks
3183	184	4184	UNKN	UNKN	1	XSM	TURT	shell	FRAG	1.2	burned
3178	184	UNKN	UNKN	UNKN	3	XSM	TURT	shell	FRAG	2.7	burned
Faunal Notation Key											
2011.28: Pechanga Cultural Resource catalogue number											
SBCM: San Bernardino Catalogue collection number											
CAT #: Catalog number											
UNIT: Location											
	According to excavation map										

TEST: Test Hole							
LEVEL: Depth							
	SURF: Surface						
	Levels 1-10 (Increments of 6 inches each level)						
QTY: Quantity							
Size Cat: Size Category							
	XSM: X-SMall 10lb or less						
	SM: Small 10-30lbs						
	MED: Medium 30-200lbs						
	LG: Large 200lb +						
	UNKN: Unknown						
	ALL: all sizes mixed						
Species:							
	Common name		Scientific name				
	BADG: Badger		Taxidea taxus				
	BCAT: Bob Cat/ WildCat		Lynx rufus				
	BHRB: Brush Rabbit		Sylvilagus bachmani				
	CHPM: Chipmunk		Tamias				
	COW: Cow		Bos primigenius				
	COYT: Coyote		Canis latrans				
	CTRB: Cotton tail Rabbit		Sylvilagus				
	DEER: Deer, mule		Odocoileus hemionus				
	FISH: Fish, Rainbow Trout		Oncorhynchus mykiss				

	GOPH: Gopher, pocket		Geomyidae				
	GRSQ: Ground Squirel		Ictidomys tridecemlineatus				
	GYSQ: Grey Squirel		Sciurus carolinensis				
	HORS: Horse		Equua ferus caballus				
	JKRB: Jack CTRBit		Lepus				
	KRAT: Kangaroo Rat		Dipodys				
	MAML: Mammal		Mammalia				
	MOUS: Mouse		Mus musculus				
	MTLI: Mountain Lion		Puma concolor				
	PIG: Pig		Sus				
	RACC: Raccoon		Procyon lotor				
	RAT: Rat		Rattus				
	RD: Rodent		Rodentia				
	SHEP: Sheep		Ovis aries				
	SKUK: Skunk		Mephitidae				
	TURT: Turtle, Western Pond		Actinemys marmorata				
	WRAT: Wood Rat		Neotoma				

Bone Type:

	Femur								
	Humerus								
	Incisors								
	Long: Long bone								
	Mandible								

	Maxillary								
	Metacarpal								
	Metapodial								
	Pelvic girdle								
	Phalange								
	Radius								
	Rib								
	Scapula								
	Shell								
	skull								
	Teeth								
	Tibia								
	Ulna								
	Vert: Vertebra								
	Vert-Cervical								
	Vert-Lumbar								
	Vert-Thoraic								
COND: Condition									
	WHLE: Whole								
	FRAG: Fragment								
WT/g: Weight measured in grams									
Comments:									
	burned								

	Cut Marks								
	tooth								

APPENDIX Y

SHELL BEADS

Appendix Y: Shell Beads

2011.28	SBCM	Cat #	Unit	Level	Qty	MTRL	TYPE	COND	Part	Period	Sour	Hole	Descriptions	L/ MM	W/ MM	HL/ MM	Wt/g
1990	184	3776	UNKN	UNKN	1	OLVL	A1c	WHLE	WHLE	ALL	SCAL	PUCH	spire removed	12	11	12	1.1
1991	184	3776	UNKN	UNKN	1	OLVL	A1b	WHLE	WHLE	ALL	SCAL	PUCH	spire removed	14	8	2	1.1
1992	184	3776	UNKN	UNKN	1	OLVL	A1c	WHLE	WHLE	ALL	SCAL	PUCH	spire removed	16	11	3	0.6
1993	184	3776	UNKN	UNKN	1	OLVL	A1c	WHLE	WHLE	ALL	SCAL	PUCH	spire removed	16.5	11	1.5	1
1994	184	3776	UNKN	UNKN	1	OLVL	A1c	WHLE	WHLE	ALL	SCAL	PUCH	spire removed	14	11	3	0.6
1995	184	3776	UNKN	UNKN	1	OLVL	A1c	WHLE	WHLE	ALL	SCAL	PUCH	spire removed	19	11	1.5	1.3
1996	184	3776	UNKN	UNKN	1	OLVL	A1c	WHLE	WHLE	ALL	SCAL	PUCH	spire removed	21	12	2	1.5
1997	184	3776	UNKN	UNKN	1	OLVL	N3	NRCP	WHLE	ALL	SNIS	SAWD	spire removed, blank .5x3mm	15	7	0.5	0.7
1998	184	3776	UNKN	UNKN	1	OLVL	A1c	WHLE	WHLE	ALL	SCAL	PUCH	spire removed	21	10	1.5	1.4
1999	184	3776	UNKN	UNKN	1	OLVL	A1c	WHLE	WHLE	ALL	SCAL	PUCH	spire removed, slant	11	10	0.1	1
2001	184	3776	UNKN	UNKN	1	OLVL	A1c	WHLE	WHLE	ALL	SCAL	PUCH	spire removed	20	11	4	1.5
2002	184	3776	UNKN	UNKN	1	OLVL	A1c	WHLE	WHLE	ALL	SCAL	PUCH	spire removed	19	11	4	1
2003	184	3776	UNKN	UNKN	1	OLVL	A1c	WHLE	WHLE	ALL	SCAL	PUCH	spire removed	20	12	5	2
2004	184	3776	UNKN	UNKN	1	OLVL	A1b	WHLE	WHLE	ALL	SCAL	PUCH	spire removed	16	9	1	0.7
2005	184	3776	UNKN	UNKN	1	OLVL	A1c	WHLE	WHLE	ALL	SCAL	PUCH	spire removed	21	11	2	1.4

2011.28	SBCM	Cat #	Unit	Level	Qty	MTRL	TYPE	COND	Part	Period	Sour	Hole	Descriptions	L/ MM	W/ MM	HL/ MM	Wt/g
2011	184	6039	UNKN	1,4	1	OLVL	H1b	WHLE	WALL	LATE	SCAL	BCOL	spire	4	N/A	1	0.01
2095	184	6004	UNKN	1,4	1	OLVL	E1a	WHLE	WALL	LATE	SCAL	CONL	chipped, burned	5	5	1	0.01
2096	184	4569	20G5	2	1	OLVL	E1a	WHLE	WALL	LATE	SCAL	BCOL	central perforation drilled	7	5	3	0.1
2097	184	6024	UNKN	1,4	1	OLVL	E1a	WHLE	APEX	MIDL	CECA	CONL	Spire removed perpen-dicular	5	4	1	0.01
2098	184	6000	UNKN	1,4	1	OLVL	H2	WHLE	WALL	LATE	CECA	BCOL	burned	5	4	1	0.01
2099	184	6018	UNKN	1,4	1	OLVL	H2	WHLE	WALL	LATE	CECA	BCOL	chipped	5	4	1	0.01
2100	184	6034	UNKN	1,4	1	OLVL	H2	WHLE	APEX	LATE	CECA	CONL	Spire removed perpen-dicular	4	3	1	0.01
2101	184	6012	UNKN	1,4	1	OLVL	H2	WHLE	CALS	LATE	SCAL	CONL	chipped	5	N/A	1	0.01
2102	184	6030	UNKN	1,4	1	OLVL	E2b	WHLE	WALL	LATE	SCMS	CONL	ground	10	9	2	0.01
2103	184	6011	UNKN	1,4	1	OLVL	E2b	WHLE	APEX	SCMA	SCAL	BCOL	chipped	8	6	2	0.01
2104	184	6002	UNKN	1,4	1	OLVL	E2a	WHLE	WALL	LATE	SCMS	CONL		8	6	2	0.01
2105	184	6008	UNKN	1,4	1	OLVL	H1a	WHLE	WALL	LATE, HIST	CECA	BCOL	etched	2	N/A	1	0.01
2109	184	6036	UNKN	1,4	1	OLVL	H1b	WHLE	WALL	LATE	SCMS	BCOL	chippped	3	3	1	0.01
2110	184	6037	UNKN	1,4	1	OLVL	H1b	WHLE	WALL	LATE	SCMS	BCOL	chippped, burned	4.5	N/A	1.5	0.01
2112	184	6001	UNKN	1,4	1	OLVL	H1b	WHLE	WALL	LATE	SCAL	BCOL		4	3	1	0.01
2113	184	6005	UNKN	1,4	1	OLVL	H1b	WHLE	WALL	LATE	SCAL	BCOL	etched	5	N/A	1	0.01

2011.28	SBCM	Cat #	Unit	Level	Qty	MTRL	TYPE	COND	Part	Period	Sour	Hole	Descriptions	L/ MM	W/ MM	HL/ MM	Wt/g
2114	184	5999	UNKN	1,4	1	OLVL	H1b	WHLE	WALL	LATE	SCAL	BCOL	chipped	4.5	4	1	0.01
2115	184	6003	UNKN	1,4	1	OLVL	K3	WHLE	WALL	LATE	SCAL	BCOL	chipped	3	N/A	1	0.01
2116	184	6026	UNKN	1,4	1	OLVL	K1	WHLE	CALS	LATE, HIST	SCAL	CONL	chipped	4	N/A	2.5	0.01
2117	184	6032	UNKN	1,4	1	OLVL	K1	WHLE	WALL	SCMA	SCAL	BCOL	chipped	5	N/A	3	0.01
2118	184	5998	UNKN	1,4	1	OLVL	K1	WHLE	WALL	LATE	SCAL	BCOL	ground	5	4	1	0.01
2119	184	6010	UNKN	1,4	1	OLVL	J	WHLE	WALL	LATE	SCAL	CONL	ground	3	N/A	1	0.01
2120	184	6014	UNKN	1,4	1	OLVL	J	WHLE	WALL	LATE	SCAL	CONL	ground	4.5	N/A	1	0.01
2121	184	6031	UNKN	1,4	1	OLVL	J	WHLE	WALL	LATE	SCAL	CONL	chipped	5	4	1	0.01
2122	184	6021	UNKN	1,4	1	OLVL	J	WHLE	WALL	SCMA	SCAL	BCOL	chipped	4	4	1	0.01
2123	184	6023	UNKN	1,4	1	OLVL	J	WHLE	WALL	LATE	SCAL	BCOL	Burned, chipped	4	N/A	1	0.01
2124	184	6007	UNKN	1,4	1	OLVL	J	WHLE	WALL	MIDL, LATE	SCAL	CONL	ground	4	3	2	0.01
2125	184	6009	UNKN	1,4	1	OLVL	J	WHLE	WALL	LATE	SCAL	BCOL	chipped	4.5	N/A	1	0.01
2126	184	6027	UNKN	1,4	1	OLVL	J	WHLE	WALL	LATE	SCAL	BCOL	chipped	4.5	N/A	1.5	0.01
2127	184	631	85I	1	1	OLVL	PREF	WHLE	APEX	LATE	SCAL	BCOL	Round, perforation drilled	8	7	2	0.01
2128	184	5698	30I	2	1	OLVL	PREF	WHLE	APEX	LATE	SCAL	BCOL	Flat, circular, ground	7	5	1	0.01
2129	184	6033	UNKN	1,4	1	OLVL	G1	WHLE	CALS	MIDL	SCAL	CONL	central perforation, money	2	N/A	1	0.01

2011.28	SBCM	Cat #	Unit	Level	Qty	MTRL	TYPE	COND	Part	Period	Sour	Hole	Descriptions	L/ MM	W/ MM	HL/ MM	Wt/g
2130	184	6029	UNKN	1,4	1	OLVL	G1	WHLE	WALL	LATE	SCAL	BCOL	ground, chipped	2	N/A	1	0.01
2131	184	6020	UNKN	1,4	1	OLVL	G1	WHLE	WALL	LATE	SCAL	CONL	ground, broken, burned	2	N/A	1	0.01
2132	184	6015	UNKN	1,4	1	OLVL	G1	WHLE	WALL	ALL	SCAL	CONL	partly ground	3	N/A	2	0.01
2133	184	6025	UNKN	1,4	1	OLVL	G1	WHLE	CALS	LATE, HIST	CECA	CONL	ground	4	N/A	1	0.01
2134	184	6017	UNKN	1,4	1	OLVL	G1	WHLE	WALL	LATE	SCAL	BCOL	chipped	3	N/A	2	0.01
2135	184	6016	UNKN	1,4	1	OLVL	G1	WHLE	CALS	LATE	SCAL	CONL	ground	2	N/A	1	0.01
2136	184	4794	75H5	2	1	OLVL	A1c	WHLE	WHLE	LATE	SCAL	BCOL	chipped	19	9	10	0.9
2137	184	5996	UNKN	1,4	1	OLVL	A1a	WHLE	WALL	SCMA	SCAL	BCOL	chipped	15	6	1	0.2
2138	184	6019	UNKN	1,4	1	OLVL	G1	WHLE	WALL	LATE	SCAL	BCOL	chipped, burned	3	N/A	1	0.01
2139	184	6038	UNKN	UNKN	1	OLVL	G1	WHLE	WALL	LATE	SCMS	BCOL	chipped,burned, ectched	3	N/A	1	0.01
2140	184	6028	UNKN	1,4	1	OLVL	J	WHLE	WALL	LATE	SCMS	BCOL	chipped, burned	5	N/A	2	0.01
2141	184	6006	UNKN	1,4	1	OLVL	H1b	WHLE	WALL	LATE	SCAL	CONL	ectched, burned	4	N/A	1	0.01
2142	184	3775	UNKN	UNKN	1	OLVL	J	WHLE	WALL	LATE	SCMS	CONL	burned	4	N/A	1	0.1

Shell Bead Notation Key

2011.28: Pechanga Cultural Resource catalogue number

APPENDIX Y

SBCM: San Bernardino Catalogue collection number										
CAT #: Catalog number										
UNIT: Location										
According to excavation map										
LEVEL: Depth										
SURF: Surface										
Levels 1-10 (Increments of 6 inches each level)										
QTY: Quantity										
MTRL: Material										
OLVLL: Olivella										
TYPE:										
A1a: Small spire lopped										
A1b: Medium spire lopped										
A1c: Large spire lopped										
E1a: Semi-ground disk										
E2a: Full Lipped										
E2b: Deep Lipped										

	G1: Tiny Saucer										
	H1a: Ground disk										
	H1b: Semi-ground disk										
	H2: Rough Disk										
	J: Wall Disk										
	K1: Cupped										
	K3: Cylinder										
	N3: Grooved rectangle										
	PREF: Shell bead preform										
COND: Condition											
	WHLE: Whole										
	NRCP: Nearly Complete										
PART: Part of the Olivella shell											
	CALS: Callus										
	WALL: Wall										
	WHLE: Whole Olivella shell										
	APEX: Apex of Spire										

Period:											
	EALY: EALY										
	MIDL: Middle										
	LATE: LATE										
	ALL: Late, Middle and Early										
	SCMA: Southern California Mission										
	HIST: HIST										
SOUR: Source											
	SCAL: Southern California										
	CECA: Central CAifornia										
	SCMS: Southern California Mission										
	SNIS: San Nicolas Island										
HOLE: Hole Drilled											
	CONL: Conical										
	BCOL: Biconical										
	PUCH: Punched										
	SAWD: Sawed										

Description:											
	Spire removed										
	Ground: edges ground										
	Chipped: chipped edges										
	Burned										
	etched: Incised with diagonal lines										
	Money										
	Blank: Bead Blank										
L/mm: Length measured in mm from end to edge											
W/mm: Width measured in mm from edge to edge											
HLE/MM: Hole measured in mm from top to bottom											
WT/g: Weight measured in grams											

APPENDIX Z

SHELLS

Appendix Z: Shells									
2011.28	SBCM	Cat #	Unit	Level	Qty	Type	COND	Wt/g	Comments
2059	184	5762	105E	3	1	BECM	FRAG	0.5	
2008	184	987	55H5	2	2	BECM	FRAG	0.2	
1842	184	1392	55J5	3	1	BECM	FRAG	0.2	
1955	184	4364	UNKN	UNKN	2	BECM	FRAG	0.5	
1865	184	639	100D	4	1	BKAL	FRAG	0.01	
2022	184	2610	100D	4	1	BKAL	FRAG	0.2	
2045	184	5081	100D	7	1	BKAL	FRAG	0.01	
2041	184	4896	100D	8	10+	BKAL	FRAG	0.01	
2019	184	3071	100D5	1	1	BKAL	FRAG	0.2	
2027	184	955	105D5	1	1	BKAL	FRAG	0.2	
2018	184	541	105D5	5	1	BKAL	FRAG	0.2	
2036	184	5762	105E	3	1	BKAL	FRAG	0.2	
1984	184	869	105F	3	1	BKAL	FRAG	0.3	
2040	184	1485	105F5	1	1	BKAL	FRAG	0.4	
1881	184	1548	110-5	1	4	BKAL	FRAG	0.5	
2026	184	4217	110D	2	1	BKAL	FRAG	0.2	
2028	184	5338	110D	3	1	BKAL	FRAG	0.1	
2020	184	2106	110D5	4	1	BKAL	FRAG	0.2	
2025	184	5733	110E5	2	6	BKAL	FRAG	0.1	
2043	184	1093	110E5	4	1	BKAL	FRAG	1	
2039	184	5038	110E5	5	8+	BKAL	FRAG	1.5	

2011.28	SBCM	Cat #	Unit	Level	Qty	Type	COND	Wt/g	Comments
2042	184	5059	110G	1	1	BKAL	FRAG	1.4	
2033	184	5515	115B	3,4	4	BKAL	FRAG	0.1	
2044	184	1559	115D5	2	1	BKAL	FRAG	0.01	
2021	184	4882	115E	6	1	BKAL	FRAG	0.2	
2093	184	380	115E5	9	1	BKAL	FRAG	0.01	
2030	184	5329	115F5	6	2	BKAL	FRAG	0.5	
2038	184	5954	120D	1	2	BKAL	FRAG	0.2	
2091	184	2327	120D	7	1	BKAL	FRAG	0.5	
1928	184	2961	120G/ 120F5	3	2	BKAL	FRAG	0.1	
1885	184	2183	120J5	UNKN	2	BKAL	FRAG	0.5	
1919	184	2073	125G	1,2,3	1	BKAL	FRAG	3	
1926	184	4841	125G5	3	1	BKAL	FRAG	0.4	
1918	184	3734	125G5	4	4+	BKAL	FRAG	0.1	
1921	184	5125	140H5	1,2	2	BKAL	FRAG	0.5	
1917	184	1724	140I	2	1	BKAL	FRAG	7	
1920	184	3996	155H	3	12+	BKAL	FRAG	0.08	
1927	184	570	165H	1	4	BKAL	FRAG	0.01	
1924	184	560	165H5	1	2	BKAL	FRAG	0.01	
1922	184	2592	175H	3	2+	BKAL	FRAG	0.7	
1925	184	3385	175I	1	1	BKAL	FRAG	0.2	
1923	184	5210	175I5	1	1	BKAL	FRAG	0.5	
1916	184	5548	175I5	2	1	BKAL	FRAG	0.1	

2011.28	SBCM	Cat #	Unit	Level	Qty	Type	COND	Wt/g	Comments
1877	184	1569	40I	3	1	BKAL	FRAG	0.01	
1868	184	6059	55H5	3	5+	BKAL	FRAG	0.8	
1869	184	2043	55I	1	1	BKAL	FRAG	0.9	
1866	184	527	55I	4	3	BKAL	FRAG	0.1	
1876	184	612	55I	4	1	BKAL	FRAG	0.3	
1872	184	2742	55I5	2	10+	BKAL	FRAG	0.5	
1875	184	2714	55I5	3	1	BKAL	FRAG	0.3	
1871	184	1714	55J	1	1	BKAL	FRAG	0.01	
1870	184	1950	60H5	1	1	BKAL	FRAG	0.8	
1880	184	1596	60I5	3	3+	BKAL	FRAG	0.2	
1867	184	12	65H5	2	1	BKAL	FRAG	0.01	
1884	184	80	65H5	3,4	11	BKAL	FRAG	0.4	
1878	184	6189	65I	1	5+	BKAL	FRAG	0.5	
1873	184	3372	65I	2	10+	BKAL	FRAG	0.4	
2013	184	1783	70C5	3	2+	BKAL	FRAG	0.1	
2014	184	842	75C5	2	1	BKAL	FRAG	1.6	
1874	184	1433	75N	1	1	BKAL	FRAG	0.01	
2012	184	732	80D5	1	1	BKAL	FRAG	4.1	
2031	184	1469	80D5	1	3	BKAL	FRAG	1.1	
2015	184	1074	80D5	2	7+	BKAL	FRAG	4.1	
1887	184	597	80H	3	5	BKAL	FRAG	0.1	
1882	184	1502	80H5	1,2	1	BKAL	FRAG	0.2	

2011.28	SBCM	Cat #	Unit	Level	Qty	Type	COND	Wt/g	Comments
2035	184	113	85D5	UNKN	3	BKAL	FRAG	0.5	
1883	184	1765	85G5	3	1	BKAL	FRAG	0.1	
2034	184	3521	90D	4	1	BKAL	FRAG	0.6	
2032	184	3154	90E	3	1	BKAL	FRAG	0.9	
2029	184	2902	90F	2	2	BKAL	FRAG	0.8	
1888	184	5624	90I	2	1	BKAL	FRAG	8.2	
2037	184	2124	95D5	2	1	BKAL	FRAG	0.2	
2024	184	2383	95E	1	2	BKAL	FRAG	0.4	
2023	184	2137	95E	4	2	BKAL	FRAG	0.2	
1886	184	3628	95I	1	11+	BKAL	FRAG	0.7	
2092	184	3608	9D	3	1	BKAL	FRAG	0.4	
1981	184	3247	UNKN	2	1	BKAL	FRAG	0.3	
1983	184	2907	UNKN	3,4	1	BKAL	FRAG	0.5	
1980	184	1039	UNKN	UNKN	1	BKAL	FRAG	2.6	
1982	184	1170	UNKN	UNKN	2+	BKAL	FRAG	0.3	burned
1985	184	1199	UNKN	UNKN	25+	BKAL	FRAG	1	
1989	184	3719	UNKN	UNKN	1	BKAL	FRAG	0.01	
1976	184	3749	UNKN	UNKN	32+	BKAL	FRAG	5.8	
1974	184	3779	UNKN	UNKN	1	BKAL	FRAG	0.2	
1986	184	3802	UNKN	UNKN	1	BKAL	FRAG	0.4	
1975	184	4183	UNKN	UNKN	1	BKAL	FRAG	1	
1979	184	4364	UNKN	UNKN	20+	BKAL	FRAG	4.1	

2011.28	SBCM	Cat #	Unit	Level	Qty	Type	COND	Wt/g	Comments
1973	184	4511	UNKN	UNKN	7	BKAL	FRAG	1	cremation pt., 4-42"
1977	184	5157	UNKN	UNKN	7	BKAL	FRAG	1.6	
1988	184	5936	UNKN	UNKN	1	BKAL	FRAG	0.3	
1978	184	6362	UNKN	UNKN	1	BKAL	FRAG	0.2	
1889	184	UNKN	UNKN	UNKN	1	CLCM	FRAG	3.7	
1954	184	4361	UNKN	UNKN	1	CRAB	FRAG	0.8	crab claw
2058	184	169	100D5	3	1	FWCM	FRAG	0.01	
2069	184	142	100D5	4	6	FWCM	FRAG	0.01	
2062	184	1048	100E5	3	2	FWCM	FRAG	0.01	
1964	184	869	105F	3	1	FWCM	FRAG	0.4	
1914	184	5717	110I	1	1	FWCM	FRAG	2.1	
2064	184	532	115D	1	5	FWCM	FRAG	0.5	
2060	184	2953	115F	4	1	FWCM	FRAG	0.1	
2065	184	1647	115F5	3	5	FWCM	FRAG	0.4	
2071	184	6171	115F5	5	1	FWCM	FRAG	2	
1853	184	2442	120D	6	9+	FWCM	FRAG	0.7	
1948	184	688	120G	1	1	FWCM	FRAG	0.01	
2056	184	943	120G	1	2	FWCM	FRAG	0.01	
1950	184	3322	120G	2	10+	FWCM	FRAG	0.2	
1945	184	471	120G5	2	1	FWCM	FRAG	0.01	
1949	184	4609	125G	2	1	FWCM	FRAG	0.1	
1941	184	2471	160H5	1	1	FWCM	FRAG	0.1	

2011.28	SBCM	Cat #	Unit	Level	Qty	Type	COND	Wt/g	Comments
1940	184	447	165H	2	2	FWCM	FRAG	0.01	
1938	184	501	165H	3	3+	FWCM	FRAG	0.01	
1946	184	2243	170H	2	2	FWCM	FRAG	0.2	
1943	184	1894	170H5	1	2	FWCM	FRAG	0.1	
1936	184	3371	175H	1	8	FWCM	FRAG	1	
1939	184	3255	175H5	1	3	FWCM	FRAG	0.4	
1942	184	3602	175H5	3	1	FWCM	FRAG	0.5	
1947	184	2971	175I	1	1	FWCM	FRAG	0.1	
1944	184	3341	175I	2	1	FWCM	FRAG	0.1	
1848	184	4568	20G5	2	1	FWCM	FRAG	0.1	
1845	184	1635	40	2	1	FWCM	FRAG	0.1	
1851	184	6350	40H5	1	1	FWCM	FRAG	0.1	
1851	184	635	45F5	6	1	FWCM	FRAG	2.1	
1852	184	2172	55H5	2	1	FWCM	FRAG	0.15	
2055	184	988	55I	2	1	FWCM	FRAG	0.01	
1850	184	2000	55I	2	1	FWCM	FRAG	0.2	
1937	184	1724	55J	1	1	FWCM	FRAG	0.1	
1841	184	6189	65I	1	1	FWCM	FRAG	0.01	
1849	184	6106	65I	2	1	FWCM	FRAG	0.01	
1874	184	2728	70I	2	1	FWCM	FRAG	0.3	
1890	184	101	70I	3	1	FWCM	FRAG	0.01	
1891	184	4623	75H	1,2	1	FWCM	FRAG	0.01	

2011.28	SBCM	Cat #	Unit	Level	Qty	Type	COND	Wt/g	Comments
1892	184	597	80H	3	3	FWCM	FRAG	0.1	
1894	184	1862	80I	1	4	FWCM	FRAG	0.01	
2061	184	887	85F	2	4	FWCM	FRAG	0.01	
2066	184	3369	85G	2	4	FWCM	FRAG	0.8	
2057	184	1599	85G5	2	1	FWCM	FRAG	0.8	
1897	184	65	85G5	4	6	FWCM	FRAG	0.01	
1895	184	486	85H	3	2	FWCM	FRAG	0.01	
1893	184	631	85I	1	1	FWCM	FRAG	0.01	
2059	184	3350	90D	2	1	FWCM	FRAG	0.2	
2070	184	3276	90E	2	1	FWCM	FRAG	0.8	
1896	184	4535	90G	2	1	FWCM	FRAG	0.1	
2067	184	1992	95D	5	2	FWCM	FRAG	0.01	
2712	184	2186	95D	3,4	3	FWCM	FRAG	0.3	
2063	184	2187	95D	3,4	6+	FWCM	FRAG	2.9	
2068	184	5377	95D	3,4	1	FWCM	FRAG	0.3	
1965	184	4660	TEST	UNKN	14	FWCM	FRAG	0.8	
1966	184	4772	TEST	UNKN	3	FWCM	FRAG	0.8	
2247	184	663	UNKN	1	3	FWCM	FRAG	0.01	
1963	184	1199	UNKN	UNKN	25+	FWCM	FRAG	1	
1967	184	2779	UNKN	UNKN	1	FWCM	FRAG	0.2	
1969	184	4364	UNKN	UNKN	1	FWCM	FRAG	1.5	
1968	184	4364	UNKN	UNKN	1	FWCM	FRAG	1.5	

2011.28	SBCM	Cat #	Unit	Level	Qty	Type	COND	Wt/g	Comments
1951	184	5210	UNKN	UNKN	1	FWCM	FRAG	0.5	
1962	184	6362	UNKN	UNKN	1	FWCM	FRAG	0.3	
2094	184	768	100F5	8	8+	GNAL	FRAG	0.8	
1987	184	4364	UNKN	UNKN	2	GNAL	FRAG	0.5	
1959	184	254	0-G	UNKN	1	HSCM	FRAG	1.5	
1854	184	639	100D	4	1	HSCM	FRAG	0.01	
2072	184	968	100E	2	1	HSCM	FRAG	0.7	
2073	184	955	105D5	1	1	HSCM	FRAG	0.3	
2088	184	2203	120D	5	1	HSCM	FRAG	2.6	
1929	184	3614	125G5	4	1	HSCM	FRAG	1.2	
1930	184	5430	155F5	1,2,3	1	HSCM	FRAG	0.1	
1932	184	2885	175H	1	2	HSCM	FRAG	2.8	
1931	184	3602	175H5	3	1	HSCM	FRAG	0.5	
2171	184	6350	40H5	1	1	HSCM	FRAG	0.1	
1856	184	4450	55	2	1	HSCM	FRAG	0.2	
1857	184	2172	55H5	2	1	HSCM	FRAG	0.15	
1905	184	1622	55J	1	1	HSCM	FRAG	0.1	
1855	184	4441	55J5	5	1	HSCM	FRAG	0.3	
2009	184	4814	65E5	2	2	HSCM	FRAG	1.3	
1904	184	80	65H5	3,4	1	HSCM	FRAG	0.1	
2010	184	3382	70C	2	2	HSCM	FRAG	1	
2638	184	2735	70E	3	1	HSCM	FRAG	0.5	

2011.28	SBCM	Cat #	Unit	Level	Qty	Type	COND	Wt/g	Comments
2172	184	2277	70I	1	1	HSCM	FRAG	0.15	
1908	184	101	70I	3	1	HSCM	FRAG	0.01	
1906	184	190	75I	3	1	HSCM	FRAG	0.3	
2089	184	3858	80D	6,7	1	HSCM	FRAG	0.8	
1909	184	4182	90I5	2	1	HSCM	FRAG	0.3	
2713	184	2186	95D	3,4	2	HSCM	FRAG	0.1	
1907	184	3628	95I	1	1	HSCM	FRAG	0.2	
1960	184	2779	UNKN	UNKN	1	HSCM	FRAG	0.2	
1970	184	3749	UNKN	UNKN	1	HSCM	FRAG	0.2	
1958	184	3777	UNKN	UNKN	3	HSCM	FRAG	1.4	
1957	184	3802	UNKN	UNKN	1	HSCM	FRAG	0.3	
1971	184	4364	UNKN	UNKN	1	HSCM	FRAG	0.5	
2053	184	1032	70E5	2	1	MATC	FRAG	3.3	
1956	184	2907	UNKN	3,4	8	MUSS	FRAG	1.5	
1952	184	3749	UNKN	UNKN	1	MUSS	FRAG	0.5	
2087	184	3780	UNKN	UNKN	1	MUSS	FRAG	4.5	
2108	184	1894	170H5	1	1	OLVA	FRAG	0.1	
2007	184	3776	UNKN	UNKN	1	OLVA	FRAG	1.5	
2006	184	3776	UNKN	UNKN	1	OLVA	FRAG	3.5	
2000	184	3776	UNKN	UNKN	1	OLVA	FRAG	1.4	
2083	184	2610	100D	4	2	PECT	FRAG	0.6	
2075	184	968	100E	2	1	PECT	FRAG	0.5	

2011.28	SBCM	Cat #	Unit	Level	Qty	Type	COND	Wt/g	Comments
2078	184	980	105D5	2	1	PECT	FRAG	0.01	
2081	184	5762	105E	3	1	PECT	FRAG	0.3	
2076	184	4217	110D	2	2	PECT	FRAG	0.4	
2085	184	3166	115F	5	1	PECT	FRAG	0.9	
2077	184	2442	120D	6	1	PECT	FRAG	0.3	
2090	184	2327	120D	7	2	PECT	FRAG	0.5	
1911	184	2183	120J5	UNKN	1	PECT	FRAG	0.5	
2579	184	1729	140I	2	1	PECT	FRAG	0.3	burned
1913	184	3996	155H	3	3	PECT	FRAG	0.03	
1915	184	570	165H	1	1	PECT	FRAG	0.01	
1912	184	2592	175H	3	1	PECT	FRAG	0.05	
2080	184	2346	58E5	UNKN	3	PECT	FRAG	2.5	
2084	184	4558	65E	1	1	PECT	FRAG	0.2	
1844	184	12	65H5	2	1	PECT	FRAG	0.01	
2011	184	6539	70C	1	1	PECT	FRAG	0.4	
2636	184	5949	70C	2	1	PECT	FRAG	0.4	
2620	184	2868	70E	2	1	PECT	FRAG	0.3	
2082	184	5636	70E	5	1	PECT	FRAG	0.3	burned
2074	184	731	75D	3	4	PECT	FRAG	8.4	
1843	184	5609	75J	1	1	PECT	FRAG	0.1	
2714	184	2186	95D	3,4	1	PECT	FRAG	0.1	
2079	184	2187	95D	3,4	6+	PECT	FRAG	3	

2011.28	SBCM	Cat #	Unit	Level	Qty	Type	COND	Wt/g	Comments
1910	184	5260	95H5	2	1	PECT	FRAG	0.4	burned
2048	184	825	105E5	1	1	PSCM	FRAG	3.2	
1900	184	5373	110-5	2	2	PSCM	FRAG	2	
2049	184	1776	110D5	3	1	PSCM	FRAG	0.1	
1899	184	1909	110H	1	1	PSCM	FRAG	1.5	
1901	184	5717	110I	1	1	PSCM	FRAG	1.5	
2051	184	1196	115B	3,4	2	PSCM	FRAG	0.7	
2047	184	4882	115E	6	1	PSCM	FRAG	1	
2050	184	5219	120F5	1	2	PSCM	FRAG	4	
1934	184	5125	140H5	1,2	2	PSCM	FRAG	0.5	
2517	184	1729	140I	2	1	PSCM	FRAG	0.4	
1933	184	6527	140I5	1	1	PSCM	FRAG	4.8	
1935	184	3255	175H5	1	2	PSCM	FRAG	0.2	
1860	184	636	40I	1	1	PSCM	FRAG	1.5	
1861	184	2043	55I	1	1	PSCM	FRAG	1	
1859	184	612	55I	4	1	PSCM	FRAG	0.1	
1863	184	2477	55I	4	1	PSCM	FRAG	0.8	
1862	184	1622	55J	2	1	PSCM	FRAG	0.3	
1864	184	1950	60H5	1	2	PSCM	FRAG	0.1	
1858	184	2577	70I	1	1	PSCM	FRAG	0.15	
2046	184	3350	90D	2	1	PSCM	FRAG	0.2	
1902	184	1807	90I	3	2	PSCM	FRAG	0.6	

2011.28	SBCM	Cat #	Unit	Level	Qty	Type	COND	Wt/g	Comments
2052	184	3133	95E5	3	1+	PSCM	FRAG	3.6	
1898	184	858	95G5	1	1	PSCM	FRAG	2.7	
1972	184	2907	UNKN	3,4	1	PSCM	FRAG	0.5	
1961	184	1039	UNKN	UNKN	1	PSCM	FRAG	1.5	
2017	184	2929	100D5	3	1	RDAL	FRAG	5.9	
1879	184	1034	70J	1	2	RDAL	FRAG	0.01	
2016	184	2346	85E	UNKN	2	RDAL	FRAG	1.1	
1953	184	3780	UNKN	UNKN	1	SADL	FRAG	10.1	
2086	184	3780	UNKN	UNKN	1	VLLT	FRAG	4	
Shell Notation Key									
2011.28: Pechanga Cultural Resource catalogue number									
SBCM: San Bernardino Catalogue collection number									
CAT: Catalog number									
UNIT: Location									
	According to excavation map								
	TEST: Test Hole								
LEVEL: Depth									
	SURF: Surface								
	Levels 1-10								
QTY: Quantity									
Type:									

	Common name		Scientific name				
	FWCM: Fresh Water Clam		Ano donta				
	BECM: Bean Clam		Donax gouldii				
	HSCM: Hard Shell Clam		Chione succincta				
	BKAL: Black Abalone		Haliotis cracherodii				
	RDAL: Red Abalone		Haliotis rufescens				
	GNAL: Green Abalone		Haliotis fulfens				
	PECT: Pecten		Pectinidae				
	MUSS: Mussel		Mytilus sp.				
	OLVA: Olivella		Olivella biplicata				
	MATC: California Mactra		Mactrotoma californica				
	PSCM: Pismo Clam		Tivela stultorum				
	CLCM: California Clam		Mytilus californianus				
	VLLT: Volcano Limpet		Fissurella volcano				
	SADL: Sand Dollar		Clypeasteroida				
	CRAB: Crab		Brachyura				
	UNKN: Unknown						
COND: Condition							
	FRAG: Fragment						
WT/g: Weight measured in grams							
Comment:							
	Specific location						
	burned						

APPENDIX AA

POTTERY

Appendix AA: Pottery										
2011.28	SBCM	Cat #	Unit	Level	Qty	MTRL	COND	Vess Part	Wt/g	Comments
717	184	1633	40	2	9	TIZON	FRAG	BODY	27.2	
718	184	1637	40	2	1	TIZON	FRAG	RIM	3.6	
863	184	4447	55	2	4	TIZON	FRAG	BODY	28.5	
728	184	672	115	1	25	TIZON	FRAG	BODY	278	
415	184	673	115	1	1	TIZON	FRAG	RIM	3.7	5% of rim
417	184	676	115	1	1	TIZON	FRAG	RIM	6.8	5% of rim
437	184	674	115	1	1	TIZON	FRAG	RIM	6	5% of rim
175	184	677	115	1	1	TIZON	FRAG	RIM	4	
204	184	675	115	1	1	TIZON	FRAG	RIM	7.6	
466	184	678	115	1	1	TIZON	FRAG	RIM	3.4	
801	184	2134	1105	1	1	TIZON	FRAG	RIM	7	
1651	184	5367	1105	2	9	TIZON	FRAG	BODY	63.2	
295	184	255	0-G	UNKN	11	TIZON	FRAG	BODY	58	
347	184	252	0-G	UNKN	1	TIZON	FRAG	RIM	2.4	5% of rim
308	184	251	0-G		1	TIZON	FRAG	RIM	5.5	
616	184	2260	100A	UNKN	1	TIZON	FRAG	RIM	1.8	5% of rim
96	184	6262	100A20	1	8	TIZON	FRAG	BODY	39.2	
345	184	2258	100A40	UNKN	1	TIZON	FRAG	RIM	5.6	5% of rim
133	184	2257	100A40	UNKN	1	TIZON	FRAG	RIM	6.5	
148	184	2256	100A40	UNKN	1	TIZON	FRAG	RIM	10.7	
195	184	2253	100A40	UNKN	1	TIZON	FRAG	RIM	303.2	

2011.28	SBCM	Cat #	Unit	Level	Qty	MTRL	COND	Vess Part	Wt/ g	Comments
666	184	2259	100A40	UNKN	1	TIZON	FRAG	RIM	4.8	
195	184	2253	100A40		66	TIZON	FRAG	BODY	303.2	
196	184	2253	100A40		1	TIZON	FRAG	BODY	1.1	
722	184	2254	100A40		1	TIZON	FRAG	RIM	29.5	5% of rim
533	184	1815	100A6	1	6	TIZON	FRAG	BODY	18.5	
803	184	1816	100A6	1	1	TIZON	FRAG	RIM	7.8	5% of rim
500	184	344	100D	1	1	BUFF	FRAG	BODY	1.1	
499	184	344	100D	1	50	TIZON	FRAG	BODY	137.4	
501	184	344	100D	1	1	TIZON	FRAG	BODY	2.9	
1383	184	2698	100D	1	5	TIZON	FRAG	BODY	5.4	
505	184	346	100D	1	1	TIZON	FRAG	RIM	3.2	5% of rim
499	184	344	100D	1	2	TIZON	FRAG	RIM	137.4	
503	184	347	100D	1	1	TIZON	FRAG	RIM	7.3	
504	184	345	100D	1	1	TIZON	FRAG	RIM	0.8	
136	184	185	100D	2	19	TIZON	FRAG	BODY	76.1	
86	184	187	100D	2	1	TIZON	FRAG	RIM	3.2	10% of rim
1156	184	2855	100D	3	11	TIZON	FRAG	BODY	28	
1251	184	2856	100D	3	1	TIZON	FRAG	RIM	5.3	
429	184	644	100D	4	15	TIZON	FRAG	BODY	27.1	
1501	184	2612	100D	4	3	TIZON	FRAG	BODY	13.1	
1509	184	642	100D	4	1	TIZON	FRAG	RIM	16.7	less than 5% of rim
473	184	2919	100D	5	1	TIZON	FRAG	BODY	2.1	

2011.28	SBCM	Cat #	Unit	Level	Qty	MTRL	COND	Vess Part	Wt/ g	Comments
474	184	235	100D	5	28	TIZON	FRAG	BODY	102.1	
1502	184	3130	100D	SURF	3	TIZON	FRAG	BODY	16.3	
492	184	216	100D5	1	1	BUFF	FRAG	BODY	1.4	
49	184	217	100D5	1	1	TIZON	FRAG	BODY	2	
491	184	216	100D5	1	58	TIZON	FRAG	BODY	212.8	
1343	184	2538	100D5	1	1	TIZON	FRAG	BODY	4	
1382	184	3065	100D5	1	2	TIZON	FRAG	BODY	7.8	
490	184	217	100D5	1	1	TIZON	FRAG	RIM	2	
1161	184	2631	100D5	2	2	BUFF	FRAG	BODY	2	
116	184	2631	100D5	2	55	TIZON	FRAG	BODY	224	
1716	184	2632	100D5	2	1	TIZON	FRAG	RIM	7.3	5% of rim
1089	184	2635	100D5	2	1	TIZON	FRAG	RIM	1.9	5% of rim
1046	184	2634	100D5	2	1	TIZON	FRAG	RIM	3.1	
1079	184	2636	100D5	2	1	TIZON	FRAG	RIM	8	
1091	184	2633	100D5	2	1	TIZON	FRAG	RIM	4.5	
1122	184	2638	100D5	2	1	TIZON	FRAG	RIM	4.9	
1587	184	2637	100D5	2	1	TIZON	FRAG	RIM	5.3	
1270	184	2927	100D5	3	1	BUFF	FRAG	BODY	2	
126	184	133	100D5	3	65	TIZON	FRAG	BODY	327.8	
127	184	133	100D5	3	1	TIZON	FRAG	BODY	7.7	
293	184	165	100D5	3	2	TIZON	FRAG	BODY	10	
4	184	2104	100D5	3	21	TIZON	FRAG	BODY	112	

2011.28	SBCM	Cat #	Unit	Level	Qty	MTRL	COND	Vess Part	Wt/ g	Comments
401	184	2104	100D5	3	2	TIZON	FRAG	BODY	5.7	
1269	184	2927	100D5	3	8	TIZON	FRAG	BODY	28	
1456	184	2927	100D5	3	1	TIZON	FRAG	BODY	5.4	
402	184	2105	100D5	3	1	TIZON	FRAG	RIM	3.2	
137	184	4101	100D5	4	1	BUFF	FRAG	RIM	14	
138	184	817	100D5	4	6	TIZON	FRAG	BODY	12.6	
385	184	140	100D5	4	1	TIZON	FRAG	RIM	6	5% of rim
390	184	137	100D5	4	1	TIZON	FRAG	RIM	6	5% of rim
446	184	141	100D5	4	1	TIZON	FRAG	RIM	6	5% of rim
442	184	138	100D5	4	1	TIZON	FRAG	RIM	4	10% of rim
514	184	139	100D5	4	1	TIZON	FRAG	RIM	7.5	7% of rim
559	184	1958	100D5	5	3	TIZON	FRAG	BODY	13.2	
592	184	1962	100D5	5	1	TIZON	FRAG	RIM	3.9	5% of rim
83	184	2288	100D5	6	2	TIZON	FRAG	BODY	4.7	
517	184	893	100D5	8	1	TIZON	FRAG	BODY	5	
178	184	919	100E	1	1	BUFF	FRAG	BODY	1.3	
179	184	919	100E	1	1	BUFF	FRAG	BODY	3	
177	184	919	100E	1	2	TIZON	FRAG	BODY	1.4	
214	184	211	100E	1	39	TIZON	FRAG	BODY	78.4	
194	184	970	100E	2	1	BUFF	FRAG	BODY	4.3	
193	184	970	100E	2	1	TIZON	FRAG	BODY	1.1	
189	184	358	100E	3	1	BUFF	FRAG	BODY	1.4	

2011.28	SBCM	Cat #	Unit	Level	Qty	MTRL	COND	Vess Part	Wt/ g	Comments
12	184	442	100E	3	13	TIZON	FRAG	BODY	75.7	
188	184	358	100E	3	35	TIZON	FRAG	BODY	119.8	
391	184	1050	100E	3	9	TIZON	FRAG	BODY	12	
495	184	1052	100E	3	1	TIZON	FRAG	RIM	3.6	
1324	184	2915	100E	4	4	TIZON	FRAG	BODY	13	
1324	184	2915	100E	4	1	TIZON	FRAG	RIM	13	
1348	184	3006	100E	5	4	TIZON	FRAG	BODY	5	
152	184	838	100E	6	1	BUFF	FRAG	BODY	1	
274	184	214	100F	1	3	TIZON	FRAG	BODY	14.5	
432	184	177	100F	1	1	TIZON	FRAG	BODY	0.8	
304	184	176	100F	1	1	TIZON	FRAG	RIM	2	5% of rim
623	184	2324	100F	3	1	TIZON	FRAG	BODY	5	
416	184	781	100F5	1	24	TIZON	FRAG	BODY	125.4	
1438	184	787	100F5	1	1	TIZON	FRAG	RIM	6.9	
453	184	666	100F5	3	25	TIZON	FRAG	BODY	140.4	
461	184	774	100F5	3	15	TIZON	FRAG	BODY	49.3	
462	184	774	100F5	3	1	TIZON	FRAG	BODY	2.5	
469	184	666	100F5	3	1	TIZON	FRAG	BODY	2.5	
313	184	670	100F5	3	1	TIZON	FRAG	RIM	4.6	5% of rim
359	184	780	100F5	3	1	TIZON	FRAG	RIM	1.8	5% of rim
234	184	779	100F5	3	1	TIZON	FRAG	RIM	5.6	
488	184	671	100F5	3	1	TIZON	FRAG	RIM	2.1	

2011.28	SBCM	Cat #	Unit	Level	Qty	MTRL	COND	Vess Part	Wt/ g	Comments
356	184	814	100F5	4	3	TIZON	FRAG	BODY	13.6	
1309	184	2680	100F5	5	2	TIZON	FRAG	BODY	8.6	
1697	184	3788	100F5	6	3	TIZON	FRAG	BODY	12.9	
596	184	1058	100O5	7	4	TIZON	FRAG	BODY	12.3	
216	184	1020	100O5	9	1	TIZON	FRAG	BODY	1.7	
911	184	4514	105B	1	3	TIZON	FRAG	BODY	7.2	
613	184	4414	105B	2	3	TIZON	FRAG	BODY	15.5	
851	184	2364	105D	1	12	TIZON	FRAG	BODY	54	
342	184	578	105D5	1	102	TIZON	FRAG	BODY	295.1	
364	184	578	105D5	1	1	TIZON	FRAG	BODY	1	
365	184	578	105D5	1	2	TIZON	FRAG	BODY	5.8	
346	184	580	105D5	1	1	TIZON	FRAG	RIM	6	5% of rim
1480	184	579	105D5	1	1	TIZON	FRAG	RIM	5	
13	184	984	105D5	2	37	TIZON	FRAG	BODY	181.5	
245	184	985	105D5	2	1	TIZON	FRAG	RIM	2.4	
45	184	496	105D5	3	7	TIZON	FRAG	BODY	12.7	
515	184	717	105D5	4	7	TIZON	FRAG	BODY	27.5	
15	184	719	105D5	4	1	TIZON	FRAG	RIM	5.8	
908	184	4802	105D5	5	1	BUFF	FRAG	BODY	11.1	
1222	184	2490	105D5	5	25	TIZON	FRAG	BODY	110	
1056	184	2489	105D5	5	1	TIZON	FRAG	RIM	19	
348	184	540	105D5		1	TIZON	FRAG	BODY	6.5	

2011.28	SBCM	Cat #	Unit	Level	Qty	MTRL	COND	Vess Part	Wt/ g	Comments
298	184	363	105E	1	1	BUFF	FRAG	BODY	0.8	
370	184	1006	105E	1	2	BUFF	FRAG	BODY	2.1	
368	184	1006	105E	1	1	TIZON	FRAG	BODY	49.5	13% of vessel
27	184	831	105E	1	1	TIZON	FRAG	BODY	0.5	
297	184	363	105E	1	2	TIZON	FRAG	BODY	4	
299	184	363	105E	1	52	TIZON	FRAG	BODY	94	
367	184	1006	105E	1	54	TIZON	FRAG	BODY	134	
369	184	1006	105E	1	2	TIZON	FRAG	BODY	2.3	
571	184	1846	105E	1	5	TIZON	FRAG	BODY	6.8	
301	184	365	105E	1	1	TIZON	FRAG	RIM	6	5% of rim
300	184	364	105E	1	1	TIZON	FRAG	RIM	2.4	
781	184	1847	105E	1	1	TIZON	FRAG	RIM	2.4	
604	184	1227	105E	2	11	TIZON	FRAG	BODY	19	
605	184	1227	105E	2	1	TIZON	FRAG	BODY	0.5	
628	184	1229	105E	2	1	TIZON	FRAG	RIM	2.4	5% of rim
572	184	1228	105E	2	1	TIZON	FRAG	RIM	1.2	
332	184	224	105E	3	1	BUFF	FRAG	BODY	1.3	
202	184	2355	105E	3	81	TIZON	FRAG	BODY	214.7	
329	184	224	105E	3	55	TIZON	FRAG	BODY	197.6	
33	184	224	105E	3	3	TIZON	FRAG	BODY	6.2	
331	184	224	105E	3	1	TIZON	FRAG	BODY	4	
333	184	224	105E	3	1	TIZON	FRAG	BODY	4.1	

2011.28	SBCM	Cat #	Unit	Level	Qty	MTRL	COND	Vess Part	Wt/ g	Comments
1555	184	5746	105E	3	7	TIZON	FRAG	BODY	11.7	
296	184	226	105E	3	1	TIZON	FRAG	RIM	4.1	5% of rim
310	184	2358	105E	3	1	TIZON	FRAG	RIM	1.7	
1427	184	2357	105E	3	1	TIZON	FRAG	RIM	1.3	
1470	184	2356	105E	3	1	TIZON	FRAG	RIM	5.2	
1724	184	5754	105E	3	1	TIZON	FRAG	RIM	3.8	
618	184	1086	105E	4	9	TIZON	FRAG	BODY	29.7	
156	184	4576	105E	5	4	TIZON	FRAG	BODY	42	
640	184	1486	105F	1	2	BUFF	FRAG	BODY	5.6	
715	184	1004	105F	1	1	BUFF	FRAG	BODY	3.2	
627	184	1486	105F	1	13	TIZON	FRAG	BODY	65	
714	184	1004	105F	1	10	TIZON	FRAG	BODY	33.6	
751	184	796	105F	1	1	TIZON	FRAG	BODY	3.3	
752	184	796	105F	1	13	TIZON	FRAG	BODY	64.3	
121	184	2572	105F	1	8	TIZON	FRAG	BODY	22	
316	184	799	105F	1	1	TIZON	FRAG	RIM	13.8	
219	184	868	105F	3	4	TIZON	FRAG	BODY	26.4	
650	184	878	105F	4	2	BUFF	FRAG	BODY	9	
649	184	878	105F	4	2	TIZON	FRAG	BODY	7.3	
1421	184	1479	105F5	1	1	TIZON	FRAG	RIM	16	12% of rim
291	184	711	105F5	2	1	BUFF	FRAG	BODY	6	
292	184	711	105F5	2	14	TIZON	FRAG	BODY	74	

2011.28	SBCM	Cat #	Unit	Level	Qty	MTRL	COND	Vess Part	Wt/ g	Comments
438	184	713	105F5	2	1	TIZON	FRAG	RIM	10	5% of rim
46	184	898	105F5	3	12	TIZON	FRAG	BODY	87	
227	184	861	105F5	4	1	TIZON	FRAG	BODY	1.8	
378	184	622	105F5	5	1	TIZON	FRAG	BODY	4	
1761	184	4452	105G	1	1	TIZON	FRAG	RIM	32.8	drill holes
1742	184	5256	10G	3	4	TIZON	FRAG	BODY	16.3	
1659	184	5254	10G(?)5	3	1	TIZON	FRAG	RIM	5.3	
818	184	1550	110-5	1	2	TIZON	FRAG	BODY	6	
327	184	351	110D	1	1	BUFF	FRAG	BODY	4.3	
82	184	350	110D	1	2	TIZON	FRAG	BODY	23.4	
281	184	348	110D	1	20	TIZON	FRAG	BODY	80.6	
326	184	351	110D	1	58	TIZON	FRAG	BODY	200	
282	184	349	110D	1	1	TIZON	FRAG	RIM	2	
255	184	4215	110D	2	2	TIZON	FRAG	BODY	8.7	
82	184	2067	110D	2	3	TIZON	FRAG	BODY	12.1	
821	184	2067	110D	2	2	TIZON	FRAG	BODY	8.4	
114	184	4202	110D	2	36	TIZON	FRAG	BODY	180	
262	184	4208	110D	2	1	TIZON	FRAG	RIM	6.2	5% of rim
1152	184	4216	110D	2	1	TIZON	FRAG	RIM	4.2	5% of rim
1391	184	4207	110D	2	1	TIZON	FRAG	RIM	5.7	5% of rim
254	184	4215	110D	2	1	TIZON	FRAG	RIM	5.5	
1235	184	4211	110D	2	1	TIZON	FRAG	RIM	3	

2011.28	SBCM	Cat #	Unit	Level	Qty	MTRL	COND	Vess Part	Wt/ g	Comments
48	184	223	110D	3	14	TIZON	FRAG	BODY	50.4	
1683	184	5348	110D	3	6	TIZON	FRAG	BODY	18	
531	184	1553	110D	4	2	TIZON	FRAG	BODY	7.9	
104	184	6100	110D	5	2	TIZON	FRAG	BODY	9.5	
1616	184	5432	110D	6	1	TIZON	FRAG	BODY	2.9	
47	184	354	110D5	1	46	TIZON	FRAG	BODY	192.3	
1384	184	3149	110D5	1	1	TIZON	FRAG	BODY	1.6	
1386	184	3151	110D5	1	1	TIZON	FRAG	RIM	9.5	5% of rim
6	184	1777	110D5	3	2	TIZON	FRAG	BODY	5	
763	184	2109	110D5	4	10	TIZON	FRAG	BODY	57.1	
802	184	2110	110D5	4	1	TIZON	FRAG	BODY	2.6	
675	184	2111	110D5	4	1	TIZON	FRAG	RIM	22.9	5% of rim
802	184	2110	110D5	4	1	TIZON	FRAG	RIM	2.6	ground
1153	184	2988	110D5	5	8	TIZON	FRAG	BODY	32	
1224	184	3548	110E	1	14	TIZON	FRAG	BODY	48	
1346	184	3549	110E	1	1	TIZON	FRAG	RIM	8.8	
68	184	6122	110E	2	7	BUFF	FRAG	BODY	16.1	
69	184	6122	110E	2	1	BUFF	FRAG	BODY	5.4	
7	184	6122	110E	2	1	TIZON	FRAG	BODY	7.4	sharply curved
17	184	221	110E	2	27	TIZON	FRAG	BODY	72.7	
67	184	6122	110E	2	25	TIZON	FRAG	BODY	156.5	
449	184	592	110E	2	10	TIZON	FRAG	BODY	39.5	

2011.28	SBCM	Cat #	Unit	Level	Qty	MTRL	COND	Vess Part	Wt/ g	Comments
34	184	6127	110E	2	1	TIZON	FRAG	RIM	3.5	less than 5%
81	184	6123	110E	2	1	TIZON	FRAG	RIM	10.2	10% of rim
16	184	222	110E	2	1	TIZON	FRAG	RIM	2.7	
64	184	6124	110E	2	1	TIZON	FRAG	RIM	4.4	
230	184	435	110E	3	1	TIZON	FRAG	RIM	23	10% of rim
168	184	441	110E	3	1	TIZON	FRAG	RIM	11.7	7% of rim
260	184	437	110E	3	1	TIZON	FRAG	RIM	4	
1482	184	438	110E	3	1	TIZON	FRAG	RIM	7.3	
259	184	1094	110E	4	2	TIZON	FRAG	BODY	4	
913	184	5019	110E	5	1	BUFF	FRAG	BODY	3.1	
1760b	184	5275	110E	5	1	TIZON	FRAG	BODY	12.1	parallel lines/chevron pattern
1642	184	5278	110E	5	11	TIZON	FRAG	BODY	43.2	
646	184	5043	110E	7	1	TIZON	FRAG	BODY	11.3	
909	184	5019	110E	7	15	TIZON	FRAG	BODY	62.9	
963	184	5063	110E	7	3	TIZON	FRAG	BODY	14.6	
1493	184	5062	110E	7	1	TIZON	FRAG	BODY	3.4	
1299	184	5064	110E	7	1	TIZON	FRAG	RIM	6.5	pottery patch
1538	184	6425	110F	3	2	TIZON	FRAG	BODY	4.5	
39	184	6146	110F	4	2	TIZON	FRAG	BODY	7.3	
659	184	1221	110F	6	1	TIZON	FRAG	BODY	3	
1322	184	3321	110F5	3	3	TIZON	FRAG	BODY	27.5	
1135	184	3184	110F5	4	17	TIZON	FRAG	BODY	68	

2011.28	SBCM	Cat #	Unit	Level	Qty	MTRL	COND	Vess Part	Wt/ g	Comments
1291	184	3559	110F5	5	9	TIZON	FRAG	BODY	37.8	
1084	184	3560	110F5	5	1	TIZON	FRAG	RIM	4.4	
363	184	788	110F5	6	4	TIZON	FRAG	BODY	22.9	
947	184	5061	110G	1	5	TIZON	FRAG	BODY	41	
948	184	5061	110G	1	2	TIZON	FRAG	BODY	5.1	
1035	184	5055	110G	1	1	TIZON	FRAG	RIM	12.9	5% of rim
915	184	5057	110G	1	1	TIZON	FRAG	RIM	1.6	
1682	184	5230	110G	2	11	TIZON	FRAG	BODY	86	
905	184	5171	110G	3	2	BUFF	FRAG	BODY	25.2	
902	184	5171	110G	3	1	TIZON	FRAG	BODY	1.2	
1466	184	5068	110G	3	1	TIZON	FRAG	BODY	6	
1549	184	5065	110G	3	1	TIZON	FRAG	RIM	12.8	5% of rim
1602	184	5067	110G	3	1	TIZON	FRAG	RIM	13.8	
1307	184	4779	110G	5	6	TIZON	FRAG	BODY	18.2	
171	184	5810	110G5	1	1	TIZON	FRAG	BODY	9.8	
1711	184	5807	110G5	1	1	TIZON	FRAG	RIM	10	5% of rim
999	184	4866	110G5	3	1	BUFF	FRAG	BODY	3.7	
998	184	4866	110G5	3	4	TIZON	FRAG	BODY	19.8	
924	184	4867	110G5	3	1	TIZON	FRAG	RIM	4.4	5% of rim
457	184	4470	110G5	4	1	TIZON	FRAG	BODY	7.6	
573	184	1910	110H	1	2	BUFF	FRAG	BODY	6.7	
786	184	1872	110H	1	9	TIZON	FRAG	BODY	39.5	

2011.28	SBCM	Cat #	Unit	Level	Qty	MTRL	COND	Vess Part	Wt/ g	Comments
817	184	1873	110H	1	1	TIZON	FRAG	RIM	2.7	
881	184	1912	110H	2	1	BUFF	FRAG	BODY	2.6	
81	184	1912	110H	2	7	TIZON	FRAG	BODY	35.1	
815	184	1918	110H	2	1	TIZON	FRAG	RIM	17.3	5% of rim
553	184	1874	110H	3	1	BUFF	FRAG	BODY	11.5	
552	184	1874	110H	3	3	TIZON	FRAG	BODY	16	
719	184	1876	110H	3	1	TIZON	FRAG	RIM	18.7	5% of rim
185	184	1934	110H	4	3	TIZON	FRAG	BODY	5.6	
72	184	6210	110H5	1	1	TIZON	FRAG	RIM	7	5% of rim
84	184	6208	110H5	1	1	TIZON	FRAG	RIM	8.8	7% of rim
1568	184	5983	110H5	2	1	BUFF	FRAG	BODY	5.3	
1567	184	5983	110H5	2	5	TIZON	FRAG	BODY	39.5	
1560	184	5982	110H5	2	1	TIZON	FRAG	RIM	0	7% of rim
676	184	1920	110H5	5	2	TIZON	FRAG	BODY	4.5	
794	184	1794	110H5	5	5	TIZON	FRAG	BODY	23.9	
157	184	5712	110I	1	8	TIZON	FRAG	BODY	57	
1545	184	5716	110I	1	1	TIZON	FRAG	RIM	18.6	13% of rim
1674	184	5718	110I	1	1	TIZON	FRAG	RIM	11.8	8% of rim
698	184	1419	110I	2	1	TIZON	FRAG	BODY	17.5	
169	184	5990	110I	4	1	TIZON	FRAG	BODY	7	
711	184	1532	110I5	1	1	BUFF	FRAG	BODY	0.7	
71	184	1532	110I5	1	8	TIZON	FRAG	BODY	122.5	

2011.28	SBCM	Cat #	Unit	Level	Qty	MTRL	COND	Vess Part	Wt/ g	Comments
1448	184	1532	110I5	1	1	TIZON	FRAG	BODY	5	
657	184	1534	110I5	1	1	TIZON	FRAG	RIM	2.9	5% of rim
664	184	1533	110I5	1	1	TIZON	FRAG	RIM	6.7	5% of rim
525	184	1535	110I5	1	1	TIZON	FRAG	RIM	5.3	
654	184	1536	110I5	1	1	TIZON	FRAG	RIM	2.2	
1635	184	5561	110I5	2	3	BUFF	FRAG	BODY	4.5	
1634	184	5561	110I5	2	5	TIZON	FRAG	BODY	32.2	
1708	184	5562	110I5	2	1	TIZON	FRAG	RIM	8.9	5% of rim
56	184	6249	110I5	3	2	TIZON	FRAG	BODY	13.1	
37	184	6246	110I5	3	1	TIZON	FRAG	RIM	4.3	
647	184	1522	110I5	4	6	TIZON	FRAG	BODY	41.4	
1059	184	2996	110I5	4	13	TIZON	FRAG	BODY	55.3	
1389	184	2997	110I5	4	1	TIZON	FRAG	RIM	2.5	
33	184	5826	110J5	1	1	BUFF	FRAG	BODY	1.5	
32	184	5826	110J5	1	4	TIZON	FRAG	BODY	34.7	
1519	184	5318	110J5	3	2	TIZON	FRAG	BODY	10	
1632	184	5186	110J5	UNKN	1	TIZON	FRAG	RIM	3.1	
1729	184	5189	110J5		2	TIZON	FRAG	BODY	28.4	
1528	184	5581	115B	3,4	4	BUFF	FRAG	BODY	8.5	
1513	184	5588	115B	3,4	1	BUFF	FRAG	RIM	2.1	5% of rim
1529	184	5581	115B	3,4	2	TIZON	FRAG	BODY	62	parallel lines
149	184	7025	115B	3,4	1	TIZON	FRAG	BODY	19.8	

2011.28	SBCM	Cat #	Unit	Level	Qty	MTRL	COND	Vess Part	Wt/ g	Comments
1527	184	5581	115B	3,4	114	TIZON	FRAG	BODY	491.7	
1601	184	5593	115B	3,4	1	TIZON	FRAG	RIM	3.4	10% of rim
1654	184	5590	115B	3,4	1	TIZON	FRAG	RIM	8.2	6% of rim
1605	184	5587	115B	3,4	1	TIZON	FRAG	RIM	9.1	5% of rim
1686	184	5584	115B	3,4	1	TIZON	FRAG	RIM	9.8	19% of rim
1667	184	5585	115B	3,4	1	TIZON	FRAG	RIM	1.9	5% of rim
1582	184	5583	115B	3,4	1	TIZON	FRAG	RIM	10.3	
1660	184	5592	115B	3,4	1	TIZON	FRAG	RIM	3.4	
1693	184	3354	115B	3,4	1	TIZON	FRAG	RIM	4.5	
134	184	537	115D	1	5	TIZON	FRAG	BODY	4.7	
35	184	538	115D	1	1	TIZON	FRAG	RIM	3.6	
867	184	415	115D	2	55	TIZON	FRAG	BODY	656	
793	184	1561	115D5	2	1	BUFF	FRAG	BODY	2.1	
792	184	1561	115D5	2	13	TIZON	FRAG	BODY	61.7	
721	184	1563	115D5	2	1	TIZON	FRAG	RIM	38.7	5% of rim
522	184	1564	115D5	2	1	TIZON	FRAG	RIM	7.5	12% of rim
1469	184	1562	115D5	2	1	TIZON	FRAG	RIM	43.4	5% of rim
1522	184	405	115D5	3	2	BUFF	FRAG	BODY	10	
1521	184	405	115D5	3	35	TIZON	FRAG	BODY	220.4	
201	184	411	115D5	3	1	TIZON	FRAG	RIM	9.5	16% of rim
163	184	412	115D5	3	1	TIZON	FRAG	RIM	11.6	10% of rim
266	184	414	115D5	3	1	TIZON	FRAG	RIM	6.3	

2011.28	SBCM	Cat #	Unit	Level	Qty	MTRL	COND	Vess Part	Wt/ g	Comments
324	184	413	115D5	3	1	TIZON	FRAG	RIM	7.6	
489	184	407	115D5	3	1	TIZON	FRAG	RIM	7.3	
784	184	763	115D5	4	2	BUFF	FRAG	BODY	8.2	
783	184	763	115D5	4	18	TIZON	FRAG	BODY	102.7	
785	184	763	115D5	4	1	TIZON	FRAG	BODY	70	
169	184	4008	115E	1	17	TIZON	FRAG	BODY	116.3	
283	184	4005	115E	1	1	TIZON	FRAG	RIM	2.4	
46	184	6463	115E	2	1	BUFF	FRAG	BODY	2	
1657	184	5728	115E	2	1	BUFF	FRAG	BODY	0.6	
45	184	6463	115E	2	26	TIZON	FRAG	BODY	174.9	
1726	184	6469	115E	2	1	TIZON	FRAG	RIM	5.2	5% of rim
1704	184	6466	115E	2	1	TIZON	FRAG	RIM	24.4	8% of rim
1646	184	6470	115E	2	1	TIZON	FRAG	RIM	2.9	
1778	184	3984	115E	3	1	BUFF	FRAG	BODY	9.1	
1755	184	3982	115E	3	1	TIZON	FRAG	BODY	20.2	parallel lines
1756	184	3985	115E	3	1	TIZON	FRAG	BODY	7.9	parallel lines
1753	184	3981	115E	3	1	TIZON	FRAG	BODY	19.5	parallel lines
1754	184	3983	115E	3	1	TIZON	FRAG	BODY	5	parallel lines
1760a	184	3980	115E	3	2	TIZON	FRAG	BODY	48.4	parallel lines/chevron pattern
854	184	3979	115E	3	44	TIZON	FRAG	BODY	339.3	
643	184	4886	115E	6	3	TIZON	FRAG	BODY	10.3	
1640	184	5142	115E	7	1	BUFF	FRAG	BODY	1.4	

2011.28	SBCM	Cat #	Unit	Level	Qty	MTRL	COND	Vess Part	Wt/ g	Comments
1639	184	5142	115E	7	7	TIZON	FRAG	BODY	23.6	
1562	184	5140	115E	7	1	TIZON	FRAG	RIM	3.6	
1759	184	6310	115E	9	1	BUFF	FRAG	BODY	13.2	painted horizontal stripes, triangles in brown
665	184	5249	115E	3,4	1	TIZON	FRAG	BODY	0.7	
161	184	396	115F	1	2	BUFF	FRAG	BODY	7.7	
679	184	2162	115F	1	2	BUFF	FRAG	BODY	2.5	
16	184	396	115F	1	21	TIZON	FRAG	BODY	128.6	
678	184	2162	115F	1	12	TIZON	FRAG	BODY	64.3	
906	184	2163	115F	1	1	TIZON	FRAG	RIM	9.9	7% of rim
87	184	403	115F	1	1	TIZON	FRAG	RIM	7	
111	184	4052	115F	2	22	TIZON	FRAG	BODY	104.5	
1377	184	3174	115F	2	1	TIZON	FRAG	BODY	6.9	
1126	184	3175	115F	2	1	TIZON	FRAG	RIM	7.9	5% of rim
217	184	4057	115F	2	1	TIZON	FRAG	RIM	1.6	
399	184	4056	115F	2	1	TIZON	FRAG	RIM	5.6	
1101	184	3017	115F	3	6	TIZON	FRAG	BODY	19.1	
1177	184	2956	115F	4	3	TIZON	FRAG	BODY	16.4	
1294	184	3168	115F	5	2	TIZON	FRAG	BODY	11.8	
811	184	1650	115F5	3	9	TIZON	FRAG	BODY	63	
849	184	1738	115F5	4	9	TIZON	FRAG	BODY	62	
74	184	6166	115F5	5	6	TIZON	FRAG	BODY	38.5	
1552	184	5331	115F5	6	1	TIZON	FRAG	RIM	5.8	

2011.28	SBCM	Cat #	Unit	Level	Qty	MTRL	COND	Vess Part	Wt/ g	Comments
545	184	2133	11O5	1	18	TIZON	FRAG	BODY	68.7	
487	184	267	120-5E	3	1	TIZON	FRAG	BODY	6	
703	184	2345	120D	1	52	TIZON	FRAG	BODY	195.8	
764	184	1982	120D	2	1	BUFF	FRAG	BODY	1.1	
884	184	1982	120D	2	2	BUFF	FRAG	BODY	3.9	
765	184	1982	120D	2	25	TIZON	FRAG	BODY	106.1	
612	184	1192	120D	4	5	TIZON	FRAG	BODY	18.2	
1442	184	7027	120D	4	1	TIZON	FRAG	BODY	2.2	
1524	184	1125	120D	4	10	TIZON	FRAG	BODY	29.8	
825	184	2206	120D	5	2	TIZON	FRAG	BODY	8.1	
477	184	2446	120D	6	38	TIZON	FRAG	BODY	105.2	
478	184	2446	120D	6	3	TIZON	FRAG	BODY	2.9	
325	184	2447	120D	6	1	TIZON	FRAG	RIM	3.4	
642	184	2329	120D	7	1	TIZON	FRAG	BODY	5.3	
116	184	6230	120D5	2	7	TIZON	FRAG	BODY	41.8	
1085	184	5087	120D5	4	3	TIZON	FRAG	BODY	2.7	
568	184	2199	120D5	UNKN	1	TIZON	FRAG	RIM	4.9	
144	184	2200	120D5		2	TIZON	FRAG	BODY	34	
1406	184	2849	120E	1	5	TIZON	FRAG	BODY	31.1	
1449	184	7023	120E	1	1	TIZON	FRAG	BODY	5.8	
1511	184	331	120E	1	9	TIZON	FRAG	BODY	83.9	
1437	184	327	120E	1	1	TIZON	FRAG	RIM	13.6	5% of rim

2011.28	SBCM	Cat #	Unit	Level	Qty	MTRL	COND	Vess Part	Wt/g	Comments
1481	184	328	120E	1	1	TIZON	FRAG	RIM	2.6	
107	184	2543	120E	2	6	TIZON	FRAG	BODY	32	
1214	184	2845	120E	2	43	TIZON	FRAG	BODY	458	
1233	184	2843	120E	2	1	TIZON	FRAG	RIM	4.6	5% of rim
1072	184	2842	120E	2	1	TIZON	FRAG	RIM	12	
1098	184	2841	120E	2	1	TIZON	FRAG	RIM	28	
335	184	264	120E	3	1	TIZON	FRAG	RIM	3.9	5% of rim
455	184	6044	120E	4	4	TIZON	FRAG	BODY	11.3	
51	184	170	120E	4	9	TIZON	FRAG	BODY	75.4	
277	184	172	120E	4	1	TIZON	FRAG	RIM	4	
1765	184	5289	120F	1	1	TIZON	FRAG	BODY	5.6	drill hole
1644	184	5294	120F	1	7	TIZON	FRAG	BODY	41	
1688	184	UNKN	120F	1	6	TIZON	FRAG	BODY	67.7	
.1688e	184	5300	120F	1	2	TIZON	FRAG	BODY	20	
1705	184	5295	120F	1	1	TIZON	FRAG	RIM	11.1	7% of rim
1566	184	5285	120F	1	1	TIZON	FRAG	RIM	4.5	
1688	184		120F	1	6	TIZON	FRAG	RIM	67.7	
1688a	184	5296	120F	1	1	TIZON	FRAG	RIM	23.8	
1688b	184	5297	120F	1	1	TIZON	FRAG	RIM	3.6	
1688c	184	5298	120F	1	1	TIZON	FRAG	RIM	3.3	
1688d	184	5299	120F	1	1	TIZON	FRAG	RIM	17	
456	184	721	120F	2	8	TIZON	FRAG	BODY	57.8	

2011.28	SBCM	Cat #	Unit	Level	Qty	MTRL	COND	Vess Part	Wt/ g	Comments
512	184	725	120F	2	1	TIZON	FRAG	RIM	3.5	
1758a	184	6311	120F	3	1	BUFF	FRAG	BODY	9.6	painted horizontal stripes, triangles in brown
687	184	2015	120F	3	2	BUFF	FRAG	BODY	2.9	
686	184	2015	120F	3	1	BUFF	FRAG	RIM	8.5	etched with an "X"
1758b	184	6312	120F	3	1	TIZON	FRAG	BODY	2.9	painted horizontal stripes, triangles in brown
685	184	847	120F	3	13	TIZON	FRAG	BODY	67.9	
1315	184	3303	120F	4	3	TIZON	FRAG	BODY	13.8	
242	184	1990	120F	5	1	TIZON	FRAG	BODY	4.4	
1290	184	3595	120F	5	1	TIZON	FRAG	RIM	9.4	5% of rim
583	184	1991	120F	5	1	TIZON	FRAG	RIM	4.1	
812	184	2064	120F	7	1	TIZON	FRAG	BODY	2.3	
878	184	5214	120F5	1	36	TIZON	FRAG	BODY	255.9	
1471	184	5213	120F5	1	4	TIZON	FRAG	BODY	59.2	
1472	184	5213	120F5	1	1	TIZON	FRAG	RIM	16.1	5% of rim
1473	184	5213	120F5	1	1	TIZON	FRAG	RIM	16.4	6% of rim
289	184	5215	120F5	1	1	TIZON	FRAG	RIM	4	
982	184	5217	120F5	1	1	TIZON	FRAG	RIM	5	
1474	184	5213	120F5	1	1	TIZON	FRAG	RIM	8.2	
1475	184	5213	120F5	1	1	TIZON	FRAG	RIM	7.8	
13	184	244	120F5	2	42	TIZON	FRAG	BODY	233.8	
1491	184	247	120F5	2	1	TIZON	FRAG	RIM	14.8	10% of rim
377	184	246	120F5	2	1	TIZON	FRAG	RIM	4	

2011.28	SBCM	Cat #	Unit	Level	Qty	MTRL	COND	Vess Part	Wt/ g	Comments
816	184	1488	120F5	3	4	TIZON	FRAG	BODY	16.9	
224	184	2401	120F5	6	1	TIZON	FRAG	BODY	8.2	
1598	184	5307	120F5	6	3	TIZON	FRAG	BODY	10.6	
48	184	928	120F5	7	3	TIZON	FRAG	BODY	6	
319	184	685	120G	1	36	TIZON	FRAG	BODY	146.4	
32	184	685	120G	1	1	TIZON	FRAG	BODY	7.1	
361	184	940	120G	1	32	TIZON	FRAG	BODY	135.9	
362	184	940	120G	1	2	TIZON	FRAG	BODY	3.8	
358	184	949	120G	1	1	TIZON	FRAG	RIM	4.5	5% of rim
211	184	950	120G	1	1	TIZON	FRAG	RIM	4.4	
511	184	693	120G	1	1	TIZON	FRAG	RIM	12.5	
1487	184	948	120G	1	1	TIZON	FRAG	RIM	19.8	
1097	184	3325	120G	2	1	BUFF	FRAG	BODY	2.4	
1096	184	3325	120G	2	5	TIZON	FRAG	BODY	47.8	
773	184	3324	120G	2	1	TIZON	FRAG	RIM	14.6	10% of rim
157	184	453	120G	1,2,3	5	TIZON	FRAG	BODY	36.2	
375	184	458	120G	1,2,3	1	TIZON	FRAG	RIM	9.5	5% of rim
334	184	459	120G	1,2,3	1	TIZON	FRAG	RIM	3.9	
1453	184	460	120G	1,2,3	1	TIZON	FRAG	RIM	6.3	
1114	184	2963	120G	3	8	TIZON	FRAG	BODY	30	
690	184	469	120G5	2	1	TIZON	FRAG	RIM	66.9	
69	184	469	120G5	2	16	TIZON	FRAG	BODY	66.9	

2011.28	SBCM	Cat #	Unit	Level	Qty	MTRL	COND	Vess Part	Wt/ g	Comments
574	184	462	120G5E	2	1	TIZON	FRAG	RIM	2.5	
644	184	2181	120J5		28	TIZON	FRAG	BODY	80	
823	184	1069	125D	2	14	TIZON	FRAG	BODY	83.3	
528	184	1068	125D	2	1	TIZON	FRAG	RIM	5.3	
807	184	1027	125D	3	6	TIZON	FRAG	BODY	29.1	
89	184	1027	125D	3	2	TIZON	FRAG	BODY	1.3	
529	184	1028	125D	3	1	TIZON	FRAG	RIM	2	two diagonal lines
448	184	740	125D5	1	26	TIZON	FRAG	BODY	193.9	
1425	184	745	125D5	1	1	TIZON	FRAG	RIM	14	
115	184	516	125D5	3	11	TIZON	FRAG	BODY	67.2	
210	184	517	125D5	3	1	TIZON	FRAG	RIM	7.1	
1447	184	518	125D5	3	1	TIZON	FRAG	RIM	7.4	
1023	184	4829	125E	1	12	TIZON	FRAG	BODY	68	
986	184	4835	125E	1	1	TIZON	FRAG	RIM	6	5% of rim
1036	184	4830	125E	1	1	TIZON	FRAG	RIM	3.2	
1779	184	544	125E	2	1	TIZON	FRAG	BODY	3.1	drill hole 4mm
237	184	542	125E	2	11	TIZON	FRAG	BODY	136	
916	184	4821	125E	2	17	TIZON	FRAG	BODY	116	
939	184	4826	125E	2	1	TIZON	FRAG	RIM	10	
1020	184	4707	125E	3	1	BUFF	FRAG	BODY	2	painted
173	184	428	125E	3	1	TIZON	FRAG	BODY	0.6	polished
36	184	149	125E	3	22	TIZON	FRAG	BODY	132.8	

2011.28	SBCM	Cat #	Unit	Level	Qty	MTRL	COND	Vess Part	Wt/ g	Comments
172	184	428	125E	3	39	TIZON	FRAG	BODY	113.1	
1019	184	4707	125E	3	5	TIZON	FRAG	BODY	22	
113	184	429	125E	3	1	TIZON	FRAG	RIM	2.9	
484	184	430	125E	3	1	TIZON	FRAG	RIM	4.5	
993	184	4849	125E	4	4	TIZON	FRAG	BODY	24.5	
940	184	4850	125E	4	1	TIZON	FRAG	RIM	4.4	10% of rim
978	184	4600	125G	1	1	TIZON	FRAG	RIM	5.3	5% of rim
938	184	4598	125G	2	30	TIZON	FRAG	BODY	175.4	
1483	184	4602	125G	2	2	TIZON	FRAG	BODY	15.9	
991	184	4604	125G	2	1	TIZON	FRAG	RIM	2.5	5% of rim
979	184	4605	125G	2	1	TIZON	FRAG	RIM	3.2	
980	184	4601	125G	2	1	TIZON	FRAG	RIM	6.7	
1484	184	4602	125G	2	1	TIZON	FRAG	RIM	12.8	
1485	184	4602	125G	2	1	TIZON	FRAG	RIM	7.5	
672	184	2072	125G	1,2,3	13	TIZON	FRAG	BODY	43.5	
775	184	4695	125G5	1	1	TIZON	FRAG	BODY	1.7	
897	184	4696	125G5	1	29	TIZON	FRAG	BODY	92	
898	184	4696	125G5	1	1	TIZON	FRAG	BODY	1.1	
1001	184	4468	125G5	1	9	TIZON	FRAG	BODY	46.7	
992	184	4699	125G5	1	1	TIZON	FRAG	RIM	6.1	5% of rim
1007	184	5011	125G5	3	1	BUFF	FRAG	BODY	1.9	
876	184	4836	125G5	3	1	TIZON	FRAG	BODY	19.9	traces of paint

2011.28	SBCM	Cat #	Unit	Level	Qty	MTRL	COND	Vess Part	Wt/ g	Comments
875	184	4836	125G5	3	22	TIZON	FRAG	BODY	52	
877	184	4836	125G5	3	2	TIZON	FRAG	BODY	3.2	
1006	184	4839	125G5	3	1	TIZON	FRAG	RIM	5.3	5% of rim
997	184	4843	125G5	3	1	TIZON	FRAG	RIM	8.8	
857	184	4676	125G5	4	19	TIZON	FRAG	BODY	146.9	
858	184	4676	125G5	4	1	TIZON	FRAG	BODY	56.2	
122	184	3874	125G5	4	20	TIZON	FRAG	BODY	98	
981	184	4678	125G5	4	1	TIZON	FRAG	RIM	6	5% of rim
1229	184	3873	125G5	4	1	TIZON	FRAG	RIM	5.7	5% of rim
1530	184	4677	125G5	4	1	TIZON	FRAG	RIM	14.8	pottery patch
1025	184	4857	130E	1	1	BUFF	FRAG	BODY	2.3	
1024	184	4857	130E	1	11	TIZON	FRAG	BODY	80	
1494	184	4859	130E	1	1	TIZON	FRAG	RIM	21.1	
994	184	5130	140H5	3	4	TIZON	FRAG	BODY	16.9	
1486	184	5128	140H5	3	4	TIZON	FRAG	BODY	25.5	
384	184	5131	140H5	3	1	TIZON	FRAG	RIM	4	5% of rim
1486	184	5128	140H5	3	1	TIZON	FRAG	RIM	25.5	
899	184	4922	140H5	1,2	1	BUFF	FRAG	BODY	3.3	
9	184	4922	140H5	1,2	16	TIZON	FRAG	BODY	109.9	
901	184	4922	140H5	1,2	1	TIZON	FRAG	BODY	2.1	
1420	184	4923	140H5	1,2	1	TIZON	FRAG	RIM	4.6	
862	184	5052	140I	1	11	TIZON	FRAG	BODY	50.6	

2011.28	SBCM	Cat #	Unit	Level	Qty	MTRL	COND	Vess Part	Wt/ g	Comments
907	184	5050	140I	1	1	TIZON	FRAG	RIM	3.4	
727	184	1728	140I	2	7	TIZON	FRAG	BODY	27.9	
661	184	1723	140I	2	1	TIZON	FRAG	RIM	2.7	
191	184	1802	140I	3	7	TIZON	FRAG	BODY	34.5	
192	184	1802	140I	3	1	TIZON	FRAG	BODY	1.9	
73	184	6520	140I5	1	17	TIZON	FRAG	BODY	64.6	
99	184	6523	140I5	1	1	TIZON	FRAG	RIM	26.5	15% of rim
50	184	6521	140I5	1	1	TIZON	FRAG	RIM	8.1	
91	184	6529	140I5	1	1	TIZON	FRAG	RIM	1.7	
526	184	1145	140I5	2	15	TIZON	FRAG	BODY	60.6	
976	184	4935	140I5	3	3	TIZON	FRAG	BODY	10.9	
587	184	1706	150E	1,2,3,4	12	TIZON	FRAG	BODY	69.6	
668	184	1702	150E	1,2,3,4	1	TIZON	FRAG	RIM	6.7	5% of rim
813	184	1703	150E	1,2,3,4	1	TIZON	FRAG	RIM	8.5	5% of rim
853	184	1701	150E	1,2,3,4	1	TIZON	FRAG	RIM	8	
1445	184	5173	150F5		1	TIZON	FRAG	BODY	6.4	
819	184	4571	150G5	1	1	TIZON	FRAG	RIM	10.9	5% of rim
269	184	4570	150G5	1	1	TIZON	FRAG	RIM	3	
433	184	4572	150G5	1	1	TIZON	FRAG	RIM	5.5	
689	184	4457	150H	1,2	1	TIZON	FRAG	RIM	32.9	
1740	184	5615	155E	1,2,3,4	15	BUFF	FRAG	BODY	4.7	
1739	184	5615	155E	1,2,3,4	5	TIZON	FRAG	BODY	24.3	

2011.28	SBCM	Cat #	Unit	Level	Qty	MTRL	COND	Vess Part	Wt/ g	Comments
302	184	4012	155E	UNKN	9	TIZON	FRAG	BODY	42	
1533	184	4014	155E	UNKN	1	TIZON	FRAG	BODY	10	
558	184	4016	155E	UNKN	1	TIZON	FRAG	RIM	3	
827	184	4015	155E		1	TIZON	FRAG	RIM	5.1	
1649	184	5426	155F5	1,2,3	20	TIZON	FRAG	BODY	70.8	
1604	184	5427	155F5	1,2,3	1	TIZON	FRAG	RIM	3.5	5% of rim
1363	184	3998	155H	3	1	TIZON	FRAG	BODY	2.9	
1311	184	4001	155H	3	1	TIZON	FRAG	RIM	1.9	
312	184	2559	160H	1	11	TIZON	FRAG	BODY	46	
431	184	2560	160H	1	1	TIZON	FRAG	RIM	4.2	
158	184	19	160H	2	8	TIZON	FRAG	BODY	28.8	
1439	184	20	160H	2	1	TIZON	FRAG	RIM	3.3	
769	184	2472	160H5	1	8	TIZON	FRAG	BODY	28.2	
183	184	2524	160H5	2	7	TIZON	FRAG	BODY	40.9	
271	184	2523	160H5	2	1	TIZON	FRAG	RIM	7.5	
1636	184	6370	160I	1	15	TIZON	FRAG	BODY	56	
1706	184	6378	160I	1	1	TIZON	FRAG	RIM	4.7	5% of rim
1441	184	6376	160I	1	1	TIZON	FRAG	RIM	2.9	
707	184	2763	160I	2	10	TIZON	FRAG	BODY	35	
62	184	6060	160I5	1	12	TIZON	FRAG	BODY	94.8	
63	184	6060	160I5	1	2	TIZON	FRAG	BODY	9.7	
1536	184	5524	160I5	2	9	TIZON	FRAG	BODY	54.8	

2011.28	SBCM	Cat #	Unit	Level	Qty	MTRL	COND	Vess Part	Wt/ g	Comments
1537	184	5524	160I5	2	4	TIZON	FRAG	BODY	24.7	
123	184	6440	160J	1	17	TIZON	FRAG	BODY	67.9	
124	184	6440	160J	1	1	TIZON	FRAG	BODY	1.9	
52	184	6398	160J5	1	30	TIZON	FRAG	BODY	151.8	
54	184	6398	160J5	1	2	TIZON	FRAG	BODY	4	
1512	184	6403	160J5	1	1	TIZON	FRAG	RIM	7.2	10% of rim
55	184	6398	160J5	1	1	TIZON	FRAG	RIM	3.8	
1609	184	6404	160J5	1	1	TIZON	FRAG	RIM	6.3	
524	184	1159	160J5	2	16	TIZON	FRAG	BODY	70	
832	184	1160	160J5	2	1	TIZON	FRAG	RIM	4.4	
1738	184	5004	160J5	3	3	TIZON	FRAG	BODY	24.9	
1614	184	5002	160J5	3	1	TIZON	FRAG	RIM	12.9	
1643	184	5006	160J5	3	1	TIZON	FRAG	RIM	5.7	
1663	184	5009	160J5	3	1	TIZON	FRAG	RIM	2	
1516	184	6091	160K	1	3	BUFF	FRAG	BODY	11.2	
1515	184	6091	160K	1	11	TIZON	FRAG	BODY	56	
1539	184	6088	160K	1	1	TIZON	FRAG	BODY	15.3	
78	184	5845	160K	UNKN	1	BUFF	FRAG	BODY	6	
77	184	5845	160K	UNKN	9	TIZON	FRAG	BODY	81.9	
1517	184	6344	160K	UNKN	6	TIZON	FRAG	BODY	34.1	
1561	184	5844	160K	UNKN	1	TIZON	FRAG	RIM	14.7	less than 5%
1600	184	5838	160K	UNKN	1	TIZON	FRAG	RIM	6.8	

2011.28	SBCM	Cat #	Unit	Level	Qty	MTRL	COND	Vess Part	Wt/ g	Comments
1701	184	5834	160K		1	TIZON	FRAG	RIM	12	5% of rim
322	184	565	165H	1	1	BUFF	FRAG	BODY	1.6	
321	184	565	165H	1	23	TIZON	FRAG	BODY	92.2	
903	184	566	165H	1	1	TIZON	FRAG	RIM	3.7	
222	184	620	165H	2	7	TIZON	FRAG	BODY	30.9	
246	184	448	165H	2	12	TIZON	FRAG	BODY	61.4	
307	184	445	165H	2	1	TIZON	FRAG	RIM	6	5% of rim
218	184	446	165H	2	1	TIZON	FRAG	RIM	5.4	
467	184	444	165H	2	1	TIZON	FRAG	RIM	7	
472	184	449	165H	2	1	TIZON	FRAG	RIM	2.3	
468	184	500	165H	3	4	TIZON	FRAG	BODY	27.1	
341	184	557	165H5	1	12	TIZON	FRAG	BODY	45.4	
154	184	563	165H5	1	1	TIZON	FRAG	RIM	4.2	20% of rim
1075	184	2618	165I	2	1	BUFF	FRAG	BODY	6	
1074	184	2618	165I	2	10	TIZON	FRAG	BODY	44	
1188	184	2619	165I	2	1	TIZON	FRAG	RIM	11.6	5% of rim
1360	184	2620	165I	2	1	TIZON	FRAG	RIM	9.8	
1137	184	2645	165I	UNKN	17	TIZON	FRAG	BODY	74	
1136	184	2645	165I	UNKN	1	TIZON	FRAG	RIM	4	10% of rim
1137	184	2645	165I	UNKN	1	TIZON	FRAG	RIM	74	
1395	184	2647	165I	UNKN	1	TIZON	FRAG	RIM	8.4	
294	184	159	165I5	1	19	TIZON	FRAG	BODY	98	

2011.28	SBCM	Cat #	Unit	Level	Qty	MTRL	COND	Vess Part	Wt/ g	Comments
140	184	163	165I5	1	1	TIZON	FRAG	RIM	2	20% of rim
387	184	162	165I5	1	1	TIZON	FRAG	RIM	4	5% of rim
424	184	161	165I5	1	1	TIZON	FRAG	RIM	8.7	5% of rim
173	184	2496	165I5	2	10	TIZON	FRAG	BODY	43.8	
1523	184	2646	165I5	UNKN	1	TIZON	FRAG	RIM	3.7	
286	184	550	165J	1	19	TIZON	FRAG	BODY	108.9	
386	184	553	165J	1	1	TIZON	FRAG	RIM	4	5% of rim
150	184	552	165J	1	1	TIZON	FRAG	RIM	2.9	25% of rim
539	184	551	165J	1	1	TIZON	FRAG	RIM	3.7	5% of rim
1065	184	2755	165J	2	1	TIZON	FRAG	RIM	4	5% of rim
353	184	2837	165J	3	18	TIZON	FRAG	BODY	81.3	
1223	184	2754	165J5	2	13	TIZON	FRAG	BODY	40	
264	184	36	165J5	2	12	TIZON	FRAG	RIM	58.7	
458	184	44	165K	1	6	TIZON	FRAG	BODY	24.5	
145	184	44	165K	1	1	TIZON	FRAG	BODY	3.3	
888	184	2096	170H	1	6	BUFF	FRAG	BODY	17.6	
870	184	2095	170H	1	1	BUFF	FRAG	RIM	1.4	
742	184	2096	170H	1	13	TIZON	FRAG	BODY	36.8	
543	184	2094	170H	1	1	TIZON	FRAG	RIM	14.2	5% of rim
713	184	2093	170H	1	1	TIZON	FRAG	RIM	4.4	
135	184	2233	170H	2	21	TIZON	FRAG	BODY	74.1	
569	184	2242	170H	2	1	TIZON	FRAG	RIM	10	

2011.28	SBCM	Cat #	Unit	Level	Qty	MTRL	COND	Vess Part	Wt/ g	Comments
829	184	1885	170H5	2	4	TIZON	FRAG	BODY	22.6	
1332	184	2586	170I5	1	8	TIZON	FRAG	BODY	32	
1548	184	2585	170I5	1	1	TIZON	FRAG	BODY	5.3	
1548	184	2585	170I5	1	1	TIZON	FRAG	RIM	5.3	pottery patch
1404	184	2771	170I5	2	7	TIZON	FRAG	BODY	18.5	
1462	184	2774	170I5	2	3	TIZON	FRAG	BODY	42.9	
1123	184	2773	170I5	2	1	TIZON	FRAG	RIM	5.3	5% of rim
1415	184	2772	170I5	2	1	TIZON	FRAG	RIM	1.5	7% of rim
651	184	2515	170J	1	5	BUFF	FRAG	BODY	10.4	
850	184	2433	170J	1	3	BUFF	FRAG	BODY	10.5	
843	184	1720	170J	1	17	TIZON	FRAG	BODY	72	
1479	184	2433	170J	1	1	TIZON	FRAG	BODY	12.4	
683	184	2434	170J	1	1	TIZON	FRAG	RIM	4.1	
776	184	2666	170J	2	10	TIZON	FRAG	BODY	26.2	
1086	184	2893	170J	2	4	TIZON	FRAG	BODY	13.5	
1155	184	2850	170J	2	4	TIZON	FRAG	BODY	11.5	
328	184	2667	170J	2	1	TIZON	FRAG	RIM	2.6	
1557	184	2828	170J	UNKN	1	TIZON	FRAG	RIM	0.7	10% of rim
1120	184	2826	170J	UNKN	1	TIZON	FRAG	RIM	3.1	
1052	184	2829	170J		15	TIZON	FRAG	BODY	95.1	
1090	184	2830	170J		1	TIZON	FRAG	RIM	4.5	
475	184	235	170J5	1	1	BUFF	FRAG	BODY	6.9	

2011.28	SBCM	Cat #	Unit	Level	Qty	MTRL	COND	Vess Part	Wt/ g	Comments
396	184	239	170J5	1	1	TIZON	FRAG	RIM	4	5% of rim
634	184	236	170J5	1	1	TIZON	FRAG	RIM	7.2	5% of rim
1419	184	237	170J5	1	1	TIZON	FRAG	RIM	5.6	10% of rim
518	184	238	170J5	1	1	TIZON	FRAG	RIM	3.2	
1115	184	2548	170J5	3	6	TIZON	FRAG	BODY	24.8	
1092	184	2689	170K	1	3	TIZON	FRAG	BODY	9.3	
1296	184	2691	170K	1	1	TIZON	FRAG	RIM	1.9	
1330	184	2883	175H	1	1	BUFF	FRAG	BODY	4	
1329	184	2883	175H	1	22	TIZON	FRAG	BODY	92	
1414	184	2889	175H	1	1	TIZON	FRAG	RIM	3.4	
1159	184	2675	175H	2	9	TIZON	FRAG	BODY	30	
1068	184	2673	175H	2	1	TIZON	FRAG	RIM	2	
1412	184	2595	175H	3	4	TIZON	FRAG	BODY	5.8	
1044	184	2596	175H	3	1	TIZON	FRAG	RIM	5.5	5% of rim
1168	184	3249	175H5	1	11	TIZON	FRAG	BODY	33.8	
1088	184	3606	175H5	3	6	TIZON	FRAG	BODY	27	
1236	184	3603	175H5	3	1	TIZON	FRAG	RIM	5.7	5% of rim
1216	184	2974	175I	1	16	TIZON	FRAG	BODY	50	
1060	184	2975	175I	1	1	TIZON	FRAG	RIM	3.6	5% of rim
1073	184	2976	175I	1	1	TIZON	FRAG	RIM	8	
1314	184	2977	175I	1	1	TIZON	FRAG	RIM	2.3	
1049	184	3344	175I	2	7	TIZON	FRAG	BODY	18	

2011.28	SBCM	Cat #	Unit	Level	Qty	MTRL	COND	Vess Part	Wt/ g	Comments
1180	184	3345	175I	2	1	TIZON	FRAG	RIM	25.9	5% of rim
1461	184	5208	175I5	1	1	TIZON	FRAG	BODY	8.1	
1627	184	5203	175I5	1	16	TIZON	FRAG	BODY	48.3	
1416	184	2978	175I5	1	1	TIZON	FRAG	RIM	4.8	
1712	184	5205	175I5	1	1	TIZON	FRAG	RIM	7.3	
1698	184	5543	175I5	2	1	BUFF	FRAG	RIM	1.3	
1541	184	5552	175I5	2	15	TIZON	FRAG	BODY	68	
1702	184	5545	175I5	2	1	TIZON	FRAG	RIM	15.1	7% of rim
1631	184	5540	175I5	2	1	TIZON	FRAG	RIM	4.4	5% of rim
1725	184	5544	175I5	2	1	TIZON	FRAG	RIM	4.6	
1273	184	3223	175J	2	22	TIZON	FRAG	BODY	72	
138	184	3110	175J	3	2	TIZON	FRAG	BODY	9.5	
1526	184	5528	175J5	1	1	BUFF	FRAG	BODY	1	
1766	184	5531	175J5	1	1	TIZON	FRAG	BODY	5.6	Etched, horizontal/ diagonal lines
1525	184	5528	175J5	1	23	TIZON	FRAG	BODY	108.1	
1728	184	5532	175J5	1	1	TIZON	FRAG	BODY	11.8	
1728	184	5532	175J5	1	1	TIZON	FRAG	RIM	11.8	ground
1510	184	5527	175J5	1	1	TIZON	FRAG	RIM	2.2	
1588	184	5526	175J5	1	1	TIZON	FRAG	RIM	4.2	
1613	184	5529	175J5	1	1	TIZON	FRAG	RIM	2.4	
1727	184	5533	175J5	1	1	TIZON	FRAG	RIM	2.1	
585	184	1679	175J5	2	14	TIZON	FRAG	BODY	46.8	

2011.28	SBCM	Cat #	Unit	Level	Qty	MTRL	COND	Vess Part	Wt/ g	Comments
702	184	1675	175J5	2	1	TIZON	FRAG	RIM	4	5% of rim
732	184	1678	175J5	2	1	TIZON	FRAG	RIM	3.4	5% of rim
599	184	1674	175J5	2	1	TIZON	FRAG	RIM	1.8	
669	184	1676	175J5	2	1	TIZON	FRAG	RIM	2.3	
780	184	1677	175J5	2	1	TIZON	FRAG	RIM	2.2	
159	184	5692	175K	1	12	TIZON	FRAG	BODY	29.5	
1589	184	5696	175K	1	1	TIZON	FRAG	RIM	3.8	
99	184	4559	20G5	2	5	TIZON	FRAG	BODY	35.3	
1477	184	4560	20G5	2	1	TIZON	FRAG	RIM	4.2	
513	184	2296	20J5	1	5	TIZON	FRAG	BODY	11.3	
176	184	2297	20J5	1	1	TIZON	FRAG	RIM	5.2	
895	184	4729	20J5	2	1	BUFF	FRAG	BODY	2.5	
894	184	4729	20J5	2	4	TIZON	FRAG	BODY	8.5	
565	184	2393	20J5	3	2	TIZON	FRAG	BODY	13.2	
566	184	2393	20J5	3	1	TIZON	FRAG	BODY	4.8	
19	184	4978	20N5	1	3	TIZON	FRAG	BODY	20.5	
118	184	5864	30H5	1,2,3	28	TIZON	FRAG	BODY	68.5	
119	184	5864	30H5	1,2,3	1	TIZON	FRAG	BODY	4.4	
38	184	5869	30H5	1,2,3	1	TIZON	FRAG	RIM	1.3	
1687	184	5701	30I	2	18	TIZON	FRAG	BODY	75.9	
912	184	4472	30J5	1	10	TIZON	FRAG	BODY	30	
962	184	4478	30J5	1	1	TIZON	FRAG	BODY	4.6	

2011.28	SBCM	Cat #	Unit	Level	Qty	MTRL	COND	Vess Part	Wt/ g	Comments
987	184	4741	30J5	1	10	TIZON	FRAG	BODY	18.5	
806	184	1412	30J5	3	7	TIZON	FRAG	BODY	35.5	
1252	184	3836	30K5	1	5	TIZON	FRAG	BODY	10	
1316	184	3837	30K5	1	1	TIZON	FRAG	RIM	5.2	6% of rim
1394	184	3822	30K5	2	4	TIZON	FRAG	BODY	9.6	
1733	184	6410	30M	1	3	TIZON	FRAG	BODY	18.3	
1139	184	2937	34F4	UNKN	10	TIZON	FRAG	BODY	122	
1508	184	6483	35H5	1	2	BUFF	FRAG	BODY	5	
1433	184	6489	35H5	1	1	TIZON	FRAG	BODY	5.4	
1507	184	6483	35H5	1	31	TIZON	FRAG	BODY	88	
1434	184	6489	35H5	1	1	TIZON	FRAG	RIM	3.3	
1626	184	6508	35H5	1	1	TIZON	FRAG	RIM	3.9	
9	184	6241	35H5	3	2	TIZON	FRAG	BODY	62	
1591	184	5436	35I	2	8	TIZON	FRAG	BODY	28	
1586	184	5443	35I	2	1	TIZON	FRAG	RIM	6.4	10% of rim
1569	184	5677	35I	3	12	TIZON	FRAG	BODY	25.5	
1514	184	5564	35I	4	3	TIZON	FRAG	BODY	4.7	
1553	184	6358	40H5	1	16	TIZON	FRAG	BODY	70.6	
1603	184	6352	40H5	1	1	TIZON	FRAG	RIM	3.5	
748	184	1215	40H5	3	1	TIZON	FRAG	BODY	2.2	
749	184	1215	40H5	3	7	TIZON	FRAG	BODY	20	
692	184	1756	40I	1	1	BUFF	FRAG	BODY	1.1	

2011.28	SBCM	Cat #	Unit	Level	Qty	MTRL	COND	Vess Part	Wt/ g	Comments
760	184	1898	40I	1	2	BUFF	FRAG	BODY	2.3	
691	184	1756	40I	1	15	TIZON	FRAG	BODY	57.9	
761	184	1898	40I	1	12	TIZON	FRAG	BODY	45.9	
705	184	1900	40I	1	1	TIZON	FRAG	RIM	6.6	9% of rim
834	184	1899	40I	1	1	TIZON	FRAG	RIM	5.3	
677	184	1576	40I	3	8	TIZON	FRAG	BODY	19.2	
839	184	1508	40K	1	1	BUFF	FRAG	BODY	3.1	
837	184	1508	40K	1	9	TIZON	FRAG	BODY	47.9	
629	184	1509	40K	1	1	TIZON	FRAG	RIM	11.3	5% of rim
167	184	1121	40K	2	12	TIZON	FRAG	BODY	55.4	
167	184	1121	40K	2	1	TIZON	FRAG	RIM	55.4	
755	184	1473	40K	3	8	TIZON	FRAG	BODY	19.3	
756	184	1473	40K	3	1	TIZON	FRAG	BODY	1.4	
275	184	1178	45I	4	12	TIZON	FRAG	BODY	49.1	
66	184	1185	45I	4	1	TIZON	FRAG	BODY	2	
852	184	1179	45I	4	1	TIZON	FRAG	BODY	2	
852	184	1179	45I	4	1	TIZON	FRAG	RIM	2	
809	184	1448	4-H5	22	1	BUFF	FRAG	BODY	2.7	
808	184	1448	4-H5	22	6	TIZON	FRAG	BODY	62.5	
866	184	1449	4-H5	22	1	TIZON	FRAG	RIM	2.2	
315	184	2174	55H5	2	20	TIZON	FRAG	BODY	59.5	
839	184	6054	55H5	3	3	TIZON	FRAG	BODY	3.9	

2011.28	SBCM	Cat #	Unit	Level	Qty	MTRL	COND	Vess Part	Wt/ g	Comments
84	184	6054	55H5	3	12	TIZON	FRAG	BODY	34	
388	184	2272	55H5	4,5	5	TIZON	FRAG	BODY	10	
625	184	2045	55I	1	2	BUFF	FRAG	BODY	4.3	
624	184	2045	55I	1	35	TIZON	FRAG	BODY	87.4	
695	184	2002	55I	2	8	TIZON	FRAG	BODY	22.3	
483	184	650	55I	3	12	TIZON	FRAG	BODY	31.3	
1428	184	650	55I	3	1	TIZON	FRAG	BODY	2	
1429	184	5198	55I	3	1	TIZON	FRAG	BODY	5.4	
47	184	651	55I	3	1	TIZON	FRAG	RIM	12.5	
725	184	519	55I	4	2	BUFF	FRAG	BODY	2.1	
233	184	585	55I	4	1	TIZON	FRAG	BODY	1.5	
434	184	615	55I	4	9	TIZON	FRAG	BODY	53.2	
435	184	615	55I	4	1	TIZON	FRAG	BODY	2	
724	184	519	55I	4	4	TIZON	FRAG	BODY	30.2	
1342	184	2479	55I	4	11	TIZON	FRAG	BODY	50	
824	184	2407	55I	6,7	2	TIZON	FRAG	BODY	8.6	
1208	184	2750	55I5	2	1	BUFF	FRAG	BODY	1.2	
1207	184	2750	55I5	2	23	TIZON	FRAG	BODY	60	
1272	184	2751	55I5	2	1	TIZON	FRAG	RIM	6.9	
35	184	2715	55I5	3	8	TIZON	FRAG	BODY	29	
1337	184	2816	55I5	4	9	TIZON	FRAG	BODY	36	
842	184	1720	55J	1	1	BUFF	FRAG	BODY	1.6	

2011.28	SBCM	Cat #	Unit	Level	Qty	MTRL	COND	Vess Part	Wt/ g	Comments
882	184	1720	55J	1	7	BUFF	FRAG	BODY	17.3	
841	184	1720	55J	1	24	TIZON	FRAG	BODY	55.5	
699	184	1624	55J	2	8	TIZON	FRAG	BODY	14.8	
557	184	1625	55J	2	1	TIZON	FRAG	RIM	5.1	15% of rim
314	184	4432	55J5	3	9	TIZON	FRAG	BODY	33.7	
798	184	1970	55J5	3	4	TIZON	FRAG	BODY	6.5	
95	184	4375	55J5	4	9	TIZON	FRAG	BODY	64.6	
1041	184	4711	55J5	4	10	TIZON	FRAG	BODY	31.7	
1409	184	4376	55J5	4	1	TIZON	FRAG	RIM	10	
549	184	4440	55J5	5	2	TIZON	FRAG	BODY	6.3	
54	184	1610	55K	1	13	TIZON	FRAG	BODY	41.4	
641	184	1398	55K	2	13	TIZON	FRAG	BODY	32.3	
73	184	1405	55K	3	5	TIZON	FRAG	BODY	41.7	
655	184	1381	55K	4	6	TIZON	FRAG	BODY	17	
635	184	1382	55K	4	1	TIZON	FRAG	RIM	2.1	
716	184	1591	55K5	1	12	TIZON	FRAG	BODY	24	
767	184	1664	55K5	2	3	BUFF	FRAG	BODY	5.6	
766	184	1664	55K5	2	2	TIZON	FRAG	BODY	2.8	
768	184	1664	55K5	2	26	TIZON	FRAG	BODY	79.7	
667	184	1659	55K5	2	1	TIZON	FRAG	RIM	3.5	5% of rim
782	184	1661	55K5	2	1	TIZON	FRAG	RIM	8	10% of rim
744	184	2348	58E	UNKN	5	TIZON	FRAG	BODY	6.6	

2011.28	SBCM	Cat #	Unit	Level	Qty	MTRL	COND	Vess Part	Wt/ g	Comments
745	184	2348	58E	UNKN	26	TIZON	FRAG	BODY	66.6	
.887a	184	2348	58E	UNKN	1	TIZON	FRAG	BODY	1.9	
630	184	2349	58E		1	TIZON	FRAG	RIM	6.2	
797	184	1970	60E	1	1	BUFF	FRAG	BODY	1.2	
796	184	1970	60E	1	16	TIZON	FRAG	BODY	51.4	
357	184	2225	60E	1	1	TIZON	FRAG	RIM	12.8	5% of rim
626	184	1971	60E	1	1	TIZON	FRAG	RIM	3.2	
922	184	1972	60E	1	1	TIZON	FRAG	RIM	16	
576	184	2226	60F5	1	14	TIZON	FRAG	BODY	47.5	
586	184	2226	60F5	1	1	TIZON	FRAG	BODY	1.9	
59	184	4175	60F5	1	1	TIZON	FRAG	BODY	2.5	
869	184	1945	60H5	1	1	BUFF	FRAG	BODY	1.4	
868	184	1945	60H5	1	9	TIZON	FRAG	BODY	39.4	
555	184	1948	60H5	1	1	TIZON	FRAG	RIM	8	10% of rim
575	184	2083	60H5	3	4	TIZON	FRAG	BODY	25.6	
1446	184	2084	60H5	3	1	TIZON	FRAG	RIM	11.5	
656	184	2023	60H5	4	7	TIZON	FRAG	BODY	32	
746	184	2055	60H5	6	1	BUFF	FRAG	BODY	2.3	
747	184	2055	60H5	6	18	TIZON	FRAG	BODY	53	
550	184	2058	60H5	6	1	TIZON	FRAG	RIM	5.1	10% of rim
1451	184	2056	60H5	6	1	TIZON	FRAG	RIM	14.1	
154	184	6199	60I	8	8	TIZON	FRAG	BODY	34	

2011.28	SBCM	Cat #	Unit	Level	Qty	MTRL	COND	Vess Part	Wt/ g	Comments
121	184	6200	60I	UNKN	1	TIZON	FRAG	RIM	5.2	
1465	184	7026	60I		1	TIZON	FRAG	BODY	17.9	
83	184	5909	60I5	3	9	TIZON	FRAG	BODY	40.3	
71	184	5908	60I5	3	1	TIZON	FRAG	RIM	2.3	
102	184	5817	60J	2	5	TIZON	FRAG	BODY	21	
85	184	5822	60J	2	1	TIZON	FRAG	RIM	1.4	5% of rim
288	184	375	60J5	2	18	TIZON	FRAG	BODY	91	
479	184	374	60J5	2	1	TIZON	FRAG	RIM	3	
693	184	2426	60J5	5	1	TIZON	FRAG	BODY	1	
1003	184	5161	60M8-N2	1,2	1	BUFF	FRAG	BODY	1.4	
1002	184	5161	60M8-N2	1,2	9	TIZON	FRAG	BODY	44.5	
927	184	4553	65E	1	1	BUFF	FRAG	BODY	3	
921	184	4553	65E	1	36	TIZON	FRAG	BODY	155	
1431	184	4554	65E	1	1	TIZON	FRAG	BODY	6.3	
943	184	4549	65E	1	1	TIZON	FRAG	RIM	8.5	5% of rim
1457	184	2927	65E	1	1	TIZON	FRAG	RIM	5.6	
930	184	4818	65E	2	8	BUFF	FRAG	BODY	31.7	
923	184	4818	65E	2	16	TIZON	FRAG	BODY	57.4	
960	184	4813	65E	2	1	TIZON	FRAG	RIM	3.2	
287	184	1	65H5	1	12	TIZON	FRAG	BODY	84.9	
1452	184	7022	65H5	2	1	TIZON	FRAG	BODY	12.1	
152	184	10	65H5	2	12	TIZON	FRAG	BODY	96.4	

2011.28	SBCM	Cat #	Unit	Level	Qty	MTRL	COND	Vess Part	Wt/ g	Comments
261	184	94	65H5	5	1	BUFF	FRAG	BODY	2	
463	184	79	65H5	3,4	8	TIZON	FRAG	BODY	43.1	
98	184	6181	65I	1	22	TIZON	FRAG	BODY	59.5	
14	184	6187	65I	1	1	TIZON	FRAG	RIM	4.6	
51	184	6194	65I	1	1	TIZON	FRAG	RIM	6.6	
93	184	6190	65I	1	1	TIZON	FRAG	RIM	1.4	
1246	184	6111	65I	2	1	TIZON	FRAG	BODY	2.8	
1736	184	6101	65I	2	8	TIZON	FRAG	BODY	16.1	
1681	184	6136	65I	3	7	TIZON	FRAG	BODY	28	
1719	184	6131	65I	3	1	TIZON	FRAG	RIM	3.8	
494	184	836	65I	4	1	BUFF	FRAG	BODY	1.5	
757	184	1557	65I	4	6	TIZON	FRAG	BODY	19.3	
758	184	1557	65I	4	3	TIZON	FRAG	BODY	12	
1565	184	6319	65I	4	1	TIZON	FRAG	BODY	1.1	
822	184	1558	65I	4	1	TIZON	FRAG	RIM	13.5	5% of rim
1732	184	6392	65I	5	8	TIZON	FRAG	BODY	25.1	
1625	184	6396	65I	5	1	TIZON	FRAG	RIM	1.1	
1661	184	6388	65I	5	1	TIZON	FRAG	RIM	5.2	
1707	184	6391	65I	5	1	TIZON	FRAG	RIM	0.9	
355	184	57	65J5	UNKN	1	TIZON	FRAG	RIM	2.8	5% of rim
226	184	58	65J5	UNKN	1	TIZON	FRAG	RIM	8.1	
459	184	56	65J5		21	TIZON	FRAG	BODY	99.3	polished

2011.28	SBCM	Cat #	Unit	Level	Qty	MTRL	COND	Vess Part	Wt/ g	Comments
1478	184	577	70-5	2	1	TIZON	FRAG	RIM	9.5	
1622	184	6535	70C	1	1	BUFF	FRAG	BODY	2.7	
1621	184	6535	70C	1	38	TIZON	FRAG	BODY	111	
1623	184	5303	70C	1	4	TIZON	FRAG	BODY	5.6	
1158	184	3849	70C	2	2	BUFF	FRAG	BODY	6	
1607	184	5948	70C	2	1	BUFF	FRAG	BODY	4	
1157	184	3849	70C	2	24	TIZON	FRAG	BODY	34	
1606	184	5948	70C	2	16	TIZON	FRAG	BODY	60	
1261	184	3848	70C	2	1	TIZON	FRAG	RIM	1.1	
709	184	1692	70C	3	12	TIZON	FRAG	BODY	36.4	
845	184	1834	70C5	1	25	TIZON	FRAG	BODY	118	
536	184	1842	70C5	1	1	TIZON	FRAG	RIM	1.6	
673	184	1836	70C5	1	1	TIZON	FRAG	RIM	3.1	
674	184	1835	70C5	1	1	TIZON	FRAG	RIM	3.7	
1116	184	3894	70C5	2	33	TIZON	FRAG	BODY	156.4	
1746	184	3895	70C5	2	1	TIZON	FRAG	BODY	4.1	
1411	184	3891	70C5	2	1	TIZON	FRAG	RIM	3	5% of rim
1392	184	3893	70C5	2	1	TIZON	FRAG	RIM	10	6% of rim
1081	184	3892	70C5	2	1	TIZON	FRAG	RIM	4.7	
1190	184	3890	70C5	2	1	TIZON	FRAG	RIM	3.1	
704	184	1784	70C5	3	7	TIZON	FRAG	BODY	19.1	
547	184	1785	70C5	3	1	TIZON	FRAG	RIM	7.6	5% of rim

2011.28	SBCM	Cat #	Unit	Level	Qty	MTRL	COND	Vess Part	Wt/ g	Comments
632	184	1825	70C5	5	5	TIZON	FRAG	BODY	10.5	
395	184	1826	70C5	5	1	TIZON	FRAG	RIM	2	5% of rim
1	184	5987	70D	1	13	TIZON	FRAG	BODY	54.7	
865	184	1665	70D	2	26	TIZON	FRAG	BODY	120.5	
240	184	694	70E	1	2	BUFF	FRAG	BODY	8.1	
241	184	6455	70E	1	1	BUFF	FRAG	RIM	0.8	
239	184	694	70E	1	21	TIZON	FRAG	BODY	96.7	
1265	184	2864	70E	2	10	TIZON	FRAG	BODY	26	
125	184	2741	70E	3	8	TIZON	FRAG	BODY	30	
1403	184	2740	70E	3	1	TIZON	FRAG	RIM	1.8	
1633	184	5628	70E	5	26	TIZON	FRAG	BODY	86.2	
1633	184	5628	70E	5	1	TIZON	FRAG	RIM	86.2	
1685	184	5637	70E	5	1	TIZON	FRAG	RIM	6.8	
1375	184	2551	70E	6	3	TIZON	FRAG	BODY	4.1	
1048	184	2732	70I	2	1	TIZON	FRAG	BODY	4.8	
1048	184	2732	70I	2	1	TIZON	FRAG	RIM	4.8	
1179	184	2655	70I5	4	2	TIZON	FRAG	BODY	4.9	
1401	184	2656	70I5	4	1	TIZON	FRAG	RIM	5.5	
486	184	89	70J	1	2	TIZON	FRAG	BODY	2.8	
1397	184	2504	70J5	1	1	BUFF	FRAG	BODY	0.9	
1396	184	2504	70J5	1	6	TIZON	FRAG	BODY	17.1	
423	184	25	70J5	2	9	TIZON	FRAG	BODY	28.3	

2011.28	SBCM	Cat #	Unit	Level	Qty	MTRL	COND	Vess Part	Wt/ g	Comments
235	184	29	70J5	2	1	TIZON	FRAG	RIM	7.4	5% of rim
942	184	4597	75C	1	1	TIZON	FRAG	BODY	2.3	
1028	184	4592	75C	1	31	TIZON	FRAG	BODY	98	
243	184	4396	75C	2	4	TIZON	FRAG	BODY	22.1	
984	184	4398	75C	2	1	TIZON	FRAG	RIM	6.4	
995	184	4401	75C	2	1	TIZON	FRAG	RIM	5.4	
1563	184	4400	75C	2	1	TIZON	FRAG	RIM	17.5	
1334	184	3311	75C	4	10	TIZON	FRAG	BODY	44	
1435	184	3312	75C	4	1	TIZON	FRAG	RIM	10.4	
397	184	4422	75C	6	3	TIZON	FRAG	BODY	11	
493	184	841	75C5	2	3	TIZON	FRAG	BODY	24.1	
1338	184	3580	75C5	3	3	TIZON	FRAG	BODY	12	
1355	184	3583	75C5	3	1	TIZON	FRAG	RIM	6	5% of rim
323	184	5073	75C5	5	3	TIZON	FRAG	BODY	15.7	
4882	184	5076	75C5	5	1	TIZON	FRAG	RIM	0.7	etched 2 parallel, diagonal lines
1178	184	3195	75C5	6	1	TIZON	FRAG	BODY	6.6	
1333	184	3565	75D	1	8	TIZON	FRAG	BODY	32	
1121	184	3568	75D	1	1	TIZON	FRAG	RIM	5.8	
1164	184	3201	75D	5	2	TIZON	FRAG	BODY	6.3	
1402	184	3210	75D	6	2	TIZON	FRAG	BODY	4.5	
1021	184	4526	75D5	3	19	TIZON	FRAG	BODY	134	
441	184	4529	75D5	3	1	TIZON	FRAG	RIM	6	5% of rim

2011.28	SBCM	Cat #	Unit	Level	Qty	MTRL	COND	Vess Part	Wt/ g	Comments
933	184	4528	75D5	3	1	TIZON	FRAG	RIM	32.7	5% of rim
967	184	4527	75D5	3	1	TIZON	FRAG	RIM	46.3	5% of rim
1544	184	3258	75D5	5	7	TIZON	FRAG	BODY	35.8	
1087	184	3262	75D5	5	1	TIZON	FRAG	RIM	12.6	5% of rim
1735	184	5655	75E	1	5	TIZON	FRAG	BODY	18.2	
1596	184	5654	75E	1	1	TIZON	FRAG	RIM	2.6	7% of rim
1656	184	5663	75E	1	1	TIZON	FRAG	RIM	1.6	
945	184	4795	75E	2	1	BUFF	FRAG	BODY	5.1	
944	184	4795	75E	2	9	TIZON	FRAG	BODY	66.8	
1008	184	4854	75E	6	2	TIZON	FRAG	BODY	11.7	
75	184	5929	75E	7	2	TIZON	FRAG	BODY	4.5	
104	184	4624	75H	1,2	6	TIZON	FRAG	BODY	25.4	
221	184	4619	75H	1,2	1	TIZON	FRAG	RIM	29	10% of rim
1454	184	4617	75H	1,2	1	TIZON	FRAG	RIM	11.1	
1455	184	4617	75H	1,2	1	TIZON	FRAG	RIM	6.4	
925	184	4758	75H5	1	1	BUFF	FRAG	BODY	4.5	
926	184	4758	75H5	1	5	TIZON	FRAG	BODY	22.6	
929	184	4758	75H5	1	1	TIZON	FRAG	BODY	5.3	
1022	184	4782	75H5	2	13	TIZON	FRAG	BODY	166	
1476	184	4785	75H5	2	3	TIZON	FRAG	BODY	29.9	
961	184	4789	75H5	2	1	TIZON	FRAG	RIM	7.5	
1648	184	5572	75I	1	19	TIZON	FRAG	BODY	71	

2011.28	SBCM	Cat #	Unit	Level	Qty	MTRL	COND	Vess Part	Wt/ g	Comments
1718	184	5579	75I	1	1	TIZON	FRAG	RIM	4.4	5% of rim
1542	184	5570	75I	1	1	TIZON	FRAG	RIM	13.5	7% of rim
1547	184	5569	75I	1	1	TIZON	FRAG	RIM	9.3	
1624	184	5578	75I	1	1	TIZON	FRAG	RIM	5.6	
1673	184	5573	75I	1	1	TIZON	FRAG	RIM	1.4	
471	184	192	75I	3	21	TIZON	FRAG	BODY	142.1	
464	184	189	75I5	3	1	TIZON	FRAG	RIM	3	
1676	184	5595	75J	1	20	TIZON	FRAG	BODY	100.5	
1655	184	5604	75J	1	1	TIZON	FRAG	RIM	16	15% of rim
584	184	1437	75N	1	9	TIZON	FRAG	BODY	27.4	
606	184	1436	75N	1	1	TIZON	FRAG	RIM	3.3	
1099	184	3766	80D	1	12	TIZON	FRAG	BODY	47.7	
1209	184	3840	80D	2	5	TIZON	FRAG	BODY	32	
1467	184	3839	80D	2	2	TIZON	FRAG	BODY	7.2	
1167	184	3863	80D	3	8	TIZON	FRAG	BODY	31.9	
1205	184	3800	80D	4	19	TIZON	FRAG	BODY	156	
1077	184	3799	80D	4	1	TIZON	FRAG	RIM	6	5% of rim
1094	184	3743	80D	5	2	TIZON	FRAG	BODY	6.9	
772	184	3747	80D	5	1	TIZON	FRAG	RIM	28.2	8% of rim
124	184	3616	80D	6	1	TIZON	FRAG	BODY	8	
425	184	4904	80D5	1	7	TIZON	FRAG	BODY	3.5	
426	184	4904	80D5	1	1	TIZON	FRAG	BODY	3	

2011.28	SBCM	Cat #	Unit	Level	Qty	MTRL	COND	Vess Part	Wt/g	Comments
62	184	2362	80D5	1	6	TIZON	FRAG	BODY	18.5	
977	184	4905	80D5	1	1	TIZON	FRAG	RIM	13.6	5% of rim
114	184	4902	80D5	1	1	TIZON	FRAG	RIM	6	
619	184	2363	80D5	1	1	TIZON	FRAG	RIM	1.3	
252	184	802	80D5	2	1	BUFF	FRAG	BODY	1.6	
848	184	1076	80D5	2	1	BUFF	FRAG	BODY	2	
251	184	802	80D5	2	11	TIZON	FRAG	BODY	52.5	
847	184	1076	80D5	2	23	TIZON	FRAG	BODY	134	
309	184	1078	80D5	2	1	TIZON	FRAG	RIM	7	5% of rim
509	184	811	80D5	2	1	TIZON	FRAG	RIM	8.4	10% of rim
519	184	810	80D5	2	1	TIZON	FRAG	RIM	13.7	11% of rim
577	184	1077	80D5	2	1	TIZON	FRAG	RIM	8.6	
871	184	1708	80D5	5	28	TIZON	FRAG	BODY	104	
236	184	5117	80E	1	12	TIZON	FRAG	BODY	63.4	
1653	184	5355	80E	1	7	TIZON	FRAG	BODY	28	
892	184	5113	80E	1	1	TIZON	FRAG	RIM	7.2	5% of rim
1611	184	5353	80E	1	1	TIZON	FRAG	RIM	2.3	
1204	184	4040	80E	2	2	BUFF	FRAG	BODY	4	
1203	184	4040	80E	2	11	TIZON	FRAG	BODY	34	
1217	184	4032	80E	2	6	TIZON	FRAG	BODY	20	
1581	184	5313	80E	2	5	TIZON	FRAG	BODY	16.9	
1141	184	4033	80E	2	1	TIZON	FRAG	RIM	1.7	

2011.28	SBCM	Cat #	Unit	Level	Qty	MTRL	COND	Vess Part	Wt/ g	Comments
1187	184	4045	80E	2	1	TIZON	FRAG	RIM	5.4	
1722	184	5314	80E	2	1	TIZON	FRAG	RIM	1.2	
880	184	5027	80E	3	2	BUFF	FRAG	BODY	8.2	
1680	184	6114	80E	3	1	BUFF	FRAG	BODY	5	
506	184	607	80E	3	1	BUFF	FRAG	RIM	2.5	
379	184	606	80E	3	19	TIZON	FRAG	BODY	88	
38	184	606	80E	3	1	TIZON	FRAG	BODY	4	
879	184	5027	80E	3	14	TIZON	FRAG	BODY	77.2	
1679	184	6114	80E	3	14	TIZON	FRAG	BODY	45	
1773	184	608	80E	3	1	TIZON	FRAG	RIM	2.8	pottery patch
1550	184	6118	80E	3	1	TIZON	FRAG	RIM	5.5	
1615	184	6117	80E	3	1	TIZON	FRAG	RIM	10	
1119	184	4065	80E	4	1	BUFF	FRAG	BODY	1.8	
1118	184	4065	80E	4	23	TIZON	FRAG	BODY	156.8	
382	184	4046	80E	4	1	TIZON	FRAG	RIM	6	5% of rim
831	184	4066	80E	4	1	TIZON	FRAG	RIM	31.5	
1132	184	4076	80E	4	1	TIZON	FRAG	RIM	10.1	
1151	184	4077	80E	4	1	TIZON	FRAG	RIM	7	
1744	184	5232	80E	5	1	BUFF	FRAG	BODY	0.9	
1608	184	5265	80E	5	10	TIZON	FRAG	BODY	34	
1743	184	5232	80E	5	1	TIZON	FRAG	BODY	1.1	
1647	184	5233	80E	5	1	TIZON	FRAG	RIM	8.8	6% of rim

2011.28	SBCM	Cat #	Unit	Level	Qty	MTRL	COND	Vess Part	Wt/ g	Comments
1658	184	5271	80E	5	1	TIZON	FRAG	RIM	1.3	
1675	184	6217	80E	7	5	TIZON	FRAG	BODY	15.6	
1617	184	5150	80E	1,2	9	TIZON	FRAG	BODY	59.4	
338	184	706	80H	1	7	TIZON	FRAG	BODY	28.3	
339	184	706	80H	1	1	TIZON	FRAG	BODY	3.9	
34	184	706	80H	1	1	TIZON	FRAG	BODY	5.4	
414	184	750	80H	2	1	BUFF	FRAG	BODY	5.5	
413	184	750	80H	2	12	TIZON	FRAG	BODY	115.3	
381	184	594	80H	3	5	TIZON	FRAG	BODY	44	
578	184	1500	80H5	1,2	9	TIZON	FRAG	BODY	60.9	
579	184	1500	80H5	1,2	1	TIZON	FRAG	BODY	2.2	
58	184	1500	80H5	1,2	1	TIZON	FRAG	BODY	3	
581	184	1500	80H5	1,2	1	TIZON	FRAG	BODY	2	
731	184	1503	80H5	1,2	1	TIZON	FRAG	RIM	5	
582	184	1864	80I	1	17	TIZON	FRAG	BODY	106.8	
601	184	1864	80I	1	1	TIZON	FRAG	BODY	2	
633	184	1859	80I	1	1	TIZON	FRAG	RIM	3.8	5% of rim
637	184	1860	80I	1	1	TIZON	FRAG	RIM	3.8	
1275	184	4123	80I	2	1	TIZON	FRAG	BODY	1.7	
1295	184	4119	80I	2	10	TIZON	FRAG	BODY	40.4	
1393	184	4030	80I	2	10	TIZON	FRAG	BODY	40	
27	184	421	84-85H	6	15	TIZON	FRAG	BODY	47.7	

2011.28	SBCM	Cat #	Unit	Level	Qty	MTRL	COND	Vess Part	Wt/ g	Comments
41	184	132	85D	1	9	TIZON	FRAG	BODY	32	
149	184	353	85D	3	10	TIZON	FRAG	BODY	29.5	
454	184	314	85D5	4	1	BUFF	FRAG	BODY	1.4	
465	184	314	85D5	4	7	TIZON	FRAG	BODY	35.5	
508	184	320	85D5	4	1	TIZON	FRAG	RIM	3.6	5% of rim
142	184	114	85D5	UNKN	1	BUFF	FRAG	BODY	1.6	
141	184	114	85D5	UNKN	1	TIZON	FRAG	BODY	0.6	
143	184	114	85D5	UNKN	20	TIZON	FRAG	BODY	30.5	
311	184	115	85D5		1	TIZON	FRAG	RIM	5	5% of rim
49	184	107	85E	1	3	TIZON	FRAG	BODY	3.8	
253	184	220	85E	1	4	TIZON	FRAG	BODY	23.5	
317	184	362	85E	1	14	TIZON	FRAG	BODY	75.6	
318	184	362	85E	1	2	TIZON	FRAG	BODY	7	
622	184	2671	85E	1	11	TIZON	FRAG	BODY	33.7	
1281	184	2802	85E	2	4	TIZON	FRAG	BODY	3.1	
258	184	273	85E	3	1	BUFF	FRAG	BODY	0.6	
795	184	2365	85E	3	13	TIZON	FRAG	BODY	11.8	
208	184	134	85E	4	5	BUFF	FRAG	BODY	19.8	
209	184	134	85E	4	31	TIZON	FRAG	BODY	260.3	
502	184	147	85E	4	7	TIZON	FRAG	BODY	36.1	
507	184	209	85E	4	1	TIZON	FRAG	BODY	1.2	
1559	184	5940	85E	4	6	TIZON	FRAG	BODY	30	

2011.28	SBCM	Cat #	Unit	Level	Qty	MTRL	COND	Vess Part	Wt/ g	Comments
147	184	148	85E	4	1	TIZON	FRAG	RIM	29.4	
443	184	1065	85E	6	1	TIZON	FRAG	RIM	6	5% of rim
444	184	986	85E	6	1	TIZON	FRAG	RIM	2.5	
706	184	1963	85E	2,3	9	TIZON	FRAG	RIM	37.9	9% of rim
164	184	218	85E	3, 4	12	TIZON	FRAG	BODY	55.7	
165	184	219	85E	3, 4	1	TIZON	FRAG	RIM	2.4	
1267	184	2946	85F	1	8	TIZON	FRAG	BODY	38	
1695	184	2947	85F	1	1	TIZON	FRAG	RIM	9.3	
371	184	885	85F	2	9	TIZON	FRAG	BODY	35.9	
184	184	888	85F	2	1	TIZON	FRAG	RIM	0.9	
273	184	508	85F	4	1	TIZON	FRAG	BODY	2.3	
941	184	4910	85F5	1	13	TIZON	FRAG	BODY	44.3	
105	184	3578	85F5	3	2	TIZON	FRAG	BODY	12	
1737	184	5898	85F5	3	5	TIZON	FRAG	BODY	16.4	
1612	184	5896	85F5	3	1	TIZON	FRAG	RIM	7.7	5% of rim
61	184	6271	85F5	4	1	BUFF	FRAG	BODY	1.8	
6	184	6271	85F5	4	1	TIZON	FRAG	BODY	2.5	
1005	184	4975	85F5	5	3	TIZON	FRAG	BODY	9.3	
988	184	4972	85F5	5	1	TIZON	FRAG	RIM	4	
89	184	6285	85F5	6	1	TIZON	FRAG	BODY	3.2	
91	184	4757	85G	1	1	TIZON	FRAG	BODY	2.1	
996	184	4755	85G	2	1	BUFF	FRAG	RIM	3.3	

2011.28	SBCM	Cat #	Unit	Level	Qty	MTRL	COND	Vess Part	Wt/ g	Comments
891	184	4748	85G	2	37	TIZON	FRAG	BODY	202.3	
1009	184	4751	85G	2	1	TIZON	FRAG	RIM	2.5	
1628	184	6429	85G	3	17	TIZON	FRAG	BODY	69.2	
537	184	1768	85G	3	1	TIZON	FRAG	RIM	2.8	
1418	184	6431	85G	3	1	TIZON	FRAG	RIM	10	
1042	184	4808	85G	4	9	TIZON	FRAG	BODY	22	
1033	184	4688	85G	5	5	TIZON	FRAG	BODY	6.3	
694	184	1544	85G5	1	1	TIZON	FRAG	BODY	12	
804	184	1602	85G5	2	8	TIZON	FRAG	BODY	39.2	
700	184	1597	85G5	2	1	TIZON	FRAG	RIM	10	5% of rim
770	184	1767	85G5	3	2	BUFF	FRAG	BODY	8.2	
889	184	1767	85G5	3	1	BUFF	FRAG	BODY	5.2	
771	184	1767	85G5	3	11	TIZON	FRAG	BODY	58.4	
351	184	63	85G5	4	16	TIZON	FRAG	BODY	41.9	
352	184	63	85G5	4	2	TIZON	FRAG	BODY	3.5	
966	184	4668	85G5	4	2	TIZON	FRAG	BODY	15.5	
228	184	909	85H	1	1	TIZON	FRAG	BODY	4.9	etched cross-hatch pattern
229	184	909	85H	1	7	TIZON	FRAG	BODY	28.5	
238	184	908	85H	1	1	TIZON	FRAG	RIM	52.4	18% of rim
439	184	371	85H	2	6	TIZON	FRAG	BODY	22	
44	184	371	85H	2	1	TIZON	FRAG	BODY	2	
206	184	482	85H	3	1	BUFF	FRAG	BODY	3.9	

2011.28	SBCM	Cat #	Unit	Level	Qty	MTRL	COND	Vess Part	Wt/ g	Comments
205	184	482	85H	3	1	TIZON	FRAG	BODY	4.5	
207	184	482	85H	3	6	TIZON	FRAG	BODY	53.5	
1460	184	488	85H	3	1	TIZON	FRAG	RIM	4.1	5% of rim
645	184	2181	85H5	1	24	TIZON	FRAG	BODY	122.6	
1772	184	2377	85H5	1	1	TIZON	FRAG	RIM	4	drill hole 5mm diameter
554	184	2374	85H5	1	1	TIZON	FRAG	RIM	39	10% of rim
544	184	2375	85H5	1	1	TIZON	FRAG	RIM	2.4	
602	184	2376	85H5	1	1	TIZON	FRAG	RIM	7.9	
187	184	627	85I	1	5	TIZON	FRAG	BODY	18.3	
250	184	628	85I	1	1	TIZON	FRAG	RIM	13.6	5% of rim
272	184	716	85I	2	4	TIZON	FRAG	BODY	26.3	
36	184	531	85I	3,4	5	TIZON	FRAG	BODY	15.7	
419	184	361	90D	1	12	TIZON	FRAG	BODY	46.9	
42	184	361	90D	1	1	TIZON	FRAG	BODY	2	
1498	184	3355	90D	2	1	BUFF	FRAG	RIM	4	
1331	184	3353	90D	2	25	TIZON	FRAG	BODY	64	
1692	184	3354	90D	2	1	TIZON	FRAG	RIM	3.4	
1293	184	3533	90D	4	4	BUFF	FRAG	BODY	4.8	
1292	184	3533	90D	4	41	TIZON	FRAG	BODY	172.8	
1357	184	3101	90D	4	3	TIZON	FRAG	BODY	10	
1045	184	3528	90D	4	1	TIZON	FRAG	RIM	5.1	
1047	184	3529	90D	4	1	TIZON	FRAG	RIM	3	

2011.28	SBCM	Cat #	Unit	Level	Qty	MTRL	COND	Vess Part	Wt/ g	Comments
1100	184	3530	90D	4	1	TIZON	FRAG	RIM	10.9	
393	184	359	90D5	1	1	BUFF	FRAG	BODY	1.3	
392	184	359	90D5	1	16	TIZON	FRAG	BODY	44	
28	184	203	90D5	3	21	TIZON	FRAG	BODY	134.4	
79	184	69	90D5	4	6	TIZON	FRAG	BODY	43.6	
8	184	69	90D5	4	2	TIZON	FRAG	BODY	10	
427	184	47	90D5	4	2	TIZON	FRAG	BODY	23.5	
1430	184	50	90D5	4	1	TIZON	FRAG	RIM	7.5	6% of rim
1763	184	49	90D5	4	1	TIZON	FRAG	RIM	8.1	partial drill hole
225	184	72	90D5	4	1	TIZON	FRAG	RIM	4.2	
349	184	51	90D5	4	1	TIZON	FRAG	RIM	9	
1061	184	3532	90D5	4	1	TIZON	FRAG	RIM	3.7	
1062	184	3531	90D5	4	1	TIZON	FRAG	RIM	5.6	
215	184	4462	90E	1	2	TIZON	FRAG	BODY	1.7	
421	184	366	90E	1	16	TIZON	FRAG	BODY	69.4	
422	184	366	90E	1	1	TIZON	FRAG	BODY	4.4	
1112	184	3295	90E	1	3	TIZON	FRAG	BODY	10.4	
336	184	833	90E	2	2	BUFF	FRAG	BODY	11.9	
412	184	834	90E	2	1	BUFF	FRAG	RIM	1.8	
546	184	2282	90E	2	1	TIZON	FRAG	BODY	0.2	
681	184	2070	90E	2	16	TIZON	FRAG	BODY	60.9	
1083	184	3155	90E	2	1	TIZON	FRAG	BODY	2.3	

2011.28	SBCM	Cat #	Unit	Level	Qty	MTRL	COND	Vess Part	Wt/ g	Comments
1154	184	2896	90E	2	10	TIZON	FRAG	BODY	53.7	
1213	184	3271	90E	2	5	TIZON	FRAG	BODY	28	
436	184	835	90E	2	1	TIZON	FRAG	RIM	2	
680	184	2069	90E	2	1	TIZON	FRAG	RIM	34.1	
1165	184	3278	90E	2	1	TIZON	FRAG	RIM	4.1	
872	184	800	90E	3	1	BUFF	FRAG	BODY	4	
40	184	801	90E	3	1	BUFF	FRAG	RIM	3.2	5% of rim
199	184	2317	90E	3	21	TIZON	FRAG	BODY	88.1	
2	184	2317	90E	3	1	TIZON	FRAG	BODY	69.4	
873	184	800	90E	3	24	TIZON	FRAG	BODY	170	
594	184	2318	90E	3	1	TIZON	FRAG	RIM	2.2	
337	184	837	90E	4	1	BUFF	FRAG	BODY	6.3	painted
814	184	2021	90E	4	1	TIZON	FRAG	BODY	4.3	
146	184	2416	90E	5	1	BUFF	FRAG	RIM	8.5	
743	184	2411	90E	5	5	TIZON	FRAG	BODY	15	
1206	184	3216	90E	5	11	TIZON	FRAG	BODY	32	
181	184	2040	90E	6	5	TIZON	FRAG	BODY	17.7	
1218	184	3538	90E	6	3	TIZON	FRAG	BODY	12	
1237	184	3584	90E	8	1	TIZON	FRAG	BODY	1.2	
563	184	2158	90E	9	1	TIZON	FRAG	BODY	2	
762	184	2098	90E	10	2	TIZON	FRAG	BODY	13.4	
712	184	2068	90F	1	11	TIZON	FRAG	BODY	64.5	

2011.28	SBCM	Cat #	Unit	Level	Qty	MTRL	COND	Vess Part	Wt/ g	Comments
598	184	2361	90F	2	2	TIZON	FRAG	BODY	26	
1284	184	3696	90F	2	1	TIZON	FRAG	RIM	14.1	10% of rim
1082	184	2901	90F	2	1	TIZON	FRAG	RIM	2.5	5% of rim
94	184	6207	90F	3	1	TIZON	FRAG	BODY	6.5	
95	184	6207	90F	3	5	TIZON	FRAG	BODY	33.3	
97	184	213	90F	3	2	TIZON	FRAG	BODY	17.5	
989	184	4683	90F5	1	5	TIZON	FRAG	BODY	15.5	
1026	184	4805	90F5	2	16	TIZON	FRAG	BODY	90	
1027	184	4736	90F5	2	7	TIZON	FRAG	BODY	24	
918	184	4664	90F5	3	15	TIZON	FRAG	BODY	58.5	
920	184	4655	90F5	3	1	TIZON	FRAG	RIM	5.2	
860	184	4649	90F5	5,6	1	BUFF	FRAG	BODY	4.8	
859	184	4649	90F5	5,6	21	TIZON	FRAG	BODY	97	
1489	184	4650	90F5	5,6	1	TIZON	FRAG	BODY	4	
949	184	4645	90F5	5,6	1	TIZON	FRAG	RIM	13.5	15% of rim
1038	184	4651	90F5	5,6	1	TIZON	FRAG	RIM	8	5% of rim
1029	184	4647	90F5	5,6	1	TIZON	FRAG	RIM	6	5% of rim
244	184	4643	90F5	5,6	1	TIZON	FRAG	RIM	3.6	
946	184	4646	90F5	5,6	1	TIZON	FRAG	RIM	6.4	
904	184	4480	90G	1	10	TIZON	FRAG	BODY	42.9	
985	184	4483	90G	1	1	TIZON	FRAG	BODY	2.3	
648	184	4533	90G	2	5	TIZON	FRAG	BODY	22	

2011.28	SBCM	Cat #	Unit	Level	Qty	MTRL	COND	Vess Part	Wt/ g	Comments
896	184	4539	90G	2	9	TIZON	FRAG	BODY	55.1	
1532	184	4537	90G	2	1	TIZON	FRAG	BODY	3.3	
1248	184	4538	90G	2	1	TIZON	FRAG	RIM	3.3	
1043	184	4640	90G	3	8	TIZON	FRAG	BODY	40	
220	184	4635	90G	3	1	TIZON	FRAG	RIM	8.8	
212	184	4544	90G	4	3	TIZON	FRAG	BODY	4.2	
306	184	4412	90G	5	1	TIZON	FRAG	BODY	7.2	
617	184	2414	90G	5	1	TIZON	FRAG	RIM	3.1	5% of rim
861	184	4425	90G5	1	19	TIZON	FRAG	BODY	88.2	
15	184	4426	90G5	1	1	TIZON	FRAG	BODY	5.6	
636	184	4724	90G5	3	3	TIZON	FRAG	BODY	12.5	
1670	184	5642	90H	1	2	BUFF	FRAG	BODY	6	
1424	184	5644	90H	1	3	TIZON	FRAG	BODY	14	
1669	184	5642	90H	1	16	TIZON	FRAG	BODY	58	
1638	184	5645	90H	1	1	TIZON	FRAG	RIM	14.1	6% of rim
1665	184	5650	90H	1	1	TIZON	FRAG	RIM	2.1	
893	184	4519	90H	3	12	TIZON	FRAG	BODY	47.4	
232	184	4408	90H	4	3	TIZON	FRAG	BODY	19.7	
567	184	4417	90H	5	1	TIZON	FRAG	BODY	2.3	
76	184	6382	90H5	1	14	TIZON	FRAG	BODY	68.1	
1554	184	6386	90H5	1	1	TIZON	FRAG	RIM	3.9	5% of rim
1518	184	6299	90H5	2	1	BUFF	FRAG	RIM	2.3	

2011.28	SBCM	Cat #	Unit	Level	Qty	MTRL	COND	Vess Part	Wt/ g	Comments
1618	184	6297	90H5	2	13	TIZON	FRAG	BODY	45.1	
1535	184	6300	90H5	2	1	TIZON	FRAG	RIM	4.3	
1720	184	6301	90H5	2	1	TIZON	FRAG	RIM	12.7	
57	184	6144	90H5	3	10	TIZON	FRAG	BODY	40.4	
58	184	6144	90H5	3	1	TIZON	FRAG	BODY	3.6	
59	184	6144	90H5	3	1	TIZON	FRAG	BODY	2.9	
66	184	6143	90H5	3	1	TIZON	FRAG	RIM	7.2	
1731	184	6328	90H5	4	5	TIZON	FRAG	BODY	18.2	
1664	184	6329	90H5	4	1	TIZON	FRAG	RIM	4.2	
103	184	6238	90H5	5	4	TIZON	FRAG	BODY	10.4	
1678	184	5410	90I	1	2	BUFF	FRAG	BODY	4.1	
1677	184	5410	90I	1	25	TIZON	FRAG	BODY	87.8	
1700	184	5413	90I	1	1	TIZON	FRAG	RIM	5.1	5% of rim
1443	184	5411	90I	1	1	TIZON	FRAG	RIM	15.4	
1630	184	5414	90I	1	1	TIZON	FRAG	RIM	3.7	
1689	184	5412	90I	1	1	TIZON	FRAG	RIM	3.9	
1703	184	5409	90I	1	1	TIZON	FRAG	RIM	12.8	
1652	184	5619	90I	2	19	TIZON	FRAG	BODY	132	
542	184	1809	90I	3	8	TIZON	FRAG	BODY	26.4	
1488	184	1809	90I	3	1	TIZON	FRAG	BODY	4.2	
671	184	1811	90I	3	1	TIZON	FRAG	RIM	4.8	5% of rim
723	184	1810	90I	3	1	TIZON	FRAG	RIM	3	5% of rim

2011.28	SBCM	Cat #	Unit	Level	Qty	MTRL	COND	Vess Part	Wt/ g	Comments
1713	184	5621	90I	UNKN	1	TIZON	FRAG	RIM	6.9	5% of rim
589	184	4175	90I5	1	1	BUFF	FRAG	BODY	3.7	
588	184	4175	90I5	1	19	TIZON	FRAG	BODY	116.5	
570	184	4177	90I5	1	1	TIZON	FRAG	RIM	8.5	5% of rim
1259	184	4165	90I5	2	14	TIZON	FRAG	BODY	82	
1276	184	4164	90I5	2	1	TIZON	FRAG	RIM	3.6	5% of rim
428	184	4163	90I5	2	1	TIZON	FRAG	RIM	6.9	
1241	184	4154	90I5	3	6	TIZON	FRAG	BODY	62	
1413	184	4152	90I5	3	1	TIZON	FRAG	RIM	4.3	
1585	184	4153	90I5	3	1	TIZON	FRAG	RIM	5	
1358	184	4148	90J	1	7	TIZON	FRAG	BODY	38.8	
1319	184	4144	90J	2	3	TIZON	FRAG	BODY	3.6	
128	184	4149	90J5	1	1	TIZON	FRAG	BODY	5.2	
726	184	2307	95D	2	20	TIZON	FRAG	BODY	59.9	
1546	184	2308	95D	2	1	TIZON	FRAG	RIM	3.7	
535	184	1998	95D	5	6	TIZON	FRAG	BODY	16.6	
256	184	2193	95D	3,4	36	TIZON	FRAG	BODY	113.9	
257	184	2193	95D	3,4	3	TIZON	FRAG	BODY	8	
615	184	2190	95D	3,4	1	TIZON	FRAG	RIM	2.4	
372	184	96	95D5	2	17	TIZON	FRAG	BODY	0.7	
373	184	96	95D5	2	1	TIZON	FRAG	BODY	0.8	
591	184	2126	95D5	2	1	TIZON	FRAG	BODY	6.7	

2011.28	SBCM	Cat #	Unit	Level	Qty	MTRL	COND	Vess Part	Wt/ g	Comments
171	184	2436	95D5	3	2	BUFF	FRAG	BODY	8.5	
17	184	2436	95D5	3	31	TIZON	FRAG	BODY	129.3	
790	184	2118	95D5	4	1	BUFF	FRAG	BODY	0.8	
789	184	2118	95D5	4	45	TIZON	FRAG	BODY	165.2	
564	184	2119	95D5	4	1	TIZON	FRAG	RIM	7.5	5% of rim
603	184	2120	95D5	4	1	TIZON	FRAG	RIM	11	
497	184	339	95D5	5	1	BUFF	FRAG	BODY	1.2	
496	184	339	95D5	5	34	TIZON	FRAG	BODY	94.1	
498	184	339	95D5	5	1	TIZON	FRAG	BODY	1.3	
914	184	334	95D5	5	1	TIZON	FRAG	RIM	3.4	5% of rim
155	184	332	95D5	5	1	TIZON	FRAG	RIM	1.4	
496	184	339	95D5	5	1	TIZON	FRAG	RIM	94.1	
516	184	333	95D5	5	1	TIZON	FRAG	RIM	5.3	
247	184	355	95E	1	1	BUFF	FRAG	BODY	0.9	
248	184	355	95E	1	79	TIZON	FRAG	BODY	268.2	
1063	184	3095	95E	1	114	TIZON	FRAG	BODY	324	
1185	184	3080	95E	1	1	TIZON	FRAG	RIM	20.2	4% of rim
1095	184	3081	95E	1	1	TIZON	FRAG	RIM	4.3	5% of rim
1078	184	3089	95E	1	1	TIZON	FRAG	RIM	2	7% of rim
197	184	357	95E	1	1	TIZON	FRAG	RIM	3	
198	184	356	95E	1	1	TIZON	FRAG	RIM	7.1	
248	184	355	95E	1	1	TIZON	FRAG	RIM	268.2	

2011.28	SBCM	Cat #	Unit	Level	Qty	MTRL	COND	Vess Part	Wt/ g	Comments
1069	184	3086	95E	1	1	TIZON	FRAG	RIM	1.5	
1285	184	3088	95E	1	1	TIZON	FRAG	RIM	1.5	
1138	184	3042	95E	2	70	TIZON	FRAG	BODY	330	
1124	184	3038	95E	2	1	TIZON	FRAG	RIM	10.5	5% of rim
1170	184	3029	95E	2	1	TIZON	FRAG	RIM	10.8	5% of rim
1194	184	3032	95E	2	1	TIZON	FRAG	RIM	17.2	5% of rim
1371	184	3037	95E	2	1	TIZON	FRAG	RIM	4.4	5% of rim
1264	184	3041	95E	2	1	TIZON	FRAG	RIM	22	5% of rim
1130	184	3036	95E	2	1	TIZON	FRAG	RIM	2.2	
1138	184	3042	95E	2	1	TIZON	FRAG	RIM	330	
1175	184	3039	95E	2	1	TIZON	FRAG	RIM	4	
1231	184	3034	95E	2	1	TIZON	FRAG	RIM	5.5	
1271	184	3033	95E	2	1	TIZON	FRAG	RIM	4.2	
1318	184	3030	95E	2	1	TIZON	FRAG	RIM	4.4	
1372	184	3035	95E	2	1	TIZON	FRAG	RIM	1.2	
1699	184	3031	95E	2	1	TIZON	FRAG	RIM	4.3	
1166	184	3135	95E	3	5	TIZON	FRAG	BODY	8.5	
777	184	2140	95E	4	4	BUFF	FRAG	BODY	9.2	
597	184	2144	95E	4	1	BUFF	FRAG	RIM	5.2	5% of rim
593	184	2142	95E	4	1	BUFF	FRAG	RIM	2.4	
778	184	2140	95E	4	1	TIZON	FRAG	BODY	50	
779	184	2140	95E	4	41	TIZON	FRAG	BODY	245.3	

2011.28	SBCM	Cat #	Unit	Level	Qty	MTRL	COND	Vess Part	Wt/ g	Comments
1039	184	4498	95E	4	5	TIZON	FRAG	BODY	16.4	
305	184	4500	95E	4	1	TIZON	FRAG	RIM	1.6	5% of rim
485	184	4499	95E	4	1	TIZON	FRAG	RIM	3.9	5% of rim
621	184	2141	95E	4	1	TIZON	FRAG	RIM	8.1	7% of rim
631	184	2143	95E	4	1	TIZON	FRAG	RIM	2.5	
1093	184	3286	95E	5	6	TIZON	FRAG	BODY	19.7	
1219	184	3231	95E	5	4	TIZON	FRAG	BODY	14	
151	184	2212	95E	6	2	TIZON	FRAG	BODY	3.9	
1349	184	3334	95E	6	2	TIZON	FRAG	BODY	3.9	
1149	184	3267	95E	7	1	TIZON	FRAG	BODY	4.1	
595	184	6045	95E	8	1	TIZON	FRAG	BODY	1	
267	184	2337	95E	UNKN	1	TIZON	FRAG	RIM	3.3	
231	184	2336	95E		6	TIZON	FRAG	BODY	20.4	
1066	184	3087	95E	1	1	TIZON	FRAG	RIM	8	
1067	184	3040	95E	2	1	TIZON	FRAG	RIM	2	
1064	184	3095	95E5/ 152	1	3	BUFF	FRAG	BODY	12	
1221	184	3105	95G	3	4	TIZON	FRAG	BODY	4	
828	184	1627	95G	4	2	TIZON	FRAG	BODY	4.3	
708	184	1498	95G5	3	4	TIZON	FRAG	BODY	5.8	
614	184	1530	95G5	4	2	TIZON	FRAG	BODY	14.3	
556	184	1734	95H	2	4	TIZON	FRAG	BODY	25.8	
532	184	1735	95H	2	1	TIZON	FRAG	RIM	7.1	

2011.28	SBCM	Cat #	Unit	Level	Qty	MTRL	COND	Vess Part	Wt/ g	Comments
548	184	1686	95H	3,4	3	TIZON	FRAG	BODY	13.7	
1741	184	5258	95H5	2	7	TIZON	FRAG	BODY	38.4	
1226	184	3630	95I	1	1	BUFF	FRAG	RIM	18	5% of rim
1339	184	3625	95I	1	18	TIZON	FRAG	BODY	112	
1129	184	3629	95I	1	1	TIZON	FRAG	RIM	8.4	
1506	184	3626	95I	1	1	TIZON	FRAG	RIM	6.7	
787	184	1110	95I	2	1	TIZON	FRAG	BODY	6.4	
788	184	1108	95I	2	11	TIZON	FRAG	BODY	88	
787	184	1110	95I	2	1	TIZON	FRAG	RIM	6.4	
1468	184	5336	95I	3	1	TIZON	FRAG	BODY	3.5	
1671	184	5337	95I	3	4	TIZON	FRAG	BODY	34	
67	184	1612	95I	4	1	TIZON	FRAG	BODY	5.2	
1212	184	3768	95I5	1	1	BUFF	FRAG	BODY	14	
1211	184	3768	95I5	1	10	TIZON	FRAG	BODY	54	
1107	184	3769	95I5	1	1	TIZON	FRAG	RIM	7.5	
1387	184	3770	95I5	1	1	TIZON	FRAG	RIM	7.8	
1341	184	3816	95I5	2	2	BUFF	FRAG	BODY	4	
134	184	3816	95I5	2	6	TIZON	FRAG	BODY	38	
527	184	1109	95I5	2	1	TIZON	FRAG	RIM	9.1	5% of rim
1620	184	5774	95I5	3	1	BUFF	FRAG	BODY	3.4	
1619	184	5774	95I5	3	9	TIZON	FRAG	BODY	57.8	
1597	184	5775	95I5	3	1	TIZON	FRAG	RIM	6.8	5% of rim

2011.28	SBCM	Cat #	Unit	Level	Qty	MTRL	COND	Vess Part	Wt/ g	Comments
1637	184	5400	95I5	4	5	TIZON	FRAG	BODY	20.9	
696	184	1642	95J	1	5	TIZON	FRAG	BODY	22.9	
541	184	1643	95J	1	1	TIZON	FRAG	RIM	3.9	
561	184	1593	95J5	2	1	BUFF	FRAG	BODY	2.7	
56	184	1593	95J5	2	1	TIZON	FRAG	BODY	2.5	
1335	184	3609	9D	3	10	TIZON	FRAG	BODY	32	
1668	184	5512	E5	5	1	BUFF	FRAG	RIM	4.3	6% of rim
1558	184	5514	E5	5	5	TIZON	FRAG	BODY	15.9	
1201	184	3162	H0E5	3	21	TIZON	FRAG	BODY	94	
855	184	4769	TEST	UNKN	19	TIZON	FRAG	BODY	53	
919	184	4655	TEST	UNKN	20	TIZON	FRAG	BODY	82.6	
917	184	4655	TEST	UNKN	2	TIZON	FRAG	BODY	2.6	
445	184	4771	TEST	UNKN	1	TIZON	FRAG	RIM	4	5% of rim
662	184	4773	TEST	UNKN	1	TIZON	FRAG	RIM	2.1	
864	184	4774	TEST	UNKN	1	TIZON	FRAG	RIM	4.7	
1336	184	3116	Tile 11	2	7	TIZON	FRAG	BODY	40	
21	184	6452	UNKN	1	4	BUFF	FRAG	BODY	8.1	
22	184	6452	UNKN	1	4	BUFF	FRAG	BODY	4.2	
23	184	6452	UNKN	1	1	BUFF	FRAG	BODY	4.8	
1031	184	2722	UNKN	1	16	BUFF	FRAG	BODY	98	
18	184	6452	UNKN	1	192	TIZON	FRAG	BODY	697	glued
19	184	6452	UNKN	1	2	TIZON	FRAG	BODY	56.4	glued

2011.28	SBCM	Cat #	Unit	Level	Qty	MTRL	COND	Vess Part	Wt/ g	Comments
2	184	6452	UNKN	1	2	TIZON	FRAG	BODY	8.6	glued
284	184	659	UNKN	1	21	TIZON	FRAG	BODY	99.1	
285	184	659	UNKN	1	2	TIZON	FRAG	BODY	10.3	
103	184	2722	UNKN	1	217	TIZON	FRAG	BODY	922	
1032	184	2722	UNKN	1	5	TIZON	FRAG	BODY	14	
24	184	115	UNKN	1	1	TIZON	FRAG	RIM	15.4	10% of rim
279	184	664	UNKN	1	1	TIZON	FRAG	RIM	10	5% of rim
1328	184	2879	UNKN	2	3	BUFF	FRAG	BODY	14	
1326	184	2879	UNKN	2	2	TIZON	FRAG	BODY	20	drill hole 4mm
1325	184	2879	UNKN	2	34	TIZON	FRAG	BODY	536	
1327	184	2879	UNKN	2	1	TIZON	FRAG	BODY	70	
1797	184	2880	UNKN	2	3	TIZON	FRAG	BODY	13.8	
1258	184	2875	UNKN	2	1	TIZON	FRAG	RIM	35.7	18% of rim
1257	184	2872	UNKN	2	1	TIZON	FRAG	RIM	29.4	5% of rim
1298	184	2870	UNKN	2	1	TIZON	FRAG	RIM	10.4	5% of rim
1071	184	2873	UNKN	2	1	TIZON	FRAG	RIM	6	7% of rim
738	184	2871	UNKN	2	1	TIZON	FRAG	RIM	42.3	9% of rim
1504	184	3245	UNKN	2	1	TIZON	FRAG	RIM	2.7	
1202	184	3162	UNKN	3	1	BUFF	FRAG	BODY	8	
846	184	1099	UNKN	4	22	TIZON	FRAG	BODY	138	
1422	184	1099	UNKN	4	2	TIZON	FRAG	BODY	20	
833	184	1100	UNKN	4	1	TIZON	FRAG	RIM	11	10% of rim

2011.28	SBCM	Cat #	Unit	Level	Qty	MTRL	COND	Vess Part	Wt/ g	Comments
1	184	4708	UNKN	5	9	TIZON	FRAG	BODY	39.7	
1011	184	4709	UNKN	5	1	TIZON	FRAG	RIM	2.3	
1464	184	5163	UNKN	1,2	1	TIZON	FRAG	RIM	5.1	
1225	184	3756	UNKN	3,4,5	12	TIZON	FRAG	BODY	68	
403	184	287	UNKN	UNKN	6	BUFF	FRAG	BODY	16.7	rounded edges
7	184	5765	UNKN	UNKN	3	BUFF	FRAG	BODY	42.8	
8	184	5765	UNKN	UNKN	1	BUFF	FRAG	BODY	22.9	
10	184	5765	UNKN	UNKN	1	BUFF	FRAG	BODY	9.2	
26	184	6175	UNKN	UNKN	5	BUFF	FRAG	BODY	25.8	
30	184	6071	UNKN	UNKN	5	BUFF	FRAG	BODY	13	
31	184	6071	UNKN	UNKN	9	BUFF	FRAG	BODY	15.4	
43	184	5811	UNKN	UNKN	11	BUFF	FRAG	BODY	19	
44	184	5811	UNKN	UNKN	16	BUFF	FRAG	BODY	32.8	
106	184	5191	UNKN	UNKN	1	BUFF	FRAG	BODY	5.3	
109	184	4491	UNKN	UNKN	13	BUFF	FRAG	BODY	26.2	
131	184	984	UNKN	UNKN	3	BUFF	FRAG	BODY	30	
406	184	287	UNKN	UNKN	1	BUFF	FRAG	BODY	0.7	
407	184	287	UNKN	UNKN	3	BUFF	FRAG	BODY	18	
408	184	287	UNKN	UNKN	6	BUFF	FRAG	BODY	32.7	
452	184	479	UNKN	UNKN	11	BUFF	FRAG	BODY	76.9	
551	184	5120	UNKN	UNKN	1	BUFF	FRAG	BODY	5.8	
608	184	1688	UNKN	UNKN	2	BUFF	FRAG	BODY	18.6	

2011.28	SBCM	Cat #	Unit	Level	Qty	MTRL	COND	Vess Part	Wt/ g	Comments
609	184	1688	UNKN	UNKN	1	BUFF	FRAG	BODY	4.5	
610	184	1688	UNKN	UNKN	2	BUFF	FRAG	BODY	1.8	
611	184	1688	UNKN	UNKN	1	BUFF	FRAG	BODY	5.1	
653	184	1251	UNKN	UNKN	1	BUFF	FRAG	BODY	1.8	
885	184	1925	UNKN	UNKN	1	BUFF	FRAG	BODY	9	
936	184	4238	UNKN	UNKN	108	BUFF	FRAG	BODY	290	
951	184	5092	UNKN	UNKN	1	BUFF	FRAG	BODY	6.1	
959	184	4092	UNKN	UNKN	14	BUFF	FRAG	BODY	52	
964	184	5015	UNKN	UNKN	1	BUFF	FRAG	BODY	3.7	
965	184	5176	UNKN	UNKN	13	BUFF	FRAG	BODY	32	
969	184	5200	UNKN	UNKN	5	BUFF	FRAG	BODY	20.9	
972	184	3965	UNKN	UNKN	22	BUFF	FRAG	BODY	79.7	
975	184	3966	UNKN	UNKN	91	BUFF	FRAG	BODY	334	
1015	184	4111	UNKN	UNKN	21	BUFF	FRAG	BODY	80	
1199	184	3791	UNKN	UNKN	7	BUFF	FRAG	BODY	32	
1239	184	3616	UNKN	UNKN	1	BUFF	FRAG	BODY	6	
1254	184	4201	UNKN	UNKN	1	BUFF	FRAG	BODY	65.6	
1256	184	4201	UNKN	UNKN	1	BUFF	FRAG	BODY	8.8	
1313	184	2786	UNKN	UNKN	3	BUFF	FRAG	BODY	9.9	
1572	184	5119	UNKN	UNKN	4	BUFF	FRAG	BODY	17	
1575	184	5159	UNKN	UNKN	1	BUFF	FRAG	BODY	0.7	
1576	184	5037	UNKN	UNKN	7	BUFF	FRAG	BODY	9.4	

2011.28	SBCM	Cat #	Unit	Level	Qty	MTRL	COND	Vess Part	Wt/ g	Comments
1578	184	5202	UNKN	UNKN	5	BUFF	FRAG	BODY	14.6	
1583	184	6416	UNKN	UNKN	1	BUFF	FRAG	BODY	16.8	
1593	184	5450	UNKN	UNKN	10	BUFF	FRAG	BODY	40	
1599	184	6415	UNKN	UNKN	1	BUFF	FRAG	BODY	16.2	
1769	184	6313	UNKN	UNKN	1	BUFF	FRAG	BODY	12.5	
800	184	4109	UNKN	UNKN	1	BUFF	FRAG	RIM	6	5%
145	184	310	UNKN	UNKN	1	BUFF	FRAG	RIM	40.5	20%
562	184	4105	UNKN	UNKN	1	BUFF	FRAG	RIM	32.3	10% of rim
92	184	6156	UNKN	UNKN	1	BUFF	FRAG	RIM	6.6	20% of rim
374	184	477	UNKN	UNKN	1	BUFF	FRAG	RIM	3.1	5% of rim
886	184	1925	UNKN	UNKN	1	BUFF	FRAG	RIM	5.3	5% of rim
1345	184	4244	UNKN	UNKN	1	BUFF	FRAG	RIM	1.6	5% of rim
1142	184	3710	UNKN	UNKN	1	BUFF	FRAG	RIM	2.7	5% of buff
734	184	295	UNKN	UNKN	1	BUFF	FRAG	RIM	33.4	more than 25% of buff
1012	184	3966	UNKN	UNKN	3	BUFF	FRAG	RIM	12	painted
1757	184	UNKN	UNKN	UNKN	9	BUFF	FRAG	RIM	68.2	painted horizontal stripes, triangles in brown
1758	184	UNKN	UNKN	UNKN	2	BUFF	FRAG	RIM	12.4	painted horizontal stripes, triangles in brown
139	184	4100	UNKN	UNKN	1	BUFF	FRAG	RIM	38.9	
180	184	299	UNKN	UNKN	1	BUFF	FRAG	RIM	9.2	
1146	184	4191	UNKN	UNKN	1	BUFF	FRAG	RIM	3.8	
1184	184	4243	UNKN	UNKN	1	BUFF	FRAG	RIM	1.6	
1495	184	4192	UNKN	UNKN	1	BUFF	FRAG	RIM	3.7	

2011.28	SBCM	Cat #	Unit	Level	Qty	MTRL	COND	Vess Part	Wt/ g	Comments
1767	184	5449	UNKN	UNKN	2	TIZON	FRAG	BODY	30.9	drill holes
2	184	5765	UNKN	UNKN	2	TIZON	FRAG	BODY	37.3	glued
25	184	6175	UNKN	UNKN	177	TIZON	FRAG	BODY	647.7	glued
1760	184		UNKN	UNKN	3	TIZON	FRAG	BODY	60.3	parallel lines in a chevron pattern
9	184	5765	UNKN	UNKN	1	TIZON	FRAG	BODY	38.1	fragment of base
4	184	5765	UNKN	UNKN	1	TIZON	FRAG	BODY	35.3	approx 18% of vessel
5	184	5765	UNKN	UNKN	1	TIZON	FRAG	BODY	41.3	approx 19% of vessel
6	184	5765	UNKN	UNKN	1	TIZON	FRAG	BODY	26.9	21% of vessel, ground
29	184	6071	UNKN	UNKN	276	TIZON	FRAG	BODY	638.2	glued
957	184	4092	UNKN	UNKN	6	TIZON	FRAG	BODY	54	glued
1757a	184	5444	UNKN	UNKN	2	TIZON	FRAG	BODY	23.1	painted horizontal stripes, triangles in brown
1757b	184	6314	UNKN	UNKN	5	TIZON	FRAG	BODY	30.7	painted horizontal stripes, triangles in brown
1757c	184	6315	UNKN	UNKN	2	TIZON	FRAG	BODY	14.3	painted horizontal stripes, triangles in brown
1776	184	3970	UNKN	UNKN	1	TIZON	FRAG	BODY	2.1	partial drill hole 4mm
1	184	5765	UNKN	UNKN	35	TIZON	FRAG	BODY	342.6	
3	184	5765	UNKN	UNKN	1	TIZON	FRAG	BODY	34.7	
42	184	5811	UNKN	UNKN	275	TIZON	FRAG	BODY	828	
65	184	6153	UNKN	UNKN	2	TIZON	FRAG	BODY	12	
101	184	5935	UNKN	UNKN	1	TIZON	FRAG	BODY	6.9	
107	184	5191	UNKN	UNKN	14	TIZON	FRAG	BODY	78	
108	184	4491	UNKN	UNKN	5	TIZON	FRAG	BODY	13.1	
112	184	4091	UNKN	UNKN	6	TIZON	FRAG	BODY	29.4	

2011.28	SBCM	Cat #	Unit	Level	Qty	MTRL	COND	Vess Part	Wt/ g	Comments
213	184	265	UNKN	UNKN	5	TIZON	FRAG	BODY	24.6	
268	184	3869	UNKN	UNKN	1	TIZON	FRAG	BODY	2	
28	184	5017	UNKN	UNKN	1	TIZON	FRAG	BODY	7.2	
343	184	4505	UNKN	UNKN	5	TIZON	FRAG	BODY	24.5	
383	184	1033	UNKN	UNKN	2	TIZON	FRAG	BODY	16	
394	184	4456	UNKN	UNKN	1	TIZON	FRAG	BODY	2	
405	184	287	UNKN	UNKN	6	TIZON	FRAG	BODY	11.4	
409	184	287	UNKN	UNKN	6	TIZON	FRAG	BODY	18.2	
41	184	287	UNKN	UNKN	176	TIZON	FRAG	BODY	740	
418	184	298	UNKN	UNKN	1	TIZON	FRAG	BODY	5.9	
451	184	479	UNKN	UNKN	14	TIZON	FRAG	BODY	98	
481	184	312	UNKN	UNKN	1	TIZON	FRAG	BODY	0.6	
482	184	4097	UNKN	UNKN	1	TIZON	FRAG	BODY	3.1	
53	184	1136	UNKN	UNKN	2	TIZON	FRAG	BODY	27	
607	184	1688	UNKN	UNKN	1	TIZON	FRAG	BODY	1.8	
638	184	1688	UNKN	UNKN	12	TIZON	FRAG	BODY	25.2	
639	184	1688	UNKN	UNKN	1	TIZON	FRAG	BODY	1.9	
652	184	1251	UNKN	UNKN	11	TIZON	FRAG	BODY	47.2	
697	184	1645	UNKN	UNKN	14	TIZON	FRAG	BODY	70.6	
701	184	5012	UNKN	UNKN	1	TIZON	FRAG	BODY	1.2	
72	184	5179	UNKN	UNKN	3	TIZON	FRAG	BODY	15	
753	184	1202	UNKN	UNKN	3	TIZON	FRAG	BODY	15	

2011.28	SBCM	Cat #	Unit	Level	Qty	MTRL	COND	Vess Part	Wt/ g	Comments
754	184	1202	UNKN	UNKN	1	TIZON	FRAG	BODY	1.1	
835	184	1169	UNKN	UNKN	5	TIZON	FRAG	BODY	16.1	
836	184	1169	UNKN	UNKN	1	TIZON	FRAG	BODY	1.8	
844	184	1426	UNKN	UNKN	11	TIZON	FRAG	BODY	88	
856	184	5071	UNKN	UNKN	6	TIZON	FRAG	BODY	35.4	
874	184	1925	UNKN	UNKN	9	TIZON	FRAG	BODY	57.8	
932	184	4238	UNKN	UNKN	15	TIZON	FRAG	BODY	22.2	
934	184	4238	UNKN	UNKN	1	TIZON	FRAG	BODY	41.1	
935	184	4238	UNKN	UNKN	652	TIZON	FRAG	BODY	2132	
952	184	4092	UNKN	UNKN	5	TIZON	FRAG	BODY	4	
953	184	4092	UNKN	UNKN	1	TIZON	FRAG	BODY	76	
954	184	4092	UNKN	UNKN	1	TIZON	FRAG	BODY	66	
955	184	4092	UNKN	UNKN	1	TIZON	FRAG	BODY	36	
956	184	4092	UNKN	UNKN	1	TIZON	FRAG	BODY	46	
958	184	4092	UNKN	UNKN	419	TIZON	FRAG	BODY	1954	
968	184	5200	UNKN	UNKN	1	TIZON	FRAG	BODY	42.4	
97	184	5200	UNKN	UNKN	80	TIZON	FRAG	BODY	684	
971	184	3965	UNKN	UNKN	216	TIZON	FRAG	BODY	1146	
974	184	3965	UNKN	UNKN	1	TIZON	FRAG	BODY	95.3	
983	184	5014	UNKN	UNKN	1	TIZON	FRAG	BODY	22.5	
1013	184	3966	UNKN	UNKN	3	TIZON	FRAG	BODY	2	
1014	184	3966	UNKN	UNKN	379	TIZON	FRAG	BODY	1136	

2011.28	SBCM	Cat #	Unit	Level	Qty	MTRL	COND	Vess Part	Wt/g	Comments
1016	184	4111	UNKN	UNKN	13	TIZON	FRAG	BODY	122	
1017	184	4111	UNKN	UNKN	74	TIZON	FRAG	BODY	450	
1034	184	5172	UNKN	UNKN	2	TIZON	FRAG	BODY	16.7	
1055	184	3362	UNKN	UNKN	3	TIZON	FRAG	BODY	0.4	
1058	184	3239	UNKN	UNKN	11	TIZON	FRAG	BODY	59.3	
1113	184	3804	UNKN	UNKN	2	TIZON	FRAG	BODY	0.4	
1117	184	3759	UNKN	UNKN	2	TIZON	FRAG	BODY	7.5	
1198	184	3791	UNKN	UNKN	102	TIZON	FRAG	BODY	756	
1215	184	4023	UNKN	UNKN	23	TIZON	FRAG	BODY	84	
1228	184	3731	UNKN	UNKN	1	TIZON	FRAG	BODY	3	
1253	184	6203	UNKN	UNKN	1	TIZON	FRAG	BODY	4	
1255	184	4201	UNKN	UNKN	36	TIZON	FRAG	BODY	358	
1262	184	5846	UNKN	UNKN	15	TIZON	FRAG	BODY	54	
1312	184	2786	UNKN	UNKN	62	TIZON	FRAG	BODY	228	
1365	184	3695	UNKN	UNKN	1	TIZON	FRAG	BODY	5.7	
1373	184	3828	UNKN	UNKN	1	TIZON	FRAG	BODY	1.1	
139	184	3694	UNKN	UNKN	1	TIZON	FRAG	BODY	2.2	
1426	184	4093	UNKN	UNKN	10	TIZON	FRAG	BODY	51	
1432	184	5176	UNKN	UNKN	182	TIZON	FRAG	BODY	844	
1444	184	5146	UNKN	UNKN	1	TIZON	FRAG	BODY	5.5	
1459	184	7024	UNKN	UNKN	1	TIZON	FRAG	BODY	25.8	
1463	184	6179	UNKN	UNKN	4	TIZON	FRAG	BODY	12.8	

2011.28	SBCM	Cat #	Unit	Level	Qty	MTRL	COND	Vess Part	Wt/ g	Comments
1492	184	3969	UNKN	UNKN	5	TIZON	FRAG	BODY	23.8	
1497	184	6417	UNKN	UNKN	1	TIZON	FRAG	BODY	10.7	
1543	184	6365	UNKN	UNKN	9	TIZON	FRAG	BODY	15.1	
1571	184	5119	UNKN	UNKN	111	TIZON	FRAG	BODY	642.3	
1573	184	5119	UNKN	UNKN	1	TIZON	FRAG	BODY	37.6	
1574	184	5159	UNKN	UNKN	122	TIZON	FRAG	BODY	599.8	
1577	184	5037	UNKN	UNKN	180	TIZON	FRAG	BODY	372.6	
158	184	5202	UNKN	UNKN	163	TIZON	FRAG	BODY	899.2	
1592	184	5450	UNKN	UNKN	216	TIZON	FRAG	BODY	570	
161	184	6342	UNKN	UNKN	1	TIZON	FRAG	BODY	2.4	
1645	184	5152	UNKN	UNKN	21	TIZON	FRAG	BODY	212.2	
165	184	1518	UNKN	UNKN	12	TIZON	FRAG	BODY	44.8	
1734	184	4958	UNKN	UNKN	35	TIZON	FRAG	BODY	119.3	
1771	184	1268	UNKN	UNKN	1	TIZON	FRAG	BODY	1.6	
1745	184	5138	UNKN	UNKN	1	TIZON	FRAG	BODY	1.2	
1747	184	3937	UNKN	UNKN	1	TIZON	FRAG	BODY	2.5	
1748	184	5036	UNKN	UNKN	1	TIZON	FRAG	BODY	0.5	
1749	184	6628	UNKN	UNKN	1	TIZON	FRAG	BODY	5.9	
1584	184	3924	UNKN	UNKN	1	TIZON	FRAG	RIM	6.9	10% of rim
276	184	296	UNKN	UNKN	1	TIZON	FRAG	RIM	8	5% of rim
303	184	308	UNKN	UNKN	1	TIZON	FRAG	RIM	5.4	5% of rim
344	184	4455	UNKN	UNKN	1	TIZON	FRAG	RIM	8	5% of rim

2011.28	SBCM	Cat #	Unit	Level	Qty	MTRL	COND	Vess Part	Wt/ g	Comments
411	184	287	UNKN	UNKN	1	TIZON	FRAG	RIM	1.8	5% of rim
447	184	287	UNKN	UNKN	1	TIZON	FRAG	RIM	11.2	5% of rim
658	184	1253	UNKN	UNKN	1	TIZON	FRAG	RIM	6.3	5% of rim
1594	184	3640	UNKN	UNKN	1	TIZON	FRAG	RIM	1.9	5% of rim
1595	184	5447	UNKN	UNKN	1	TIZON	FRAG	RIM	14	5% of rim
1672	184	4960	UNKN	UNKN	1	TIZON	FRAG	RIM	5.8	5% of rim
1696	184	3925	UNKN	UNKN	1	TIZON	FRAG	RIM	4.5	7% of rim
4812	184	4258	UNKN	UNKN	1	TIZON	FRAG	RIM	0.3	etched
1368	184	3677	UNKN	UNKN	1	TIZON	FRAG	RIM	6.1	horizontal lines 15% of rim
931	184	4238	UNKN	UNKN	1	TIZON	FRAG	RIM	24.8	painted
1579	184	5202	UNKN	UNKN	1	TIZON	FRAG	RIM	2.6	painted
1764	184	3910	UNKN	UNKN	1	TIZON	FRAG	RIM	6.4	parallel diagonal lines
1762	184	3691	UNKN	UNKN	1	TIZON	FRAG	RIM	3.1	parallel lines
1780	184	4278	UNKN	UNKN	1	TIZON	FRAG	RIM	1.8	parallel lines; 6% of rim
739	184	6453	UNKN	UNKN	7	TIZON	FRAG	RIM	43.8	10% glued
973	184	3965	UNKN	UNKN	1	TIZON	FRAG	RIM	11.9	10% of rim
1277	184	3642	UNKN	UNKN	1	TIZON	FRAG	RIM	1.4	10% of rim
1286	184	4249	UNKN	UNKN	1	TIZON	FRAG	RIM	7.9	10% of rim
1305	184	3672	UNKN	UNKN	1	TIZON	FRAG	RIM	45.5	10% of rim
1356	184	3652	UNKN	UNKN	1	TIZON	FRAG	RIM	2.5	10% of rim
1499	184	3701	UNKN	UNKN	1	TIZON	FRAG	RIM	3.2	10% of rim
774	184	3668	UNKN	UNKN	1	TIZON	FRAG	RIM	43.8	11% of rim

2011.28	SBCM	Cat #	Unit	Level	Qty	MTRL	COND	Vess Part	Wt/ g	Comments
1354	184	3705	UNKN	UNKN	1	TIZON	FRAG	RIM	29.2	12% of rim
741	184	3702	UNKN	UNKN	1	TIZON	FRAG	RIM	16.5	14% of rim
805	184	4115	UNKN	UNKN	1	TIZON	FRAG	RIM	3.7	15% of rim
1195	184	3674	UNKN	UNKN	1	TIZON	FRAG	RIM	25	15% of rim
1388	184	3959	UNKN	UNKN	1	TIZON	FRAG	RIM	5.7	15% of rim
736	184	3675	UNKN	UNKN	1	TIZON	FRAG	RIM	76.2	16% of rim
521	184	1520	UNKN	UNKN	1	TIZON	FRAG	RIM	10.3	18% of rim
733	184	3706	UNKN	UNKN	1	TIZON	FRAG	RIM	13.3	18% of rim
1197	184	3693	UNKN	UNKN	1	TIZON	FRAG	RIM	36.2	18% of rim
1303	184	3671	UNKN	UNKN	1	TIZON	FRAG	RIM	25.2	18% of rim
1171	184	3660	UNKN	UNKN	1	TIZON	FRAG	RIM	7.3	2.5% of rim
1176	184	3655	UNKN	UNKN	1	TIZON	FRAG	RIM	3.2	2.5% of rim
75	184	6152	UNKN	UNKN	1	TIZON	FRAG	RIM	40.4	20% of rim
144	184	310	UNKN	UNKN	1	TIZON	FRAG	RIM	5.8	20% of rim
166	184	3689	UNKN	UNKN	1	TIZON	FRAG	RIM	16.9	20% of rim
122	184	6178	UNKN	UNKN	1	TIZON	FRAG	RIM	5.2	25% of rim
1230	184	3690	UNKN	UNKN	1	TIZON	FRAG	RIM	5.5	3% of rim
1193	184	3650	UNKN	UNKN	1	TIZON	FRAG	RIM	6.2	4% of rim
1037	184	5145	UNKN	UNKN	1	TIZON	FRAG	RIM	6	5% of rim
1053	184	3683	UNKN	UNKN	1	TIZON	FRAG	RIM	2.2	5% of rim
1057	184	3698	UNKN	UNKN	1	TIZON	FRAG	RIM	9.9	5% of rim
1076	184	2785	UNKN	UNKN	1	TIZON	FRAG	RIM	6	5% of rim

2011.28	SBCM	Cat #	Unit	Level	Qty	MTRL	COND	Vess Part	Wt/ g	Comments
1080	184	3673	UNKN	UNKN	1	TIZON	FRAG	RIM	6	5% of rim
1102	184	4251	UNKN	UNKN	1	TIZON	FRAG	RIM	1.5	5% of rim
1103	184	3688	UNKN	UNKN	1	TIZON	FRAG	RIM	45.7	5% of rim
1105	184	3676	UNKN	UNKN	1	TIZON	FRAG	RIM	5	5% of rim
1110	184	3646	UNKN	UNKN	1	TIZON	FRAG	RIM	9.3	5% of rim
1125	184	3664	UNKN	UNKN	1	TIZON	FRAG	RIM	4.1	5% of rim
1128	184	3919	UNKN	UNKN	1	TIZON	FRAG	RIM	5.1	5% of rim
1131	184	3679	UNKN	UNKN	1	TIZON	FRAG	RIM	20	5% of rim
1133	184	3927	UNKN	UNKN	1	TIZON	FRAG	RIM	11.7	5% of rim
1134	184	3707	UNKN	UNKN	1	TIZON	FRAG	RIM	9.2	5% of rim
1147	184	3941	UNKN	UNKN	1	TIZON	FRAG	RIM	5.3	5% of rim
1148	184	4247	UNKN	UNKN	1	TIZON	FRAG	RIM	3.6	5% of rim
1150	184	3961	UNKN	UNKN	1	TIZON	FRAG	RIM	2.8	5% of rim
1162	184	3662	UNKN	UNKN	1	TIZON	FRAG	RIM	1.5	5% of rim
1163	184	3643	UNKN	UNKN	1	TIZON	FRAG	RIM	2.5	5% of rim
1169	184	3658	UNKN	UNKN	1	TIZON	FRAG	RIM	8.9	5% of rim
1173	184	3918	UNKN	UNKN	1	TIZON	FRAG	RIM	5	5% of rim
1174	184	3967	UNKN	UNKN	1	TIZON	FRAG	RIM	3.5	5% of rim
1182	184	3645	UNKN	UNKN	1	TIZON	FRAG	RIM	2.8	5% of rim
1186	184	3943	UNKN	UNKN	1	TIZON	FRAG	RIM	2	5% of rim
1189	184	3921	UNKN	UNKN	1	TIZON	FRAG	RIM	16.1	5% of rim
1238	184	3917	UNKN	UNKN	1	TIZON	FRAG	RIM	8	5% of rim

2011.28	SBCM	Cat #	Unit	Level	Qty	MTRL	COND	Vess Part	Wt/ g	Comments
1249	184	3703	UNKN	UNKN	1	TIZON	FRAG	RIM	12.5	5% of rim
1289	184	3666	UNKN	UNKN	1	TIZON	FRAG	RIM	10.3	5% of rim
1308	184	3656	UNKN	UNKN	1	TIZON	FRAG	RIM	3.2	5% of rim
1344	184	3711	UNKN	UNKN	1	TIZON	FRAG	RIM	8	5% of rim
1361	184	3661	UNKN	UNKN	1	TIZON	FRAG	RIM	5.4	5% of rim
1366	184	4248	UNKN	UNKN	1	TIZON	FRAG	RIM	6.1	5% of rim
1410	184	3685	UNKN	UNKN	1	TIZON	FRAG	RIM	1.6	5% of rim
1691	184	5768	UNKN	UNKN	1	TIZON	FRAG	RIM	21.7	5% of rim
740	184	5766	UNKN	UNKN	1	TIZON	FRAG	RIM	37.2	50% of rim
1279	184	3956	UNKN	UNKN	1	TIZON	FRAG	RIM	2.6	6% of rim
1310	184	4239	UNKN	UNKN	1	TIZON	FRAG	RIM	2.5	6% of rim
1347	184	3669	UNKN	UNKN	1	TIZON	FRAG	RIM	10.5	6% of rim
1385	184	3639	UNKN	UNKN	1	TIZON	FRAG	RIM	0.6	6% of rim
1505	184	4246	UNKN	UNKN	1	TIZON	FRAG	RIM	1.7	6% of rim
1268	184	3651	UNKN	UNKN	1	TIZON	FRAG	RIM	2.7	7% of rim
1297	184	3911	UNKN	UNKN	1	TIZON	FRAG	RIM	6.8	7% of rim
1367	184	3635	UNKN	UNKN	1	TIZON	FRAG	RIM	3.7	7% of rim
1531	184	4242	UNKN	UNKN	1	TIZON	FRAG	RIM	1.5	7% of rim
1564	184	3654	UNKN	UNKN	1	TIZON	FRAG	RIM	6.3	7% of rim
1300	184	3678	UNKN	UNKN	1	TIZON	FRAG	RIM	7.7	8% of rim
735	184	4241	UNKN	UNKN	5	TIZON	FRAG	RIM	51.9	9% of 5 pieces glued
1381	184	3644	UNKN	UNKN	1	TIZON	FRAG	RIM	3.9	9% of rim

2011.28	SBCM	Cat #	Unit	Level	Qty	MTRL	COND	Vess Part	Wt/ g	Comments
1768	184	5032	UNKN	UNKN	1	TIZON	FRAG	RIM	4.8	cross-hatch pattern
1775	184	3968	UNKN	UNKN	1	TIZON	FRAG	RIM	1.6	decorated two parallel lines
1774	184	3944	UNKN	UNKN	1	TIZON	FRAG	RIM	4.4	decorated w/two perforations
1777	184	5030	UNKN	UNKN	1	TIZON	FRAG	RIM	1.2	Etched parallel lines, 5% of rim
1781	184	3940	UNKN	UNKN	1	TIZON	FRAG	RIM	5.7	etched parallel lines, 5% of rim
354	184	301	UNKN	UNKN	1	TIZON	FRAG	RIM	13	etched; 5% of rim
1350	184	3647	UNKN	UNKN	1	TIZON	FRAG	RIM	9	horizontal lines
1244	184	4117	UNKN	UNKN	1	TIZON	FRAG	RIM	5.4	less than 5% of rim
1245	184	3700	UNKN	UNKN	1	TIZON	FRAG	RIM	4.3	less than 5% of rim
1260	184	3648	UNKN	UNKN	1	TIZON	FRAG	RIM	7.7	less than 5% of rim
1274	184	3637	UNKN	UNKN	1	TIZON	FRAG	RIM	5.6	less than 5% of rim
1278	184	3922	UNKN	UNKN	1	TIZON	FRAG	RIM	6.2	less than 5% of rim
1302	184	3667	UNKN	UNKN	1	TIZON	FRAG	RIM	3.9	less than 5% of rim
1323	184	3692	UNKN	UNKN	1	TIZON	FRAG	RIM	13.7	less than 5% of rim
1374	184	3699	UNKN	UNKN	1	TIZON	FRAG	RIM	1.4	less than 5% of rim
1407	184	3659	UNKN	UNKN	1	TIZON	FRAG	RIM	3.3	less than 5% of rim
1417	184	3663	UNKN	UNKN	1	TIZON	FRAG	RIM	3.7	less than 5% of rim
1785	184	3846	UNKN	UNKN	1	TIZON	FRAG	RIM	8.5	less than 5% of rim
404	184	287	UNKN	UNKN	2	TIZON	FRAG	RIM	5.3	painted
1770	184	3955	UNKN	UNKN	1	TIZON	FRAG	RIM	2.2	parallel lines
1534	184	3914	UNKN	UNKN	1	TIZON	FRAG	RIM	3.7	
88	184	309	UNKN	UNKN	1	TIZON	FRAG	RIM	7.9	

2011.28	SBCM	Cat #	Unit	Level	Qty	MTRL	COND	Vess Part	Wt/ g	Comments
105	184	6163	UNKN	UNKN	1	TIZON	FRAG	RIM	2.3	
132	184	300	UNKN	UNKN	1	TIZON	FRAG	RIM	4.7	
153	184	304	UNKN	UNKN	1	TIZON	FRAG	RIM	4.2	
182	184	305	UNKN	UNKN	1	TIZON	FRAG	RIM	6.9	
186	184	302	UNKN	UNKN	1	TIZON	FRAG	RIM	9.2	
223	184	476	UNKN	UNKN	1	TIZON	FRAG	RIM	2.2	
263	184	303	UNKN	UNKN	1	TIZON	FRAG	RIM	6.5	
265	184	311	UNKN	UNKN	1	TIZON	FRAG	RIM	1.5	
278	184	297	UNKN	UNKN	1	TIZON	FRAG	RIM	6	
290	184	313	UNKN	UNKN	1	TIZON	FRAG	RIM	1.9	
398	184	4113	UNKN	UNKN	1	TIZON	FRAG	RIM	14.2	
430	184	4493	UNKN	UNKN	1	TIZON	FRAG	RIM	4.9	
476	184	307	UNKN	UNKN	1	TIZON	FRAG	RIM	3.3	
481	184	312	UNKN	UNKN	1	TIZON	FRAG	RIM	0.6	
520	184	4118	UNKN	UNKN	1	TIZON	FRAG	RIM	5.1	
523	184	474	UNKN	UNKN	1	TIZON	FRAG	RIM	9.2	
534	184	1427	UNKN	UNKN	1	TIZON	FRAG	RIM	3.8	
688	184	4106	UNKN	UNKN	1	TIZON	FRAG	RIM	11.3	
729	184	1519	UNKN	UNKN	1	TIZON	FRAG	RIM	16.5	
737	184	4112	UNKN	UNKN	3	TIZON	FRAG	RIM	56.3	
759	184	1252	UNKN	UNKN	1	TIZON	FRAG	RIM	11	
799	184	1929	UNKN	UNKN	1	TIZON	FRAG	RIM	3.6	

2011.28	SBCM	Cat #	Unit	Level	Qty	MTRL	COND	Vess Part	Wt/ g	Comments
826	184	1428	UNKN	UNKN	1	TIZON	FRAG	RIM	8.3	
928	184	5136	UNKN	UNKN	1	TIZON	FRAG	RIM	6.5	
935	184	4238	UNKN	UNKN	3	TIZON	FRAG	RIM	2132	
1004	184	4513	UNKN	UNKN	1	TIZON	FRAG	RIM	13.3	
1010	184	4509	UNKN	UNKN	1	TIZON	FRAG	RIM	2.9	
1051	184	3942	UNKN	UNKN	1	TIZON	FRAG	RIM	5.9	
1054	184	3951	UNKN	UNKN	1	TIZON	FRAG	RIM	9.9	
1104	184	4108	UNKN	UNKN	1	TIZON	FRAG	RIM	6.7	
1106	184	3755	UNKN	UNKN	1	TIZON	FRAG	RIM	2.5	
1108	184	3704	UNKN	UNKN	1	TIZON	FRAG	RIM	2.2	
1109	184	3926	UNKN	UNKN	1	TIZON	FRAG	RIM	2.7	
1111	184	3945	UNKN	UNKN	1	TIZON	FRAG	RIM	1.7	
1127	184	3665	UNKN	UNKN	1	TIZON	FRAG	RIM	4.7	
1143	184	4277	UNKN	UNKN	1	TIZON	FRAG	RIM	2	
1144	184	3684	UNKN	UNKN	1	TIZON	FRAG	RIM	2.2	
1145	184	3636	UNKN	UNKN	1	TIZON	FRAG	RIM	8.4	
1172	184	3687	UNKN	UNKN	1	TIZON	FRAG	RIM	4.1	
1181	184	3958	UNKN	UNKN	1	TIZON	FRAG	RIM	2.7	
1183	184	4322	UNKN	UNKN	1	TIZON	FRAG	RIM	2	
1191	184	3117	UNKN	UNKN	1	TIZON	FRAG	RIM	4.7	
1192	184	4025	UNKN	UNKN	1	TIZON	FRAG	RIM	2.3	
1196	184	3948	UNKN	UNKN	1	TIZON	FRAG	RIM	3.5	

2011.28	SBCM	Cat #	Unit	Level	Qty	MTRL	COND	Vess Part	Wt/ g	Comments
1227	184	2784	UNKN	UNKN	1	TIZON	FRAG	RIM	10	
1232	184	3913	UNKN	UNKN	1	TIZON	FRAG	RIM	2	
1234	184	3681	UNKN	UNKN	1	TIZON	FRAG	RIM	2.8	
1242	184	3246	UNKN	UNKN	1	TIZON	FRAG	RIM	4.3	
1243	184	3940	UNKN	UNKN	1	TIZON	FRAG	RIM	1.8	
1247	184	3686	UNKN	UNKN	1	TIZON	FRAG	RIM	1.8	
1263	184	3653	UNKN	UNKN	1	TIZON	FRAG	RIM	3.6	
1266	184	3697	UNKN	UNKN	1	TIZON	FRAG	RIM	21.4	
1282	184	3946	UNKN	UNKN	1	TIZON	FRAG	RIM	9	
1283	184	3696	UNKN	UNKN	1	TIZON	FRAG	RIM	1.5	
1287	184	4102	UNKN	UNKN	1	TIZON	FRAG	RIM	8.7	
1288	184	4102	UNKN	UNKN	1	TIZON	FRAG	RIM	0.8	
1301	184	3949	UNKN	UNKN	1	TIZON	FRAG	RIM	5.8	
1304	184	3912	UNKN	UNKN	1	TIZON	FRAG	RIM	4	
1306	184	3657	UNKN	UNKN	1	TIZON	FRAG	RIM	4	
1317	184	4245	UNKN	UNKN	1	TIZON	FRAG	RIM	3.9	
1320	184	3638	UNKN	UNKN	1	TIZON	FRAG	RIM	2.1	
1321	184	3920	UNKN	UNKN	1	TIZON	FRAG	RIM	2.5	
1351	184	4250	UNKN	UNKN	1	TIZON	FRAG	RIM	0.9	
1352	184	3923	UNKN	UNKN	1	TIZON	FRAG	RIM	3	
1353	184	3950	UNKN	UNKN	1	TIZON	FRAG	RIM	2.8	
1359	184	4240	UNKN	UNKN	1	TIZON	FRAG	RIM	8.4	

2011.28	SBCM	Cat #	Unit	Level	Qty	MTRL	COND	Vess Part	Wt/ g	Comments
1362	184	3709	UNKN	UNKN	1	TIZON	FRAG	RIM	1.3	
1364	184	3670	UNKN	UNKN	1	TIZON	FRAG	RIM	4.7	
1365	184	3695	UNKN	UNKN	1	TIZON	FRAG	RIM	5.7	
1369	184	3649	UNKN	UNKN	1	TIZON	FRAG	RIM	6.1	
1370	184	3971	UNKN	UNKN	1	TIZON	FRAG	RIM	3.9	
1376	184	3708	UNKN	UNKN	1	TIZON	FRAG	RIM	1.3	
1378	184	3952	UNKN	UNKN	1	TIZON	FRAG	RIM	3.4	
1398	184	3947	UNKN	UNKN	1	TIZON	FRAG	RIM	0	
1399	184	3960	UNKN	UNKN	1	TIZON	FRAG	RIM	2	
1400	184	3938	UNKN	UNKN	1	TIZON	FRAG	RIM	13.5	
1405	184	3634	UNKN	UNKN	1	TIZON	FRAG	RIM	2	
1408	184	3118	UNKN	UNKN	1	TIZON	FRAG	RIM	1.1	
1423	184	5158	UNKN	UNKN	1	TIZON	FRAG	RIM	16.2	
1436	184	475	UNKN	UNKN	1	TIZON	FRAG	RIM	3.9	
1458	184	306	UNKN	UNKN	1	TIZON	FRAG	RIM	5.5	
1496	184	3680	UNKN	UNKN	1	TIZON	FRAG	RIM	3.3	
1503	184	3957	UNKN	UNKN	1	TIZON	FRAG	RIM	5.4	
1551	184	3916	UNKN	UNKN	1	TIZON	FRAG	RIM	1.8	
1556	184	5767	UNKN	UNKN	1	TIZON	FRAG	RIM	36.5	
1574	184	5159	UNKN	UNKN	1	TIZON	FRAG	RIM	599.8	
1577	184	5037	UNKN	UNKN	2	TIZON	FRAG	RIM	372.6	
1580	184	5202	UNKN	UNKN	1	TIZON	FRAG	RIM	899.2	

2011.28	SBCM	Cat #	Unit	Level	Qty	MTRL	COND	Vess Part	Wt/ g	Comments
1629	184	6069	UNKN	UNKN	1	TIZON	FRAG	RIM	0.7	
1666	184	4965	UNKN	UNKN	1	TIZON	FRAG	RIM	2.3	
1684	184	4963	UNKN	UNKN	1	TIZON	FRAG	RIM	3.4	
1694	184	5446	UNKN	UNKN	1	TIZON	FRAG	RIM	2.7	
1709	184	3682	UNKN	UNKN	1	TIZON	FRAG	RIM	3.4	
1714	184	4962	UNKN	UNKN	1	TIZON	FRAG	RIM	2.5	
1715	184	4321	UNKN	UNKN	1	TIZON	FRAG	RIM	2.6	
1717	184	3954	UNKN	UNKN	1	TIZON	FRAG	RIM	2.5	
1721	184	2782	UNKN	UNKN	1	TIZON	FRAG	RIM	3.2	
1723	184	2783	UNKN	UNKN	1	TIZON	FRAG	RIM	1.5	
1379	184	2874		2	1	TIZON	FRAG		4.4	drill hole
Pottery Notation Key										
2011.28: Pechanga Cultural Resource catalogue number										
SBCM: San Bernardino Catalogue collection number										
CAT #: Catalog number										
UNIT: Location										
	According to excavation map									
LEVEL: Depth										
	SURF: Surface									
	Levels 1-10 (Increments of 6 inches each level)									
	TEST: Test Pit									

QTY: Quantity						
MTRL: Material						
	TIZON: Tizon Brown Ware					
	BUFF: Colorado Buff Ware					
COND: Condition						
	FRAG: Fragment					
Vess Part: Vessel Part						
	BODY					
	RIM					
WT/g: Weight measured in grams						
Comments:						
	Etched					
	decoration type: painted, lines etc					
	ground					
	pottery patch: used to repair pottery					
	percentage of rim					
	drill hole					
	glued					
	rounded edges					

APPENDIX BB

MINERALS

Appendix BB: Minerals							
2011.28	**SBCM**	**Cat #**	**Unit**	**Level**	**QTY**	**MTRL**	**Wt/g**
7454	184	839	70J5	2	10+	OCHR	0.2
7455	184	1753	40I	1	2	OCHR	0.8
7456	184	1969	60E5	1	1	OCHR	0.3
7457	184	2241	170H	2	1	OCHR	0.01
7458	184	4283	UNKN	UNKN	1	OCHR	5.4
7459	184	4284	UNKN	UNKN	1	OCHR	30.5
7460	184	4285	UNKN	UNKN	2	OCHR	4
7461	184	2815	55I5	5	1	TOUR	3.5
7462	184	3389	170I5	2	1	TOUR	1.9
7463	184	4625	UNKN	UNKN	3	TOUR	23.2
7464	184	5657	75E5	1	1	TOUR	2.4
7465	184	3781	UNKN	UNKN	2	TOUR	31.4
7466	184	3372	65I	2	2+	OCHR	0.2
7467	184	5546	175I5	2	1	CYSL	2
7468	184	4827	UNKN	UNKN	1	CYSL	6
7469	184	3612	9D	7	1	CYSL	2
7470	184	95	UNKN	UNKN	1	CYSL	1
7471	184	6	UNKN	UNKN	1	CYSL	0.8
7472	184	1861	80I	1	1	CYSL	2
7473	184	1396	55J5	3	1	CYSL	8

APPENDIX BB

Mineral Notation Key				
2011.28: Pechanga Cultural Resource catalogue number				
SBCM: San Bernardino Catalogue collection number				
CAT #: Catalog number				
UNIT: Location				
	According to excavation map			
LEVEL: Depth				
	SURF: Surface			
	Levels 1-10 (Increments of 6 inches each level)			
QTY: Quantity				
MTRL: Material				
	OCHR: Ochre			
	CYSL: Crystal			
	TOUR: Tourmaline			
WT/g: Weight measured in grams				

APPENDIX CC

HUMAN REMAINS

Appendix CC: Human Remains									
SBCM	**Cat #**	**Unit**	**Level**	**Bone (s)**	**COLOR**	**SURF TX**	**QTY**	**Wt/g**	**Comments**
184	2923	100D	5	Cranium	BLAK	C	1	4	cremation
184	1005	105F	1	Mandible	TABL	T	2	12	x-rayed
184	5021	1.10E+07	7	UNIDENTIFA-BLE	BLGY	T	2	1	cremation
184	2617	165I	2	UNIDENTIFA-BLE	BLWH	T	4	3	cremation
184	2973	175I	1	UNIDENTIFA-BLE	BLWH	C	10+	4	cremation
184	3520	90D	4	Vertebrae frag	BLGY	C	1	1	cremation
184	1999	95D	5	Femur-head, long frag	BLWH	C	3	3	cremation
184	2903	UNKN	3,4	CRANIUM	BLGY	T	12+	6	cremation
184	2903	UNKN	3,4	Epiphysis	BLGY	C	12	3	cremation
184	2903	UNKN	3,4	Long	BLGY	T	30+	20	cremation
184	2903	UNKN	3,4	Long/ cranium/ mandible/teeth	BLGY	C	100+	55	cremation
184	2903	UNKN	3,4	Mandible/Max-illary	BLGY	C	4	3	cremation
184	2903	UNKN	3,4	Phalanges	BLGY	C	3	1	cremation
184	2903	UNKN	3,4	Tarsals	BLGY	C	5	3	cremation
184	2903	UNKN	3,4	TEETH	BLGY	T	17	6	cremation
184	2903	UNKN	3,4	UNIDENTIFA-BLE	BLGY	C	6	4	cremation
184	2903	UNKN	3,4	Vertebra	BLGY	C	10+	4	cremation
184	1365	UNKN	UNKN	Cranium-Frontal	BLWH	C	2	8	cremation
Human Remains Notation Key									
SBCM: San Bernardino Catalogue collection number									

CAT #: Catalog number							
UNIT: Location							
	According to excavation map						
LEVEL: Depth							
	SURF: Surface						
	Levels 1-10 (Increments of 6 inches each level)						
Bone (s)							
	Cranium						
	Epiphysis						
	femur						
	Long						
	Mandible						
	Maxillary						
	Phalanges						
	Tarsals						
	Teeth						
	UNIDENTIFABLE						
	vertebrae						
COLOR:							
	BLAK: Black						
	BLGY: Blue-gray						
	BLUE: Blue						
	BLWH: Blue and White						

	TABL: Tan and Black						
	TAN: Tan						
	WHIT: White						
SURF TX: Surface Texture							
	T: Longitudinal and transverse checking						
	C: Curved cracks						
QTY: Quantity							
WT/g: Weight measured in grams							
Comments:							
	Cremation: From a cremation						

APPENDIX DD

ASSOCIATED GRAVE ITEMS

Appendix DD: Associated Grave Items										
2011.28	**SBCM**	**Cat #**	**Unit**	**Level**	**Bone (s)/ASS**	**COLOR/ MTRL**	**SURF/COND**	**Qty**	**Wt/g**	**Comments**
	184	**1005**	**105F**	**1**	**Mandible**	**TABL**	**T**	**2**	**12**	**x-rayed**
4776	184	1483	105F5	1	Awl	BONE	FRAG	1	10.9	
2040	184	1485	105F5	1	shell	BKAL	FRAG	1	0.4	
640	184	1486	105F	1	BODY	BUFF	FRAG	2	5.6	
715	184	1004	105F	1	BODY	BUFF	FRAG	1	3.2	
316	184	799	105F	1	RIM	TIZON	FRAG	1	13.8	
1421	184	1479	105F5	1	RIM	TIZON	FRAG	1	16	12% of rim
2295	184	1482	105F5	1	flake tool	MQTZ	UNFC	1	5.2	
2844	184	1483	105F5	1	MAML	bone	FRAG	3	4.4	
	184	**1999**	**95D**	**5**	**Femur-head, long frag**	**BLWH**	**C**	**3**	**3**	**cremation**
914	184	334	95D5	5	RIM	TIZON	FRAG	1	3.4	less than 5% of rim
496	184	339	95D5	5	BODY	TIZON	FRAG	34	94.1	
498	184	339	95D5	5	BODY	TIZON	FRAG	1	1.3	
497	184	339	95D5	5	BODY	BUFF	FRAG	1	1.2	
155	184	332	95D5	5	RIM	TIZON	FRAG	1	1.4	
496	184	339	95D5	5	RIM	TIZON	FRAG	1	94.1	
516	184	333	95D5	5	RIM	TIZON	FRAG	1	5.3	
	184	**2617**	**165I**	**2**	**UNIDENTIFI-ABLE**	**BLWH**	**T**	**4**	**3**	**cremation**
1188	184	2619	165I	2	RIM	TIZON	FRAG	1	11.6	5% of rim
1074	184	2618	165I	2	BODY	TIZON	FRAG	10	44	
1075	184	2618	165I	2	BODY	BUFF	FRAG	1	6	

2011.28	SBCM	Cat #	Unit	Level	Bone (s)/ASS	COLOR/ MTRL	SURF/COND	Qty	Wt/g	Comments
1360	184	2620	165I	2	RIM	TIZON	FRAG	1	9.8	
2515	184	2617	165I	2	MAML	long/skull	FRAG	37	27.6	SM/MED
2574	184	2617	165I	2	MAML	rib	FRAG	1	1.2	UNKN
3199	184	2617	165I	2	TURT	shell	FRAG	1	0.9	XSM
2568	184	2617	165I	2	MTLIn	vert	FRAG	1	11.4	MED
2600	184	2617	165I	2	CTRB	femur	FRAG	1	0.3	XSM
3560	184	2616	165I	2	CHCL	CHCL	FRAG	2	0.3	Associated with cremation
	184	**2923**	**100D**	**5**	**Cranium**	**BLAK**	**C**	**1**	**4**	**cremation**
4778	184	4898	100D	8	Awl	BONE	FRAG	1	1.8	
7416	184	230	100D	5	pendant	SLAT	FRAG	1	8.6	
2058	184	169	100D5	3	shell	FWCM	FRAG	1	0.01	
2017	184	2929	100D5	3	shell	RDAL	FRAG	1	5.9	
	184	**2973**	**175I**	**1**	**UNIDENTIFI-ABLE**	**BLWH**	**C**	**10+**	**4**	**cremation**
1925	184	3385	175I	1	shell	BKAL	FRAG	1	0.2	
1947	184	2971	175I	1	shell	FWCM	FRAG	1	0.1	
1060	184	2975	175I	1	RIM	TIZON	FRAG	1	3.6	5% of rim
1216	184	2974	175I	1	BODY	TIZON	FRAG	16	50	
1073	184	2976	175I	1	RIM	TIZON	FRAG	1	8	
1314	184	2977	175I	1	RIM	TIZON	FRAG	1	2.3	
1074	184	2618	165I	2	BODY	TIZON	FRAG	10	44	
1075	184	2618	165I	2	BODY	BUFF	FRAG	1	6	
1360	184	2620	165I	2	RIM	TIZON	FRAG	1	9.8	

2011.28	SBCM	Cat #	Unit	Level	Bone (s)/ASS	COLOR/ MTRL	SURF/COND	Qty	Wt/g	Comments
2515	184	2617	165I	2	MAML	long/skull	FRAG	37	27.6	SM/MED
2574	184	2617	165I	2	MAML	rib	FRAG	1	1.2	UNKN
3199	184	2617	165I	2	TURT	shell	FRAG	1	0.9	XSM
2568	184	2617	165I	2	MTLIn	vert	FRAG	1	11.4	MED
2600	184	2617	165I	2	CTRB	femur	FRAG	1	0.3	XSM
3560	184	2616	165I	2	CHCL	CHCL	FRAG	2	0.3	Associated with cremation
	184	**2923**	**100D**	**5**	**Cranium**	**BLAK**	**C**	**1**	**4**	**cremation**
4778	184	4898	100D	8	Awl	BONE	FRAG	1	1.8	
7416	184	230	100D	5	pendant	SLAT	FRAG	1	8.6	
2058	184	169	100D5	3	shell	FWCM	FRAG	1	0.01	
2017	184	2929	100D5	3	shell	RDAL	FRAG	1	5.9	
	184	**2973**	**175I**	**1**	**UNIDENTIFI-ABLE**	**BLWH**	**C**	**10+**	**4**	**cremation**
1925	184	3385	175I	1	shell	BKAL	FRAG	1	0.2	
1947	184	2971	175I	1	shell	FWCM	FRAG	1	0.1	
1060	184	2975	175I	1	RIM	TIZON	FRAG	1	3.6	5% of rim
1216	184	2974	175I	1	BODY	TIZON	FRAG	16	50	
1073	184	2976	175I	1	RIM	TIZON	FRAG	1	8	
1314	184	2977	175I	1	RIM	TIZON	FRAG	1	2.3	
2514	184	2973	175I	1	MAML	long	FRAG	28.8	44	SM/MED
2532	184	3387	175I	1	MAML	UNKN	FRAG	0.9	20+	UNKN
3419	184	2973	175I	1	GRSQL	mandible	FRAG	0.2	1	XSM
2499	184	5211	175I5	1	MAML	long/rib	FRAG	38	73+	SM/MED

2011.28	SBCM	Cat #	Unit	Level	Bone (s)/ASS	COLOR/ MTRL	SURF/COND	Qty	Wt/g	Comments
3538	184	2972	175I	1	CHCL	CHCL	FRAG	0.8	7	
	184	**3520**	**90D**	**4**	**Vertebrae frag**	**BLGY**	**C**	**1**	**1**	**cremation**
2034	184	3521	90D	4	shell	BKAL	FRAG	1	0.6	
2709	184	3520	90D	4	MAML	long/rib/ skull	FRAG	70+	45.8	SM/MED
	184	**5021**	**110E5**	**7**	**UNIDENTIFI-ABLE**	**BLGY**	**T**	**2**	**1**	**cremation**
7480	184	4951	110E5	8	pipe	BONE	FRAG	1	2	BURNED
1299	184	5064	110E	7	RIM	TIZON	FRAG	1	6.5	pottery patch
646	184	5043	110E	7	BODY	TIZON	FRAG	1	11.3	
909	184	5019	110E	7	BODY	TIZON	FRAG	15	62.9	
963	184	5063	110E	7	BODY	TIZON	FRAG	3	14.6	
1493	184	5062	110E	7	BODY	TIZON	FRAG	1	3.4	
2717	184	5021	110E5	7	MAML	long/rib	FRAG	39	19.9	SM/MED
2840	184	5042	110E5	7	MAML	UNKN	FRAG	2	1.7	UNKN
3061	184	5021	110E5	7	CTRB	Lt mandi-ble	FRAG	1	1	XSM
3650	184	5021	110E5	7	MAML	incisor	WHLE	1	0.9	XSM
McCown Identified			**65H5**	**1,2,3**						
1867	184	12	65H5	2	shell	BKAL	FRAG	1	0.01	
1844	184	12	65H5	2	shell	PECT	FRAG	1	0.01	
1884	184	80	65H5	3,4	shell	BKAL	FRAG	11	0.4	
1904	184	80	65H5	3,4	shell	HSCM	FRAG	1	0.1	
287	184	1	65H5	1	BODY	TIZON	FRAG	12	84.9	
1452	184	7022	65H5	2	BODY	TIZON	FRAG	1	12.1	

2011.28	SBCM	Cat #	Unit	Level	Bone (s)/ASS	COLOR/ MTRL	SURF/COND	Qty	Wt/g	Comments
152	184	10	65H5	2	BODY	TIZON	FRAG	12	96.4	
463	184	79	65H5	3,4	BODY	TIZON	FRAG	8	43.1	
2456	184	81	65H5	3, 4	MAML	skull/long/ rib	FRAG	299	129.3	SM/MED
2268	184	7	65H5	1	MAML	UNKN	FRAG	38	27.2	
2326	184	7	65H5	1	DEER	tibia	WHLE	1	2.3	MED
3279	184	7	65H5	1	HORS	tooth	FRAG	1	0.6	LG
3225	184	7	65H5	1	GRSQ	Lt mandi- ble	FRAG	1	0.4	XSM
3224	184	7	65H5	1	GRSQ	Lt mandi- ble	FRAG	1	0.1	XSM
2261	184	9	65H5	2	MAML	long/rib	FRAG	57	33.3	XSM/MED
3248	184	9	65H5	2	HORS	tooth	FRAG	1	0.8	LG
2184	184	6188	65I	1	MAML	skull	FRAG	23	11.9	
3965	184	6191	65I	1	MAML	UNKN	FRAG	1	1.4	
3984	184	6192	65I	1	MAML	UNKN	FRAG	1	3.4	
2228	184	3374	65I	1	MAML	UNKN	FRAG	1	1	
3952	184	6197	65I	1	MAML	UNKN	FRAG	1	1	
2177	184	6107	65I	2	MAML	long	FRAG	11	10.4	
3964	184	6109	65I	2	MAML	UNKN	FRAG	1	0.5	
3985	184	6110	65I	2	MAML	UNKN	FRAG	1	1.4	
3214	184	6107	65I	2	CTRBB	Lt mandi- ble	FRAG	1	0.3	XSM
2222	184	6133	65I	3	MAML	long	FRAG	25	16.4	
2213	184	6138	65I	3	MAML	UNKN	WHLE	1	1	
3970	184	6140	65I	3	MAML	UNKN	FRAG	1	0.4	

2011.28	SBCM	Cat #	Unit	Level	Bone (s)/ASS	COLOR/ MTRL	SURF/COND	Qty	Wt/g	Comments
3973	184	6141	65I	3	MAML	UNKN	FRAG	1	0.2	
3566	184	8	65H5	2	CHCL	CHCL	FRAG	28	1.6	
3570	184	82	65H5	3, 4	CHCL	CHCL	FRAG	160	14.6	
McCown Identified			**65I**	**1,2,3**						
98	184	6181	65I	1	BODY	TIZON	FRAG	22	59.5	
14	184	6187	65I	1	RIM	TIZON	FRAG	1	4.6	
51	184	6194	65I	1	RIM	TIZON	FRAG	1	6.6	
93	184	6190	65I	1	RIM	TIZON	FRAG	1	1.4	
1246	184	6111	65I	2	BODY	TIZON	FRAG	1	2.8	
1736	184	6101	65I	2	BODY	TIZON	FRAG	8	16.1	
1681	184	6136	65I	3	BODY	TIZON	FRAG	7	28	
1719	184	6131	65I	3	RIM	TIZON	FRAG	1	3.8	
7466	184	3372	65I	2	OCHR	OCHR	FRAG	2+	0.2	
3462	184	6108	65I	2	CHCL	CHCL	FRAG	4+	1.9	
3354	184	6130	65I	3	CHCL	CHCL	FRAG	20+	4.6	
McCown Identified			**100D**	**3**						
6058	184	2926	100D5	3	Point	MTVC	WHLE	1	3.4	LEARNING
6094	184	2931	100D5	3	Point	QRTZ	WHLE	1	0.6	
126	184	133	100D5	3	BODY	TIZON	FRAG	65	327.8	
127	184	133	100D5	3	BODY	TIZON	FRAG	1	7.7	
293	184	165	100D5	3	BODY	TIZON	FRAG	2	10	
4	184	2104	100D5	3	BODY	TIZON	FRAG	21	112	

2011.28	SBCM	Cat #	Unit	Level	Bone (s)/ASS	COLOR/ MTRL	SURF/COND	Qty	Wt/g	Comments
401	184	2104	100D5	3	BODY	TIZON	FRAG	2	5.7	
1269	184	2927	100D5	3	BODY	TIZON	FRAG	8	28	
1456	184	2927	100D5	3	BODY	TIZON	FRAG	1	5.4	
1270	184	2927	100D5	3	BODY	BUFF	FRAG	1	2	
402	184	2105	100D5	3	RIM	TIZON	FRAG	1	3.2	
2724	184	2860	100D	3	MAML	rib	FRAG	16	23	MED/LG
2826	184	133	100D	3	MAML	UNKN	FRAG	2	1	
3617	184	2860	100D	3	CTRBB	mandible	FRAG	1	1	XSM
McCown Identified			**105D**	**3**						
293	184	133	100D5	3	BODY	TIZON	FRAG	65	327.8	
4	184	133	100D5	3	BODY	TIZON	FRAG	1	7.7	
401	184	165	100D5	3	BODY	TIZON	FRAG	2	10	
1269	184	2104	100D5	3	BODY	TIZON	FRAG	21	112	
1456	184	2104	100D5	3	BODY	TIZON	FRAG	2	5.7	
1270	184	2927	100D5	3	BODY	TIZON	FRAG	8	28	
402	184	2927	100D5	3	BODY	TIZON	FRAG	1	5.4	
45	184	2927	100D5	3	BODY	BUFF	FRAG	1	2	
	184	2105	100D5	3	RIM	TIZON	FRAG	1	3.2	
	184	496	105D5	3	BODY	TIZON	FRAG	7	12.7	
Items Recorded with Association										
3588	184	2305	95D	2	CHCL	CHCL	FRAG	5	1.4	Associated with cremation
3571	184	1993	95D	5	CHCL	CHCL	FRAG	5+	0.7	Associated with cremation

2011.28	SBCM	Cat #	Unit	Level	Bone (s)/ASS	COLOR/ MTRL	SURF/COND	Qty	Wt/g	Comments
3586	184	2325	95D	3,4	CHCL	CHCL	FRAG	250+	43.2	Associated with cremation
3389	184	2116	95D5	4	CHCL	CHCL	FRAG	9+	0.1	Associated with cremation
	184	3097	95G	3	CHCL	CHCL	FRAG	500+	84	Associated with cremation
	184	4507	UNKN	UNKN	CHCL	CHCL	FRAG	4	0.4	Cremation

2011.3	SBCM	Cat#	Unit	Level	Qty	MTRL	Bone(s)/ ASS	COND	HOLE	LL/MM	W/MM	T/MM	WT/g	Comments
7431	184	5382	95D	3,4	1	TURT	TSR	FRAG	CONL	21.5	14.2	0.7	0.3	BURNED
7433	184	5384	95D	3,4	1	TURT	TSR	FRAG	CONL	18.9	17.8	5.1	0.7	BURNED
7436	184	5388	95D	3,4	1	TURT	TSR	FRAG	BCOL	15.9	13	2.9	0.4	BURNED
7437	184	5389	95D	3,4	2	TURT	TSR	FRAG	BCOL	25.2	10.3	2.5	0.5	BURNED
7438	184	5391	95D	3,4	1	TURT	TSR	FRAG	BCOL	15.1	14.4	2.4	0.4	BURNED
7439	184	5392	95D	3,4	1	TURT	TSR	FRAG	BCOL	12.4	12.4	4.8	0.4	BURNED
7434	184	5386	95D	3,4	1	TURT	TSR	FRAG	BOTH	22.9	19.9	3.1	0.7	BURNED, 2 HOLES
7432	184	5383	95D	3,4	1	TURT	TSR	FRAG	CONL	12.7	7.9	2	0.2	
7435	184	5387	95D	3,4	1	TURT	TSR	FRAG	CONL	17.2	14	1.7	0.3	

'Éxva Teméeku Associated Human Remain Items
2011.28: Pechanga Cultural Resource catalogue number
McCown Identified: An area McCown identified as cremation
Bolded areas are the newly identified cremation areas
Items recorded with a cremation association
SBCM: San Bernardino Catalogue collection number
CAT #: Catalog number

UNIT: Location						
LEVEL: Depth According to excavation map						
	SURF: Surface					
	Levels 1-10 (Increments of 6 inches each level)					
Bone(s)/ASS: Object name of bone(s) or associated item(s)						
	Awl: Bone Awl					
	Body					
	CHCL: Charcoal					
	Cranium: Human cranium					
	CTRB: Cotton-tail rabbit					
	CTRBB: Cotton-tail rabbit					
	DEER					
	flake tool					
	GRSQ: Grey squirrel					
	HORS: Horse					
	MAML: Mammal					
	MTLIn: Mountain lion					
	pendant					
	pipe					
	Point					
	RIM					
	shell: Shell					
	TSR: Turtle Shell Rattle					

	TURT: Western pond turtle					
COLOR/MTRL: Color or material of object						
	BKAL					
	BLAK: Black					
	BLGY: Blue-gray					
	BONE					
	BUFF					
	CHCL					
	HSCM					
	incisor					
	long					
	long/rib					
	Lt mandible					
	mandible					
	MTVC					
	OCHR					
	PECT					
	QRTZ					
	rib					
	skull/long/rib					
	TABL					
	tibia					
	TIZON					

	tooth					
SURF/COND: Surface texture or condition						
	UNKN					
	FRAG: Fragment					
	WHLE: Whole					
	C: Curved cracks					
	T: Longitudinal and transverse checking					
QTY: Quantity						
WT/g: Weight measured in grams						
Comments:						
	Associated with cremation					
	Burned					
	Learning: Learning point					
	Percentage of rim					
	Pottery patch					
	Size of faunal					
	X-Rayed					
	2 Holes					

REFERENCES

Adams, Jenny L.
2002 Ground Stone Analysis: A Technological Approach. Salt Lake City: University of Utah Press.
Andrefsky, William
2001 Lithic Debitage: Context, Form, Meaning. Salt Lake City: University of Utah Press.
Andrefsky, William
2005 Lithics: Macroscopic Approaches to Analysis. 2nd ed. New York: Cambridge University Press.
Barker, Alex W.
2003 Archaeological Ethics: Museums and Collections. Zimmerman, Larry J., Karen D. Vitelli, and Julia J. Hollowell, eds. P.p. 71-84. Walnut Creek, CA: AltaMira Press in cooperation with the Society for American Archaeology.
Bass, William M.
2009 Human Osteology A Laboratory and Field Manual. Fifth ed. Columbia, Missouri: Missouri Archaeological Society.
Bean, Lowell J., and Florence C. Shipek
1978 Luiseño. *In* Handbook of North American Indians, Vol. 8: California. Robert F. Heizer, ed. Pp. 550-563. Smithsonian Institution, Washington, D.C.
Bennyhoff, James A., and Robert F. Heizer
1958 Cross-Dating Great Basin Sites by California Shell Beads. Reports of the University of California Archaeological Survey 42: 60-92.
Bennyhoff, James A., and Richard E. Hughes
1987 Shell Bead and Ornament Exchange Networks Between California and the Western Great Basin. New York: American Museum of Natural History.
Bowden, Cheryl
2002 Site Record: P-33-000050. Record on file. The Resource Agency Department of Parks and Recreation Primary Record, California.
Bowles, L.L.
1982 Site Record: Ca-Riv-50. Record on File, Eastern Information Center.
Buikstra, Jane E., and Ubelaker, Douglas H.
1994 Standards for Data Collection from Human Skeletal Remains: Proceeding of a seminar at the Field Museum of Natural History. Little Rock, AK: Arkansas Archeological Report Research Series.
Cameron, Constance
1999 Determining Tribal Boundaries Through Potsherds-An Archaeological Perspective. Pacific Coast Archaeological Society Quarterly 35: 2-3.
Carrico, Richard
2008 Strangers in a Stolen Land: Indians in San Diego County from Prehistory to the New Deal. Second edition. San Diego: Sunbelt Publications.
Chartkoff, J.K. and L. Kona
1965 Site Record: Ca-Riv-50. Record on File, Eastern Information Center.
Dance, Peter S.
1992 Smithsonian Handbook: Shells. New York: A Dorling Kindersley Book.
Devlin, Joanne B. and Herrmann, Nicholas P.
2008 Bone Color as an Interpretive Tool of the Depositional History of Archaeological Cremains. *In* The Analysis of Burned Human Remains. Christopher W. Schimidt and Steven A. Symes, eds. Pp. 109-128. Waltham, MA: Academic Press Elsevier.
DuBois, Constance
1904 Mythology of the Mission Indians. Journal of American Folklore 17: 185-188.
DuBois, Constance
1906 Mythology of the Mission Indians. Journal of American Folklore 19:52-60.
DuBois, Constance
1908 The Religion of the Luiseño Indians of Southern California. University of California Publication in American Archaeology and Ethnology 8(3):69-186.
Elbroch, Mark

2006 Animal Skulls: A guide to North American Species. Mechanicsburg, PA: Stackpole books.
France, Diane L.
2009 Human and Nonhuman Bone Identification. New York: CRC Press.
Getches David H, Wilkinson, Charles F. and Williams, Robert A
1998 Cases and Materials on Federal Indian Law. American Casebook Series. Eagan, MN: West Publishing Co.
Glassow, Michael
1985 The Research Significance of Small Sites in Coastal California. Journal of California and Great Basin Anthropology 7:58-66.
Gilchrist, R., Mytum, H. C.
1986 Experimental Archaeology and Burnt Animal Bone from Archaeological Sites. York, UK: University of York, Micklegate House.
Gibson, R.O
1992 An Introduction to the Study of Aboriginal Beads from California. Pacific Coast Archaeological Society Quarterly 28(3): 1-46.
Iovin, June
1963 A Summary Description of Luiseño Material Culture. *In* Annual Report of the University of California Archaeological Survey. Los Angeles: University of California, Los Angeles.
Keep, Josiah A. M.
1881 Common Sea Shells of California. San Francisco: Upton Bros.
King, Chester de Witt
1990 The Evolution of Chumash Society: A Comparative Study of Artifacts Used in Social System Maintenance in the Santa Barbara Channel Region before A.D. 1804. New York: Garland.
Kroeber, A. L.
1976 [1925] Handbook of The Indians of California. New York: Dover Publications, Inc.
Luhrs, Dorothy
1940 Site Record: Ca-Riv-50. Record on file, Eastern Information Center.
Mayes, Arion T.
2010 These Bone are Read: The Science and Politics of Ancient Native America. The American Indian Quarterly 34: 2.
McCown, B. E.
1955 Temeku A Page from the History of the Luiseño Indians. Redlands, CA: Archaeological Survey Association of Southern California.
Munro, Pamela
2002 The Takic Foundation of Nicoleño Vocabulary. *In* Proceedings of the Fifth California Island Symposium: 29 March to 1 Aril, 1999. David R. Browne, Katheryn L. Michell, and Henry W. Chaney, eds. P.p. 659-668. Santa Barbara, Ca: Santa Barbara Museum of Natural History.
Odell, George H.
2003 Lithic Analysis. New York: Springer Science and Business Media.
Oxendine, Joan
1983 The Luiseño Village During the Late Prehistoric Era. Ph.D. dissertation, Department of Anthropology, University of California, Riverside.
Pilling
1952 Site Record: Ca-Riv-50. Record on file, Eastern Information Center.
Rixson, D.
1989 Butchery Evidence on Animal Bones. Ash Road Hartley, UK: Glebe House.
Schultz, John J., Warren, Michael W., and Krigbaum, John S.
2008 Analysis of Human Cremains: Gross and Chemical Methods. *In* The Analysis of Burned Human Remains. Christopher W. Schimidt and Steven A. Symes, eds. Pp 75-94. Waltham, MA: Academic Press Elsevier.
Skinner, Craig E., and Thatcher, Jennifer J.
2011 X-Ray Fluorescence Analysis and Obsidian Hydration Measurement of Artifact Obsidian from CA-RIV-50. Riverside, CA: Northwest Research Obsidian Studies Laboratory Report.
Sparkman, Philip S.
1908 The Culture of the Luiseño Indians. University of California Publications in American Archaeology and Ethnology 8(4): 187-234.

Stein, M.
1981 Site Record: Ca-Riv-50, Record on file, Eastern Information Center.
Smith, E.
1983 Anthropological Application of Optimal Foraging Theory: A Critical Review. Current Anthropology 24: 625-651.
Strong, William Duncan
1929 Aboriginal Society in Southern California. Berkeley: University of California Press.
Sutton, Mark Q., and Brooke S. Arkush
2006 Archaeological Laboratory Methods: An Introduction. 4th ed. Dubuque, IA: Kendall/Hunt Pub. Co.
Vellanoweth, R. L.
1995 New Evidence from San Nicolas Island on the Distribution of Olivella Grooved Rectangle Beads. Pacific Cost Archaeological Society Quarterly 31: 13-22.
Vellanoweth, R. L.
2001 AMS Radiocarbon Dating and Shell Bead Chronologies: Middle Holocene Trade and Interaction in Western North American. Journal of Archaeological Science 28: 941-950.
Vitelli, Karen D.
1996 Archaeological Ethics. Walnut Creek, CA: AltaMira Press.
Watkins, Joe
2003 Archaeological Ethics and American Indians. *In* Ethical Issues in Archaeology. Zimmerman, Larry J., Karen D. Vitelli, and Julia J. Hollowell, eds. P.p. 129-141. Walnut Creek, CA: AltaMira Press in cooperation with the Society for American Archaeology.
White, Raymond
1963 Luiseño Social Organization. University of California Publication in American Archaeology and Ethnology 48(2): 91-194.
White, Tim D., & Folkens, Pieter A.
2005 The Human Bone Manual. San Diego: Elsevier Academic Press.

INDEX

H

J

K

L

M

N

O

P